HISSING 히싱

Kang EunYoung

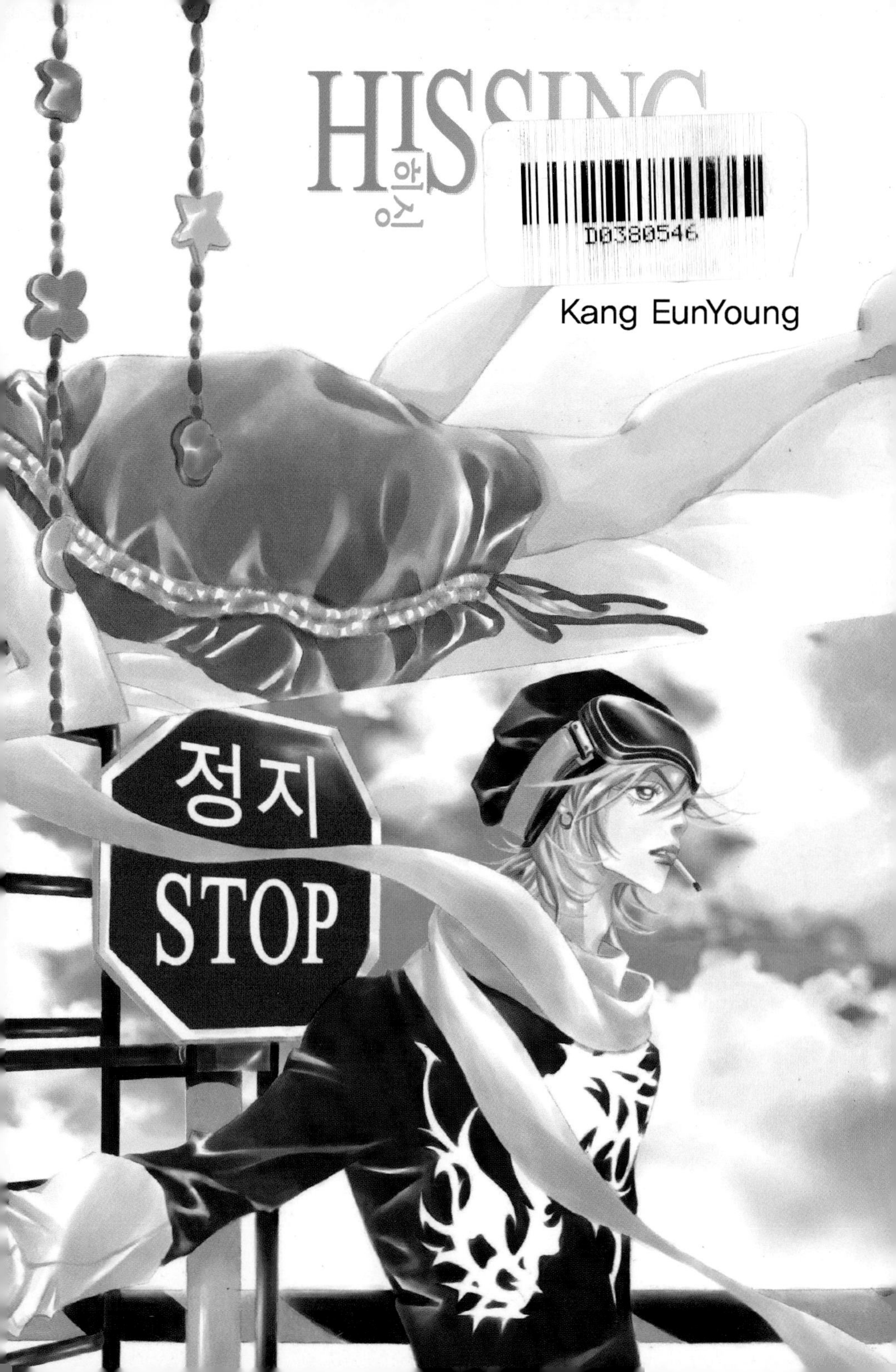
정지
STOP

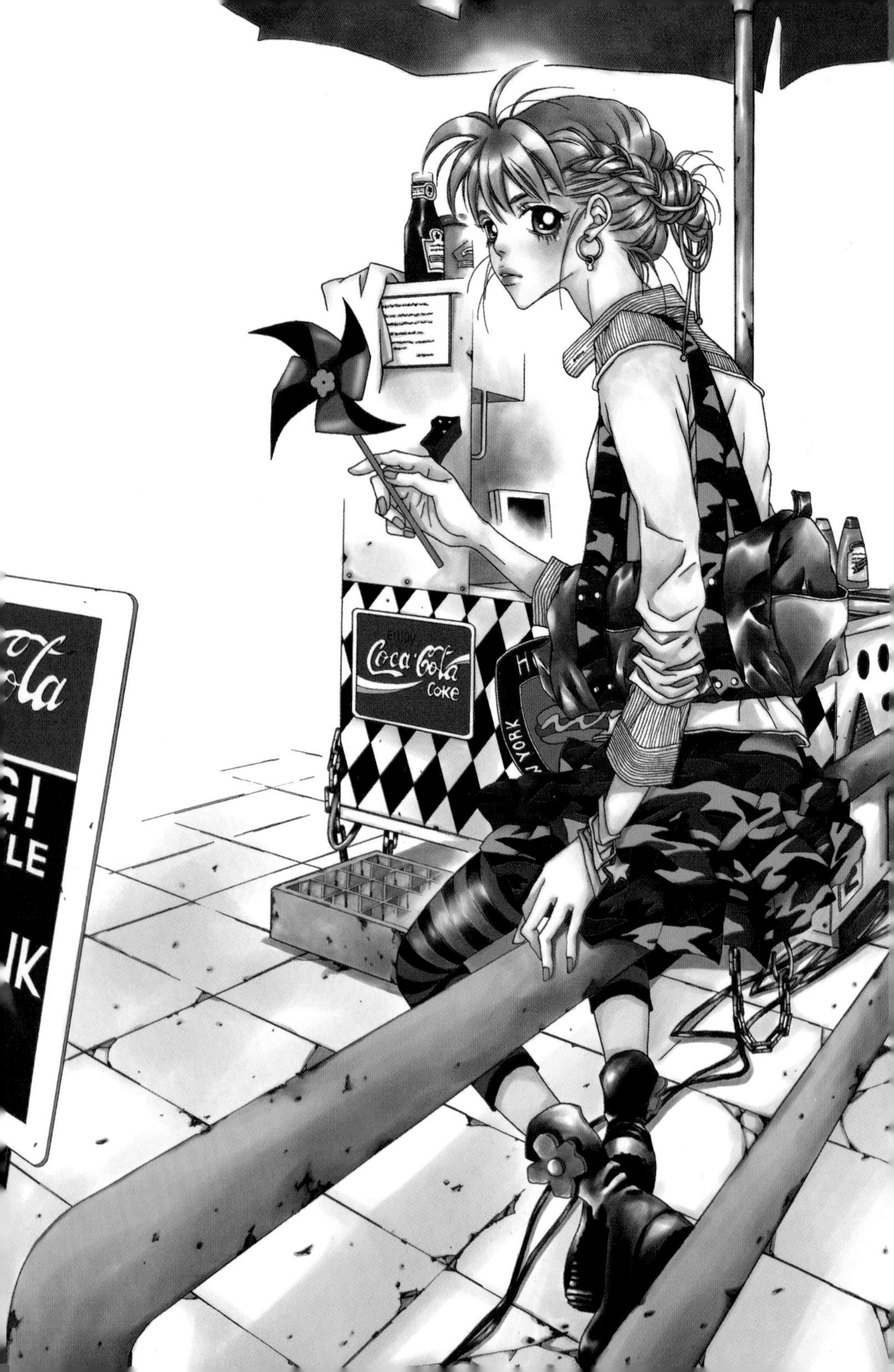
ENJOY
Coca-Cola
COKE
YORK

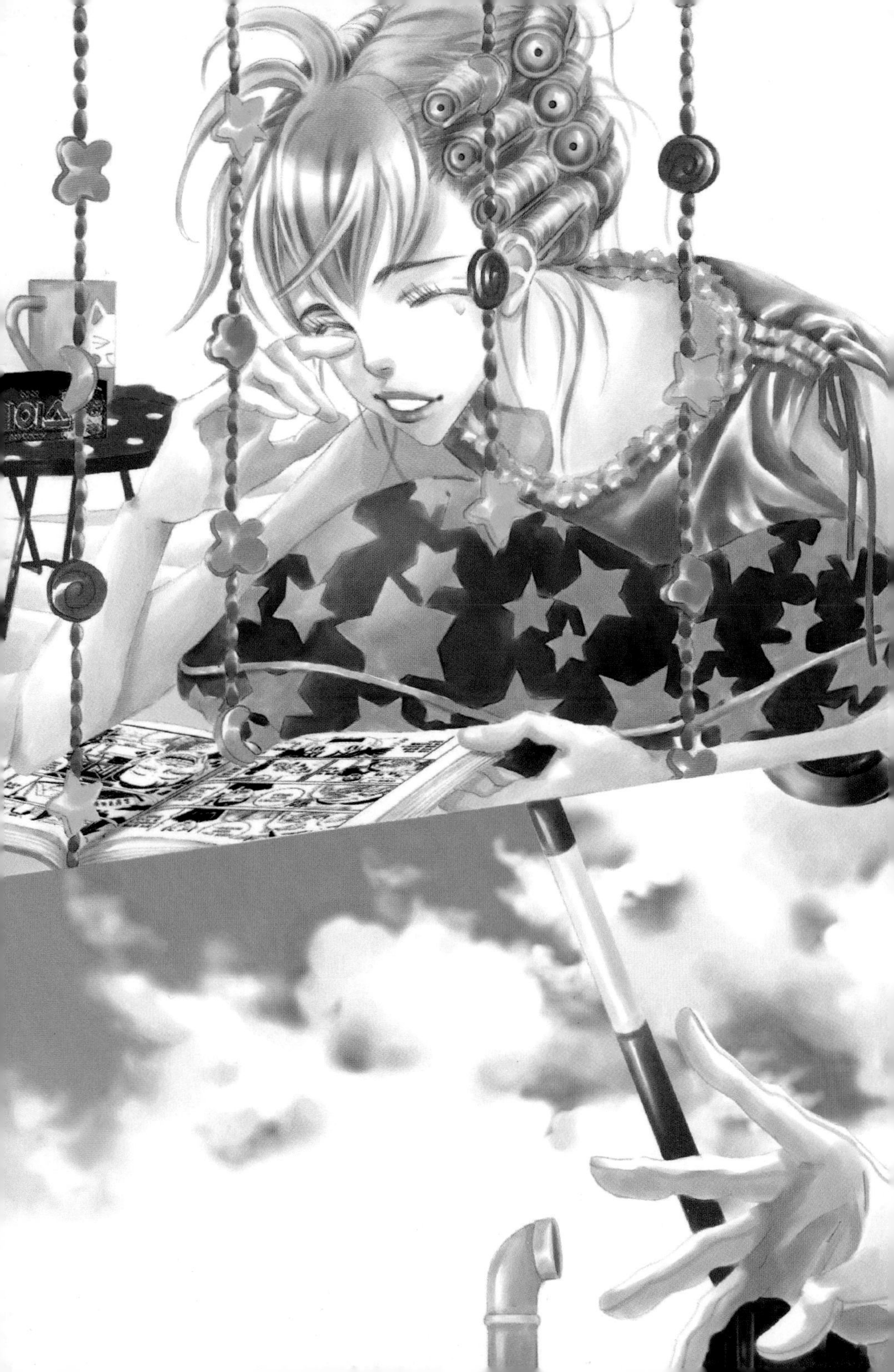

A SMALL DESK GIVEN TO ME.
IN THIS SMALL SPACE,

I STUDY,
I CHAT,
I SLEEP.
I EAT MY LUNCH...

...AND SOMETIMES,
I BECOME THE HAPPIEST
PERSON IN THE WORLD.

AS I READ MANHWA BOOKS,
CRYING, LAUGHING, AND GETTING
ANGRY...

I BECOME THE HAPPIEST
PERSON IN THE WORLD.

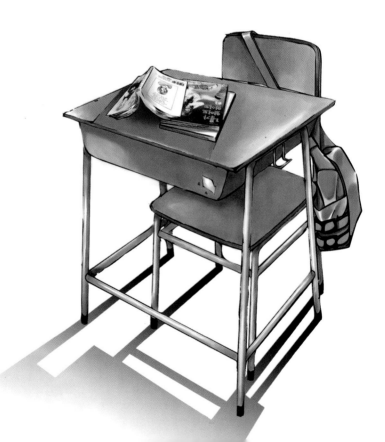

SAW A PUPPY THIS AFTERNOON.

HE MUST HAVE BEEN WAITING FOR HIS MASTER.

AFTER A LONG WAIT, IF HIS
MASTER DOESN'T RETURN,

WHAT
HAPPENS?

...BEING ALONE IS NOT SCARY.

THE THING THAT IS
REALLY SCARY IS THE
WORLD ITSELF.

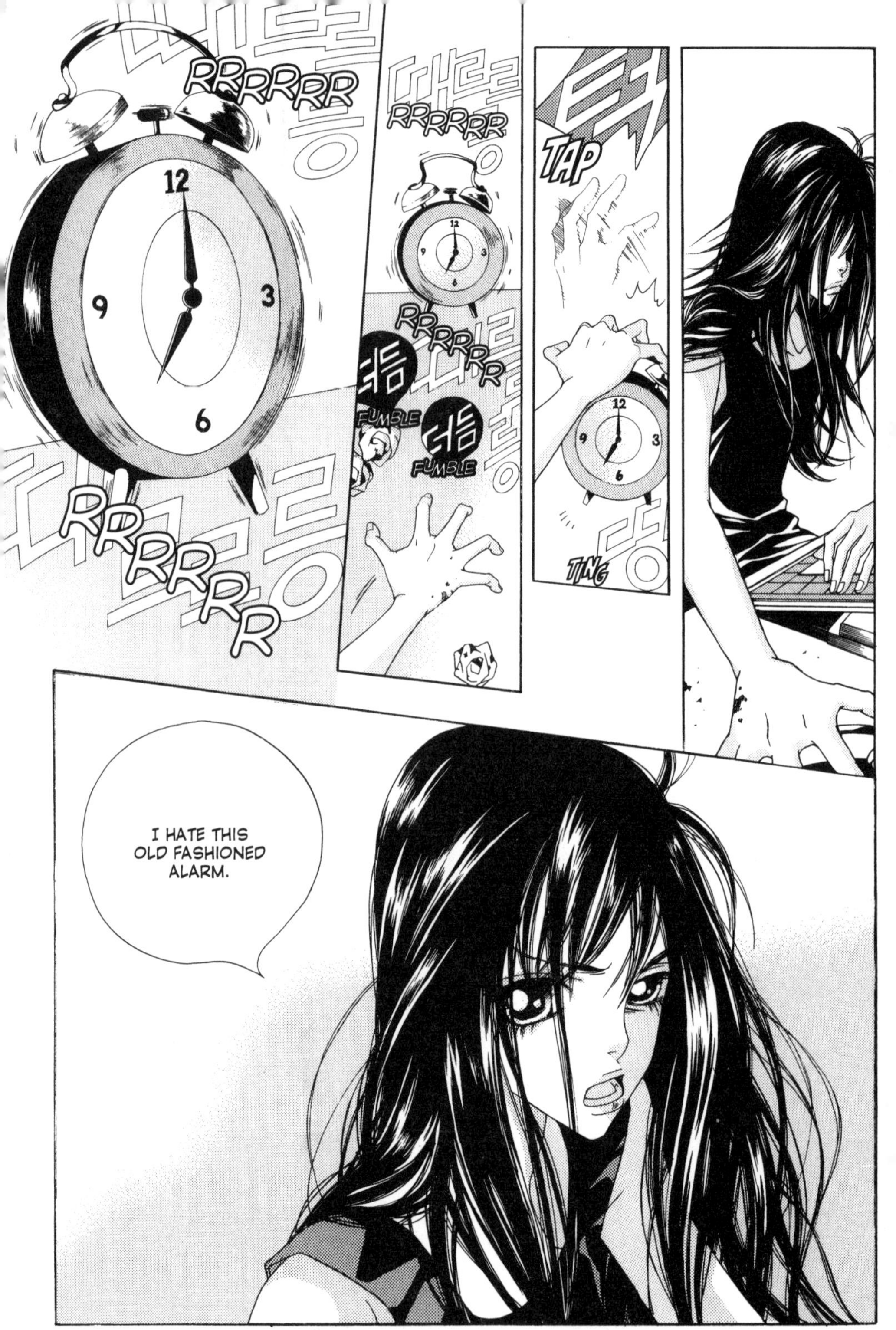
RRRRRRR
RRRRRRRR
RRRRRR
RRRRRRR
FUMBLE
FUMBLE
TAP
TING
I HATE THIS OLD FASHIONED ALARM.

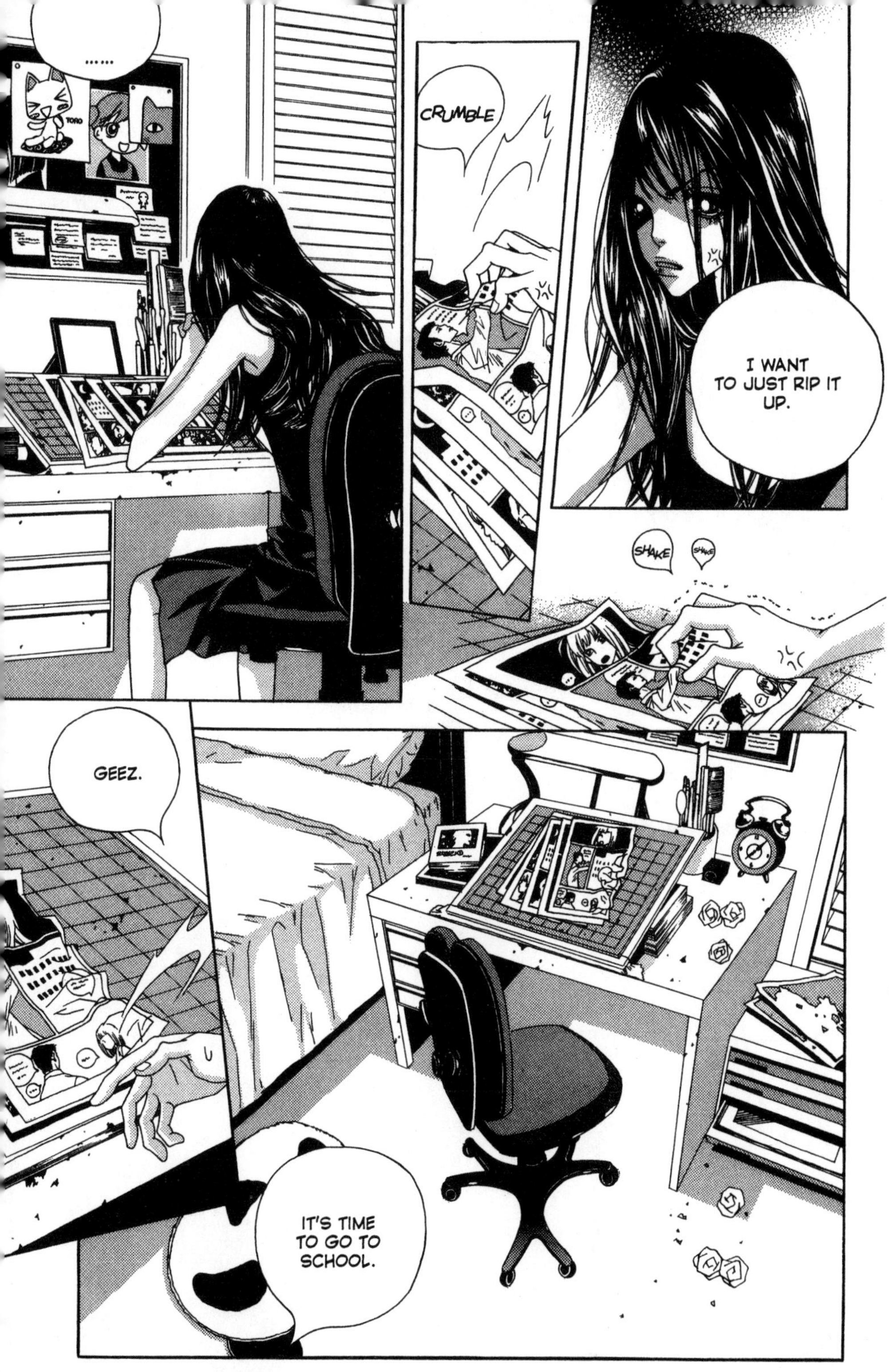
......
TORO
CRUMBLE
I WANT TO JUST RIP IT UP.
SHAKE
SHAKE
GEEZ.
IT'S TIME TO GO TO SCHOOL.

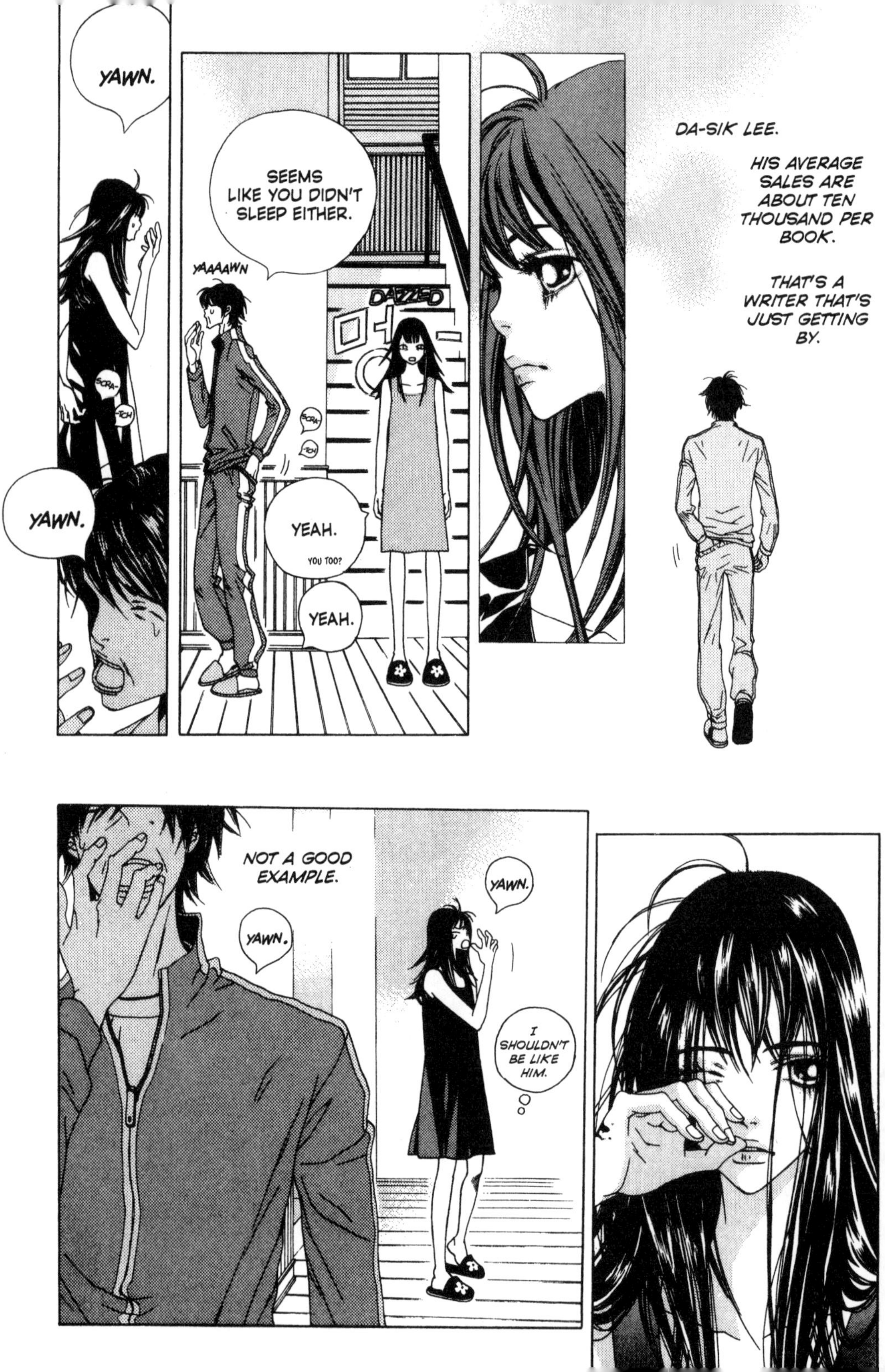
YAWN.
SCRA-
-TCH
YAWN.
SEEMS LIKE YOU DIDN'T SLEEP EITHER.
YAAAAWN
SCRA-
-TCH
DAZED
YEAH.
YOU TOO?
YEAH.
DA-SIK LEE.
HIS AVERAGE SALES ARE ABOUT TEN THOUSAND PER BOOK.
THAT'S A WRITER THAT'S JUST GETTING BY.
NOT A GOOD EXAMPLE.
YAWN.
YAWN.
I SHOULDN'T BE LIKE HIM.

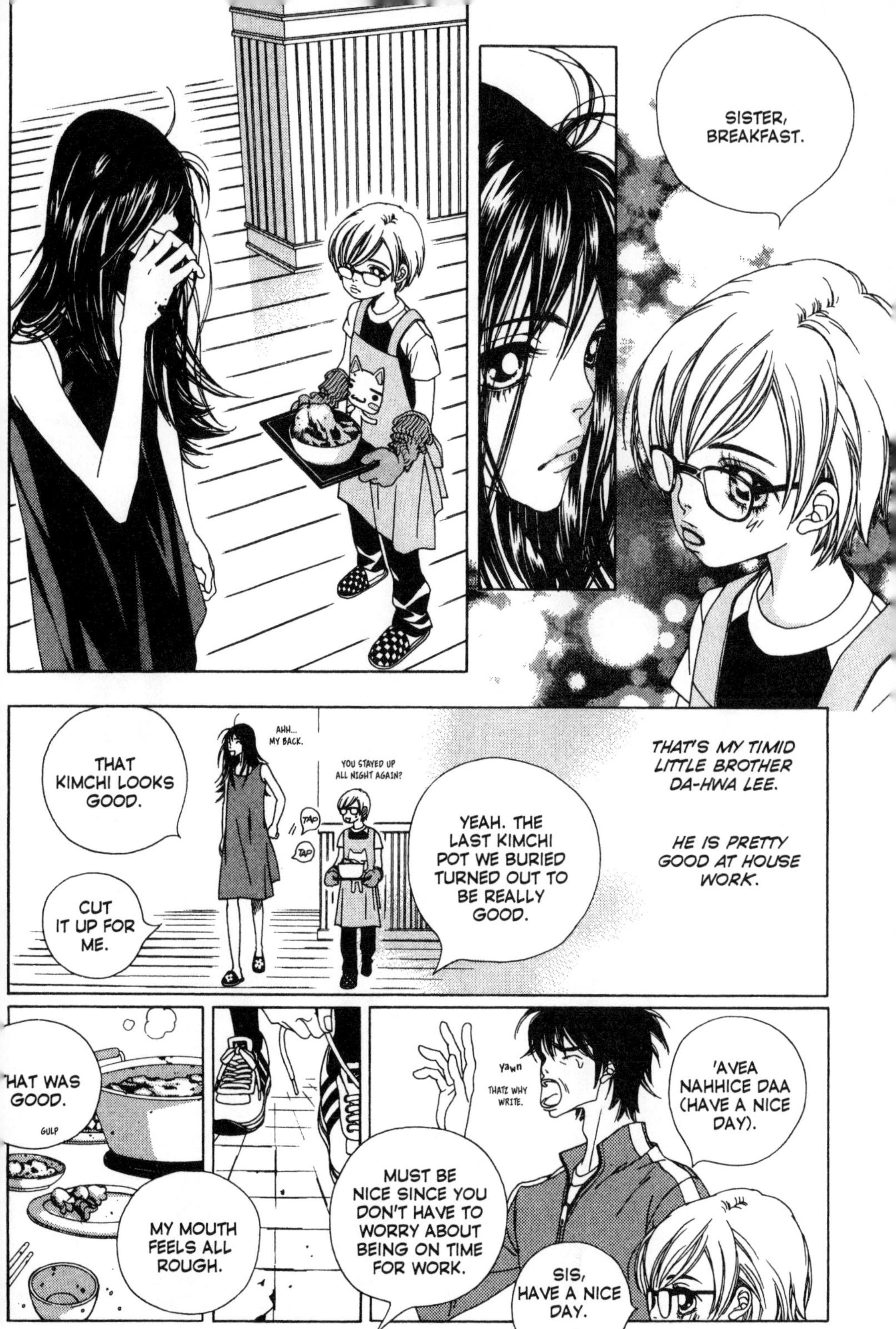
SISTER, BREAKFAST.
THAT KIMCHI LOOKS GOOD.
AHH... MY BACK.
YOU STAYED UP ALL NIGHT AGAIN?
TAP
TAP
YEAH. THE LAST KIMCHI POT WE BURIED TURNED OUT TO BE REALLY GOOD.
CUT IT UP FOR ME.
THAT'S MY TIMID LITTLE BROTHER DA-HWA LEE.
HE IS PRETTY GOOD AT HOUSE WORK.
THAT WAS GOOD.
GULP
MY MOUTH FEELS ALL ROUGH.
MUST BE NICE SINCE YOU DON'T HAVE TO WORRY ABOUT BEING ON TIME FOR WORK.
YAWN
THATZ WHY WRITE.
'AVEA NAHHICE DAA (HAVE A NICE DAY).
SIS, HAVE A NICE DAY.

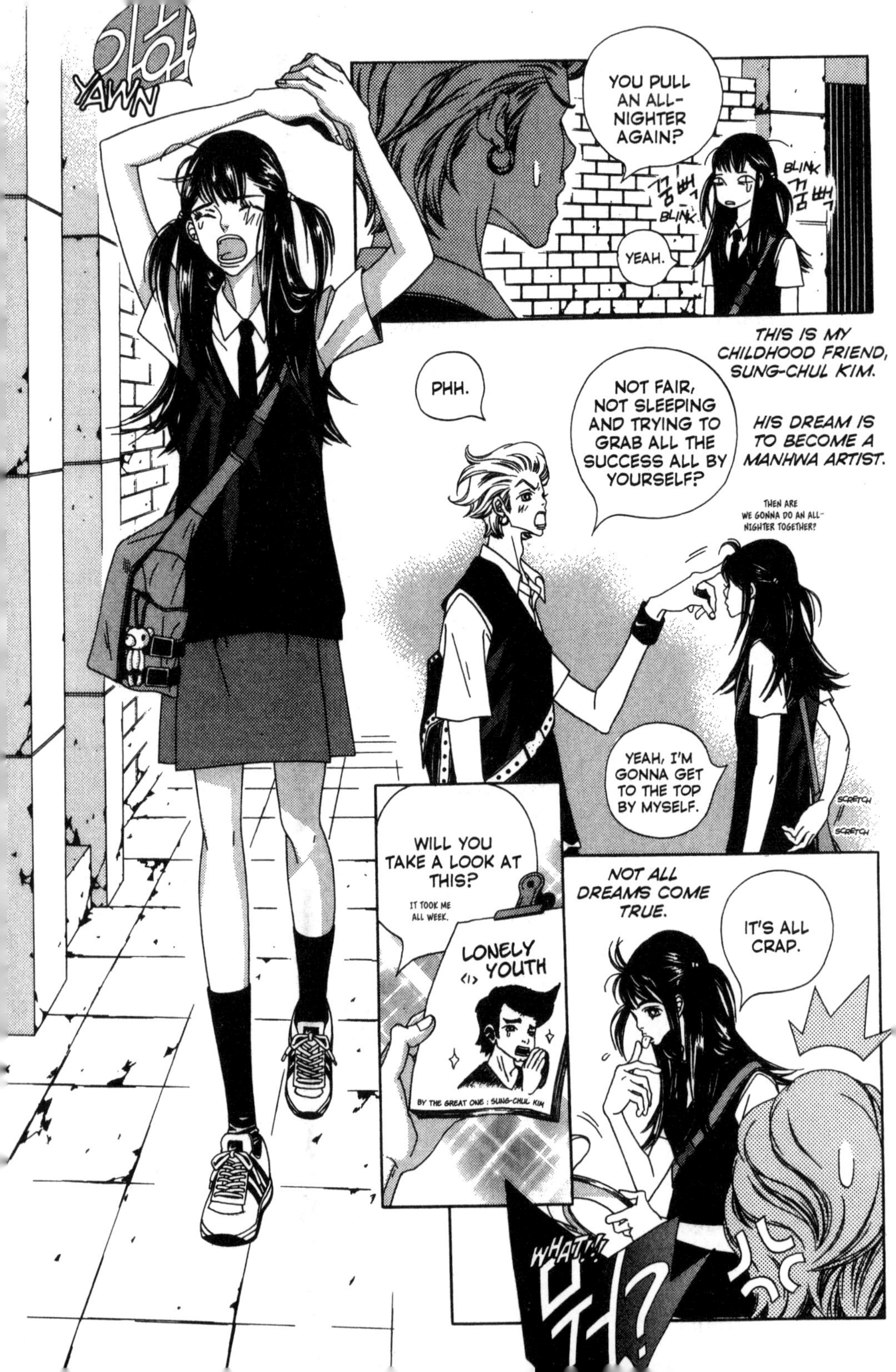
YAWN
YOU PULL AN ALL-NIGHTER AGAIN?
BLINK
BLINK
YEAH.
PHH.
NOT FAIR, NOT SLEEPING AND TRYING TO GRAB ALL THE SUCCESS ALL BY YOURSELF?
THIS IS MY CHILDHOOD FRIEND, SUNG-CHUL KIM.
HIS DREAM IS TO BECOME A MANHWA ARTIST.
THEN ARE WE GONNA DO AN ALL-NIGHTER TOGETHER?
YEAH, I'M GONNA GET TO THE TOP BY MYSELF.
SCRETCH
SCRETCH
WILL YOU TAKE A LOOK AT THIS?
IT TOOK ME ALL WEEK.
LONELY YOUTH
<1>
BY THE GREAT ONE : SUNG-CHUL KIM
NOT ALL DREAMS COME TRUE.
IT'S ALL CRAP.
WHAT!?

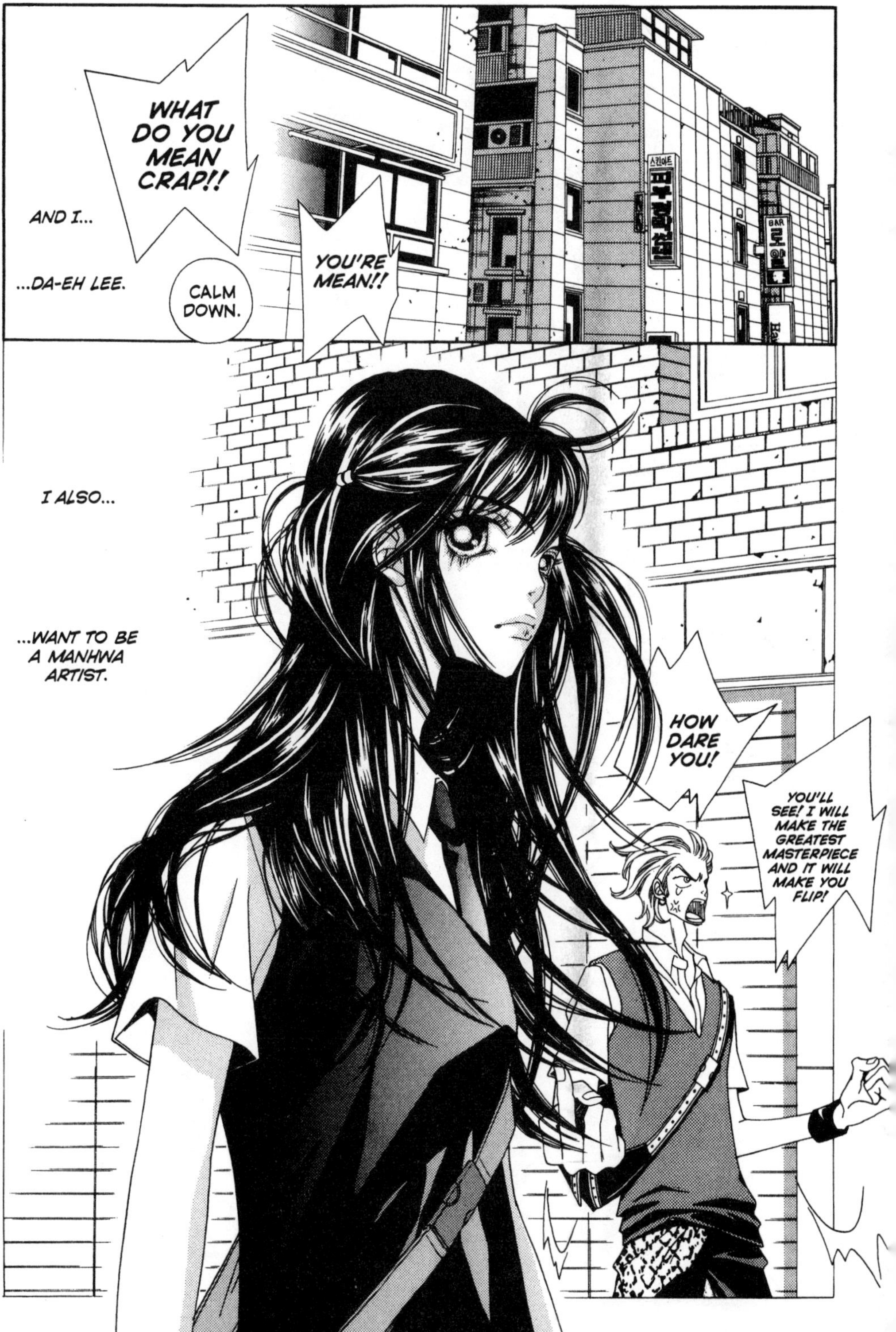
WHAT DO YOU MEAN CRAP!!
AND I...
...DA-EH LEE.
CALM DOWN.
YOU'RE MEAN!!
I ALSO...
...WANT TO BE A MANHWA ARTIST.
HOW DARE YOU!
YOU'LL SEE! I WILL MAKE THE GREATEST MASTERPIECE AND IT WILL MAKE YOU FLIP!

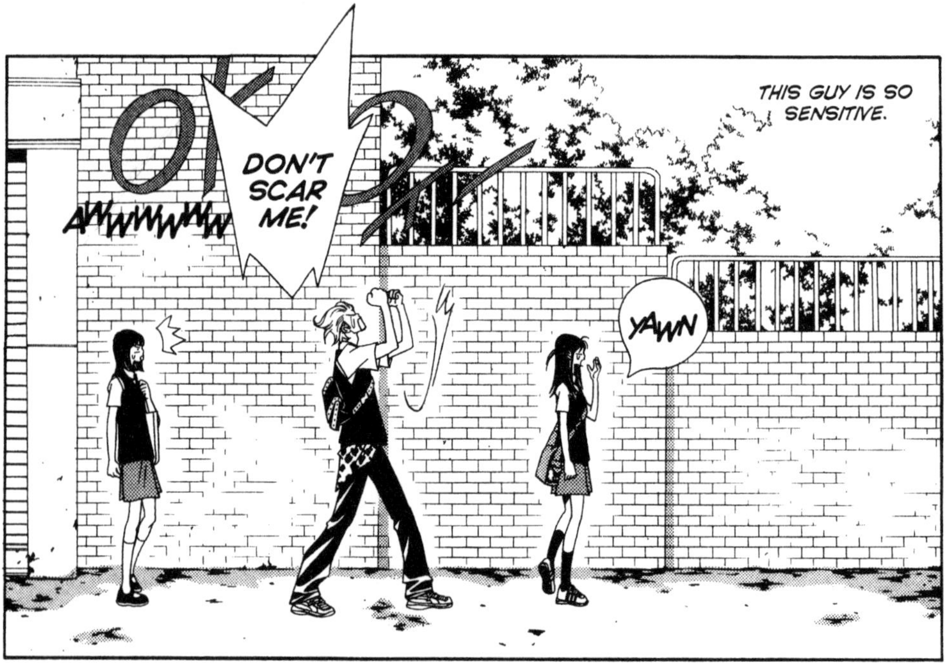
OK?
AWWWWWW
DON'T SCAR ME!
THIS GUY IS SO SENSITIVE.
YAWN
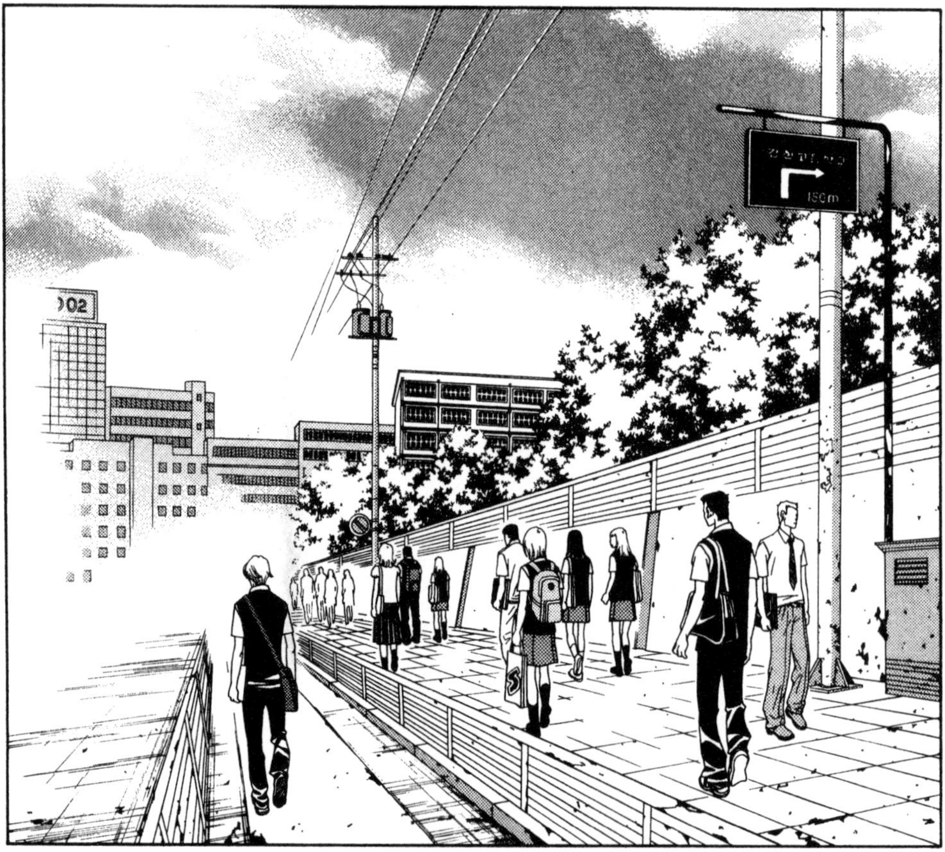
150m

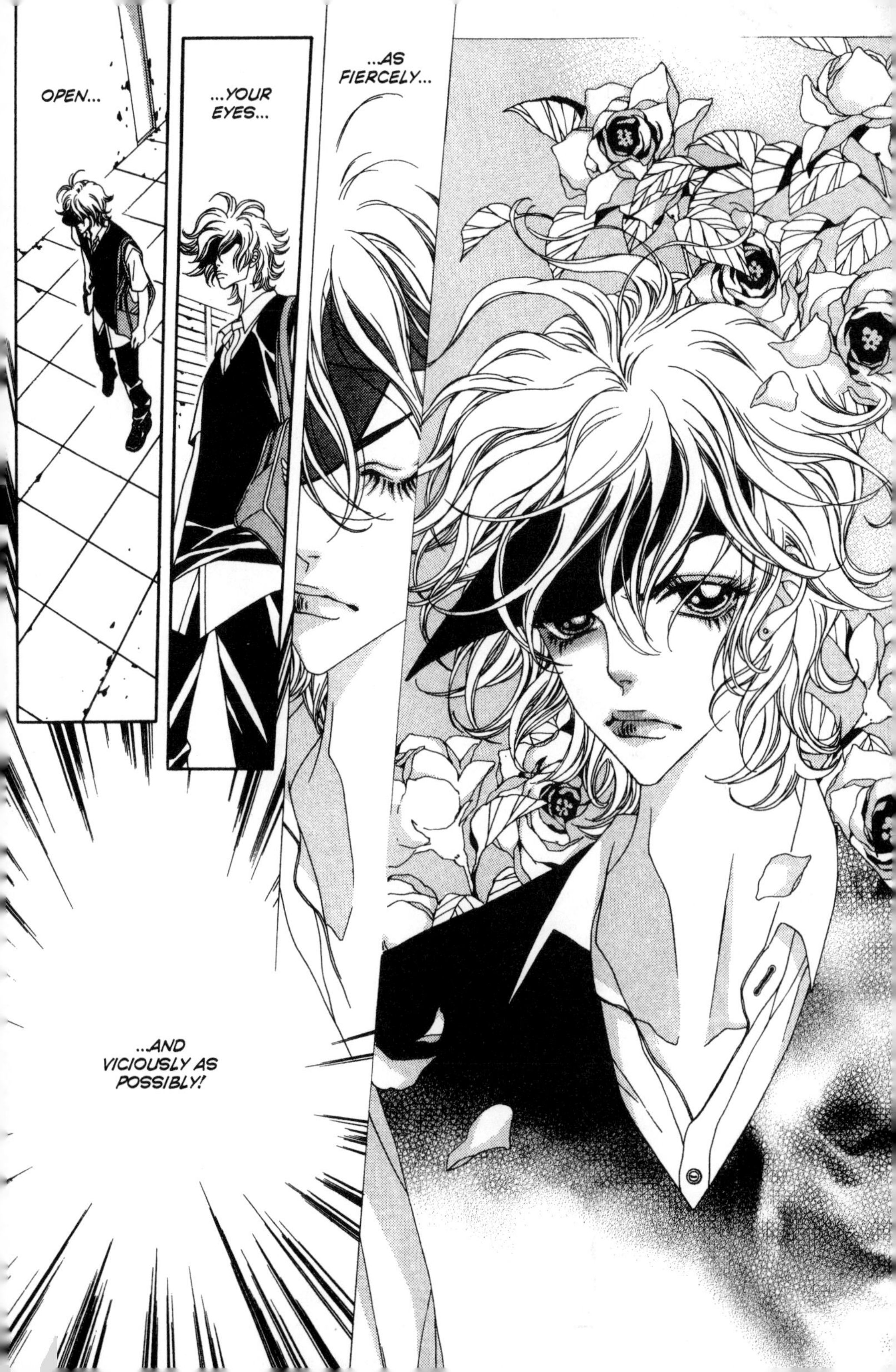
OPEN...
...YOUR EYES...
...AS FIERCELY...
...AND VICIOUSLY AS POSSIBLY!

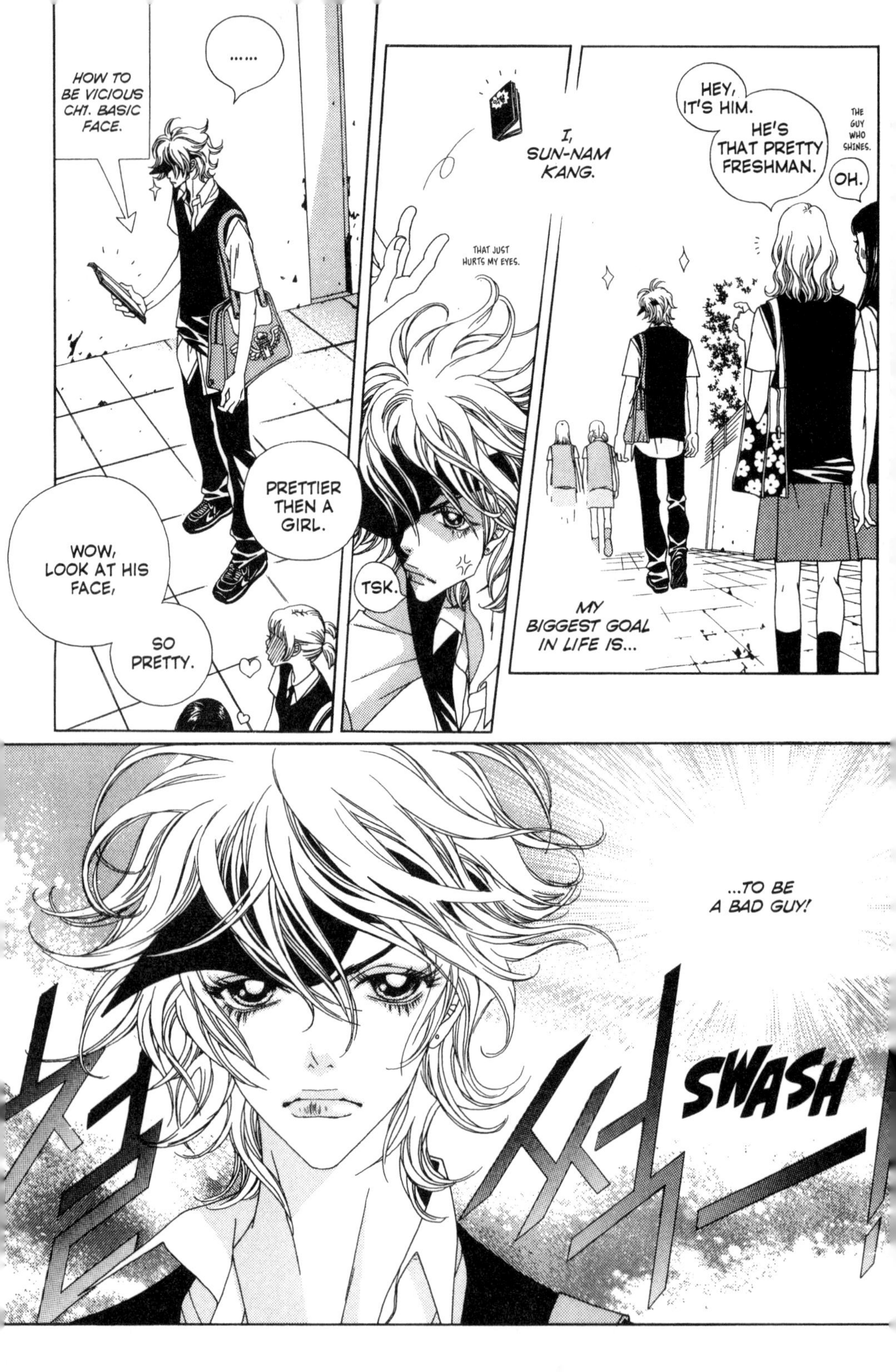
HOW TO BE VICIOUS CH1. BASIC FACE.
......
WOW, LOOK AT HIS FACE,
SO PRETTY.
PRETTIER THEN A GIRL.
I, SUN-NAM KANG.
THAT JUST HURTS MY EYES.
TSK.
HEY, IT'S HIM.
HE'S THAT PRETTY FRESHMAN.
THE GUY WHO SHINES.
OH.
MY BIGGEST GOAL IN LIFE IS...
...TO BE A BAD GUY!
SWASH

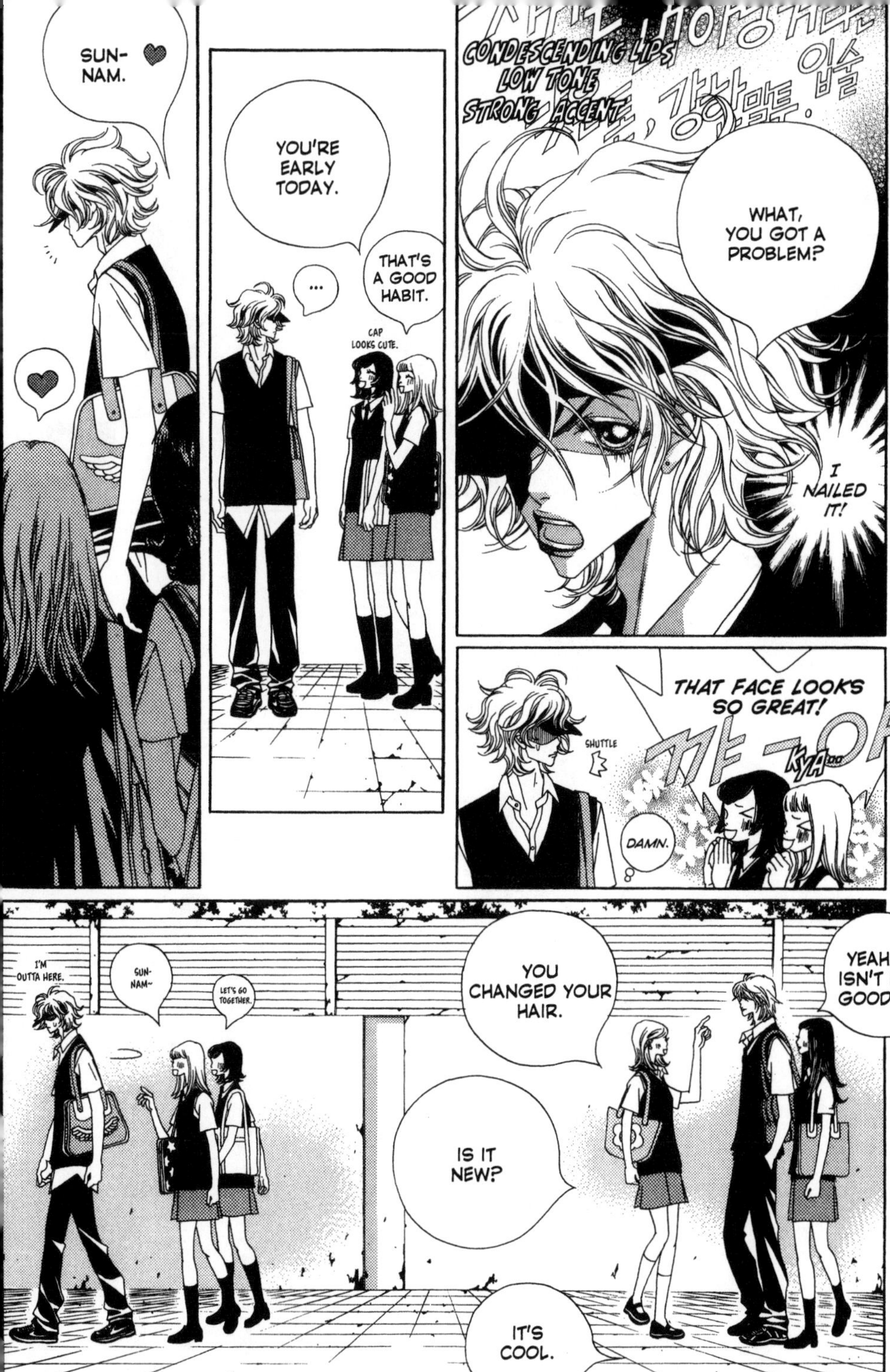
SUN-NAM. ♥
♥
YOU'RE EARLY TODAY.
...
THAT'S A GOOD HABIT.
CAP LOOKS CUTE.
CONDESCENDING LIPS
LOW TONE
STRONG ACCENT
WHAT, YOU GOT A PROBLEM?
I NAILED IT!
THAT FACE LOOKS SO GREAT!
SHUTTLE
KYA
DAMN.
I'M OUTTA HERE.
SUN-NAM~
LET'S GO TOGETHER.
YOU CHANGED YOUR HAIR.
IS IT NEW?
YEAH, ISN'T IT GOOD?
IT'S COOL.

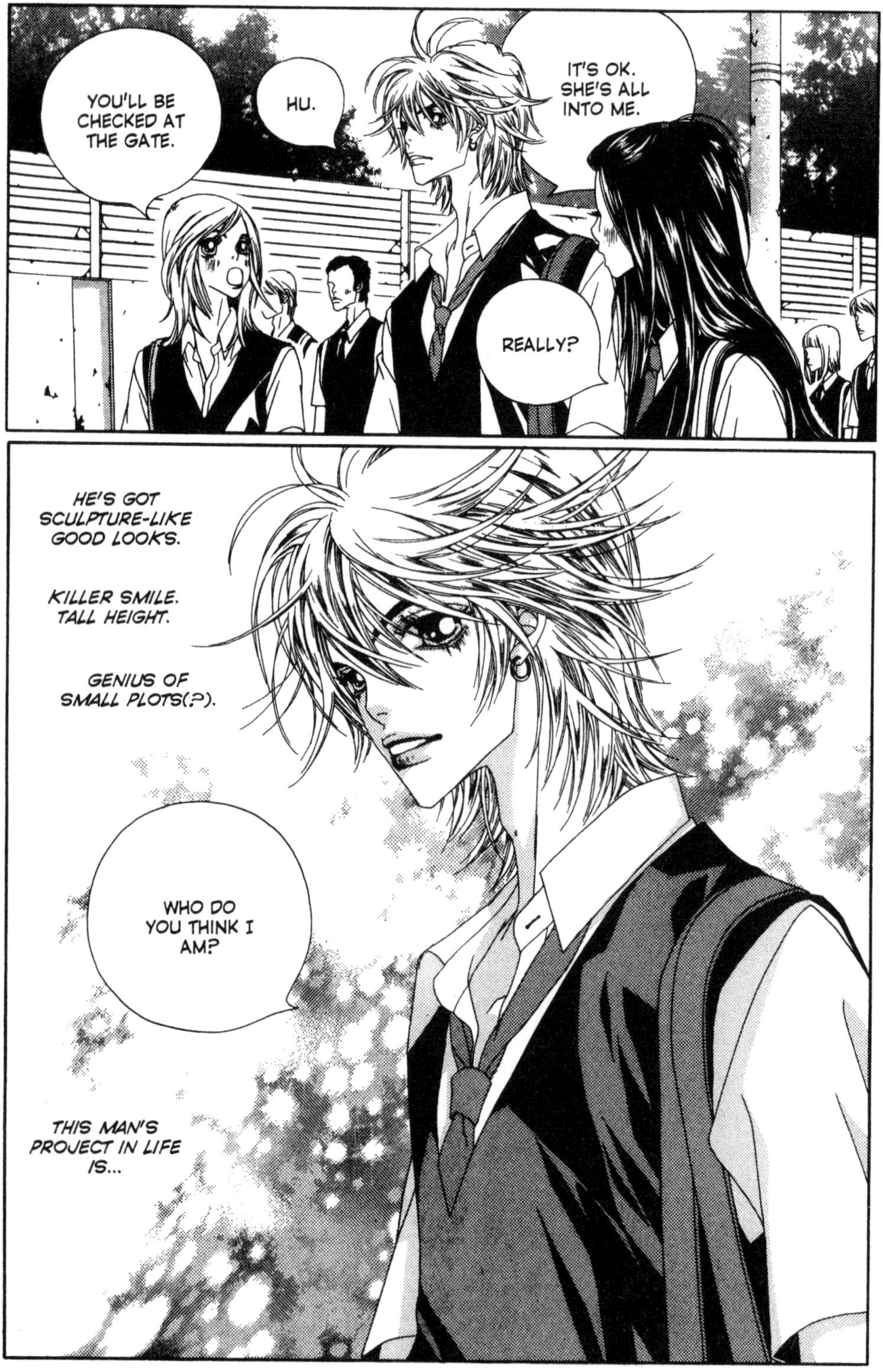
YOU'LL BE CHECKED AT THE GATE.
HU.
IT'S OK. SHE'S ALL INTO ME.
REALLY?
HE'S GOT SCULPTURE-LIKE GOOD LOOKS.
KILLER SMILE. TALL HEIGHT.
GENIUS OF SMALL PLOTS(?).
WHO DO YOU THINK I AM?
THIS MAN'S PROJECT IN LIFE IS...

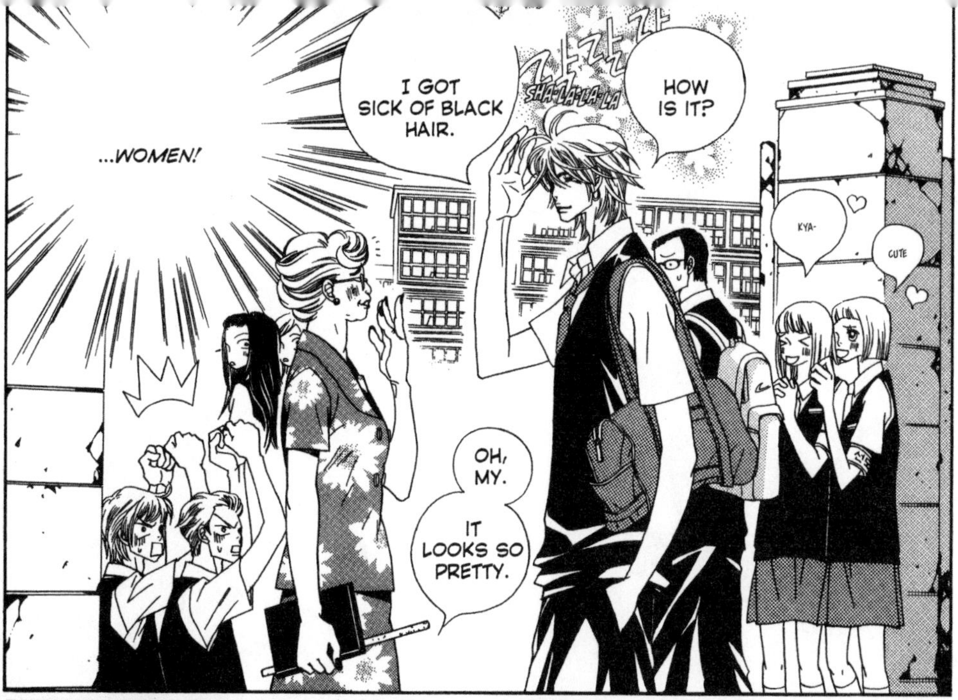
...WOMEN!
I GOT SICK OF BLACK HAIR.
SHA-LA-LA-LA
HOW IS IT?
KYA-
CUTE
OH, MY.
IT LOOKS SO PRETTY.

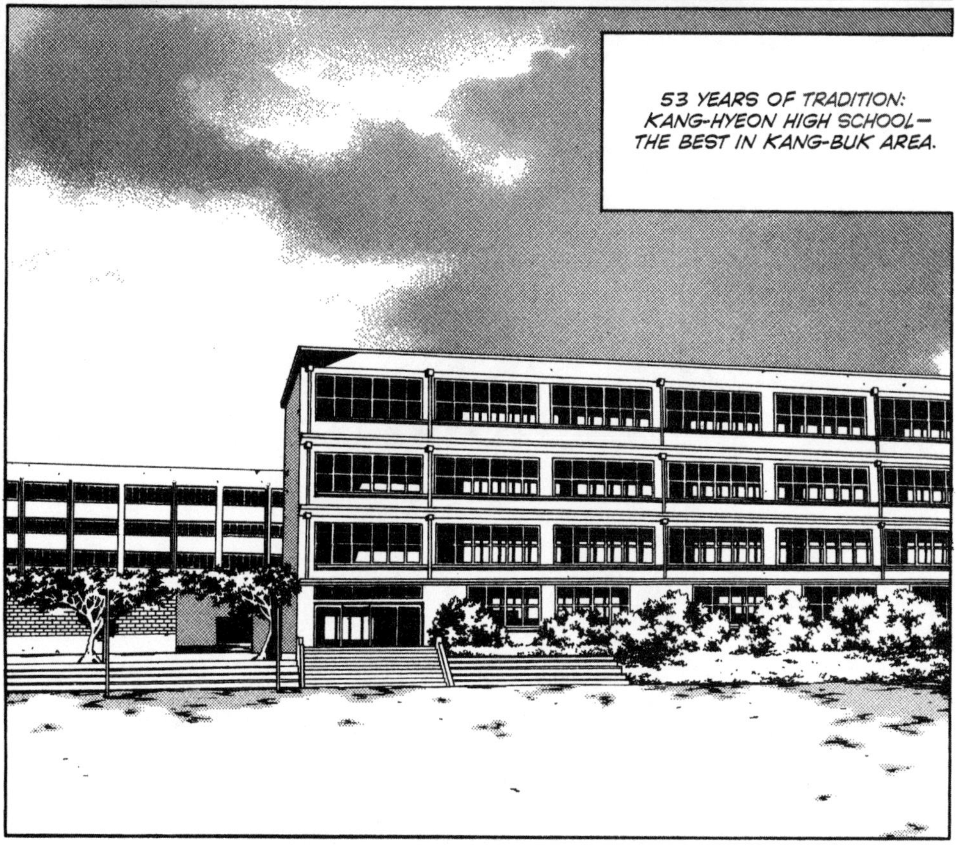
53 YEARS OF TRADITION: KANG-HYEON HIGH SCHOOL—THE BEST IN KANG-BUK AREA.

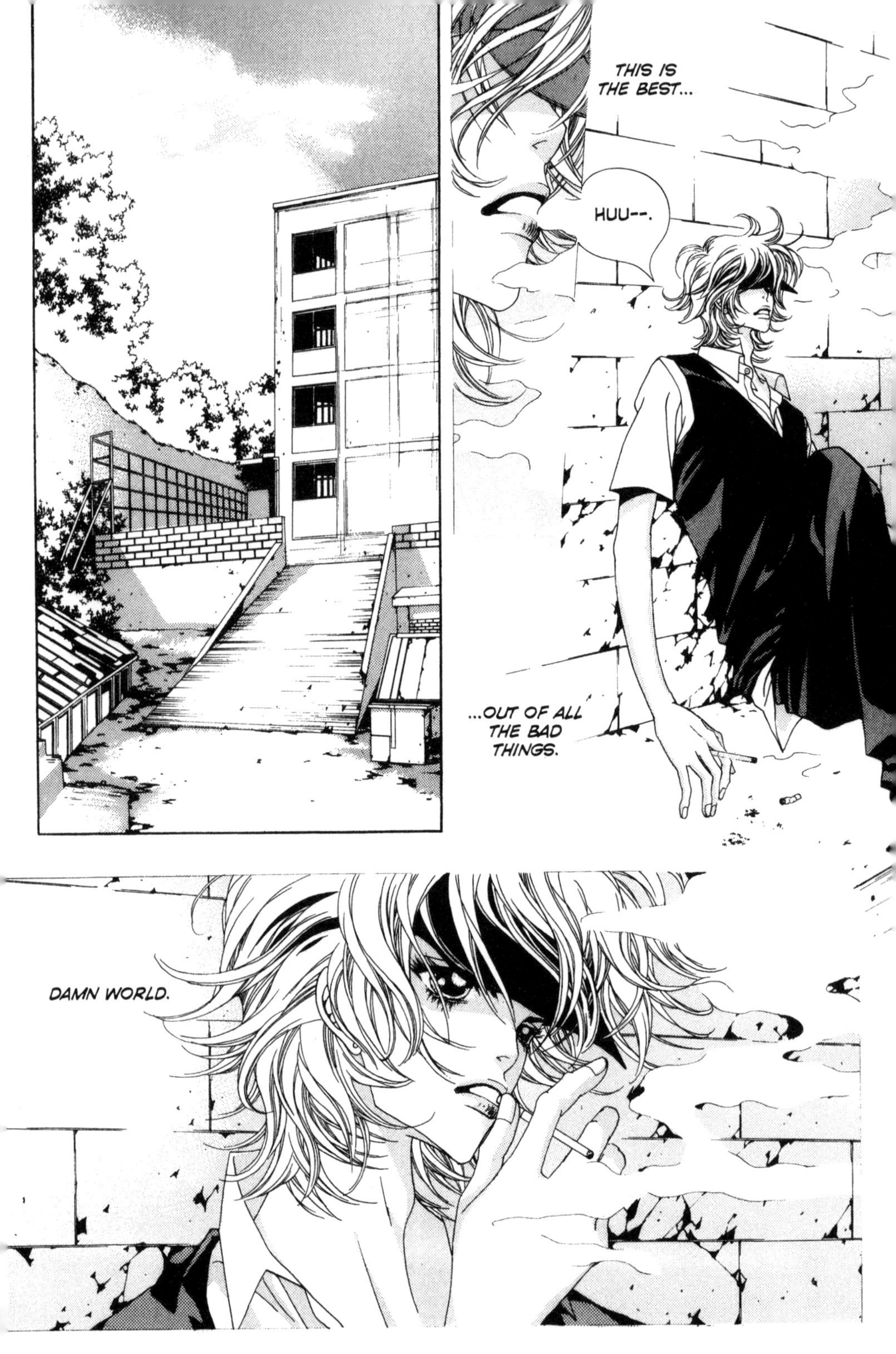
THIS IS THE BEST...
HUU--.
...OUT OF ALL THE BAD THINGS.
DAMN WORLD.

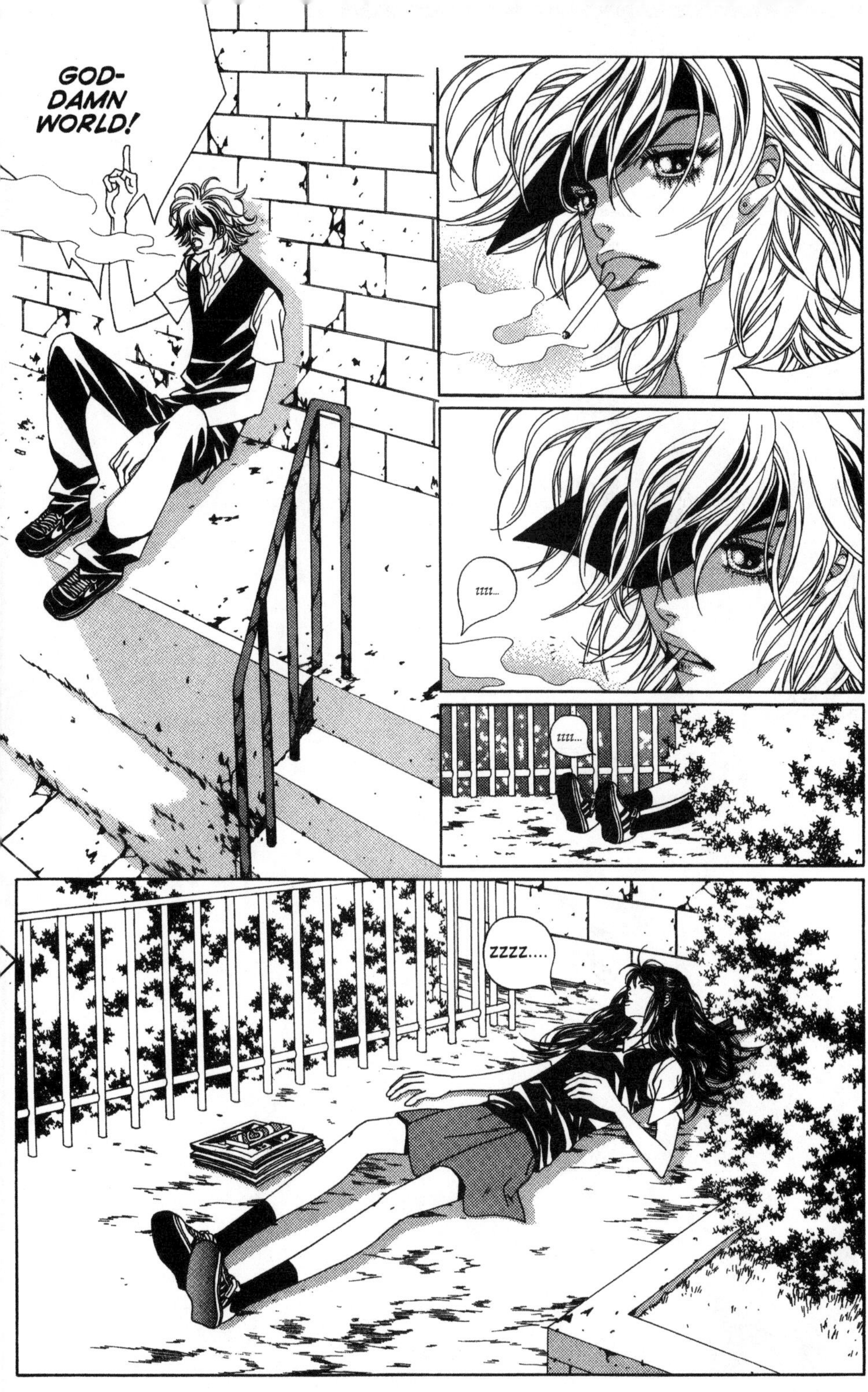
GOD-DAMN WORLD!
zzzz...
zzzz...
ZZZZ....

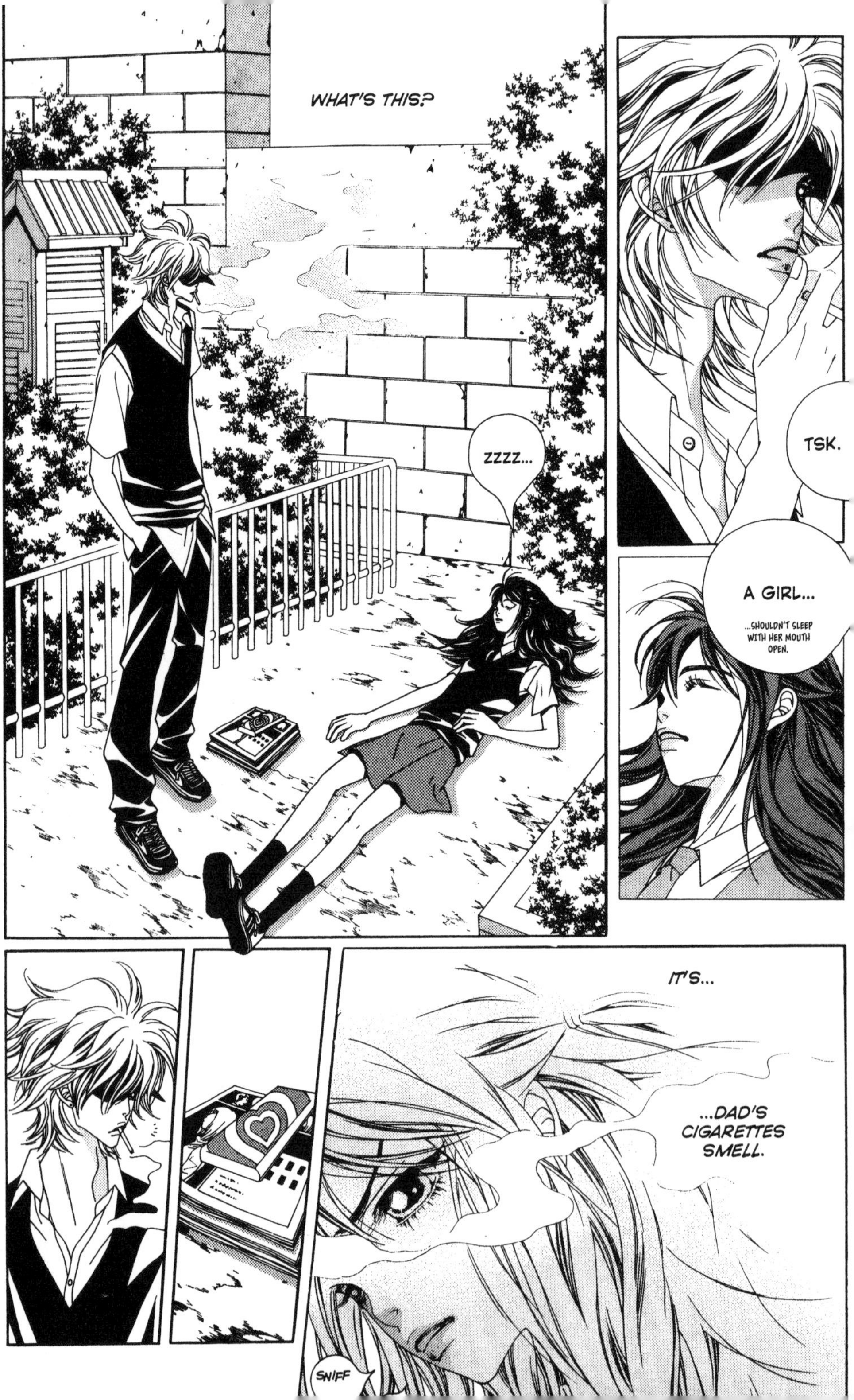
WHAT'S THIS?
ZZZZ...
TSK.
A GIRL...
...SHOULDN'T SLEEP WITH HER MOUTH OPEN.
IT'S...
...DAD'S CIGARETTES SMELL.
SNIFF

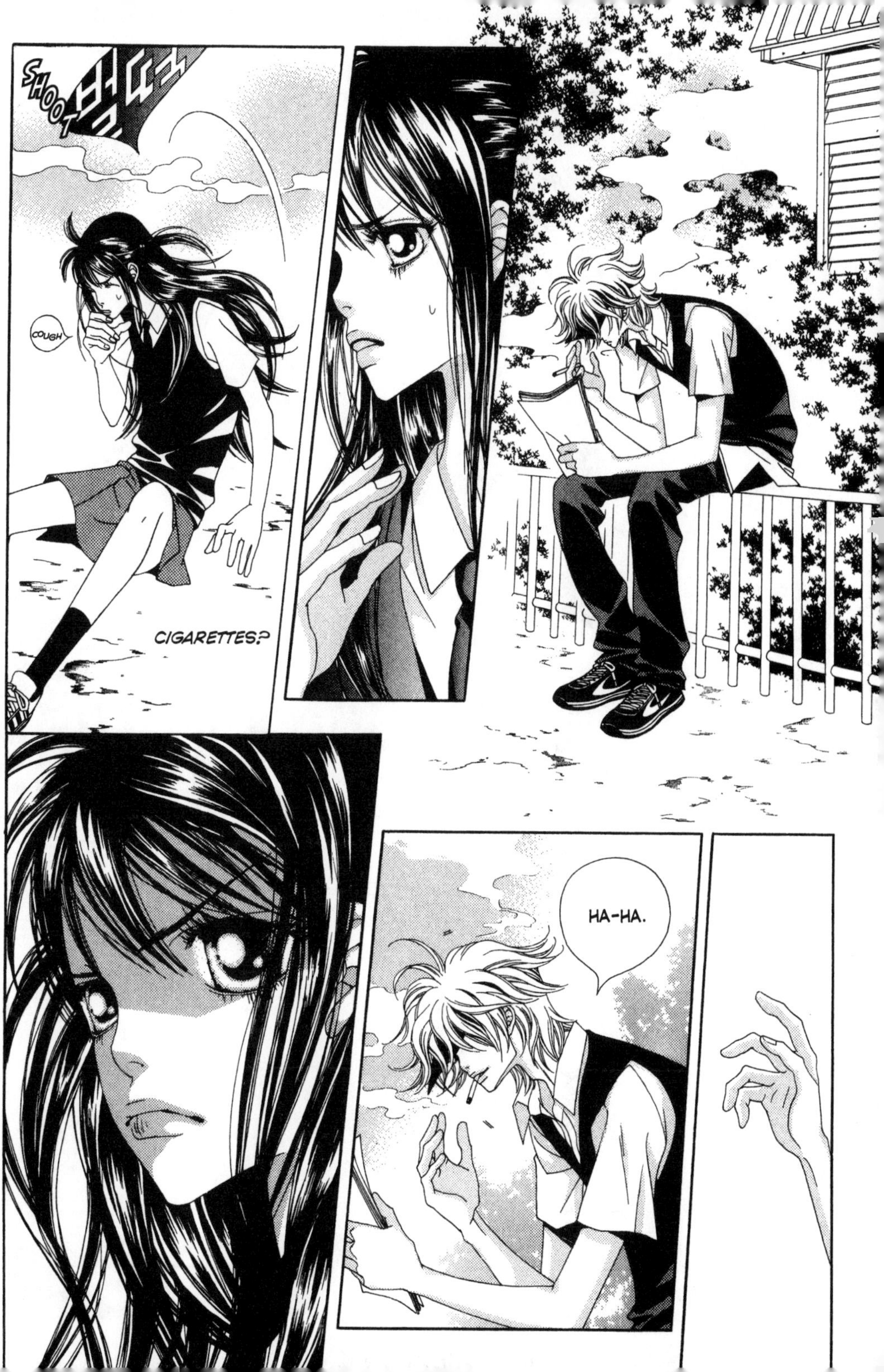
SHOOT
COUGH
CIGARETTES?
HA-HA.

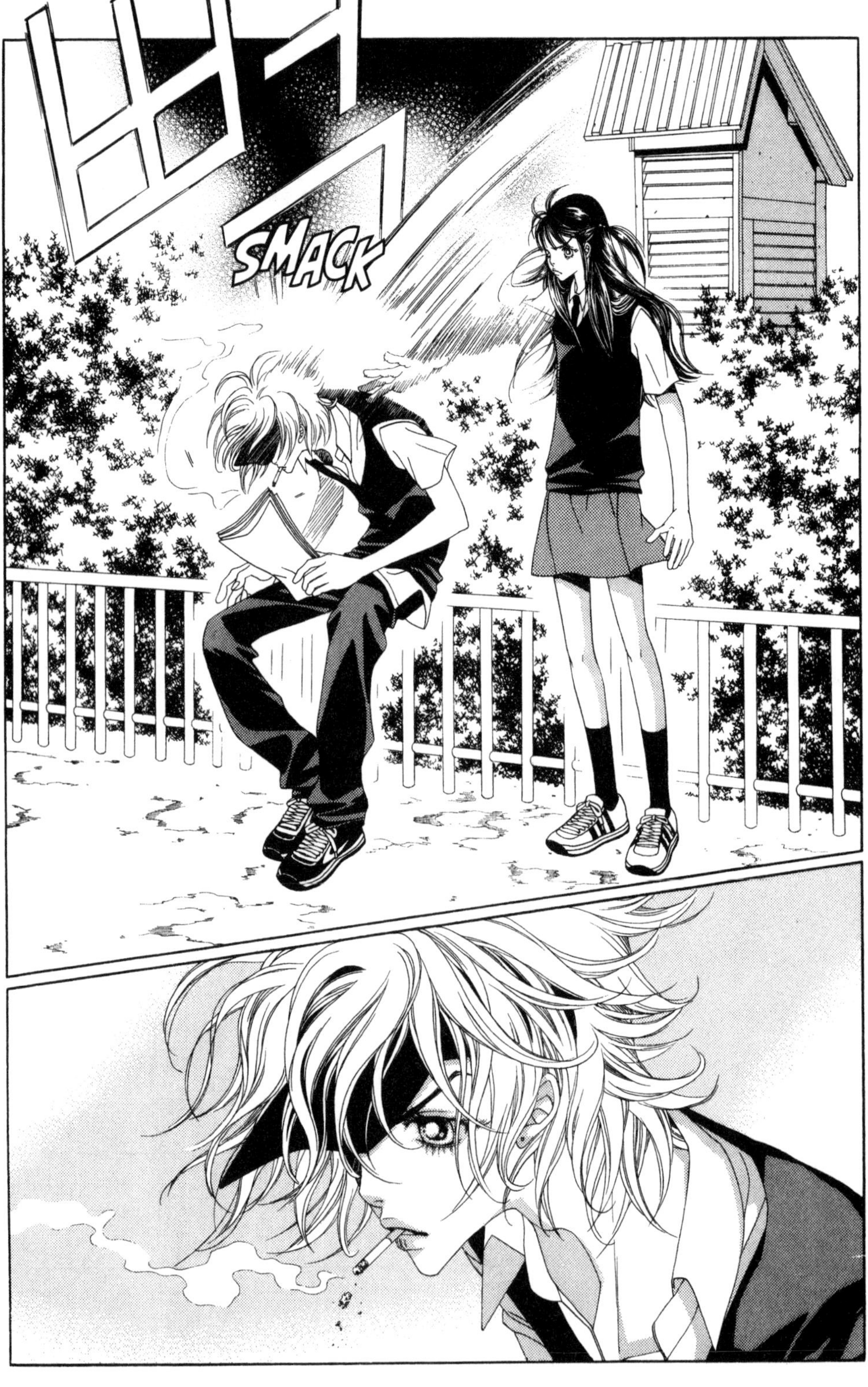
SMACK

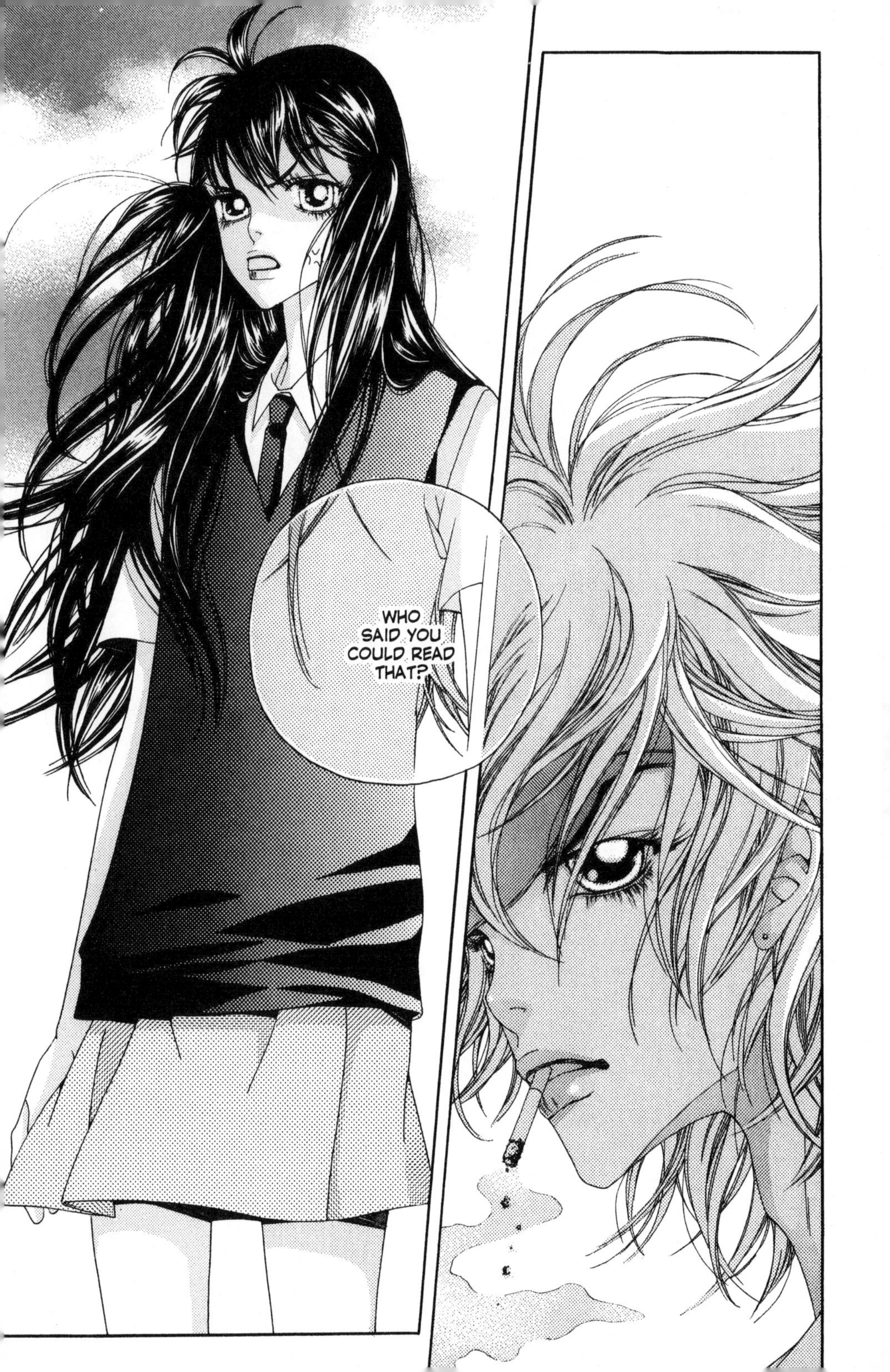
WHO SAID YOU COULD READ THAT?

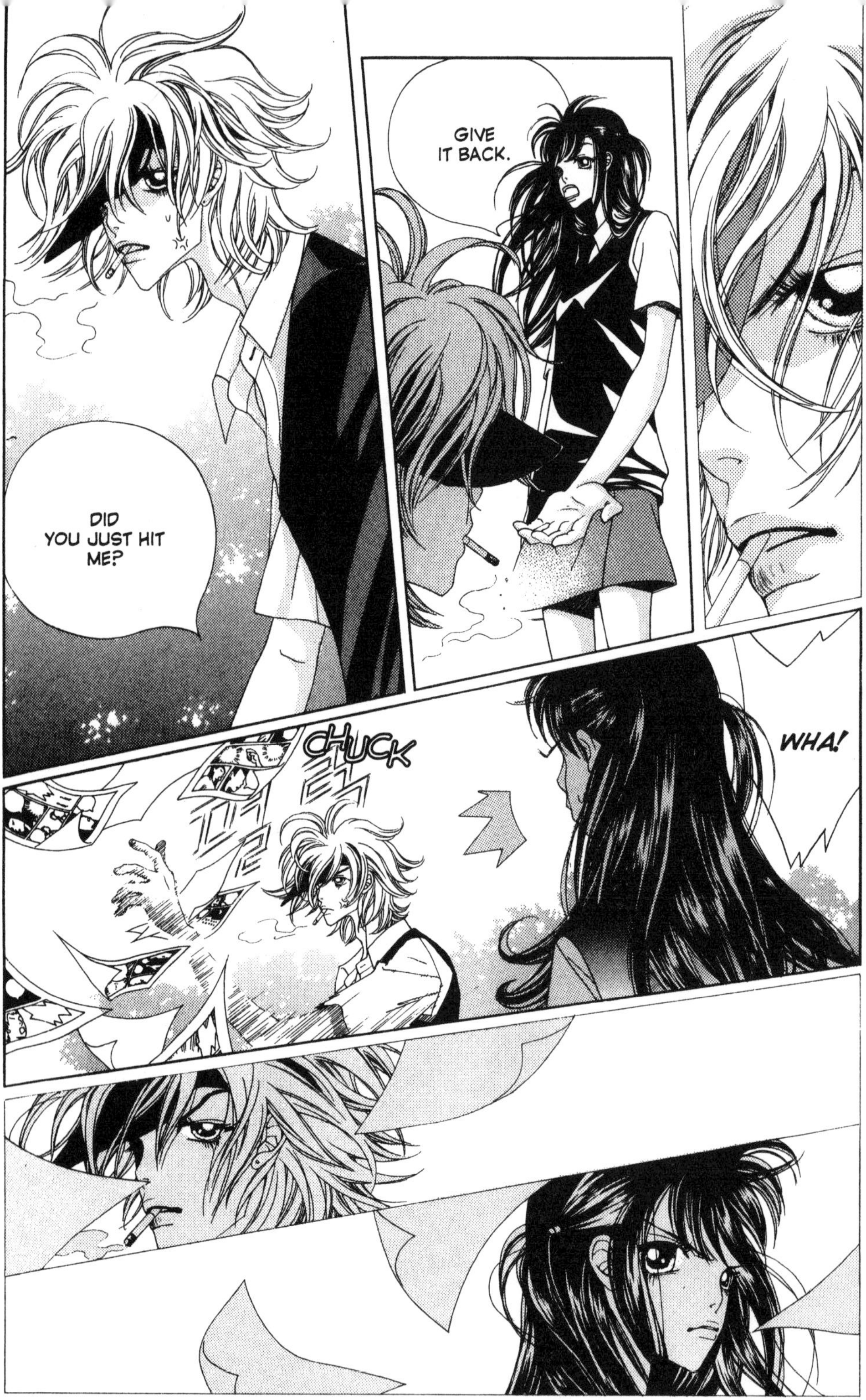
DID YOU JUST HIT ME?
GIVE IT BACK.
CHUCK
WHA!

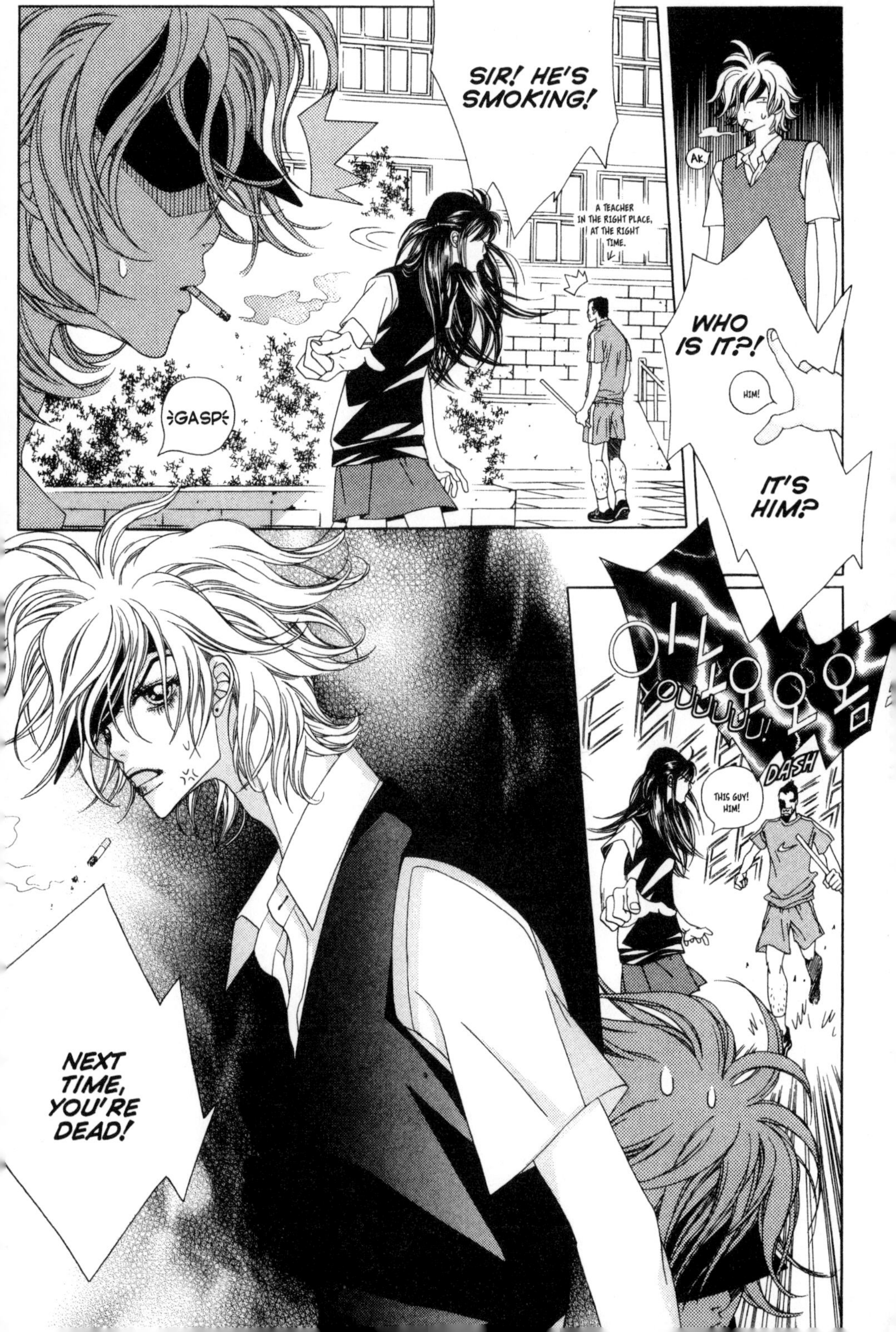
SIR! HE'S SMOKING!
GASP
A TEACHER IN THE RIGHT PLACE, AT THE RIGHT TIME.
AK.
WHO IS IT?!
HIM!
IT'S HIM?
NEXT TIME, YOU'RE DEAD!
YOUUUUU!
DASH
THIS GUY! HIM!

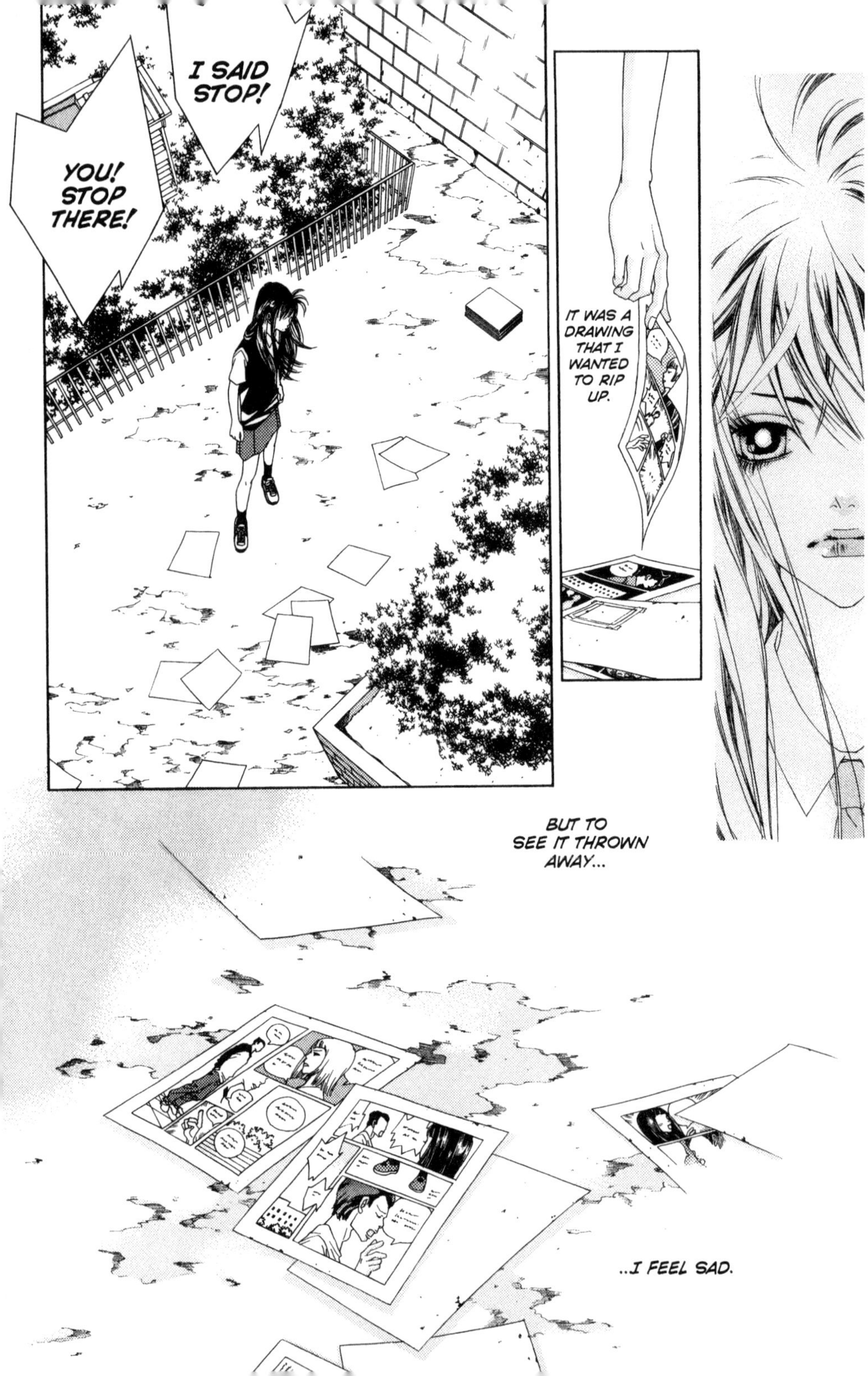
YOU! STOP THERE!
I SAID STOP!
IT WAS A DRAWING THAT I WANTED TO RIP UP.
BUT TO SEE IT THROWN AWAY...
..I FEEL SAD.

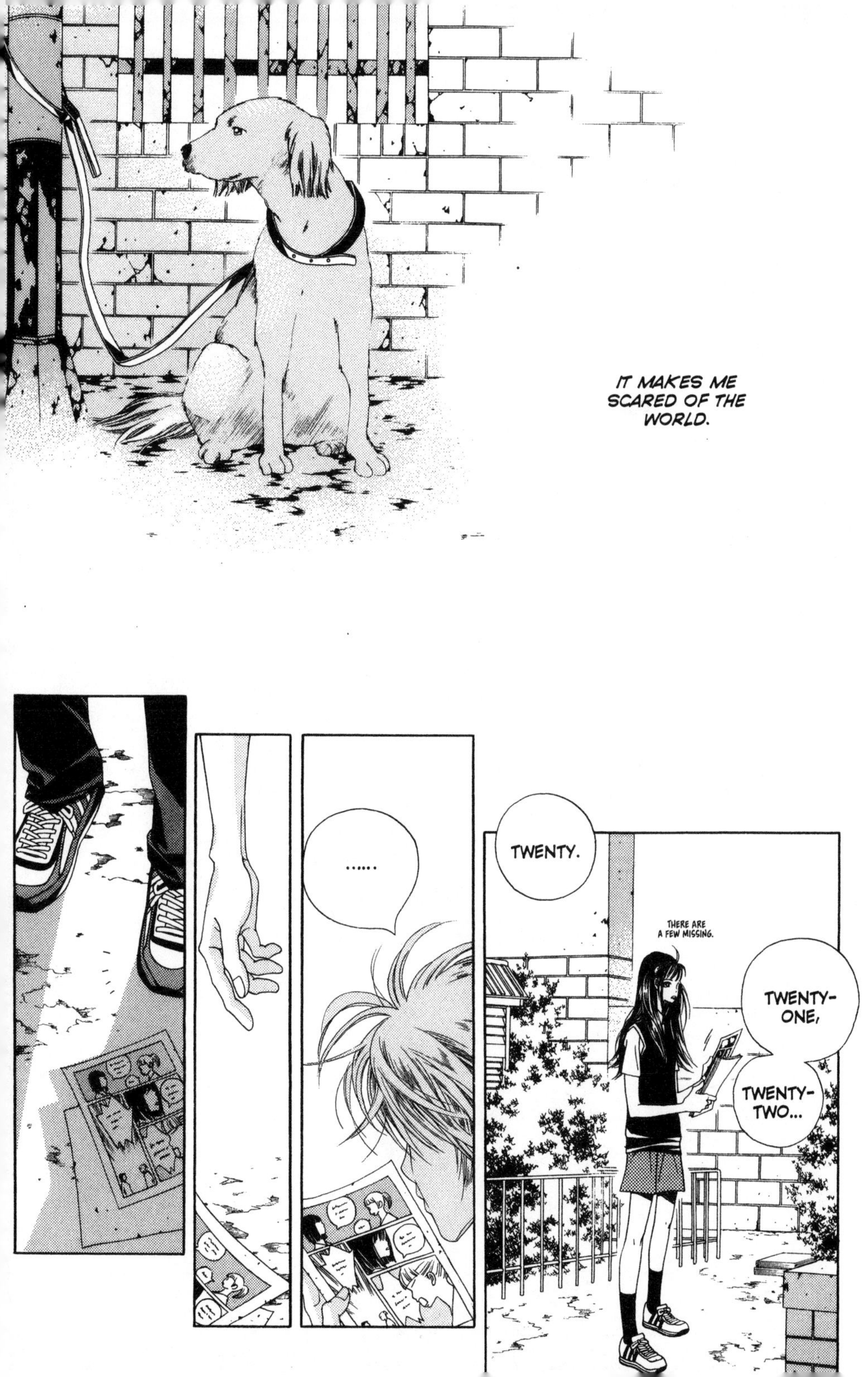
IT MAKES ME SCARED OF THE WORLD.
......
TWENTY.
THERE ARE A FEW MISSING.
TWENTY-ONE,
TWENTY-TWO...

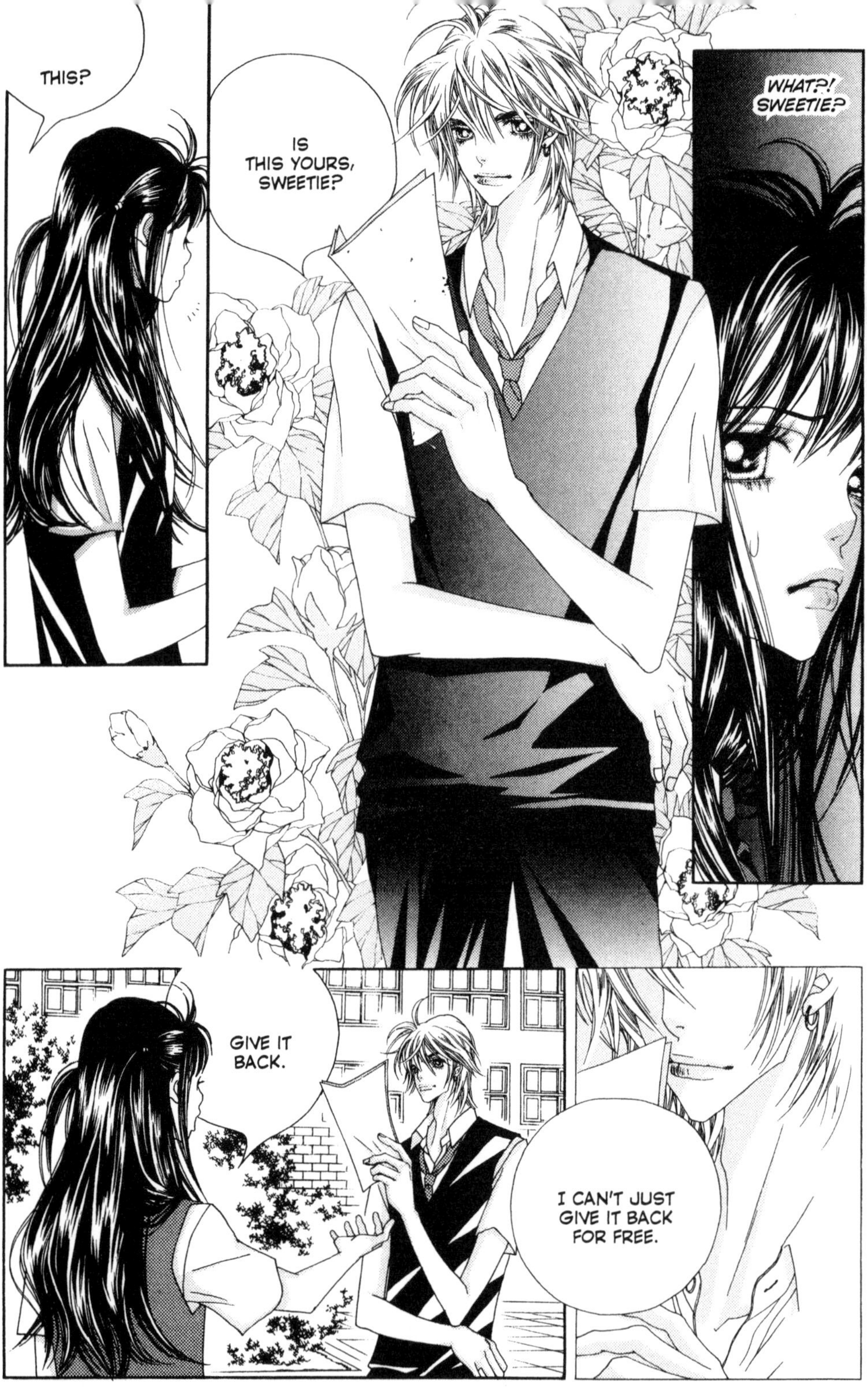
THIS?
IS THIS YOURS, SWEETIE?
WHAT?! SWEETIE?
GIVE IT BACK.
I CAN'T JUST GIVE IT BACK FOR FREE.

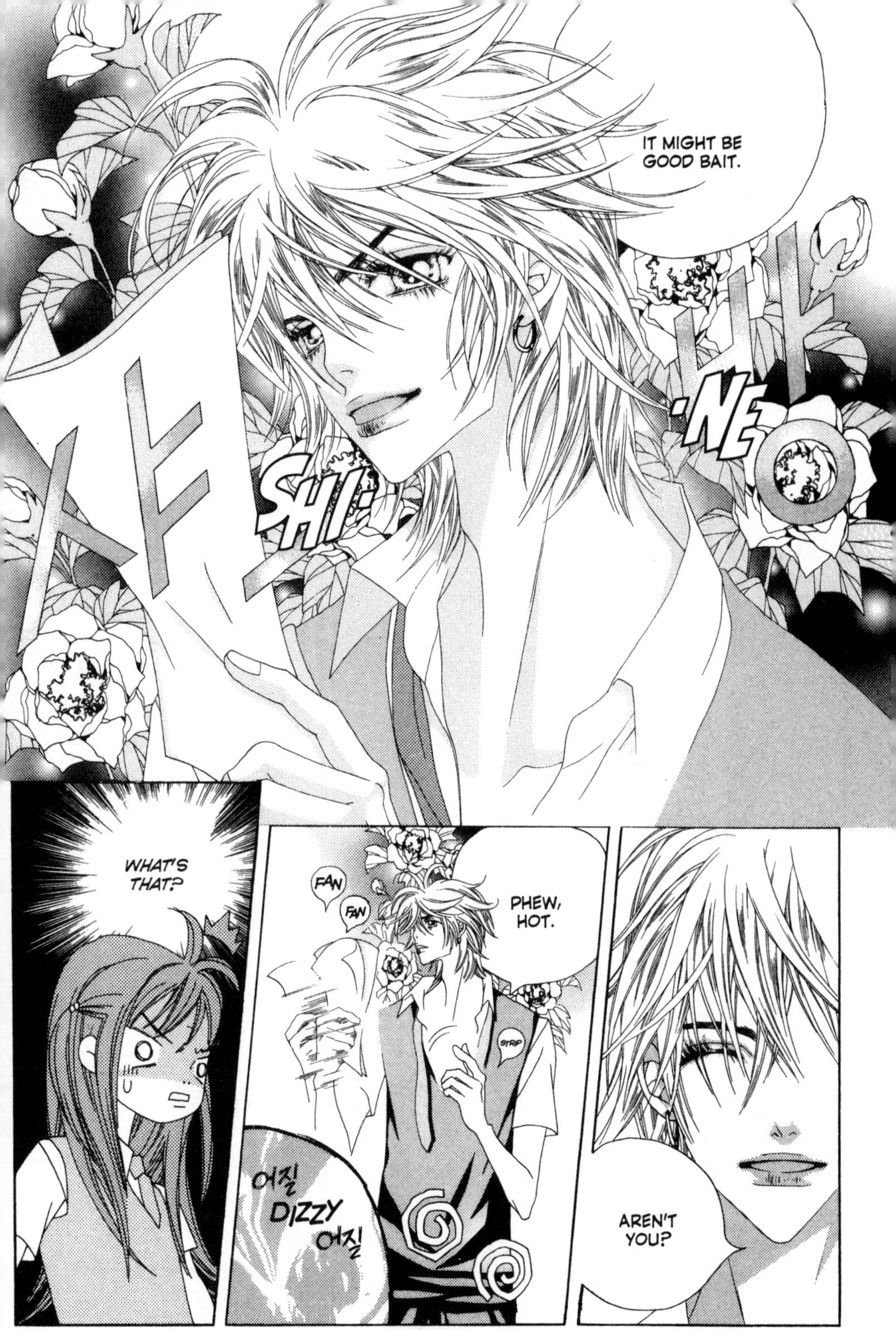
IT MIGHT BE GOOD BAIT.
SHI-
-NE
O
WHAT'S THAT?
FAN
FAN
PHEW, HOT.
STRIP
어질
DIZZY
어질!
AREN'T YOU?

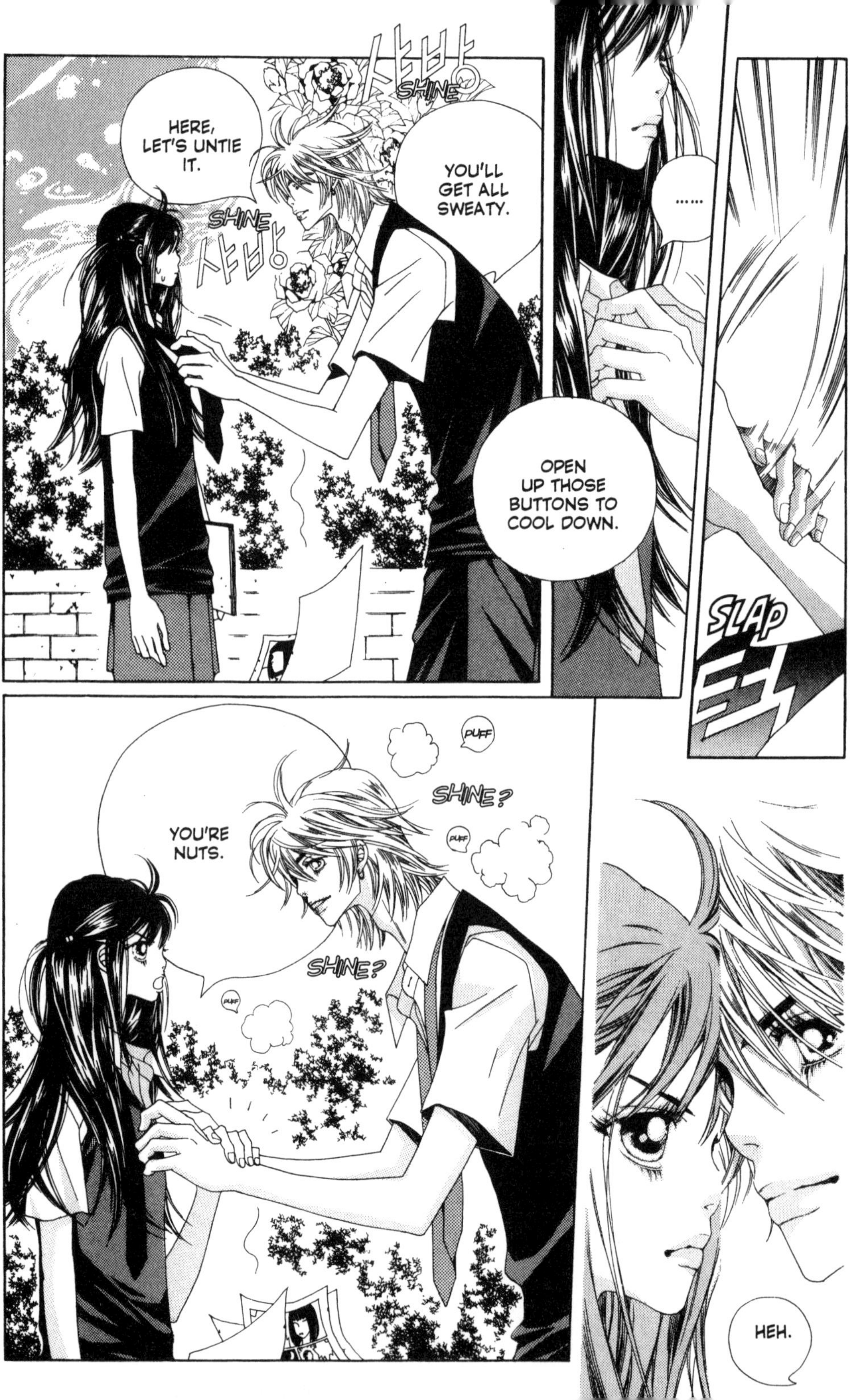
샤방
SHINE
HERE, LET'S UNTIE IT.
YOU'LL GET ALL SWEATY.
SHINE
샤방
......
OPEN UP THOSE BUTTONS TO COOL DOWN.
SLAP
YOU'RE NUTS.
PUFF
SHINE?
PUFF
SHINE?
PUFF
HEH.

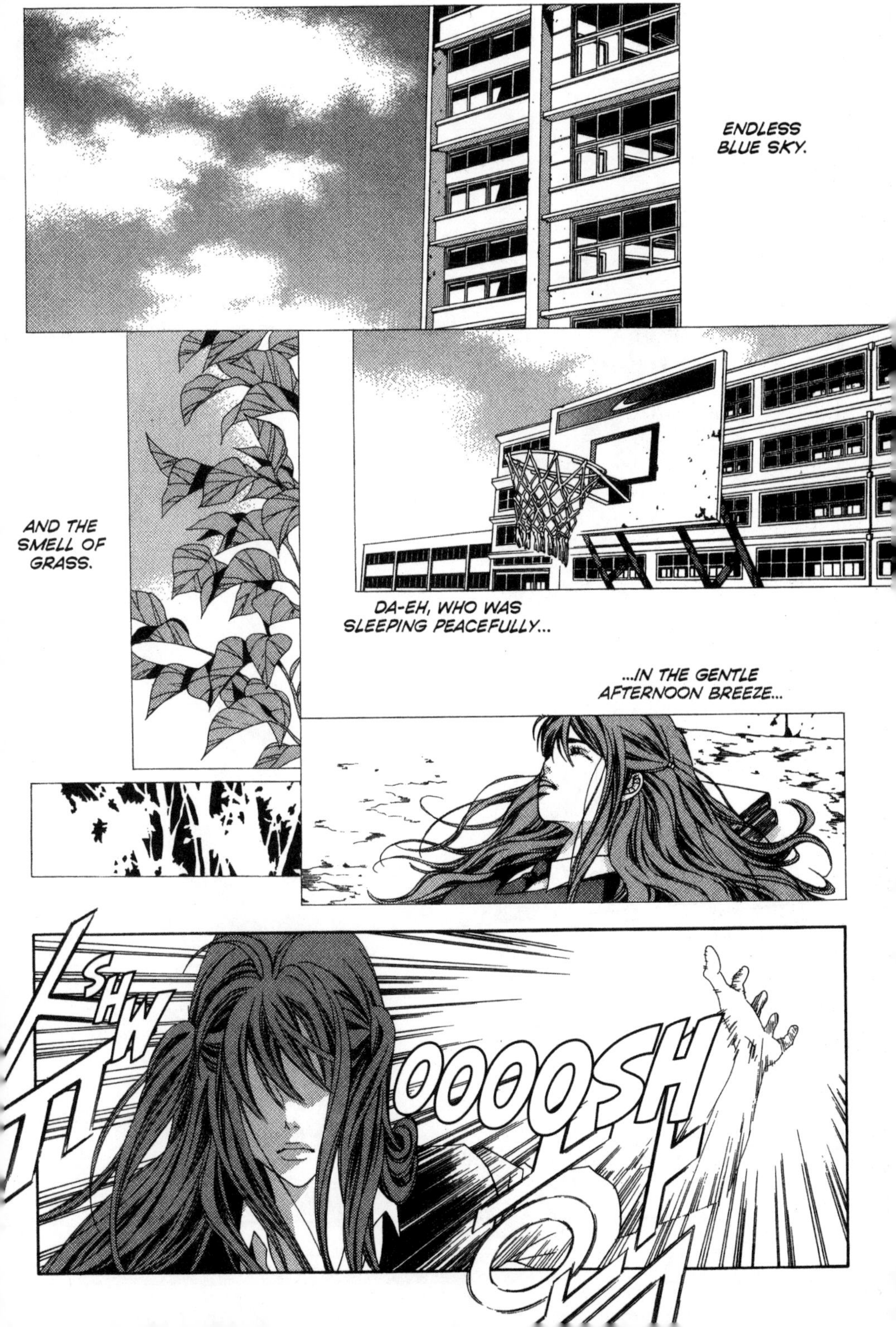
ENDLESS BLUE SKY.
AND THE SMELL OF GRASS.
DA-EH, WHO WAS SLEEPING PEACEFULLY...
...IN THE GENTLE AFTERNOON BREEZE...
SHWOOOOSH

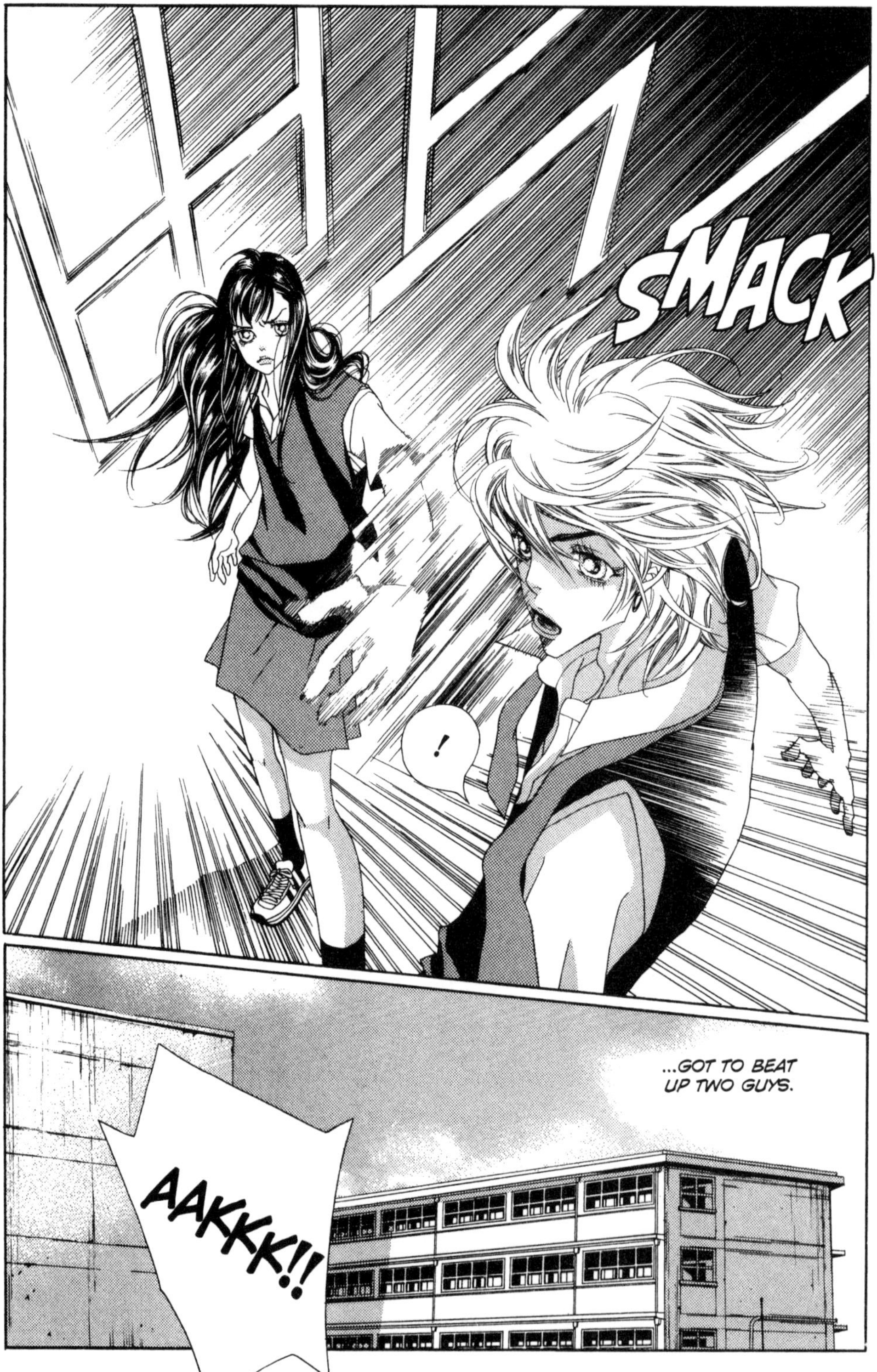
SMACK
!
AAKKK!!
...GOT TO BEAT UP TWO GUYS.

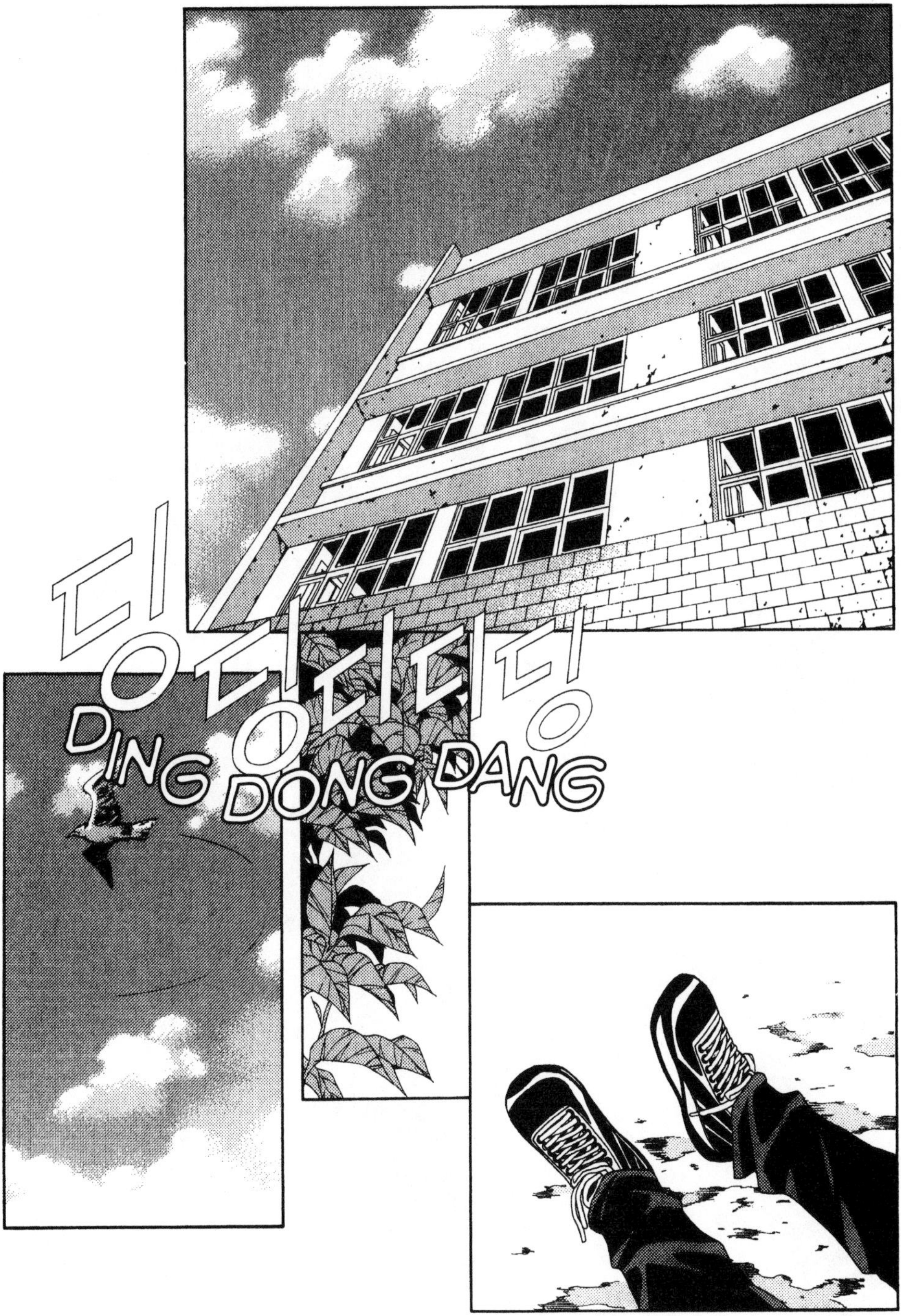
DING DONG DANG

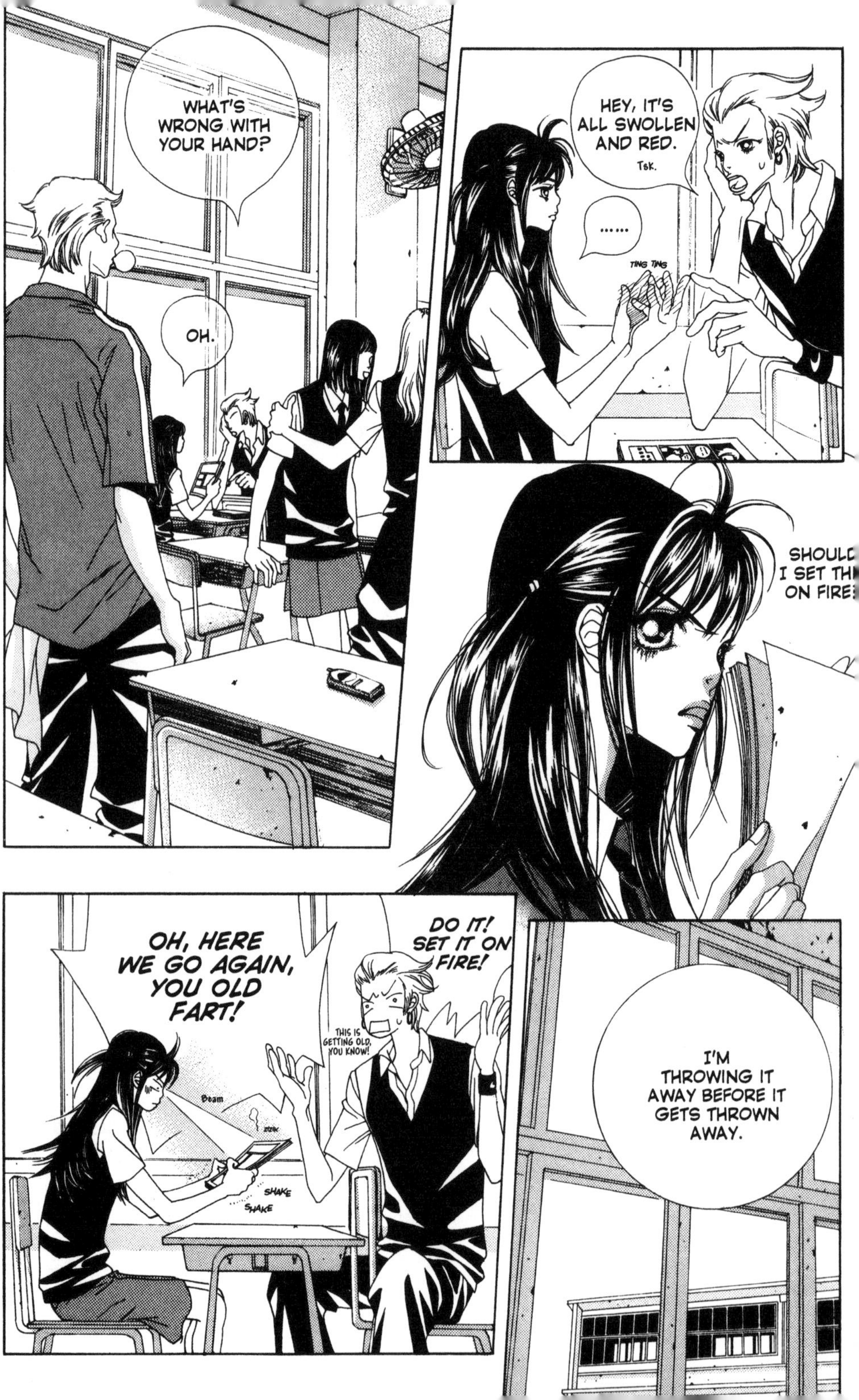
WHAT'S WRONG WITH YOUR HAND?
OH.
HEY, IT'S ALL SWOLLEN AND RED.
TSK.
......
TING TING
SHOULD I SET THI ON FIRE
OH, HERE WE GO AGAIN, YOU OLD FART!
DO IT! SET IT ON FIRE!
THIS IS GETTING OLD, YOU KNOW!
Beam
SHAKE
SHAKE
I'M THROWING IT AWAY BEFORE IT GETS THROWN AWAY.

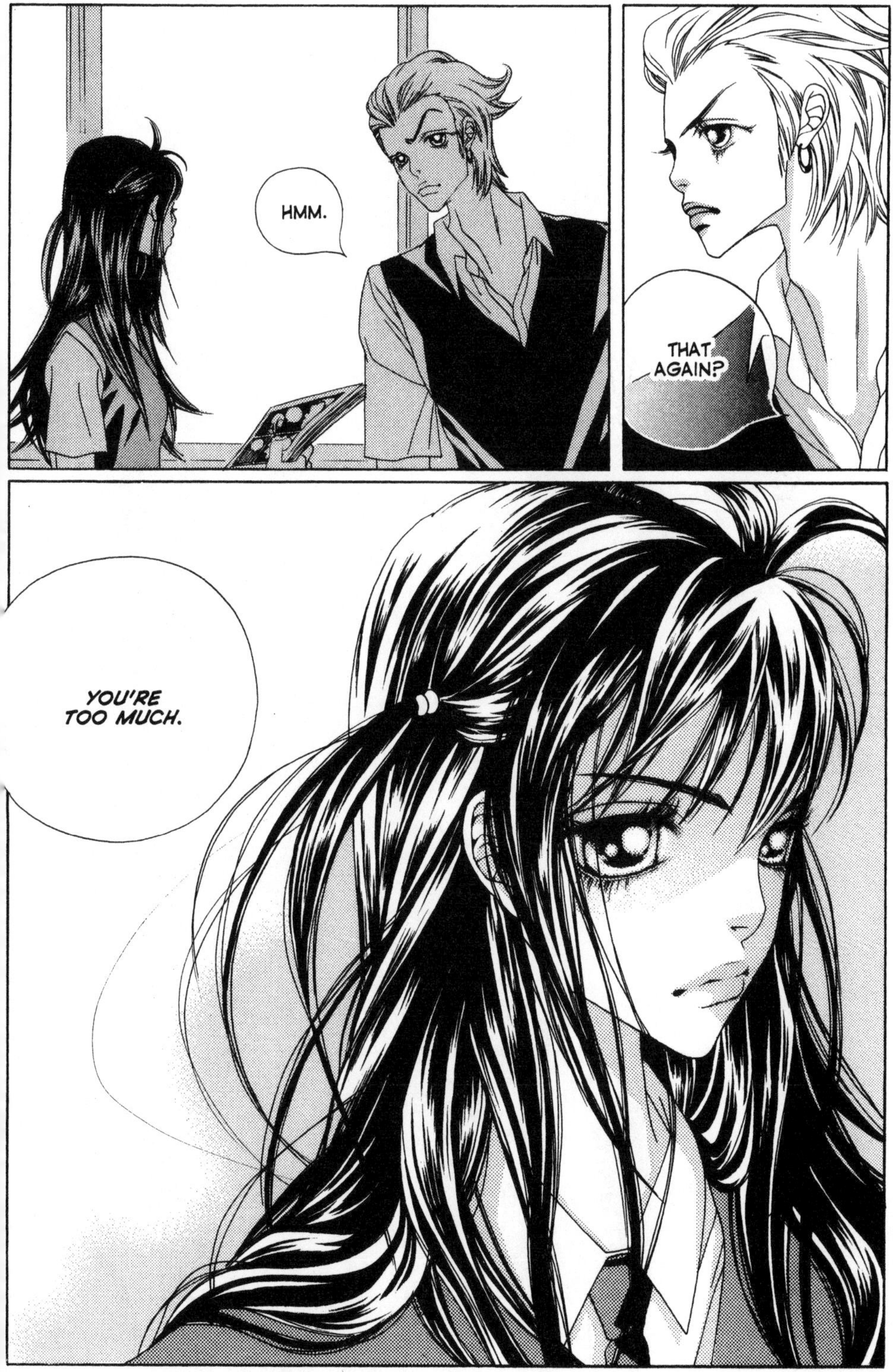
HMM.
THAT AGAIN?
YOU'RE TOO MUCH.

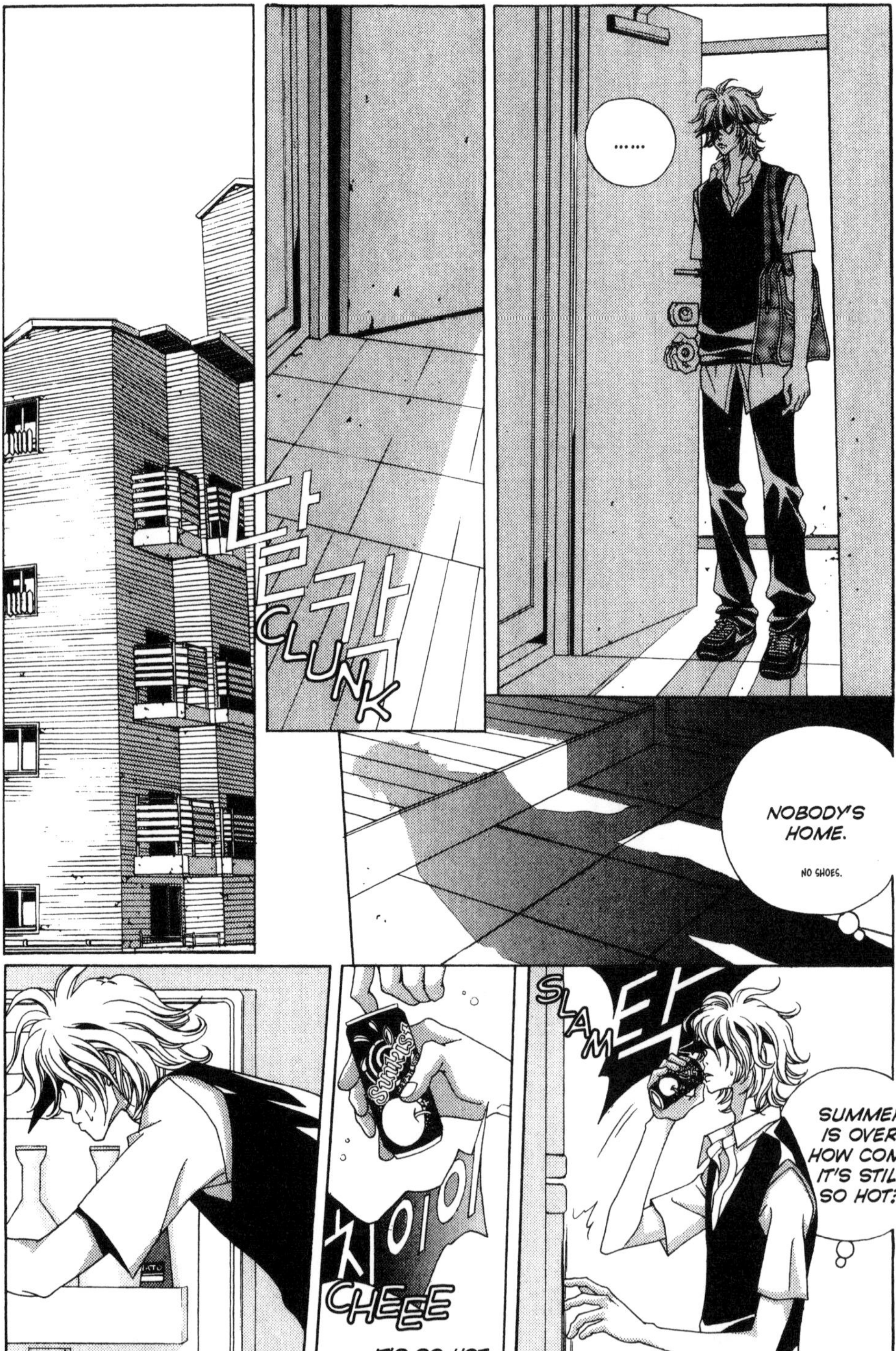
CLUNK
......
NOBODY'S HOME.
NO SHOES.
치이이이
CHEEEE
IT'S SO HOT.
탁
SLAM
SUMMER IS OVER, HOW COME IT'S STILL SO HOT?

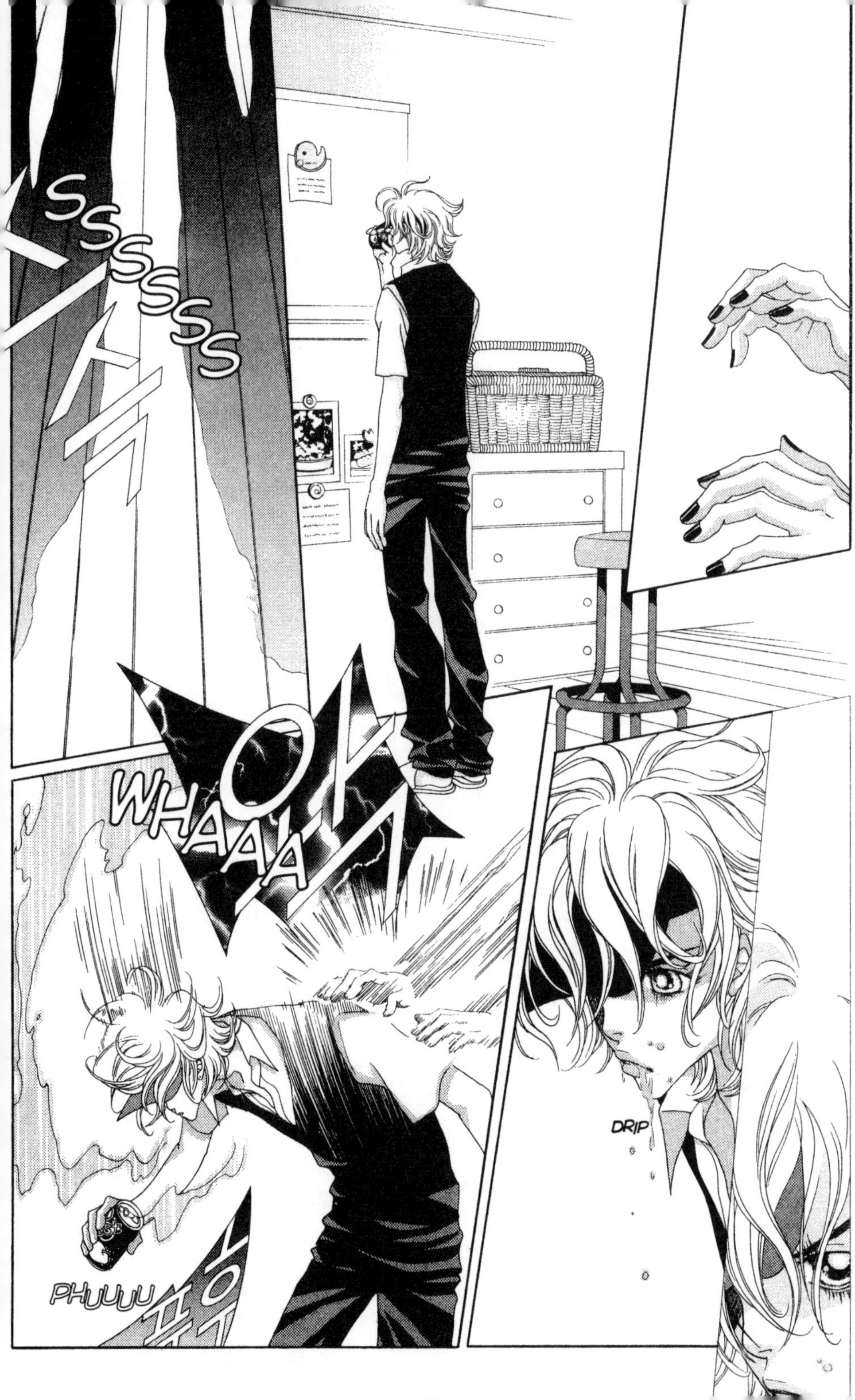
SSSSSSS
WHAAAA
DRIP
PHUUUU

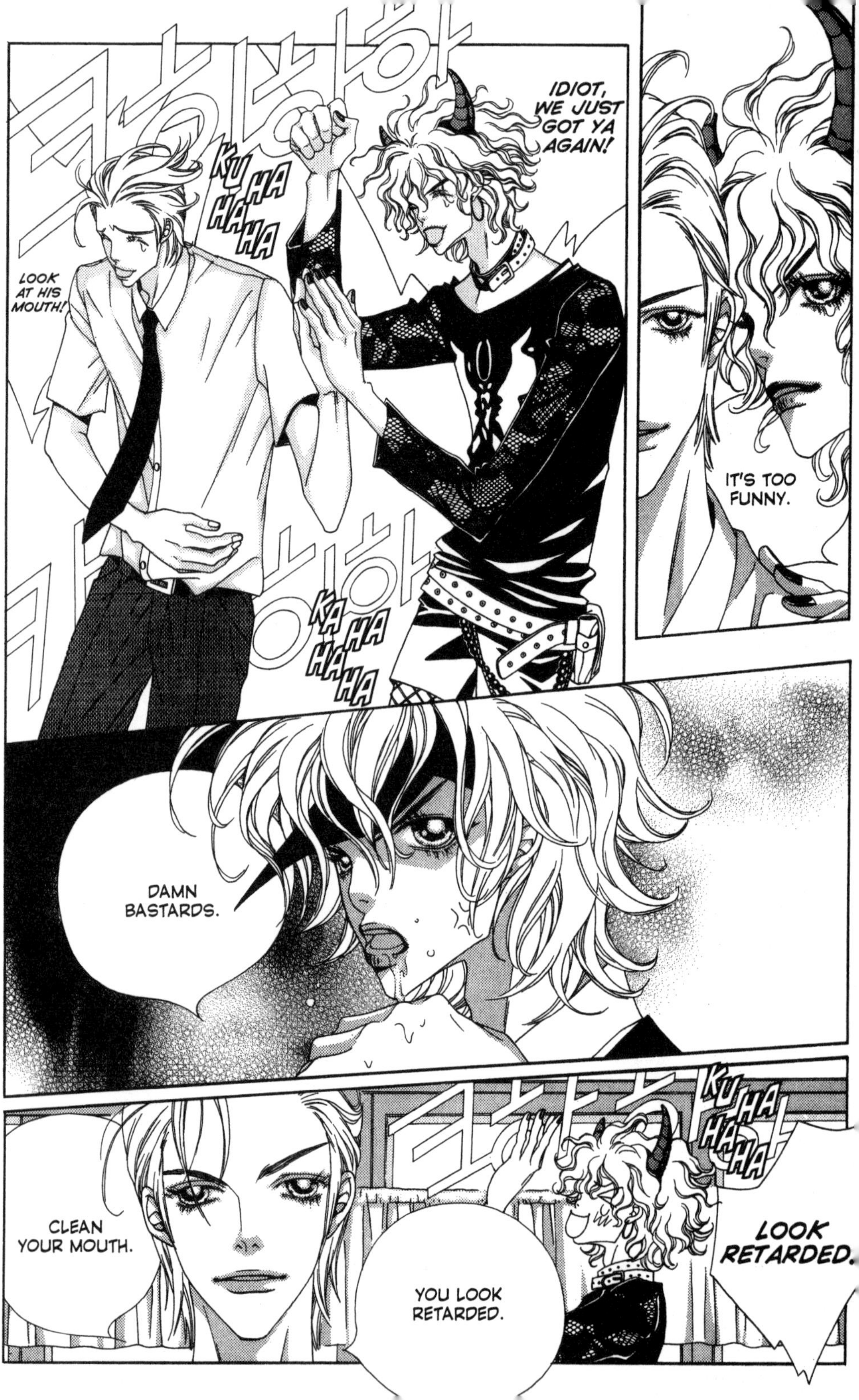
KU HA HA HA
IDIOT, WE JUST GOT YA AGAIN!
LOOK AT HIS MOUTH!
KA HA HA HA
IT'S TOO FUNNY.
DAMN BASTARDS.
CLEAN YOUR MOUTH.
KU HA HA HA
YOU LOOK RETARDED.
LOOK RETARDED.

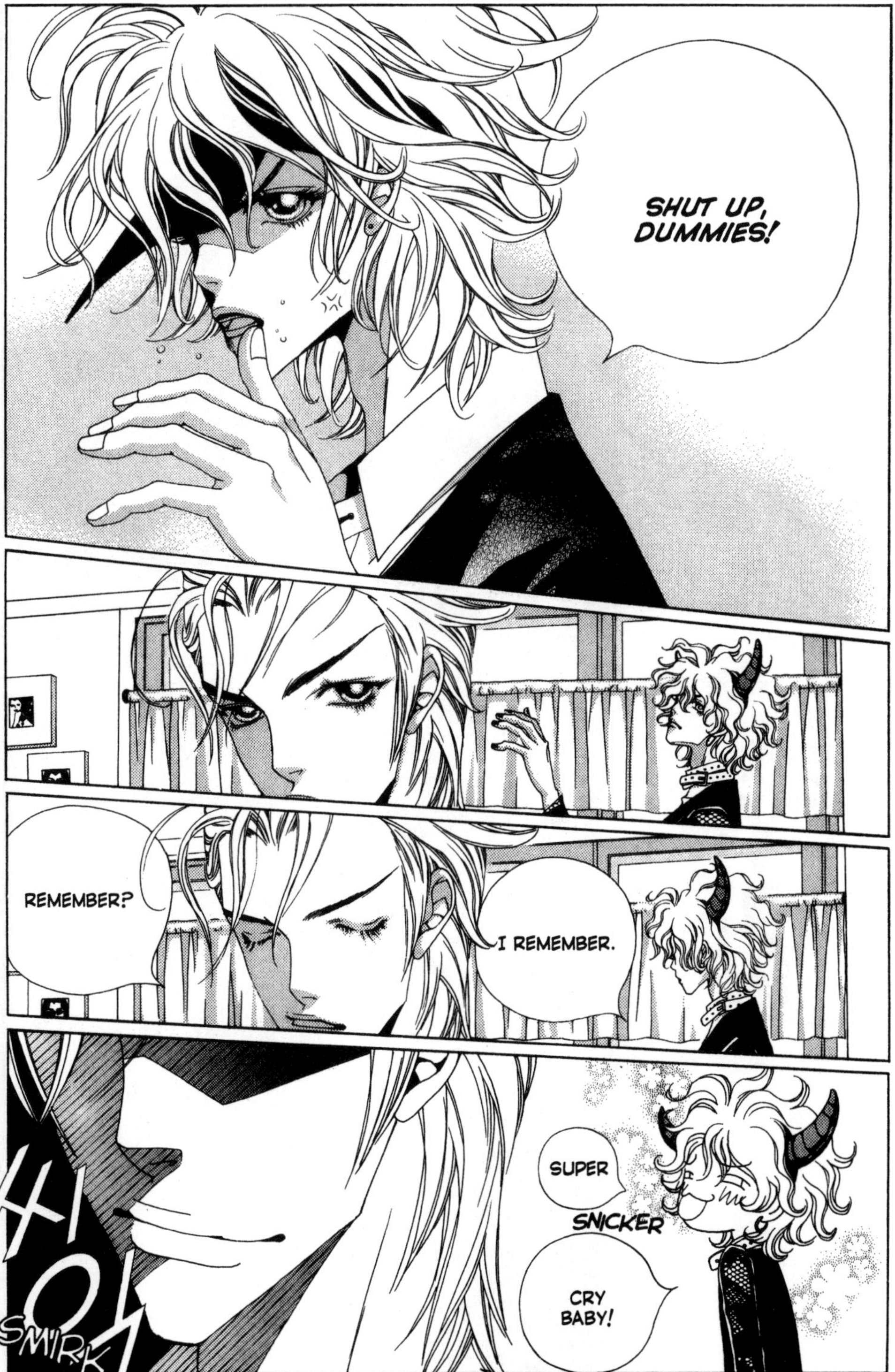
SHUT UP, DUMMIES!
REMEMBER?
I REMEMBER.
SMIRK
SUPER
SNICKER
CRY BABY!

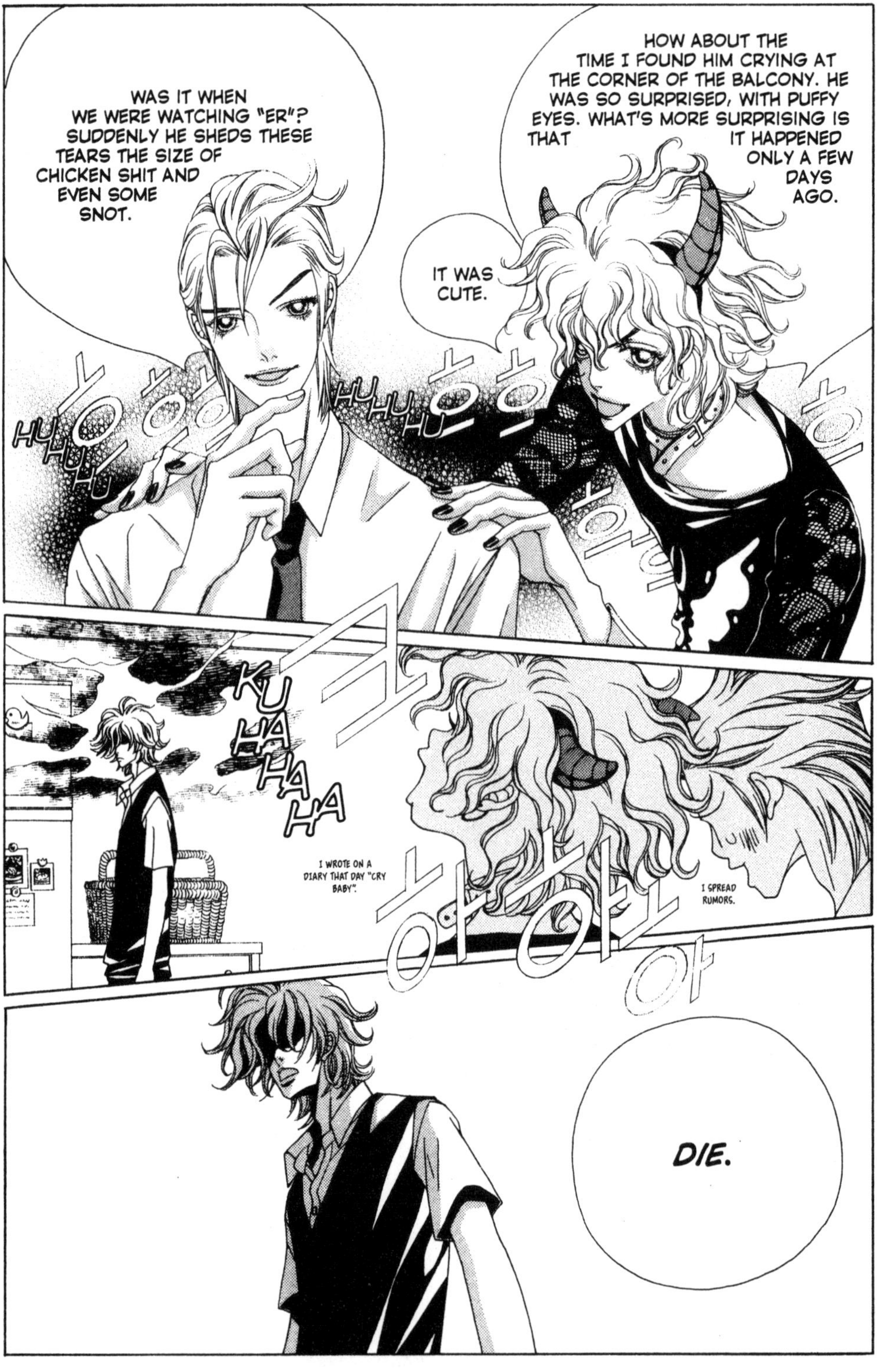
WAS IT WHEN WE WERE WATCHING "ER"? SUDDENLY HE SHEDS THESE TEARS THE SIZE OF CHICKEN SHIT AND EVEN SOME SNOT.
HUHUHU
HUHUHU
HOW ABOUT THE TIME I FOUND HIM CRYING AT THE CORNER OF THE BALCONY. HE WAS SO SURPRISED, WITH PUFFY EYES. WHAT'S MORE SURPRISING IS THAT IT HAPPENED ONLY A FEW DAYS AGO.
IT WAS CUTE.
KU HA HA HA
I WROTE ON A DIARY THAT DAY "CRY BABY".
I SPREAD RUMORS.
DIE.

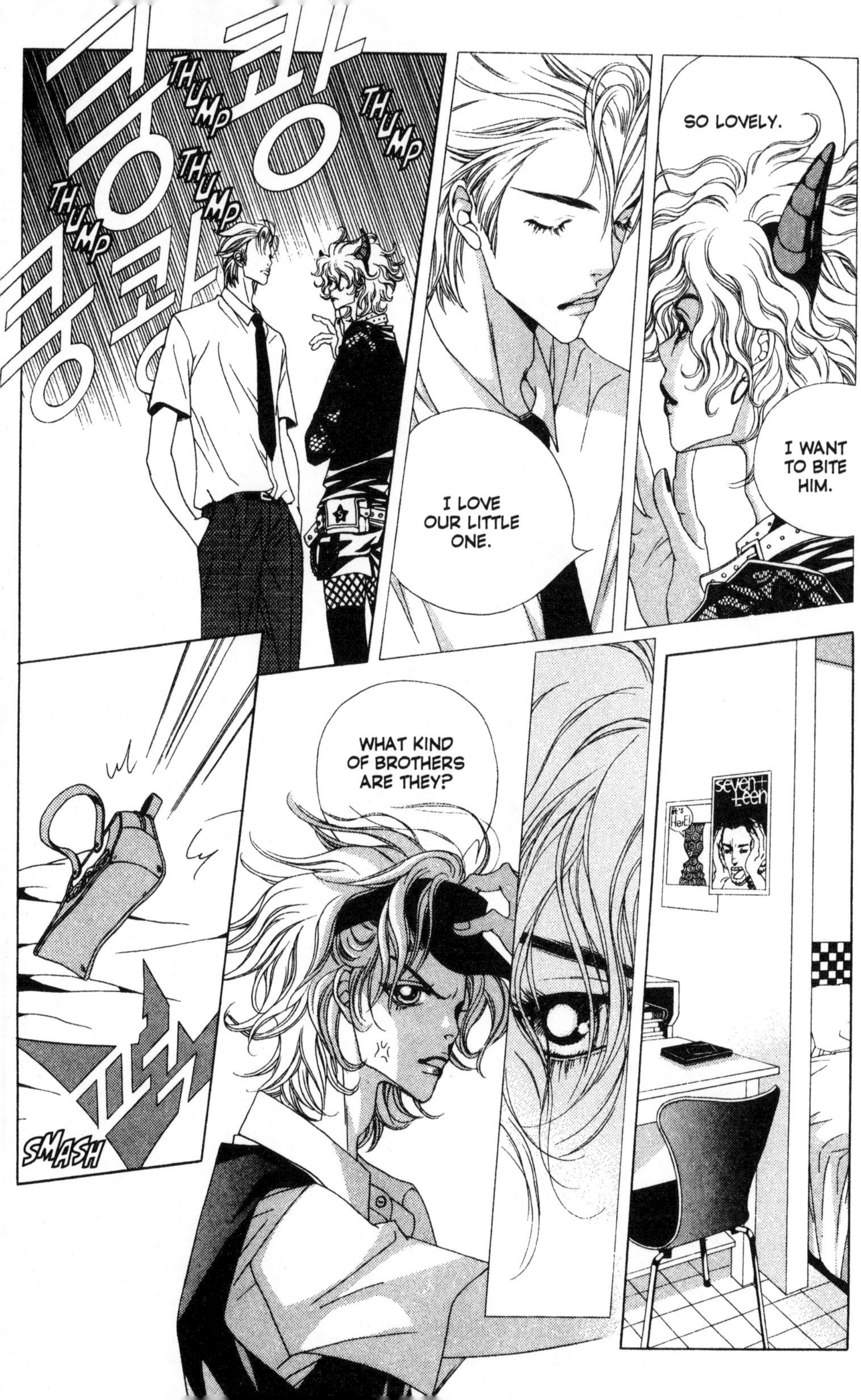
THUMP
THUMP
THUMP
THUMP
I LOVE OUR LITTLE ONE.
SO LOVELY.
I WANT TO BITE HIM.
SMASH
WHAT KIND OF BROTHERS ARE THEY?

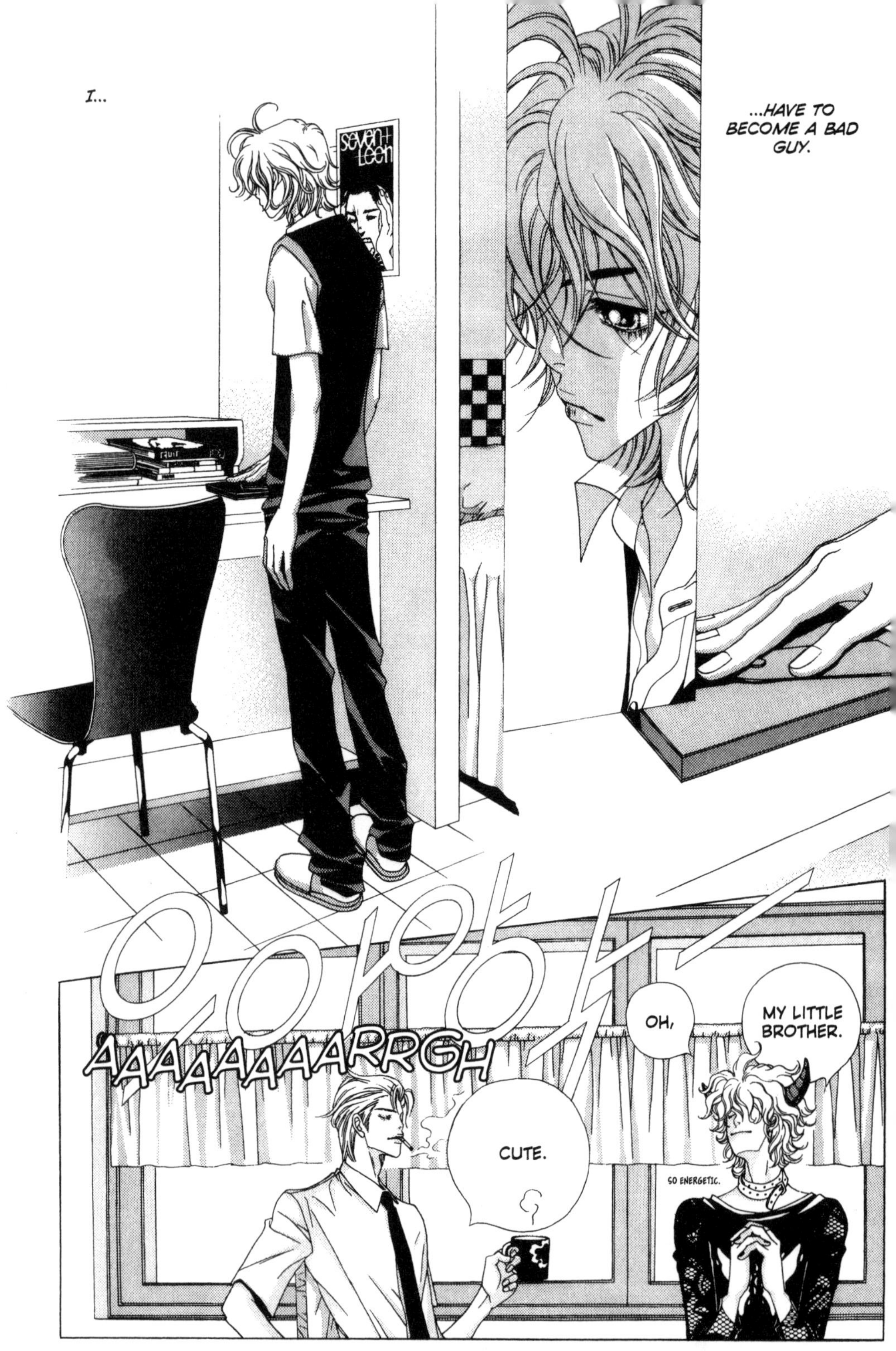
I...
...HAVE TO BECOME A BAD GUY.
AAAAAAAARRGH
OH,
MY LITTLE BROTHER.
CUTE.
SO ENERGETIC.

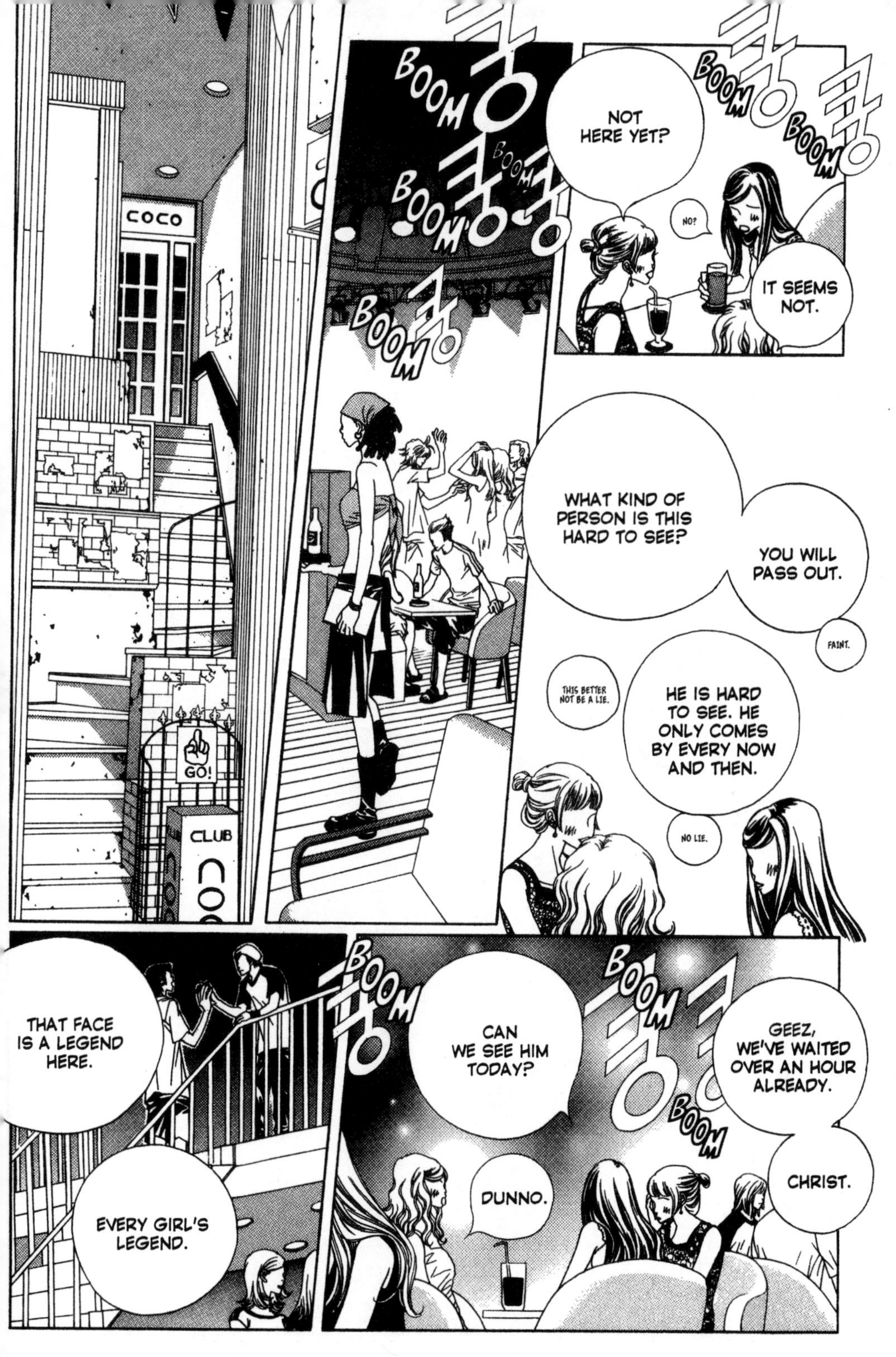
COCO
GO!
CLUB
COCO
BOOM 쿵
BOOM 쿵
BOOM 쿵
BOOM 쿵
NOT HERE YET?
BOOM 쿵
BOOM 쿵
NO?
IT SEEMS NOT.
WHAT KIND OF PERSON IS THIS HARD TO SEE?
YOU WILL PASS OUT.
FAINT.
THIS BETTER NOT BE A LIE.
HE IS HARD TO SEE. HE ONLY COMES BY EVERY NOW AND THEN.
NO LIE.
THAT FACE IS A LEGEND HERE.
EVERY GIRL'S LEGEND.
BOOM 쿵
CAN WE SEE HIM TODAY?
BOOM 쿵
BOOM 쿵
GEEZ, WE'VE WAITED OVER AN HOUR ALREADY.
DUNNO.
CHRIST.

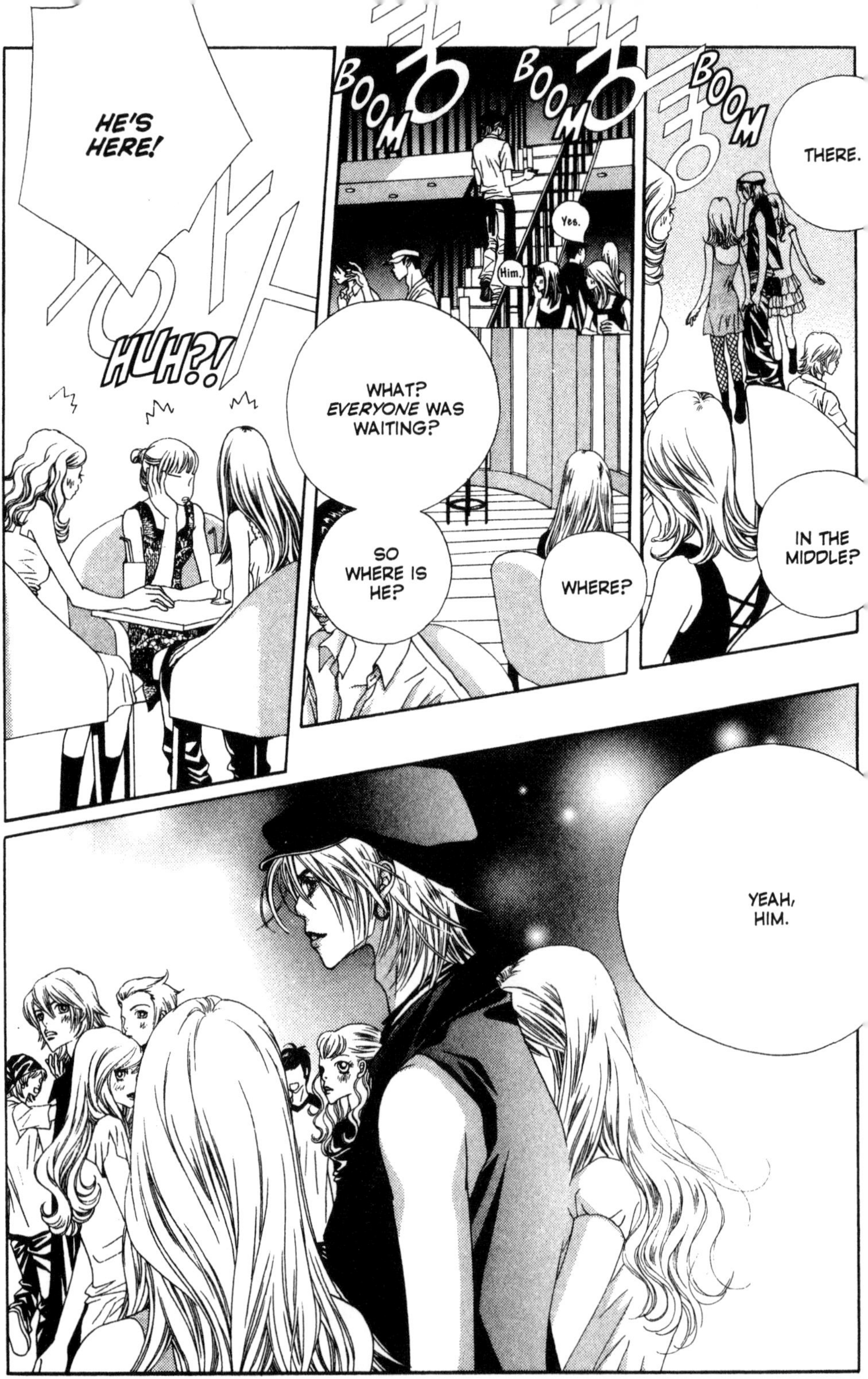
HE'S HERE!
HUH?!
BOOM
BOOM
Yes.
Him.
WHAT? EVERYONE WAS WAITING?
SO WHERE IS HE?
WHERE?
BOOM
THERE.
IN THE MIDDLE?
YEAH, HIM.

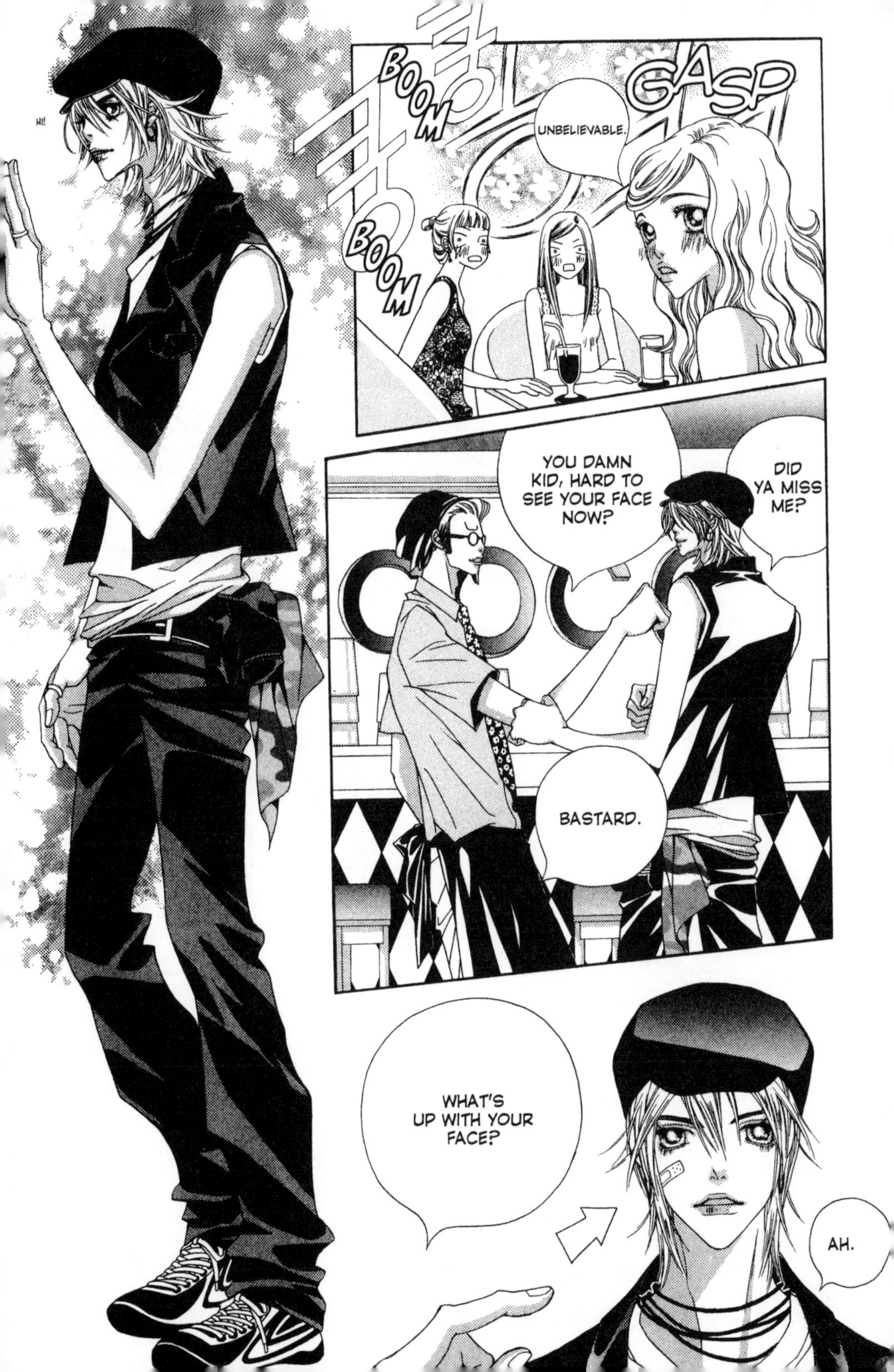
HI!
BOOM
BOOM
UNBELIEVABLE.
GASP
YOU DAMN KID, HARD TO SEE YOUR FACE NOW?
DID YA MISS ME?
BASTARD.
WHAT'S UP WITH YOUR FACE?
AH.

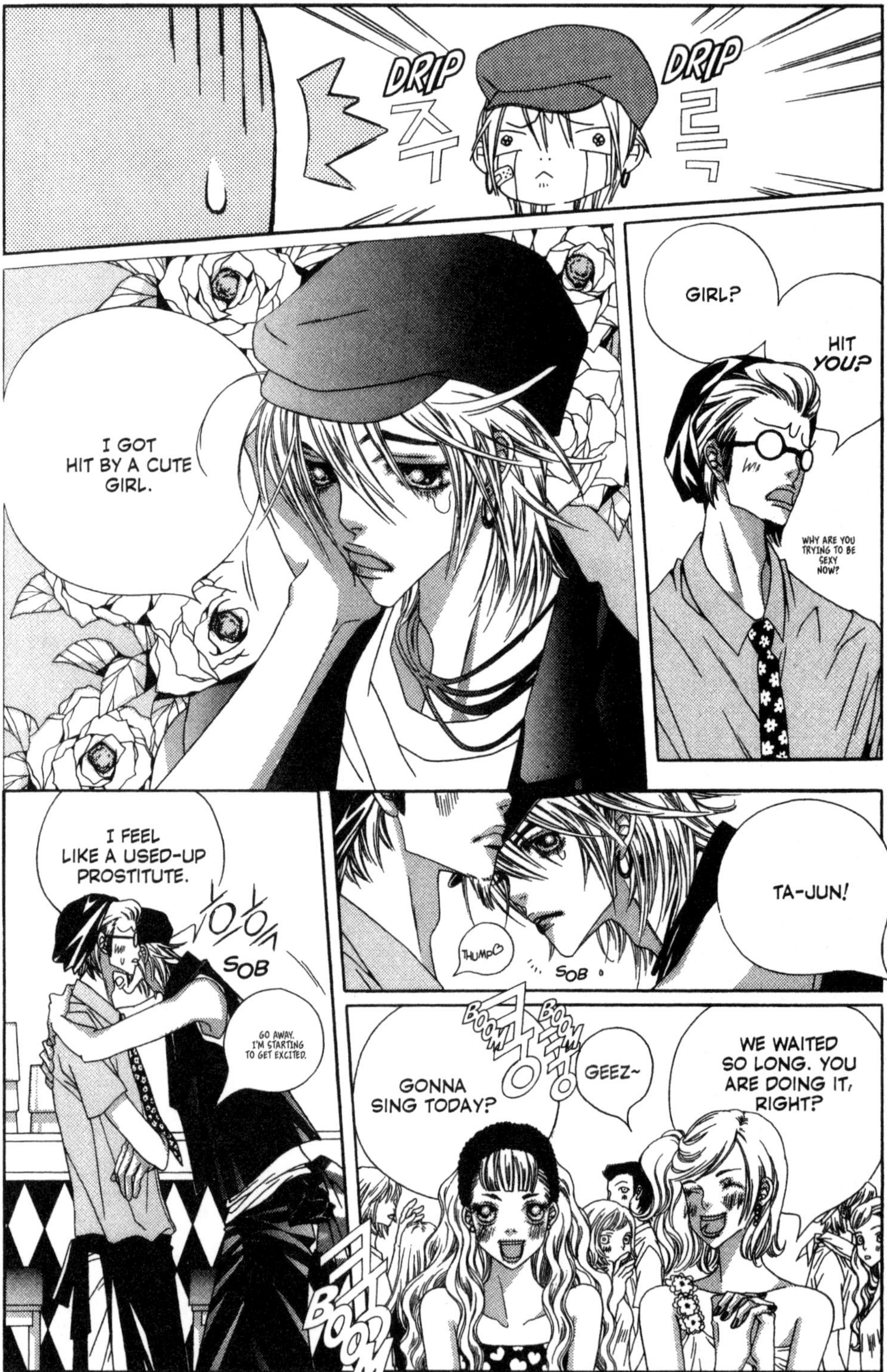
DRIP
DRIP
I GOT HIT BY A CUTE GIRL.
GIRL?
HIT YOU?
WHY ARE YOU TRYING TO BE SEXY NOW?
I FEEL LIKE A USED-UP PROSTITUTE.
SOB
GO AWAY. I'M STARTING TO GET EXCITED.
TA-JUN!
THUMP♡
SOB
BOOM
BOOM
GONNA SING TODAY?
GEEZ~
WE WAITED SO LONG. YOU ARE DOING IT, RIGHT?
BOOM

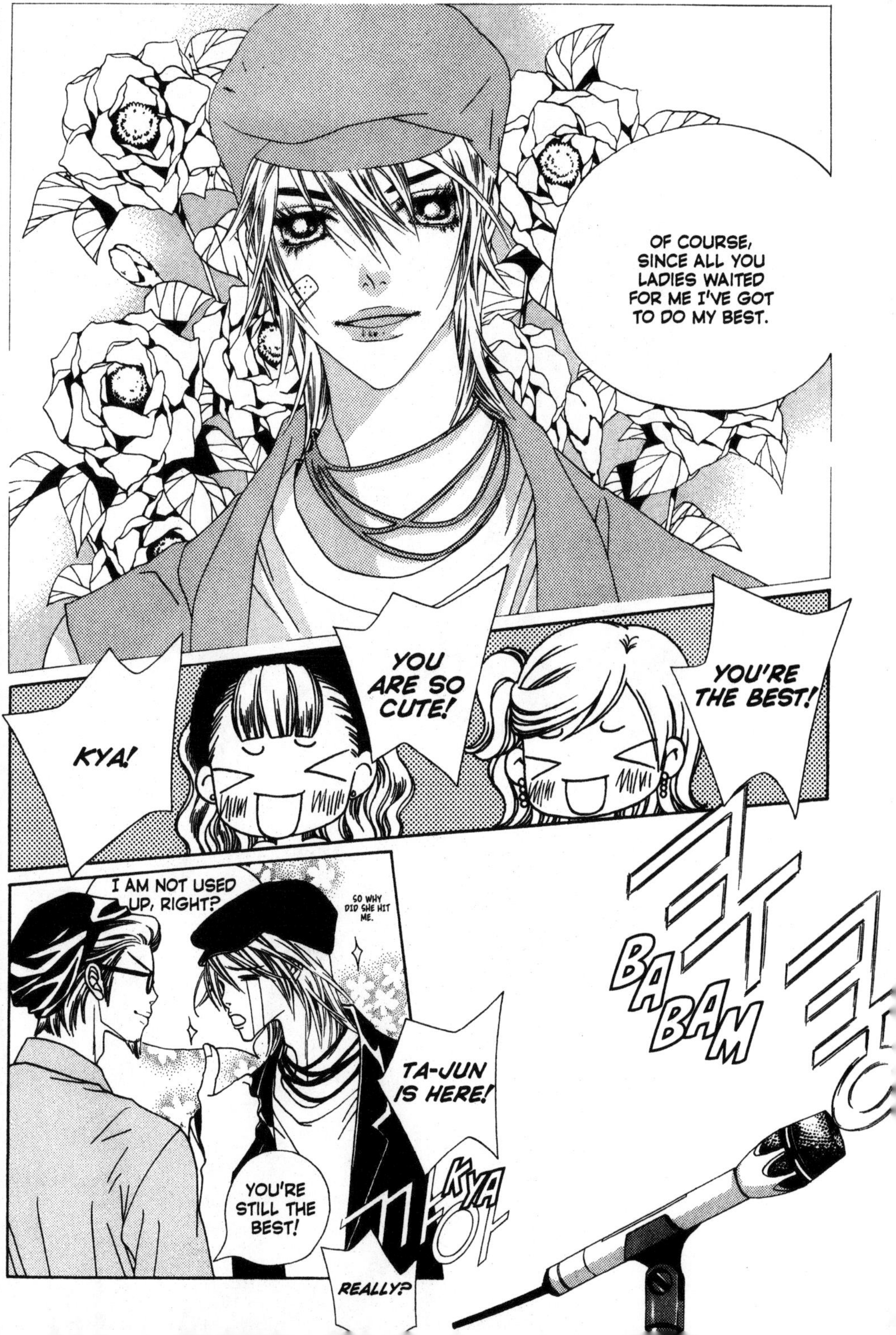
OF COURSE, SINCE ALL YOU LADIES WAITED FOR ME I'VE GOT TO DO MY BEST.
KYA!
YOU ARE SO CUTE!
YOU'RE THE BEST!
I AM NOT USED UP, RIGHT?
SO WHY DID SHE HIT ME.
TA-JUN IS HERE!
YOU'RE STILL THE BEST!
KYA
REALLY?
BABAM

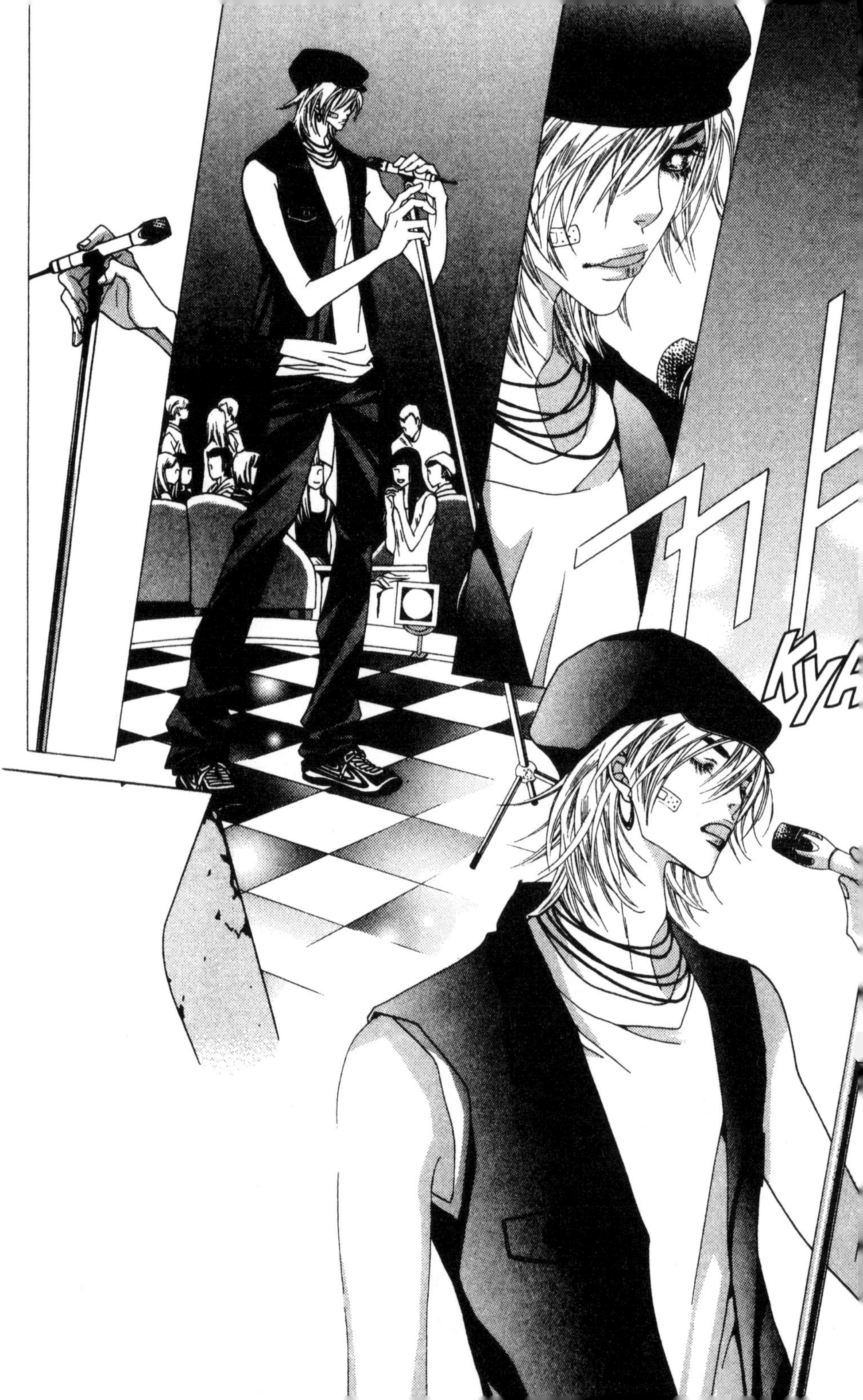
KYA

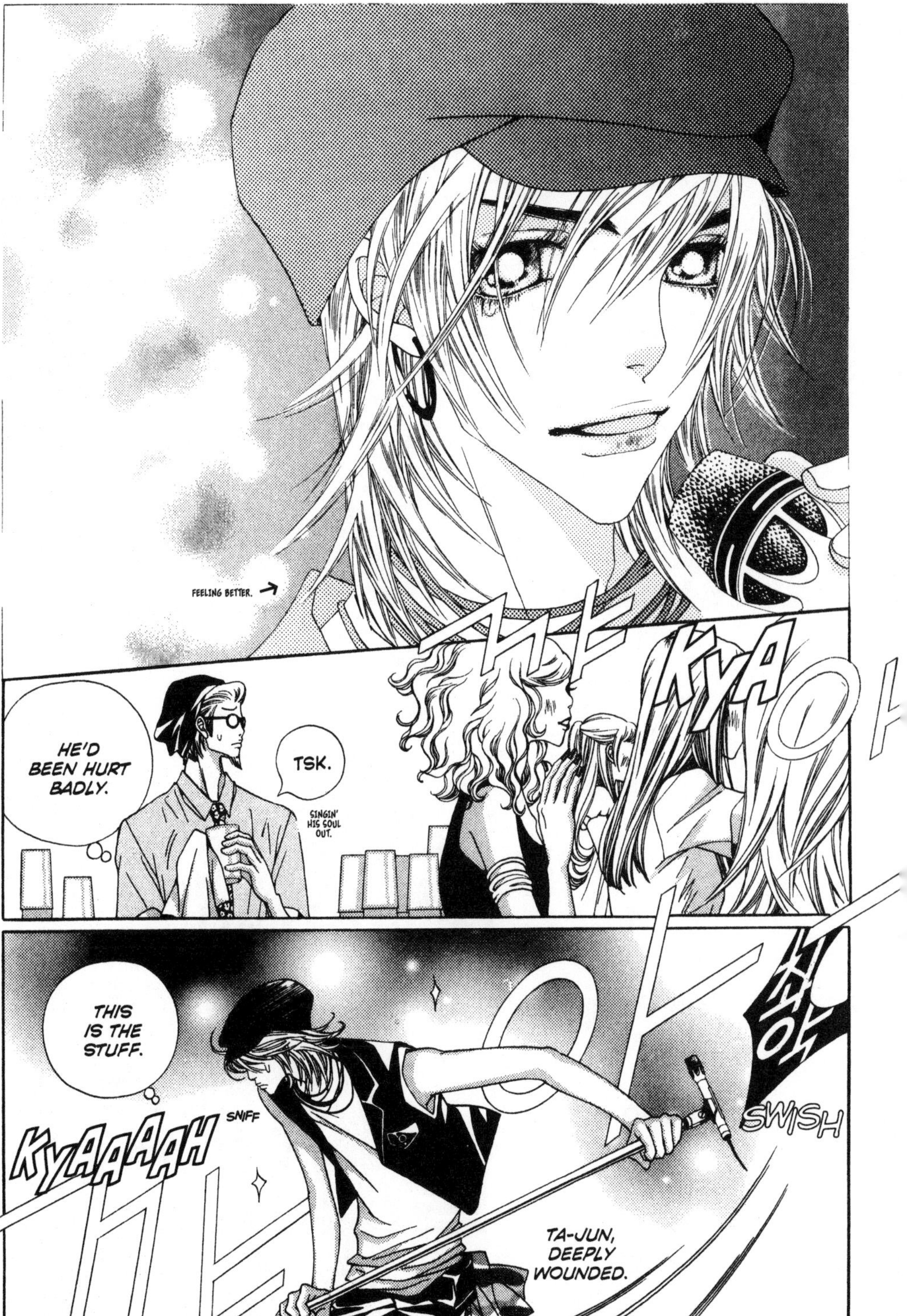
FEELING BETTER.
HE'D BEEN HURT BADLY.
TSK.
SINGIN' HIS SOUL OUT.
KYA
THIS IS THE STUFF.
SNIFF
KYAAAAH
SWISH
TA-JUN, DEEPLY WOUNDED.

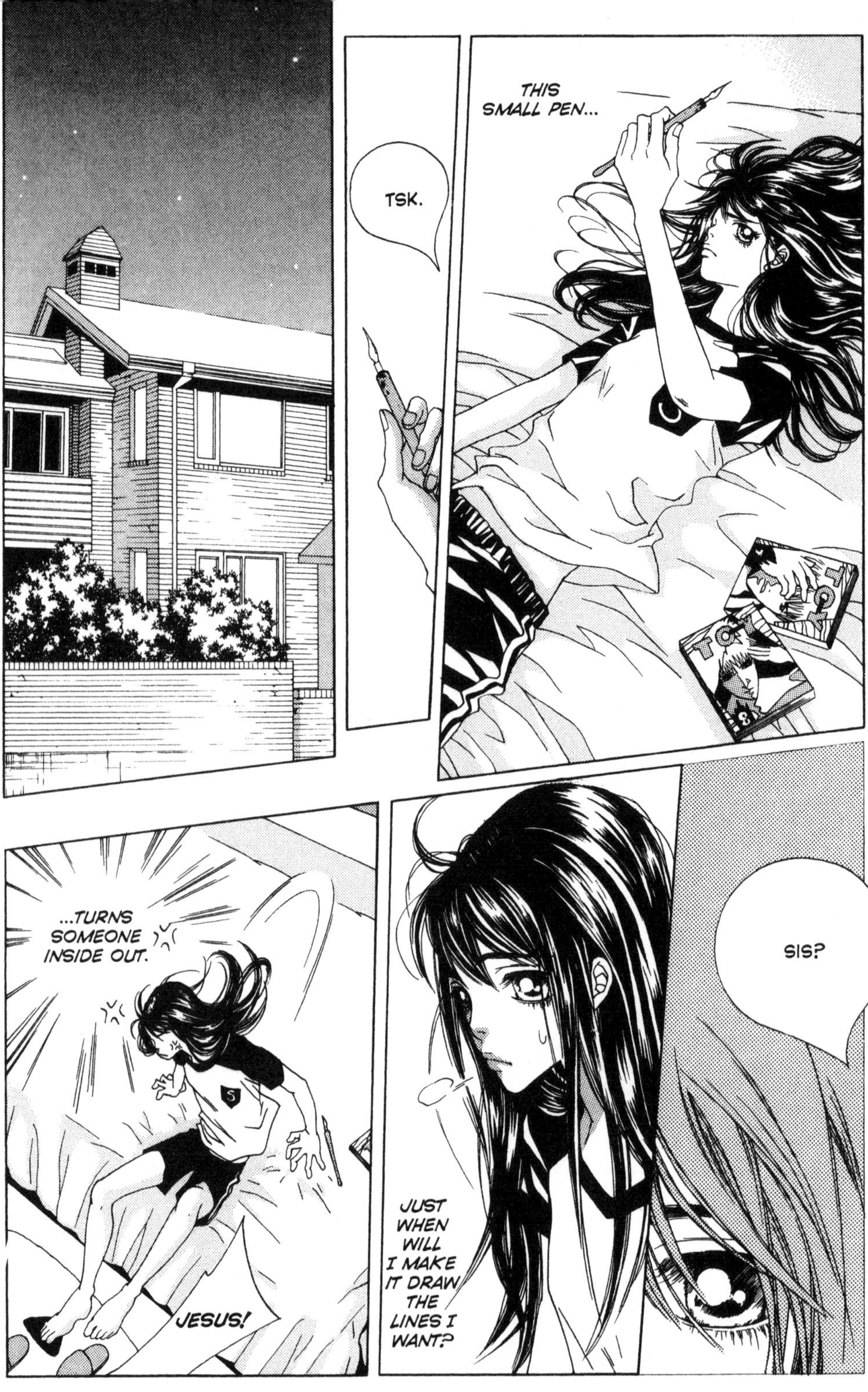
TSK.
THIS SMALL PEN...
...TURNS SOMEONE INSIDE OUT.
JESUS!
JUST WHEN WILL I MAKE IT DRAW THE LINES I WANT?
SIS?

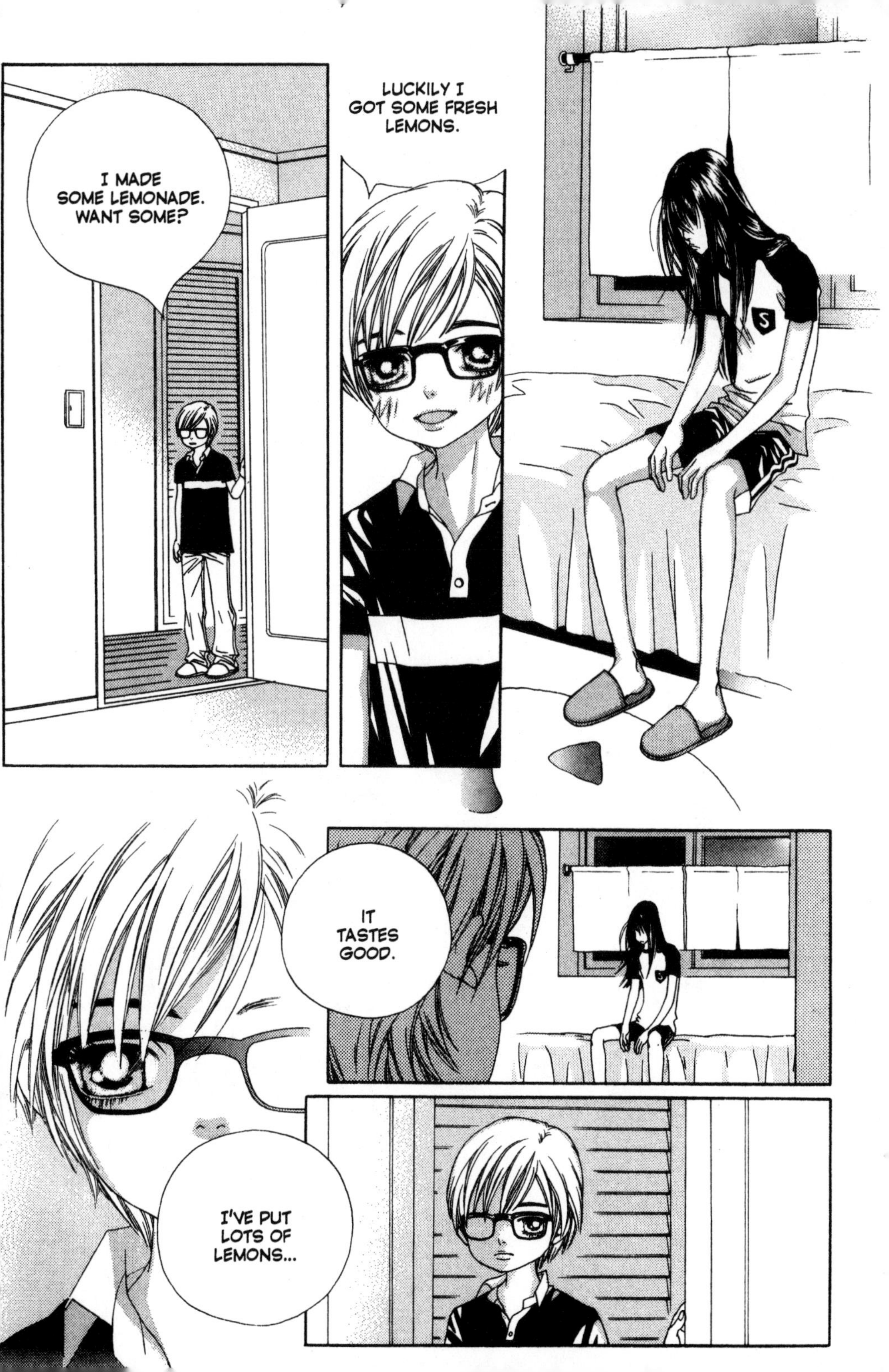
I MADE SOME LEMONADE. WANT SOME?
LUCKILY I GOT SOME FRESH LEMONS.
IT TASTES GOOD.
I'VE PUT LOTS OF LEMONS...

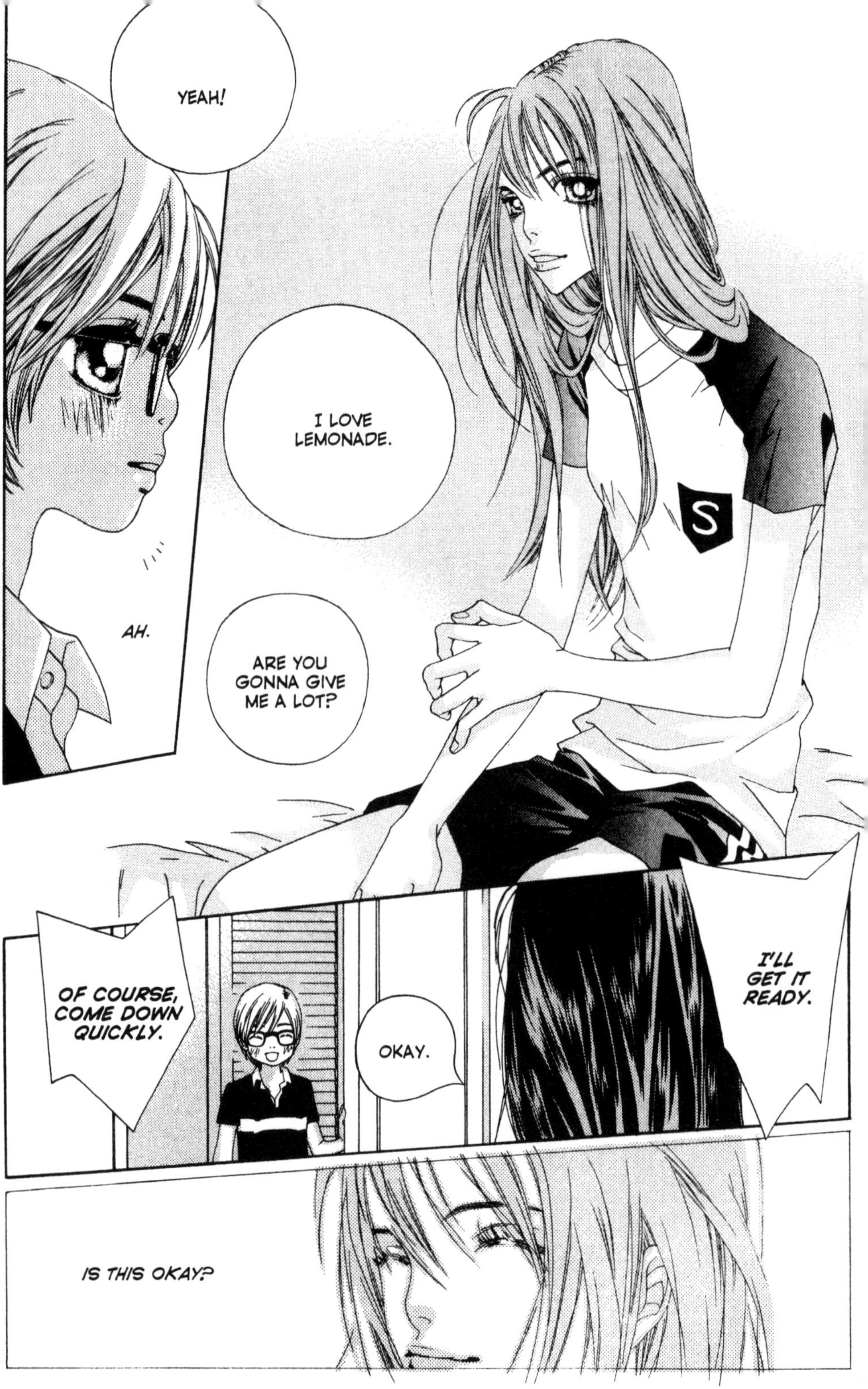
YEAH!
AH.
I LOVE LEMONADE.
ARE YOU GONNA GIVE ME A LOT?
OF COURSE, COME DOWN QUICKLY.
OKAY.
I'LL GET IT READY.
IS THIS OKAY?

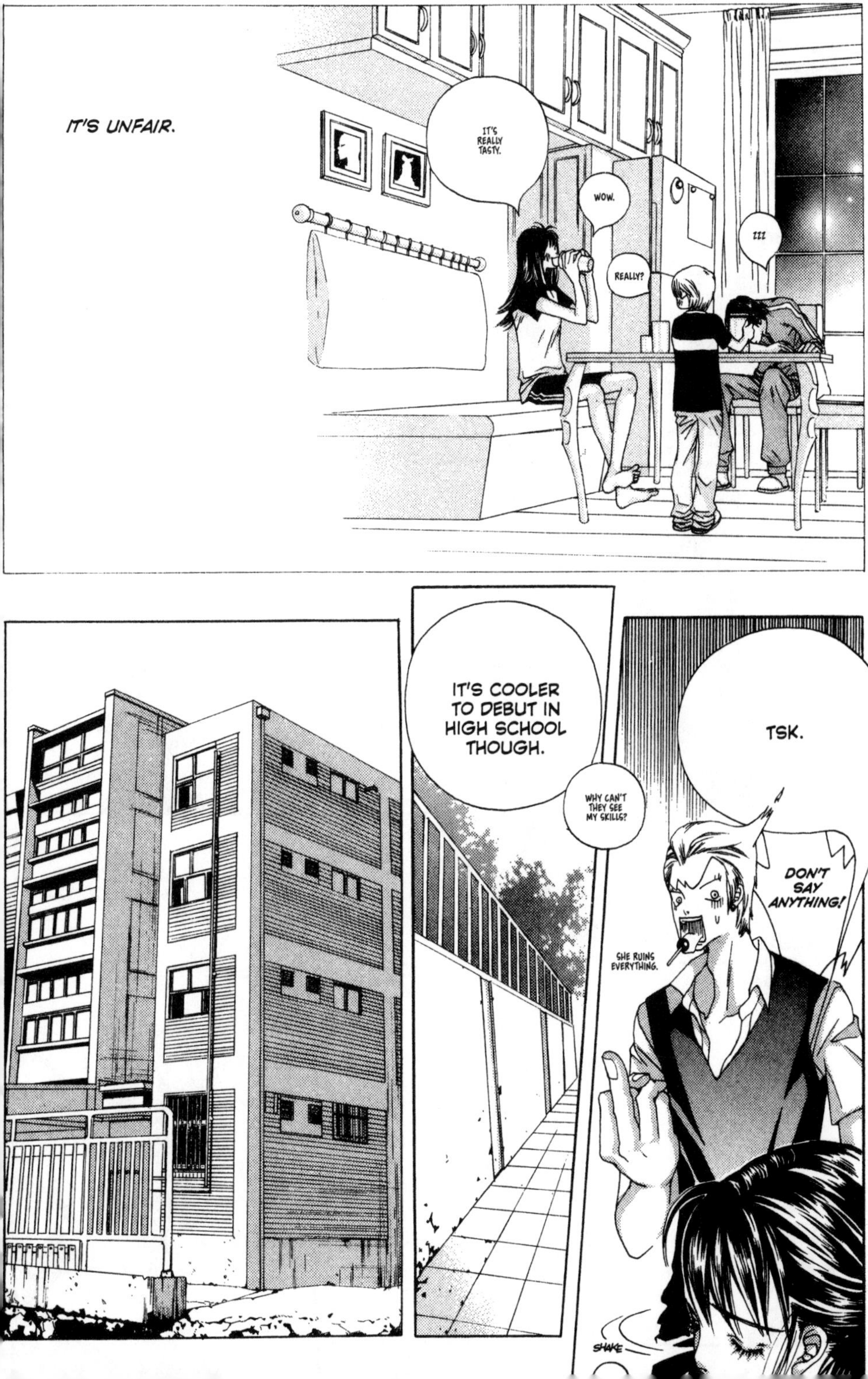
IT'S UNFAIR.
IT'S REALLY TASTY.
WOW.
REALLY?
ZZZ
IT'S COOLER TO DEBUT IN HIGH SCHOOL THOUGH.
WHY CAN'T THEY SEE MY SKILLS?
TSK.
DON'T SAY ANYTHING!
SHE RUINS EVERYTHING.
SHAKE

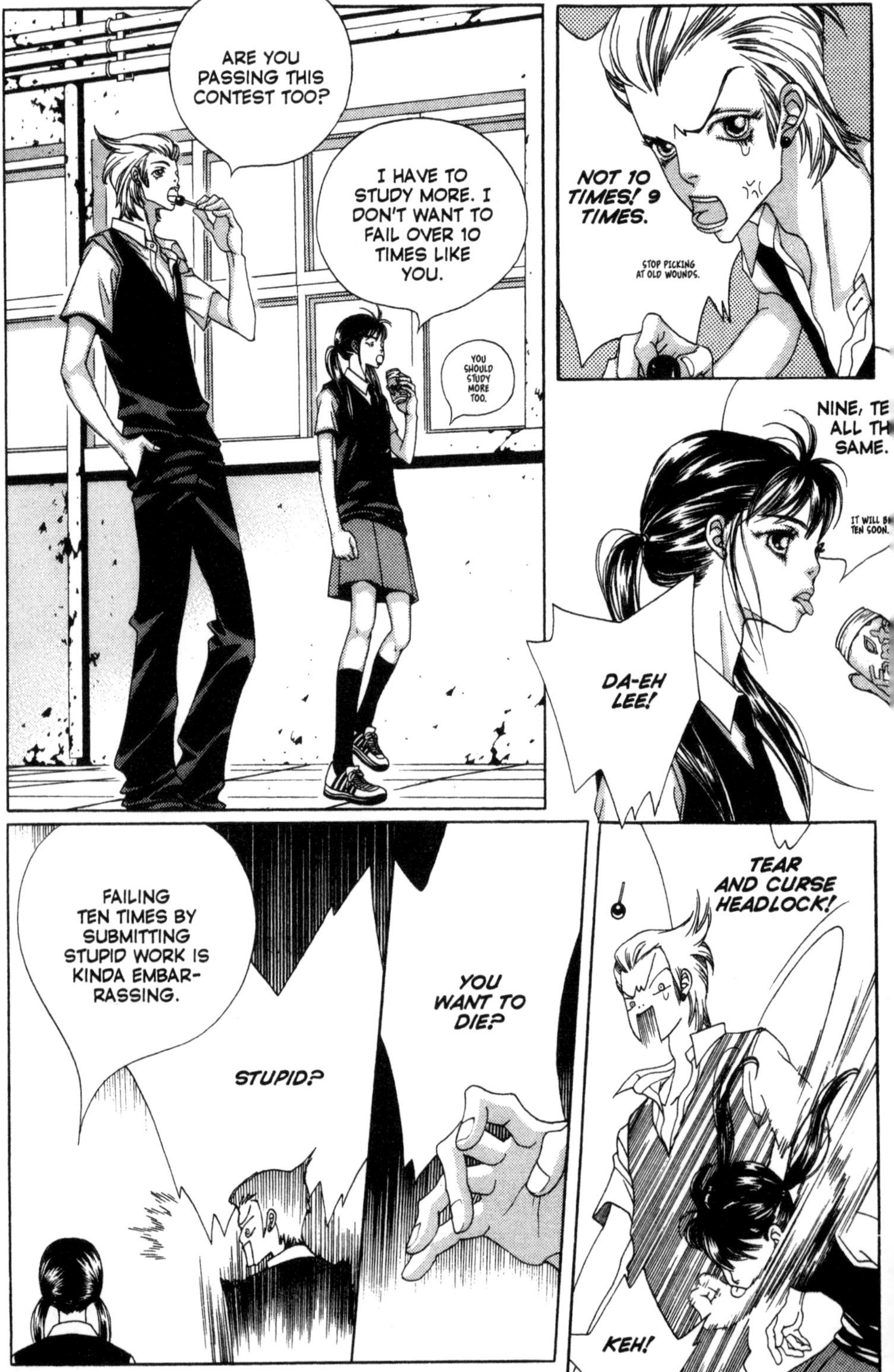
ARE YOU PASSING THIS CONTEST TOO?
I HAVE TO STUDY MORE. I DON'T WANT TO FAIL OVER 10 TIMES LIKE YOU.
YOU SHOULD STUDY MORE TOO.
NOT 10 TIMES! 9 TIMES.
STOP PICKING AT OLD WOUNDS.
NINE, TE ALL TH SAME.
IT WILL B TEN SOON.
DA-EH LEE!
FAILING TEN TIMES BY SUBMITTING STUPID WORK IS KINDA EMBAR-RASSING.
STUPID?
YOU WANT TO DIE?
TEAR AND CURSE HEADLOCK!
KEH!

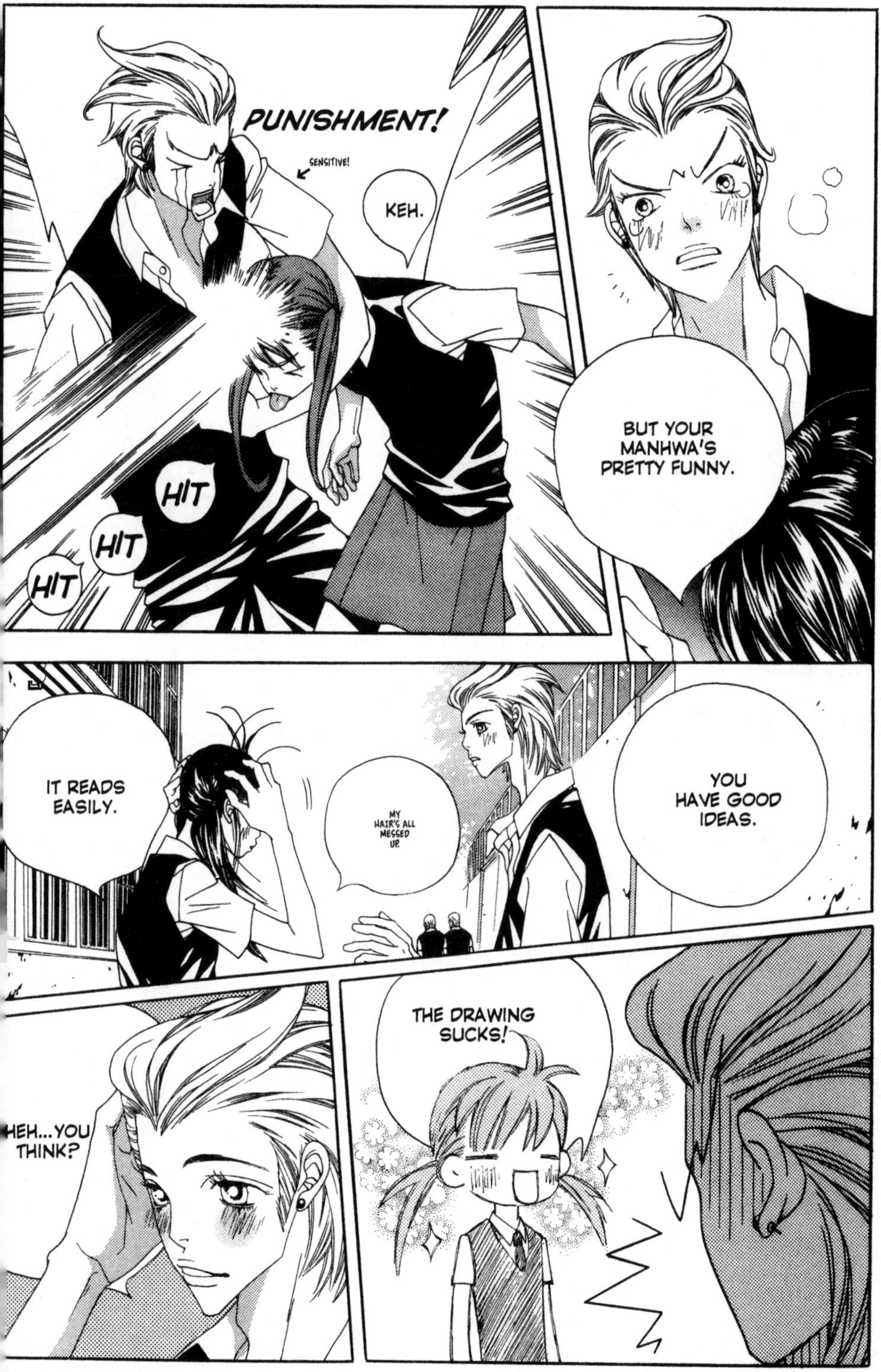
PUNISHMENT!
SENSITIVE!
KEH.
HIT
HIT
HIT
BUT YOUR MANHWA'S PRETTY FUNNY.
IT READS EASILY.
MY HAIR'S ALL MESSED UP.
YOU HAVE GOOD IDEAS.
HEH...YOU THINK?
THE DRAWING SUCKS!

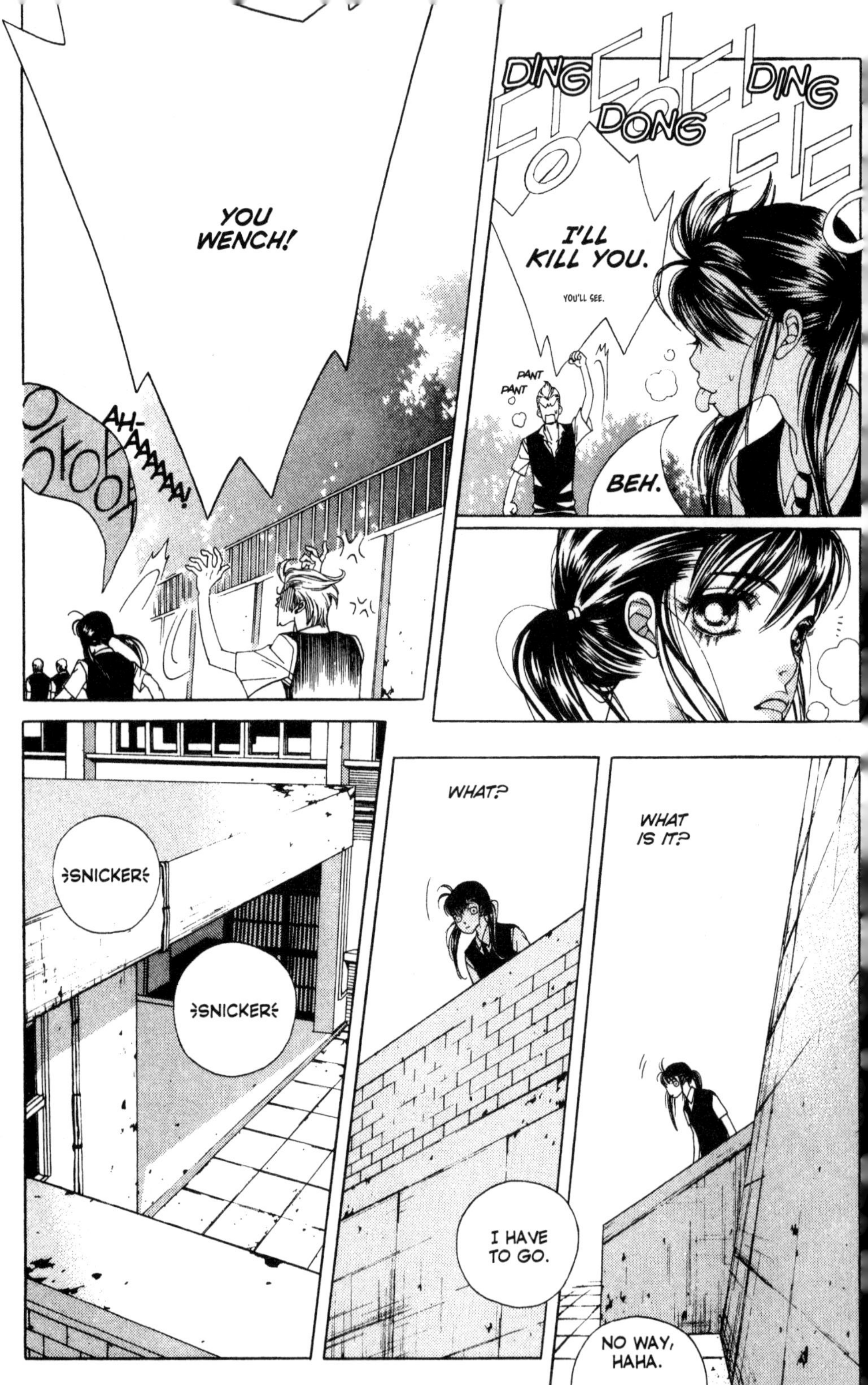
YOU WENCH!
AH-AAAAAAA!
DING DONG DING
I'LL KILL YOU.
YOU'LL SEE.
PANT PANT
BEH.
SNICKER
SNICKER
WHAT?
WHAT IS IT?
I HAVE TO GO.
NO WAY, HAHA.

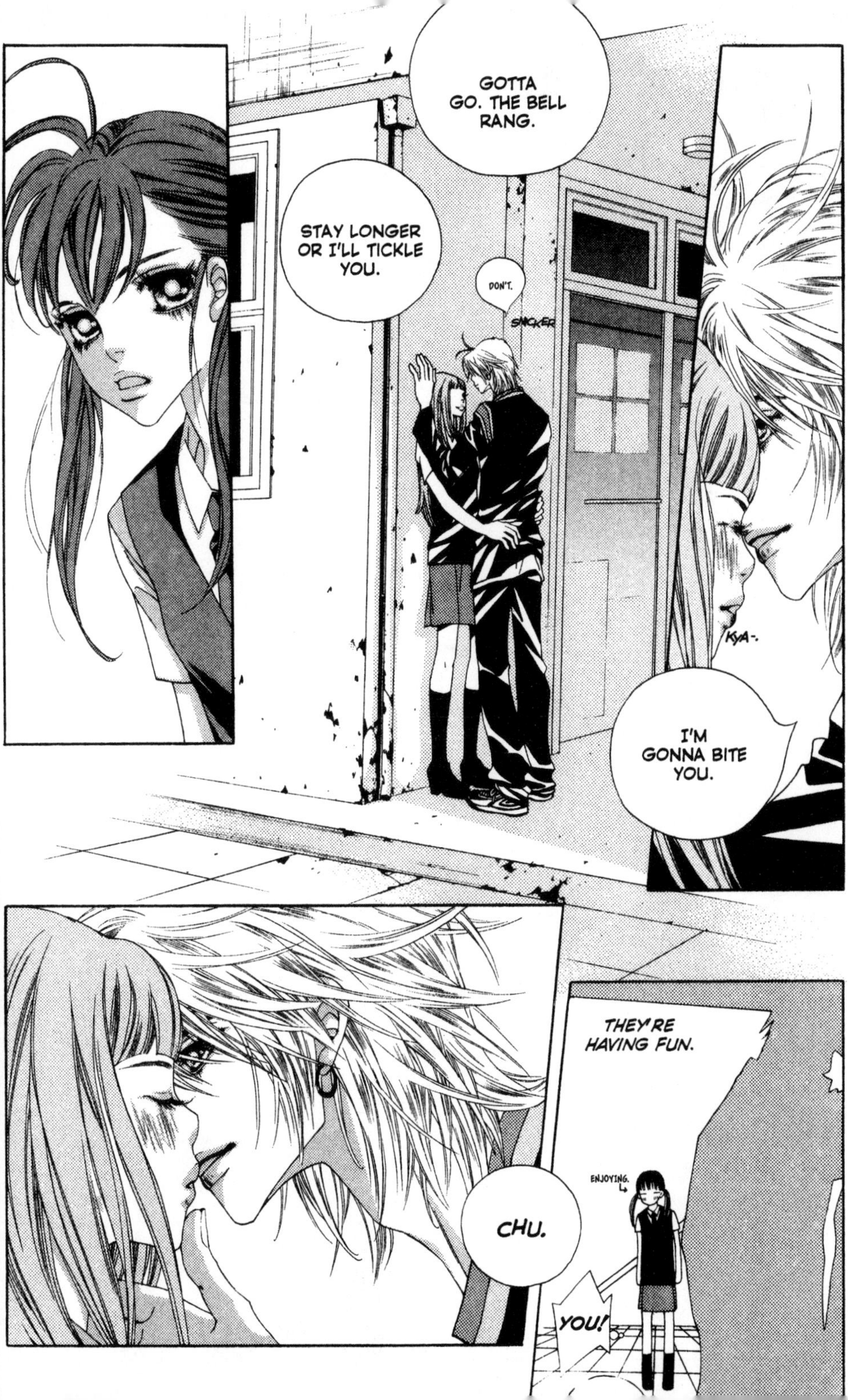

GOTTA GO. THE BELL RANG.
STAY LONGER OR I'LL TICKLE YOU.
DON'T.
SNICKER
KYA-.
I'M GONNA BITE YOU.
CHU.
THEY'RE HAVING FUN.
ENJOYING.
YOU!

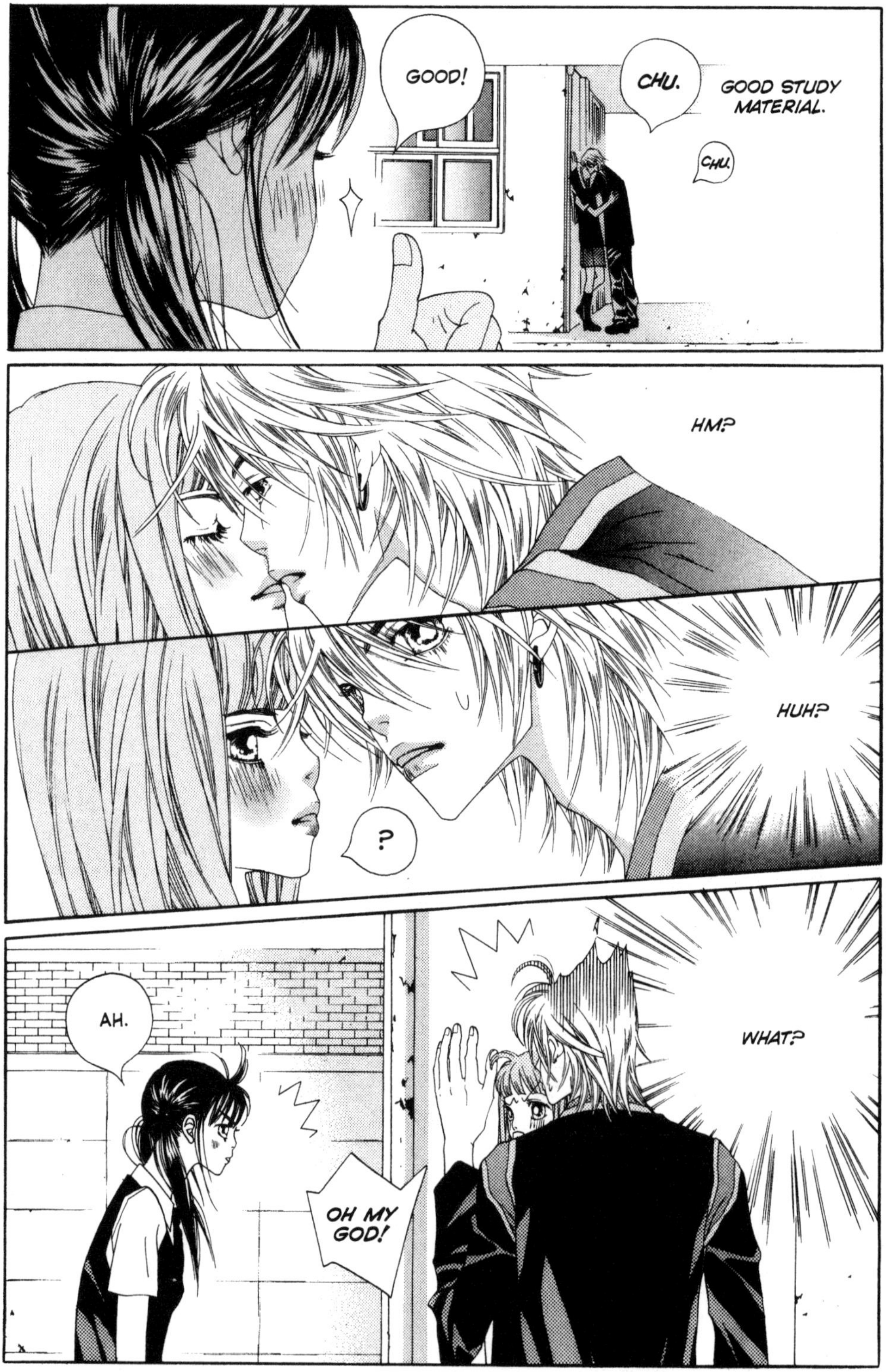

GOOD!
CHU.
GOOD STUDY MATERIAL.
CHU.
HM?
?
HUH?
AH.
OH MY GOD!
WHAT?

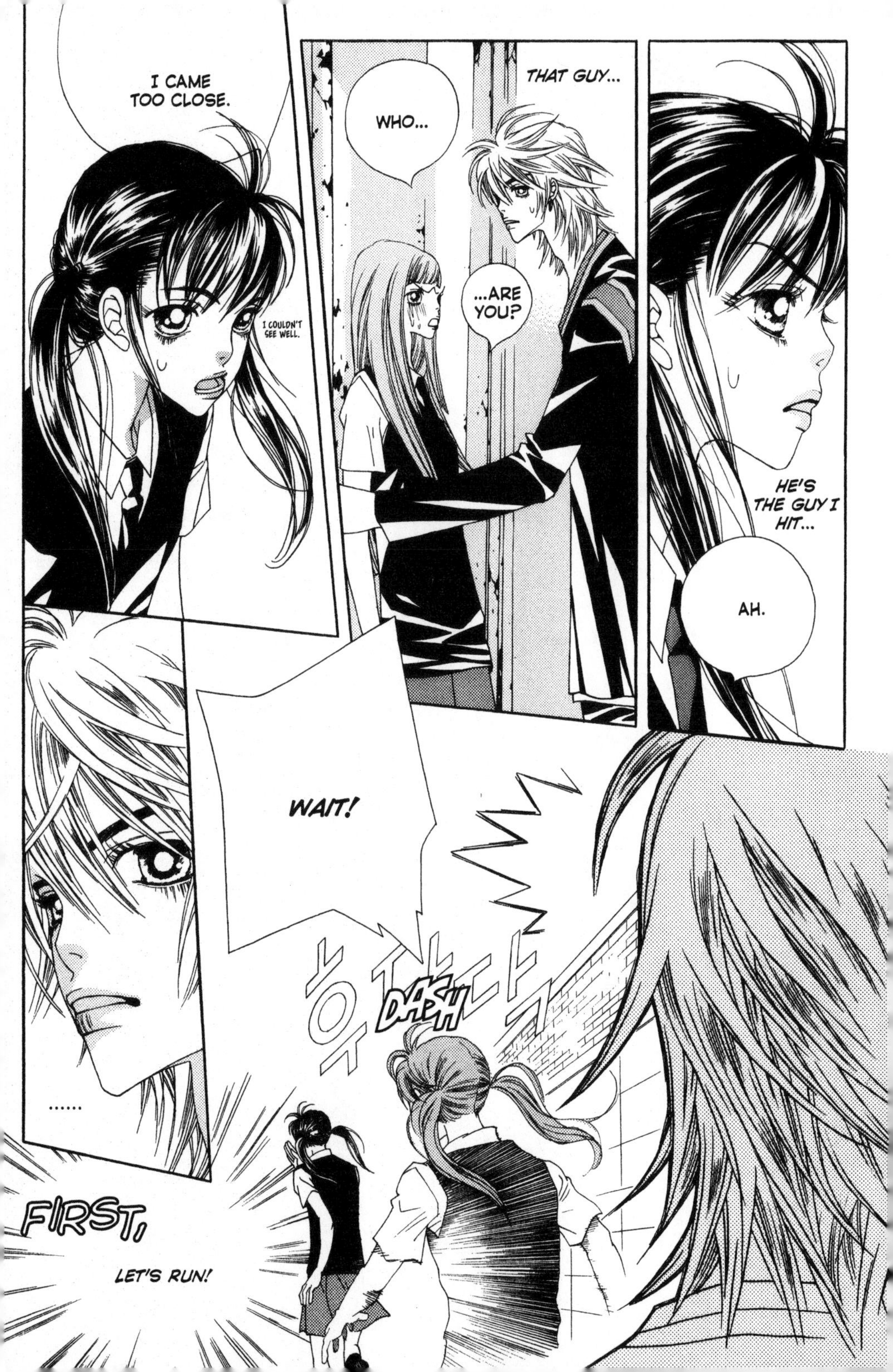
I CAME TOO CLOSE.
I COULDN'T SEE WELL.
WHO...
THAT GUY...
...ARE YOU?
HE'S THE GUY I HIT...
AH.
......
WAIT!
DASH
FIRST,
LET'S RUN!

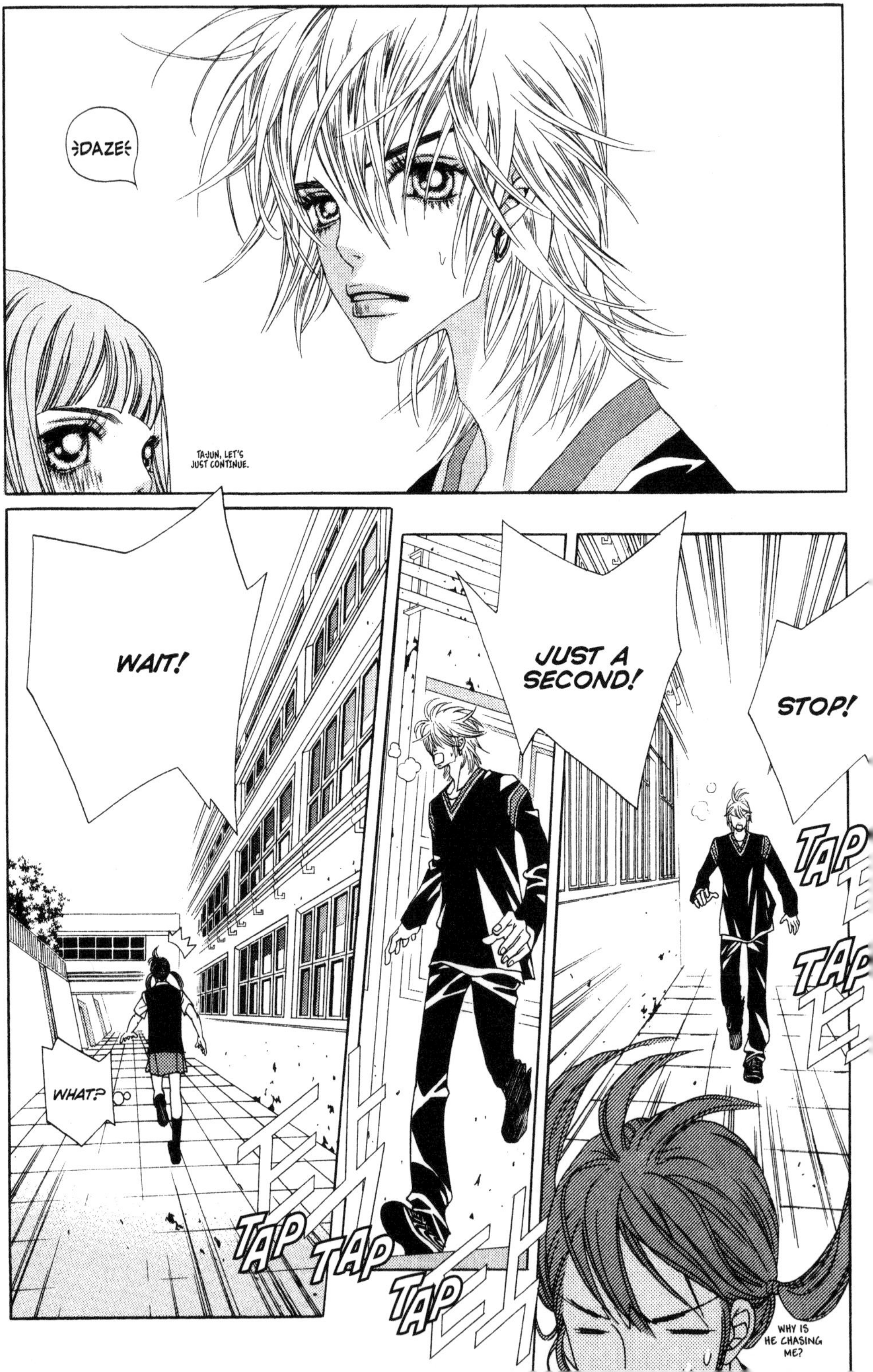
DAZE
TA-JUN, LET'S JUST CONTINUE.
WAIT!
WHAT?
TAP
TAP
TAP
JUST A SECOND!
STOP!
TAP
TAP
WHY IS HE CHASING ME?

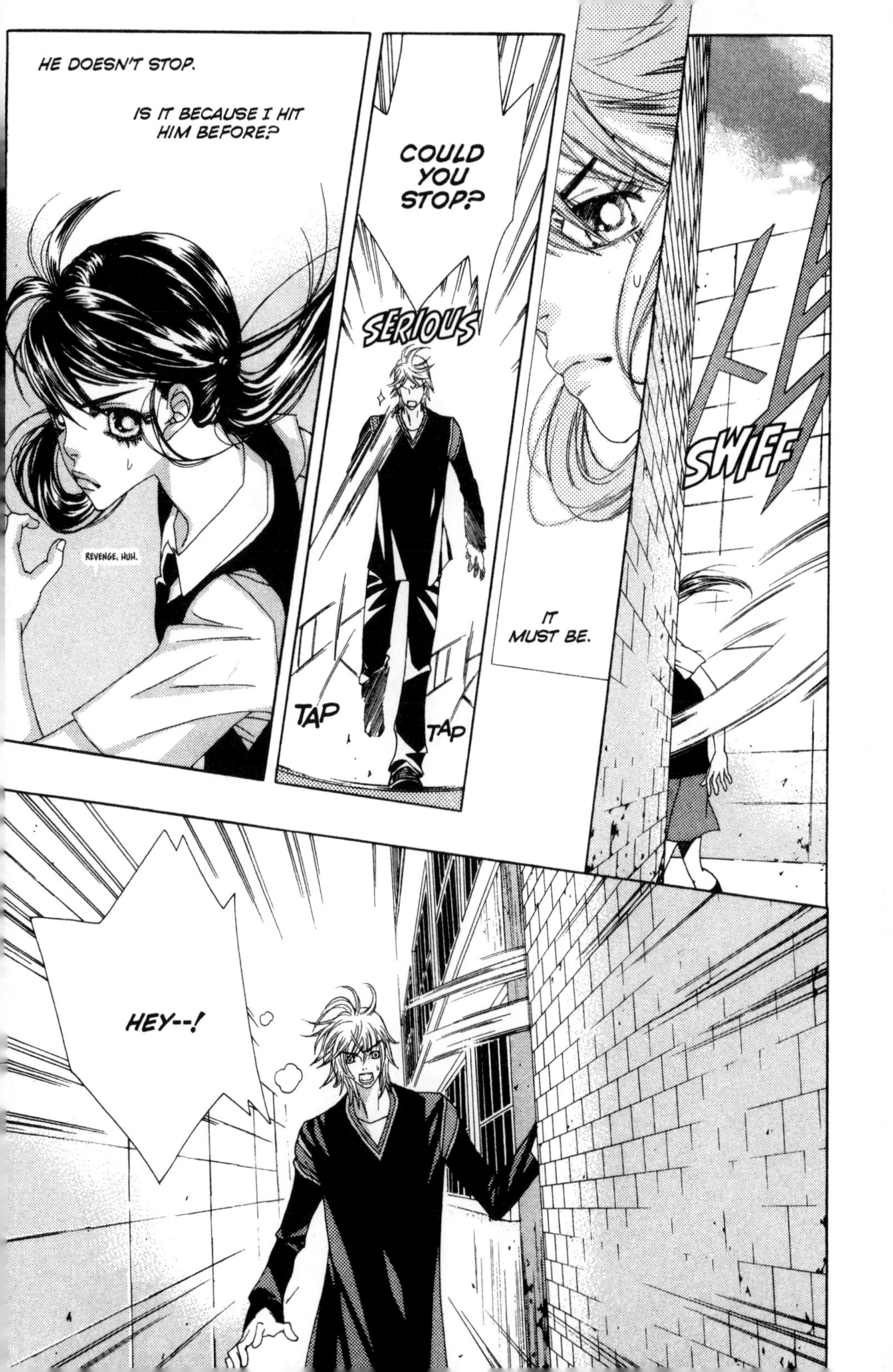
HE DOESN'T STOP.
IS IT BECAUSE I HIT HIM BEFORE?
REVENGE, HUH.
COULD YOU STOP?
SERIOUS
TAP
TAP
IT MUST BE.
SWIFF
HEY--!

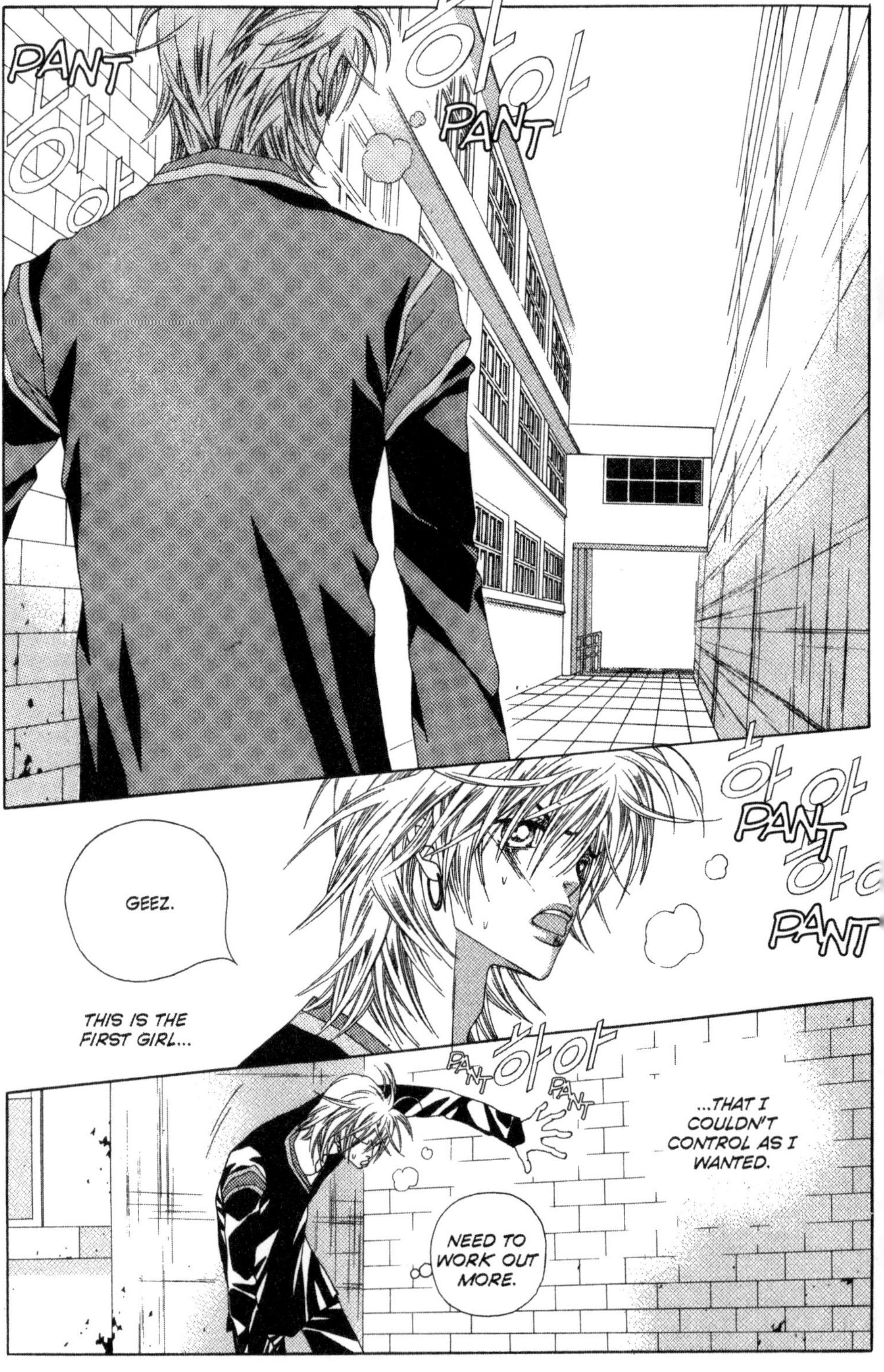
PANT
하아
하아
PANT
GEEZ.
하아
PANT
하아
PANT
THIS IS THE FIRST GIRL...
PANT
하아
PANT
...THAT I COULDN'T CONTROL AS I WANTED.
NEED TO WORK OUT MORE.

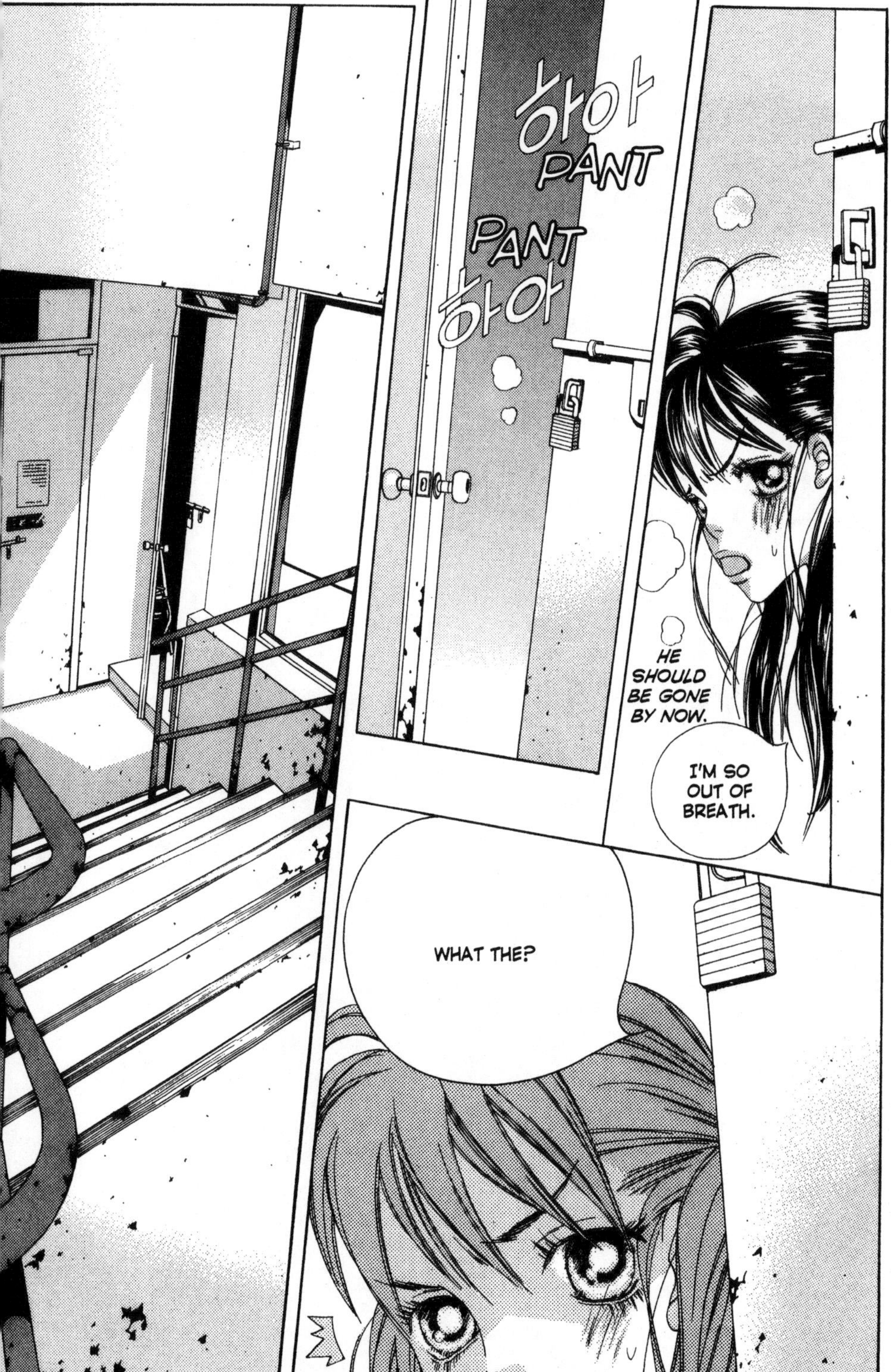
하아 PANT
PANT 하아
HE SHOULD BE GONE BY NOW.
I'M SO OUT OF BREATH.
WHAT THE?

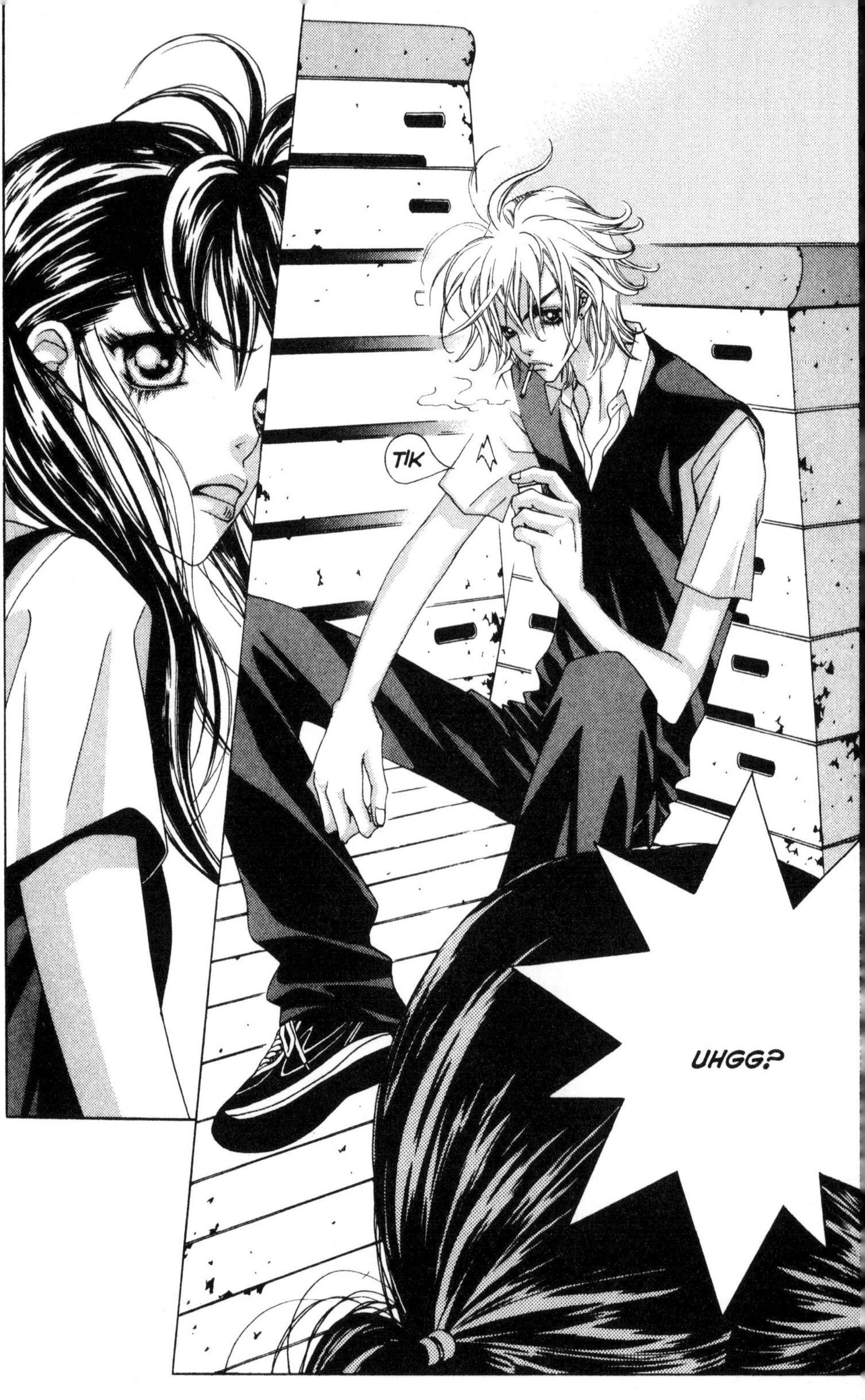
TIK
UHGG?

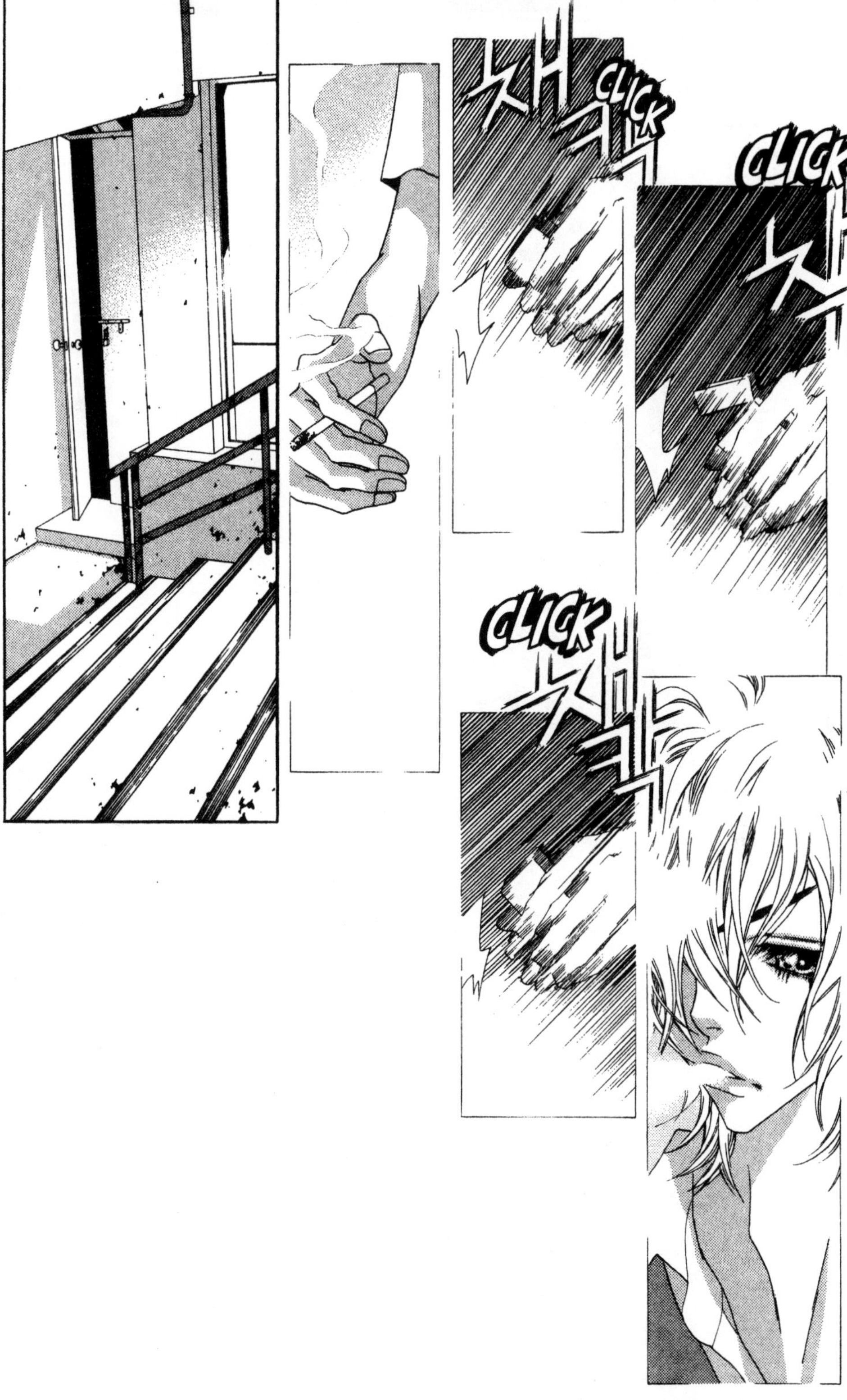
CLICK
CLICK
CLICK

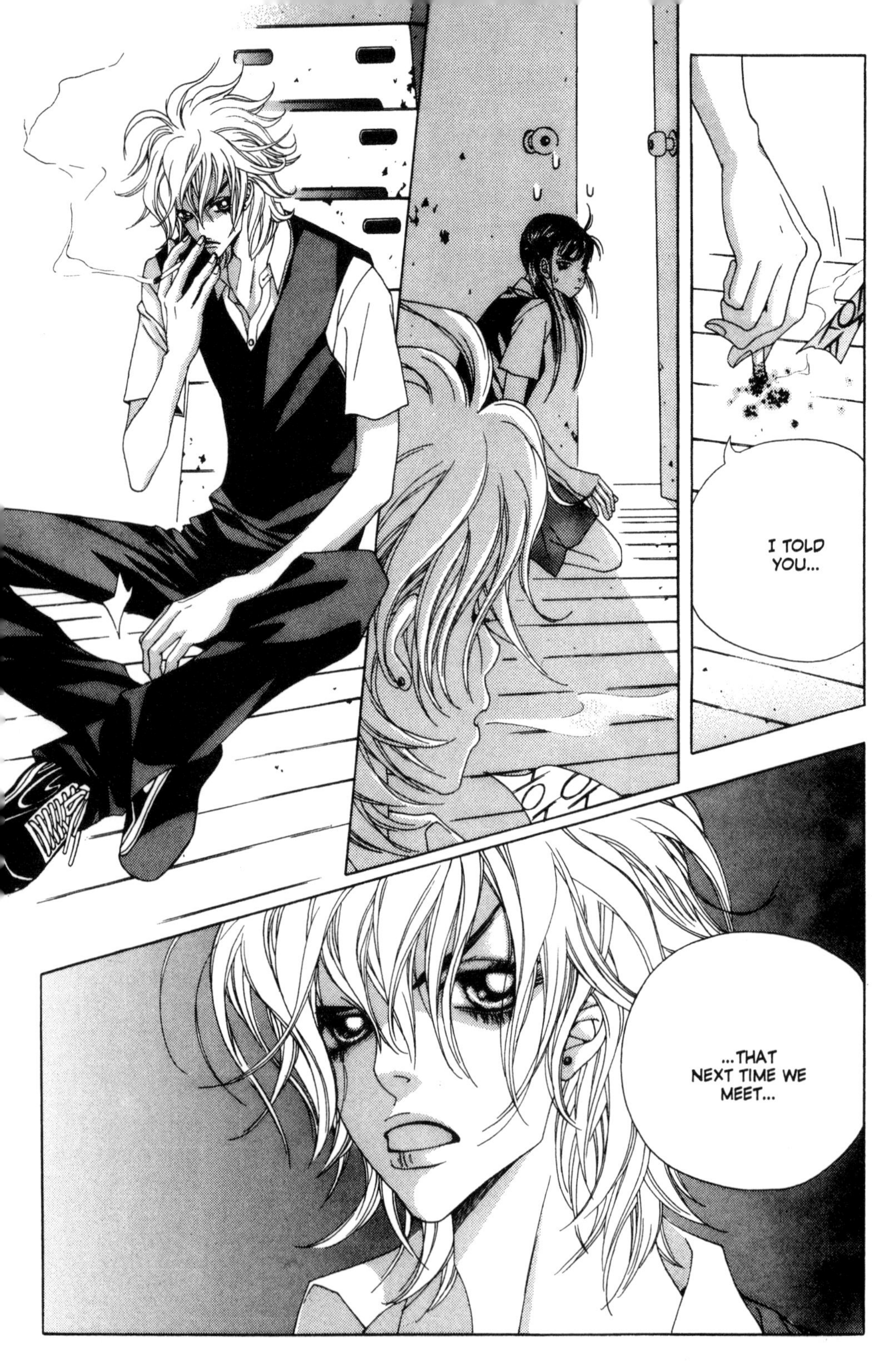
I TOLD YOU...
...THAT NEXT TIME WE MEET...

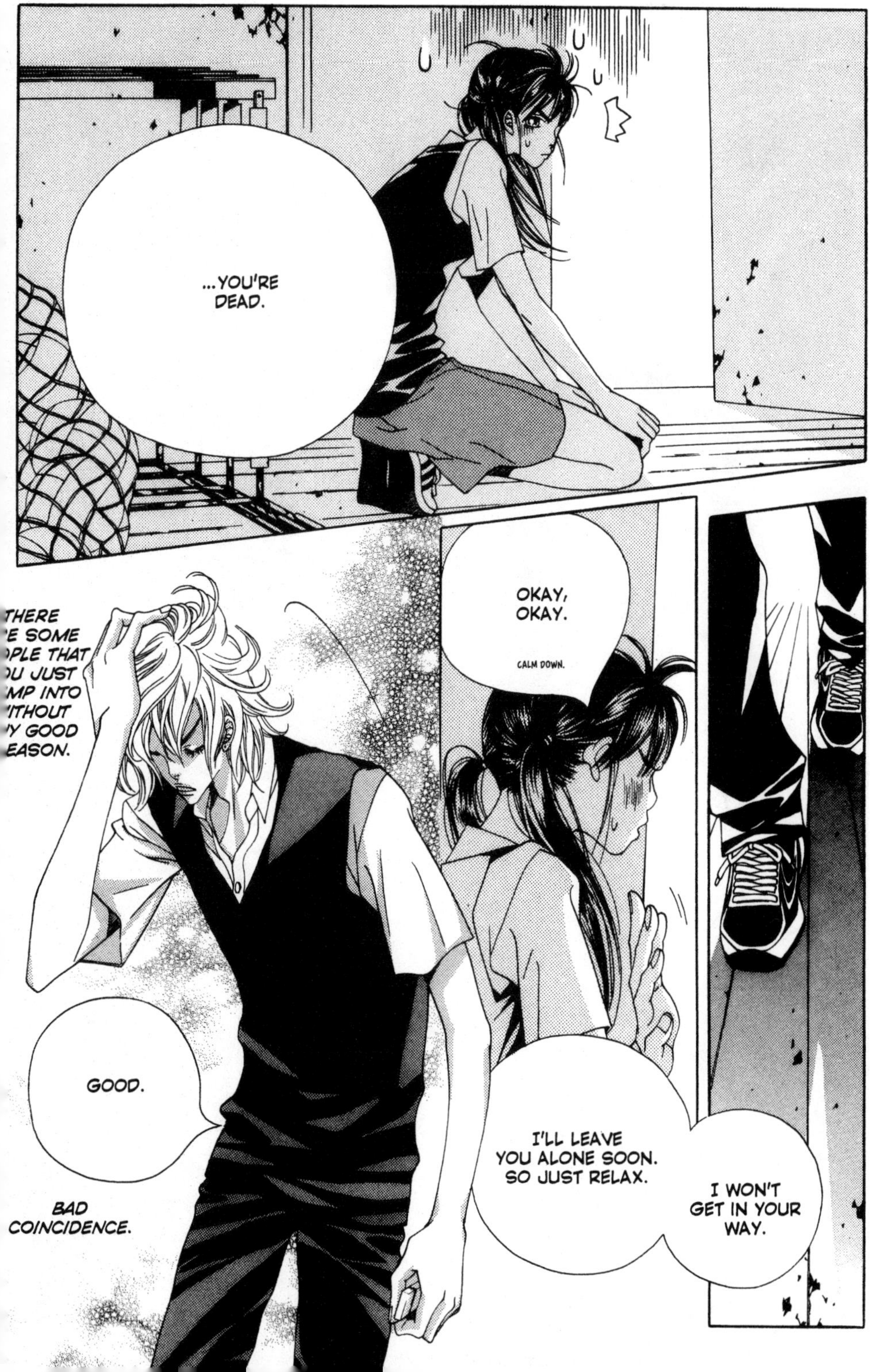
...YOU'RE DEAD.
THERE 'E SOME PLE THAT U JUST MP INTO ITHOUT Y GOOD EASON.
GOOD.
BAD COINCIDENCE.
OKAY, OKAY.
CALM DOWN.
I'LL LEAVE YOU ALONE SOON. SO JUST RELAX.
I WON'T GET IN YOUR WAY.

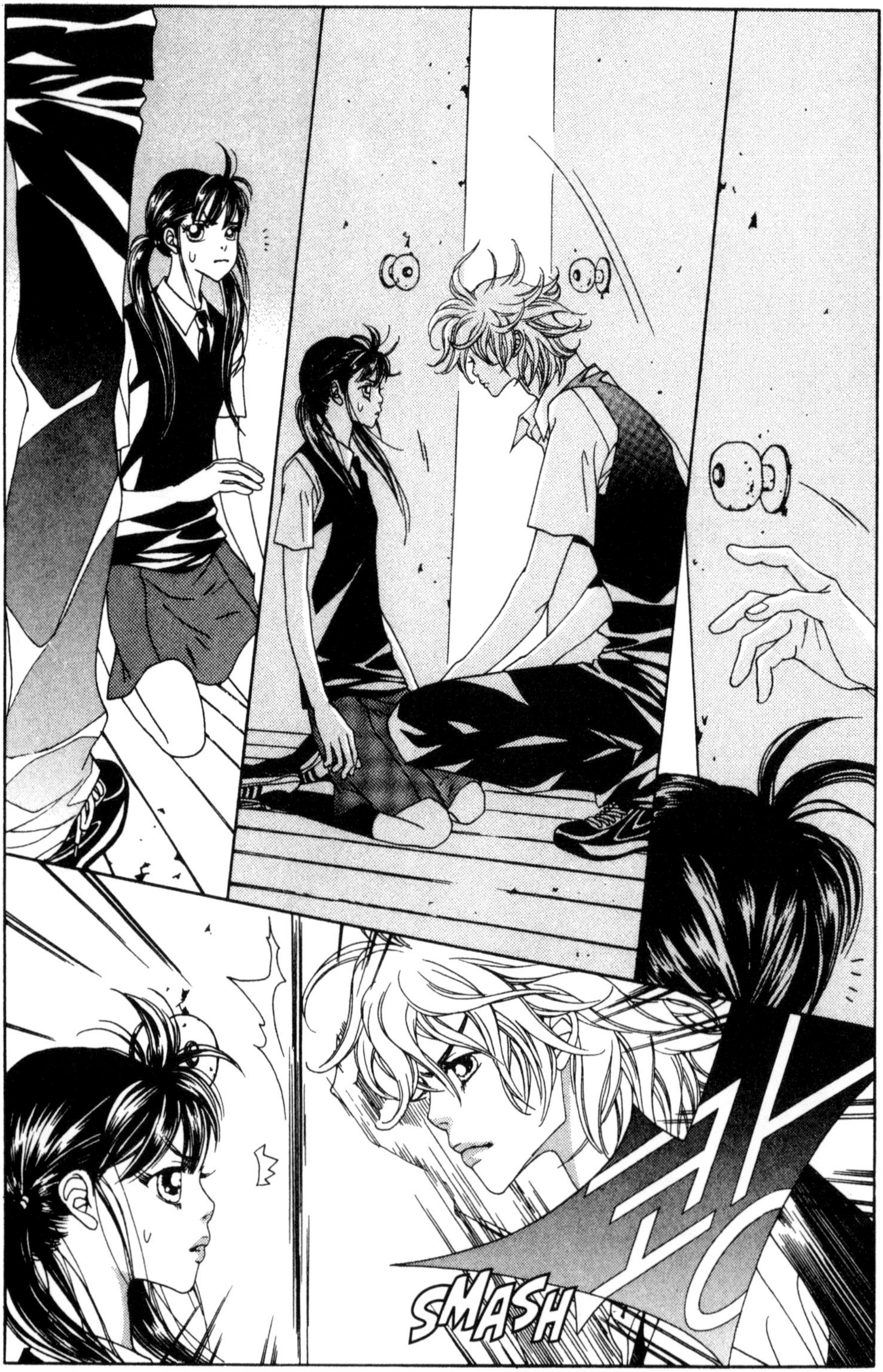
SMASH

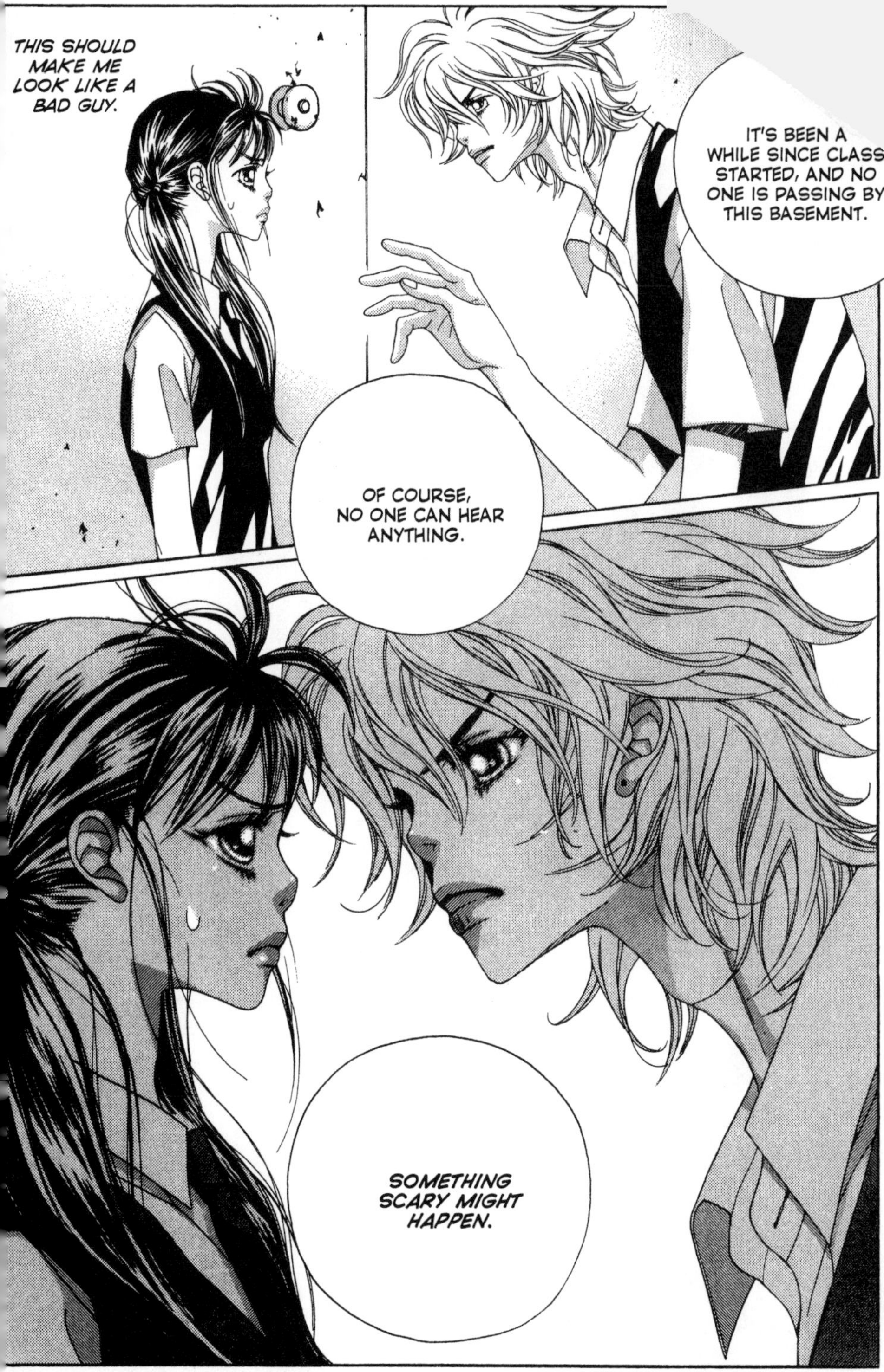
THIS SHOULD MAKE ME LOOK LIKE A BAD GUY.
IT'S BEEN A WHILE SINCE CLASS STARTED, AND NO ONE IS PASSING BY THIS BASEMENT.
OF COURSE, NO ONE CAN HEAR ANYTHING.
SOMETHING SCARY MIGHT HAPPEN.

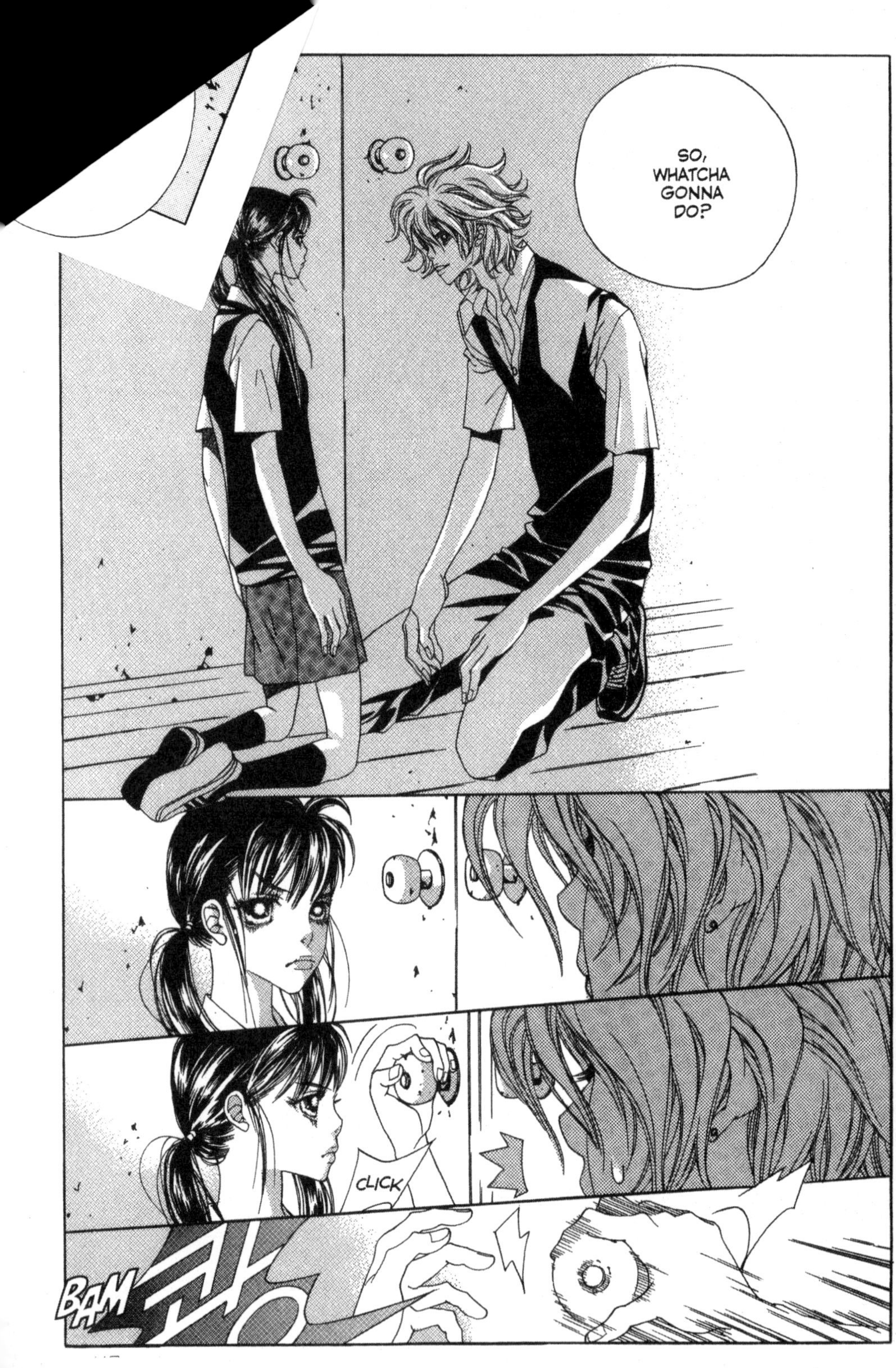
SO, WHATCHA GONNA DO?
CLICK
BAM

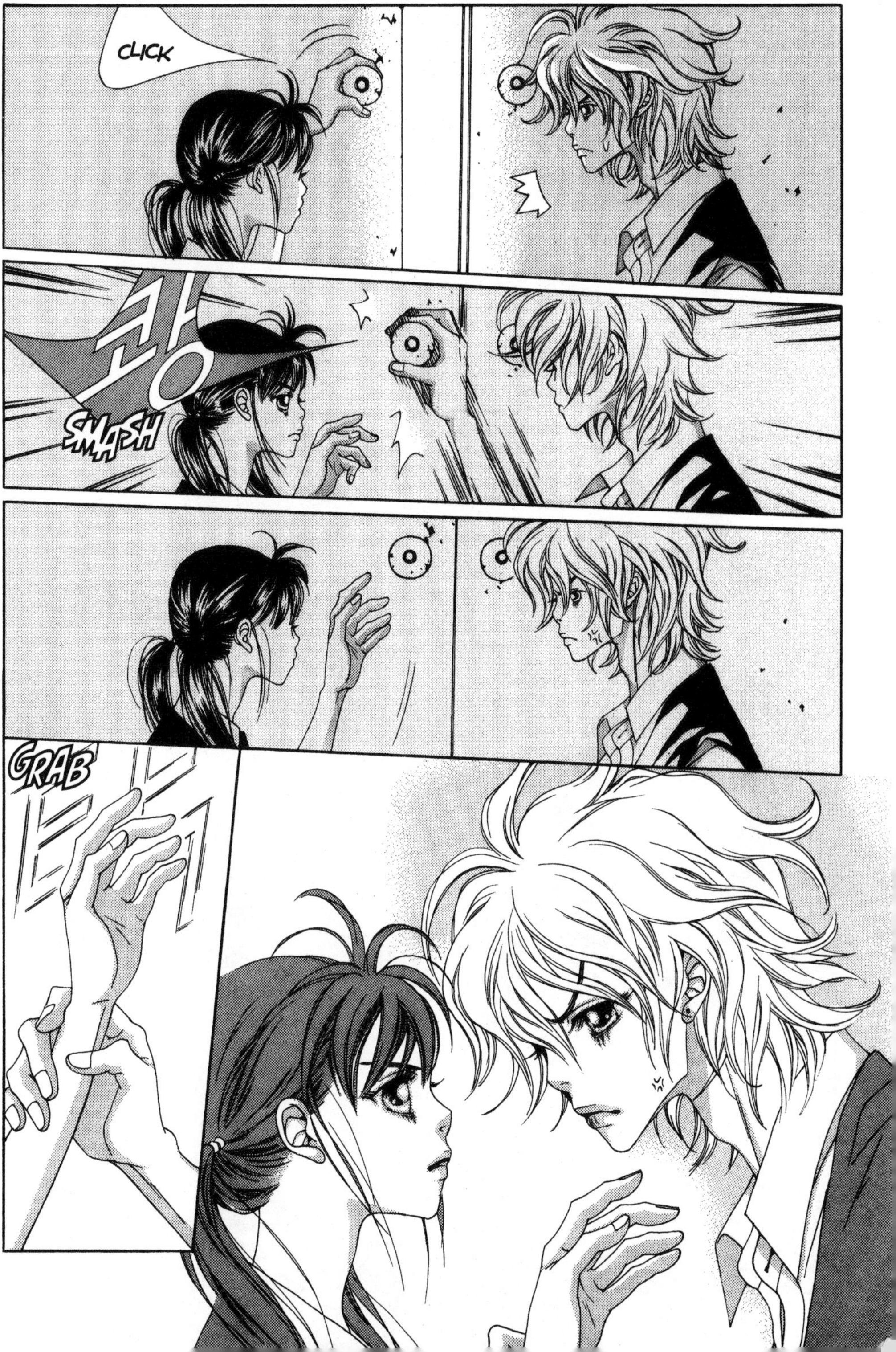
CLICK
SMASH
GRAB

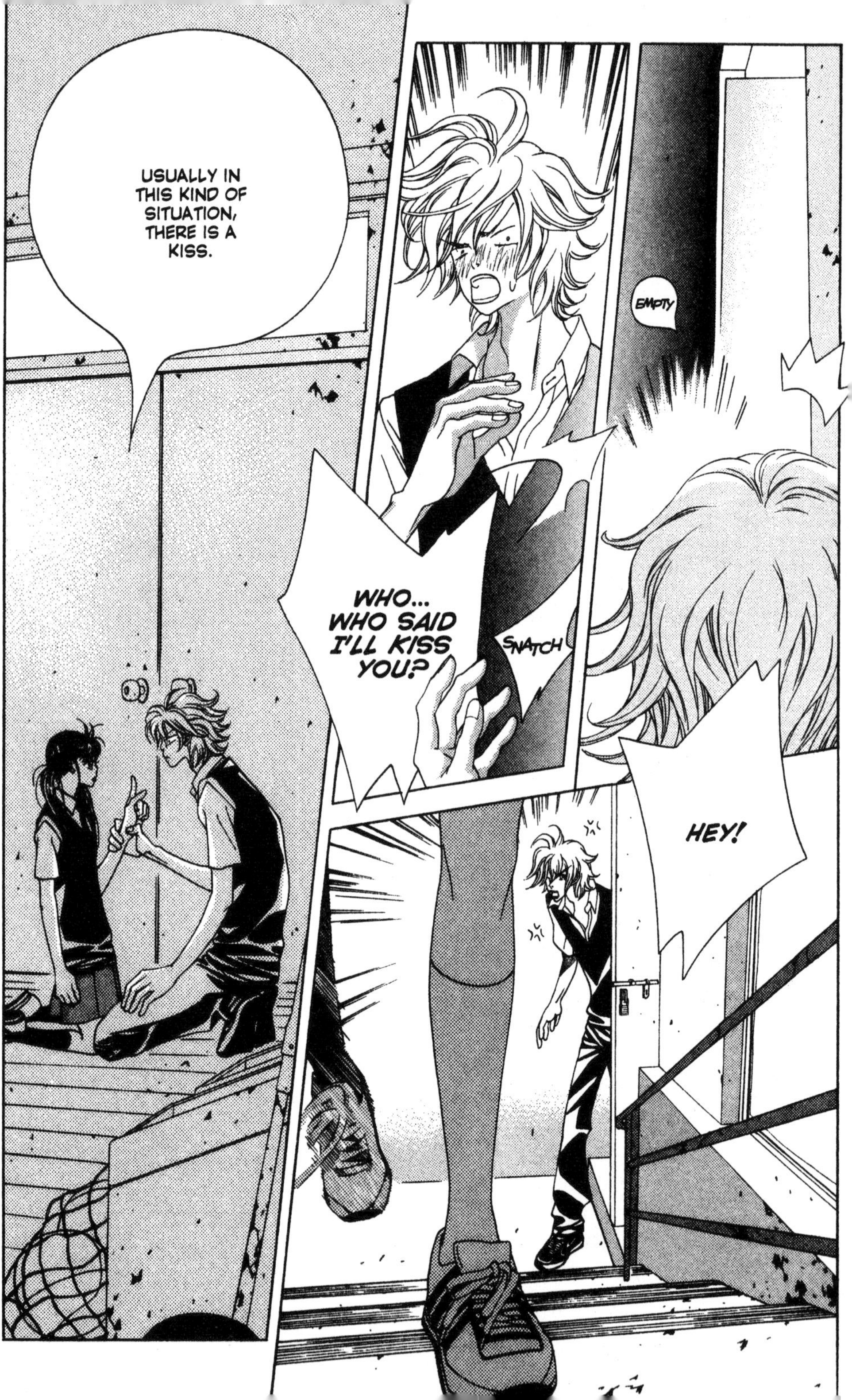
USUALLY IN THIS KIND OF SITUATION, THERE IS A KISS.
WHO... WHO SAID I'LL KISS YOU?
SNATCH
EMPTY
HEY!

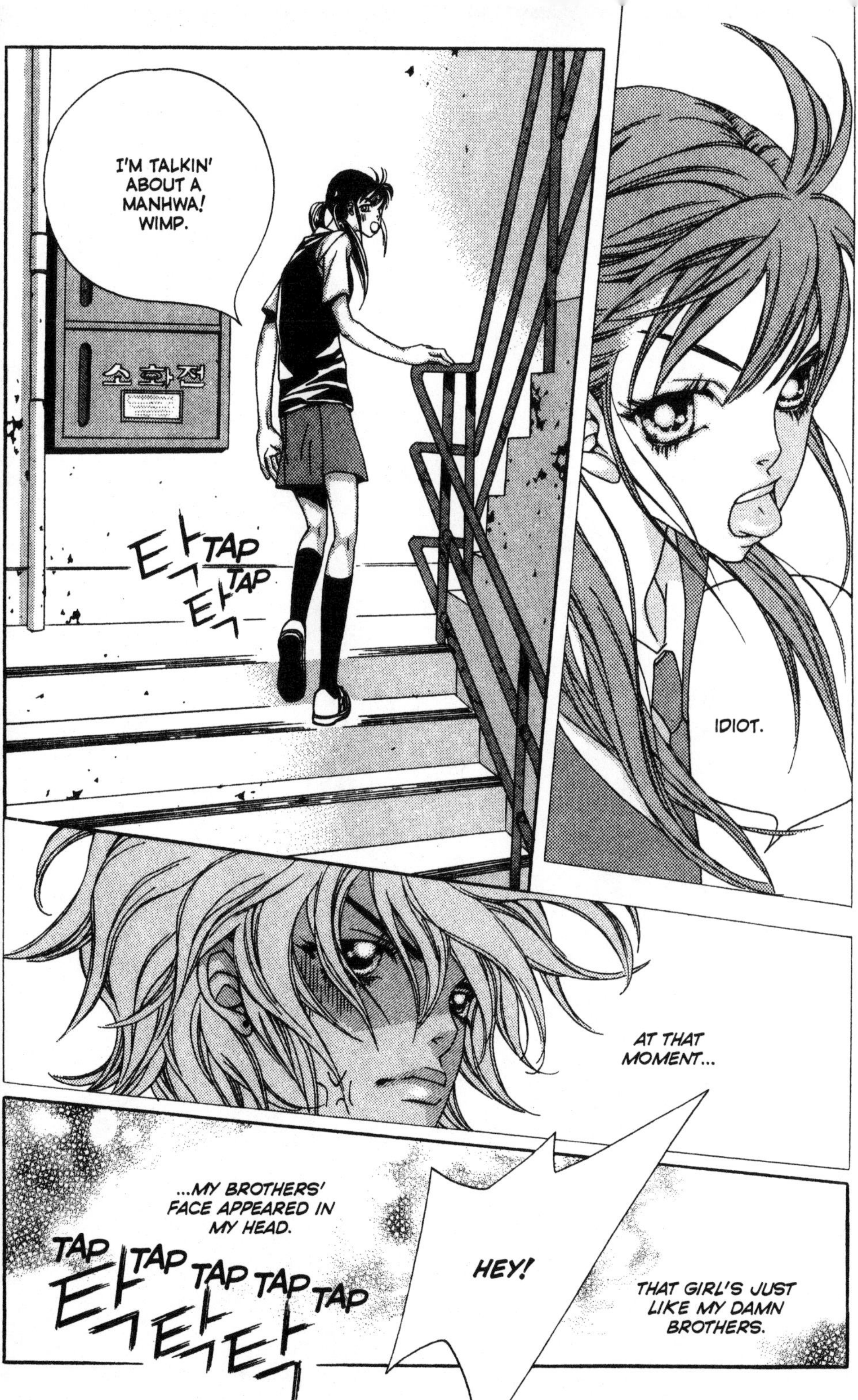
I'M TALKIN' ABOUT A MANHWA! WIMP.
소화전
탁 TAP
탁 TAP
IDIOT.
AT THAT MOMENT...
...MY BROTHERS' FACE APPEARED IN MY HEAD.
TAP TAP TAP TAP TAP
탁 탁 탁 탁
HEY!
THAT GIRL'S JUST LIKE MY DAMN BROTHERS.

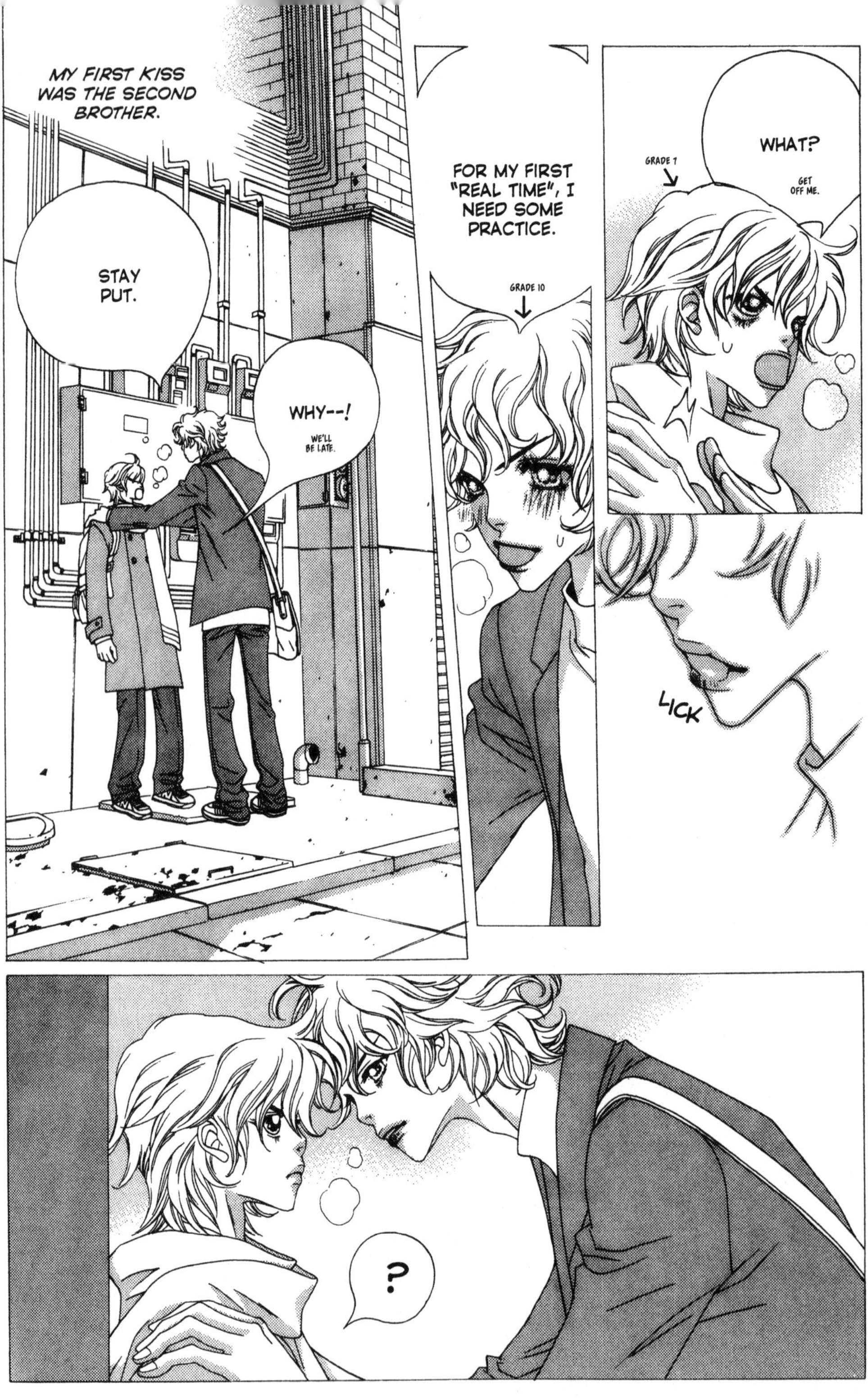
MY FIRST KISS WAS THE SECOND BROTHER.
STAY PUT.
WHY--!
WE'LL BE LATE.
FOR MY FIRST "REAL TIME", I NEED SOME PRACTICE.
GRADE 10
WHAT?
GRADE 7
GET OFF ME.
LICK
?

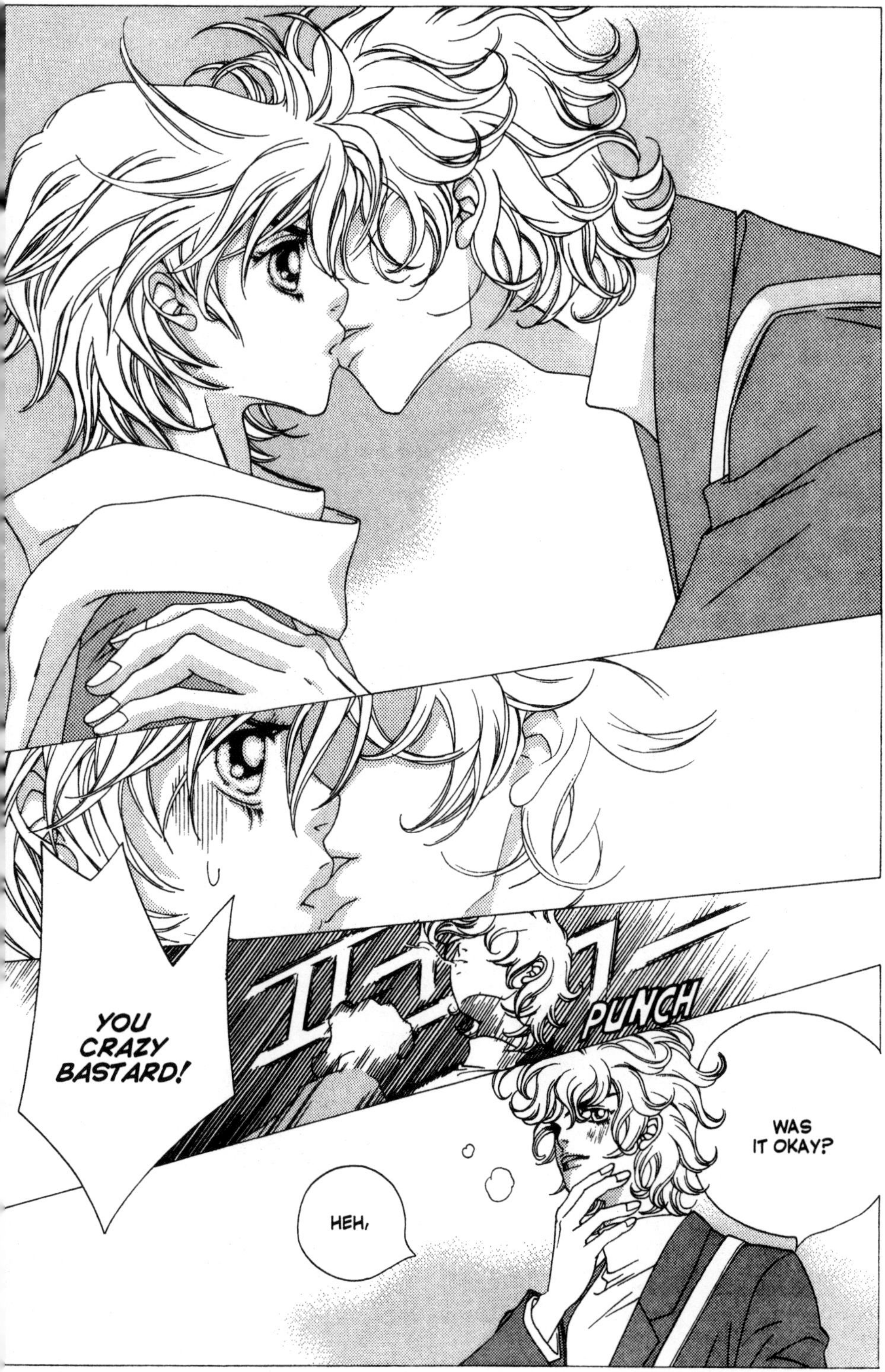
YOU CRAZY BASTARD!
PUNCH
HEH,
WAS IT OKAY?

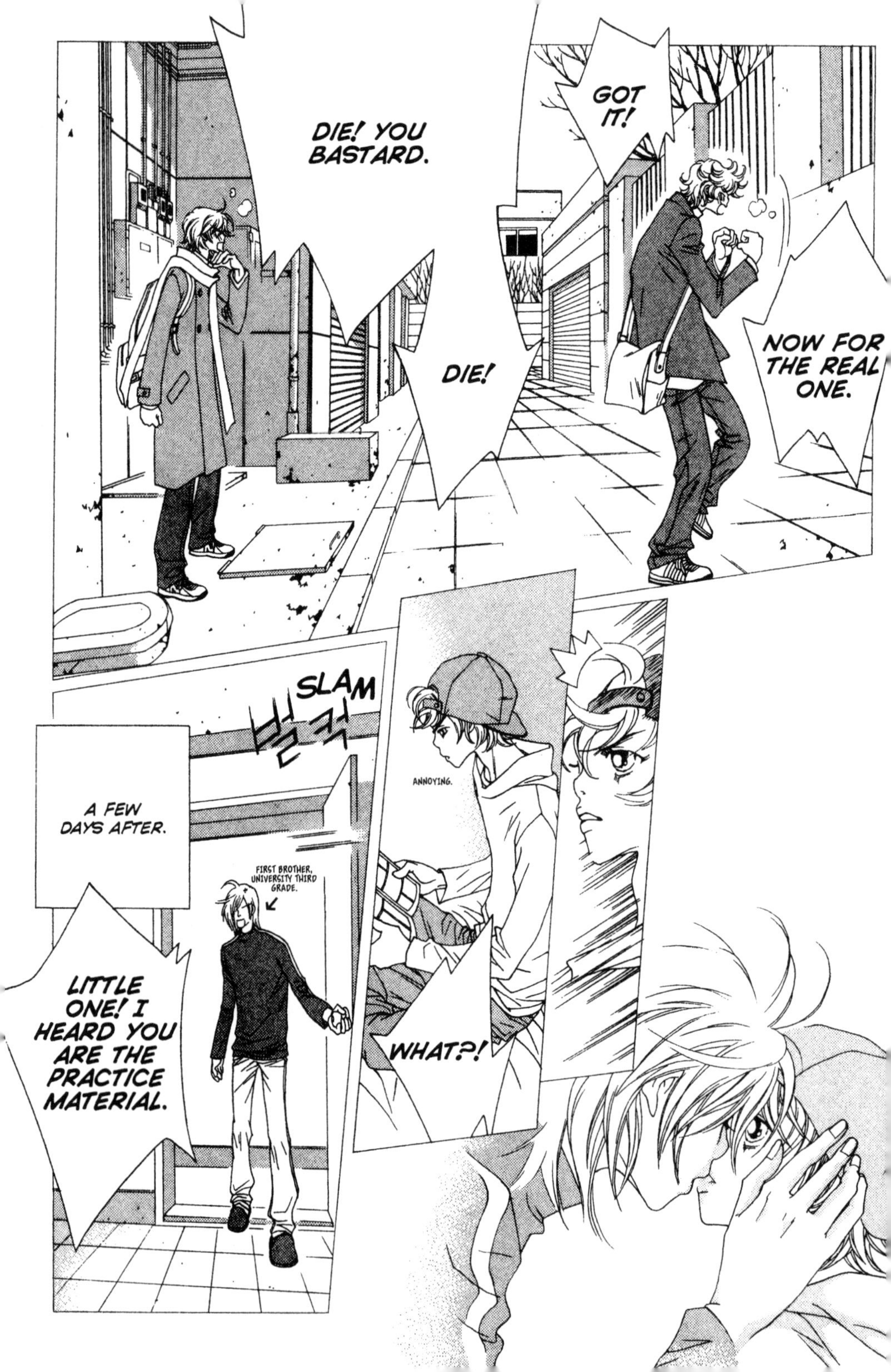
DIE! YOU BASTARD.
DIE!
GOT IT!
NOW FOR THE REAL ONE.
A FEW DAYS AFTER.
SLAM
FIRST BROTHER, UNIVERSITY THIRD GRADE.
LITTLE ONE! I HEARD YOU ARE THE PRACTICE MATERIAL.
ANNOYING.
WHAT?!

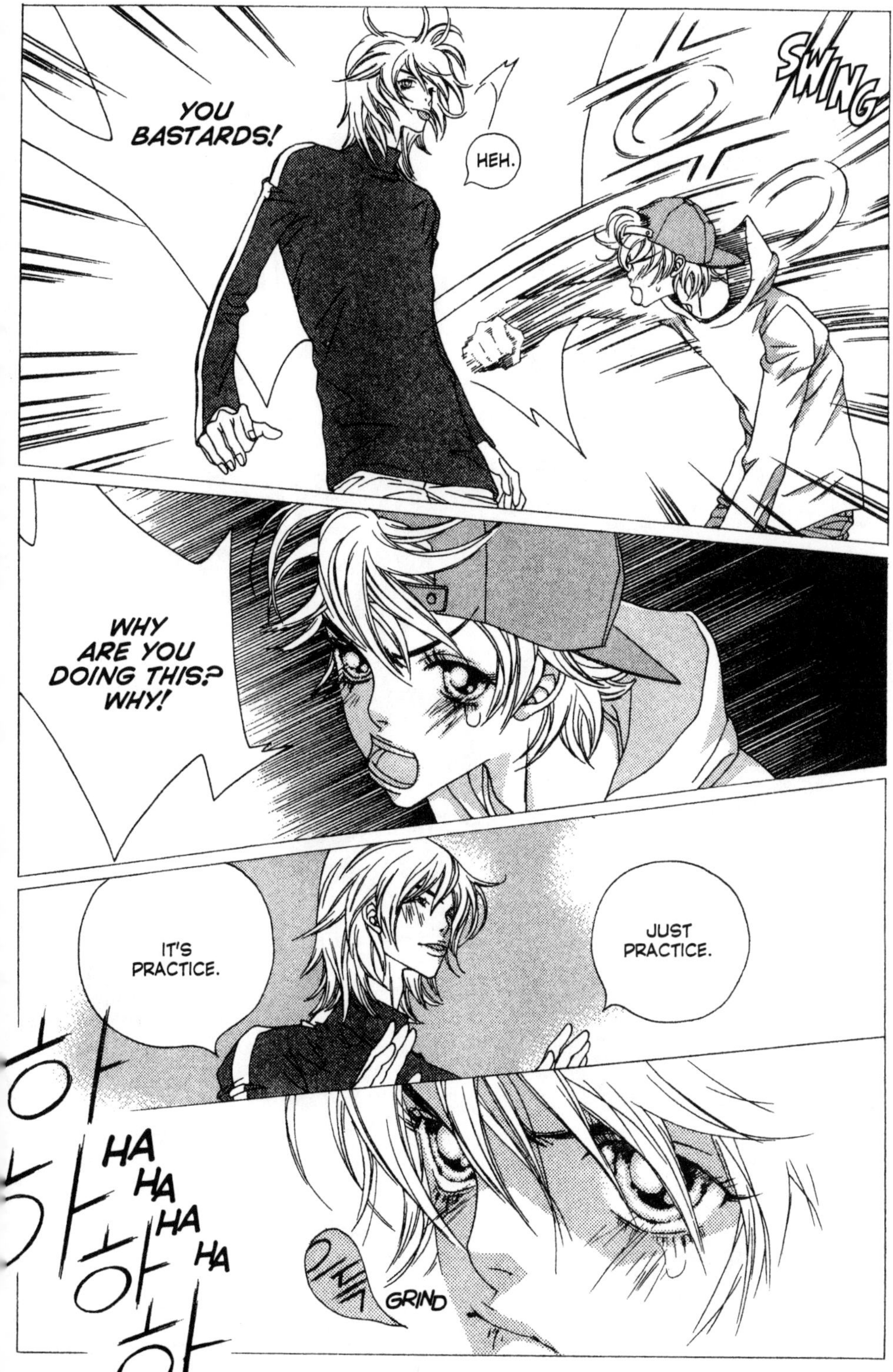
YOU BASTARDS!
HEH.
SWING
WHY ARE YOU DOING THIS? WHY!
IT'S PRACTICE.
JUST PRACTICE.
하하하하
HA HA HA HA
GRIND

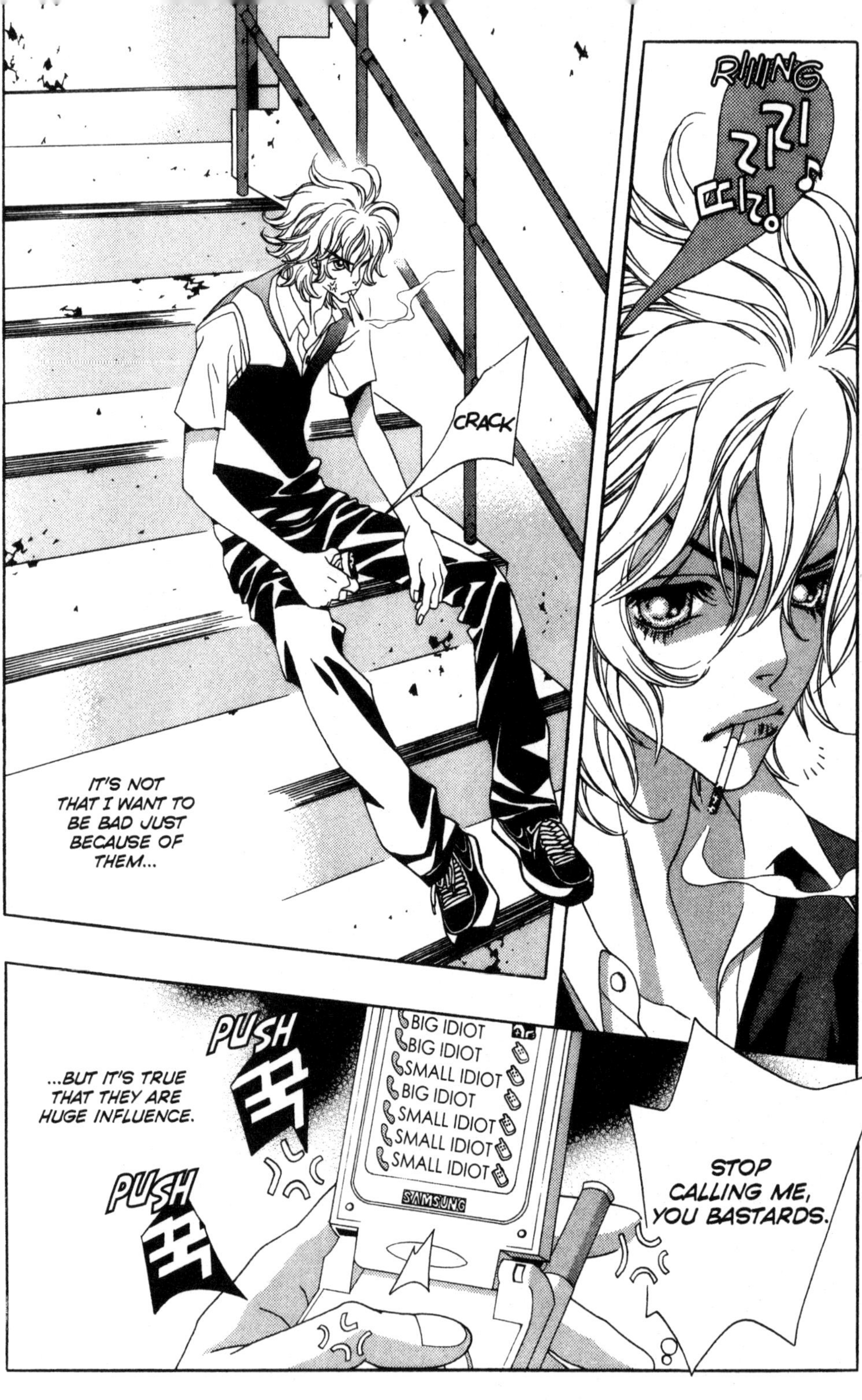
IT'S NOT THAT I WANT TO BE BAD JUST BECAUSE OF THEM...
CRACK
RIIING
...BUT IT'S TRUE THAT THEY ARE HUGE INFLUENCE.
PUSH
꾹
BIG IDIOT
BIG IDIOT
SMALL IDIOT
BIG IDIOT
SMALL IDIOT
SMALL IDIOT
SMALL IDIOT
SAMSUNG
PUSH
꾹
STOP CALLING ME, YOU BASTARDS.

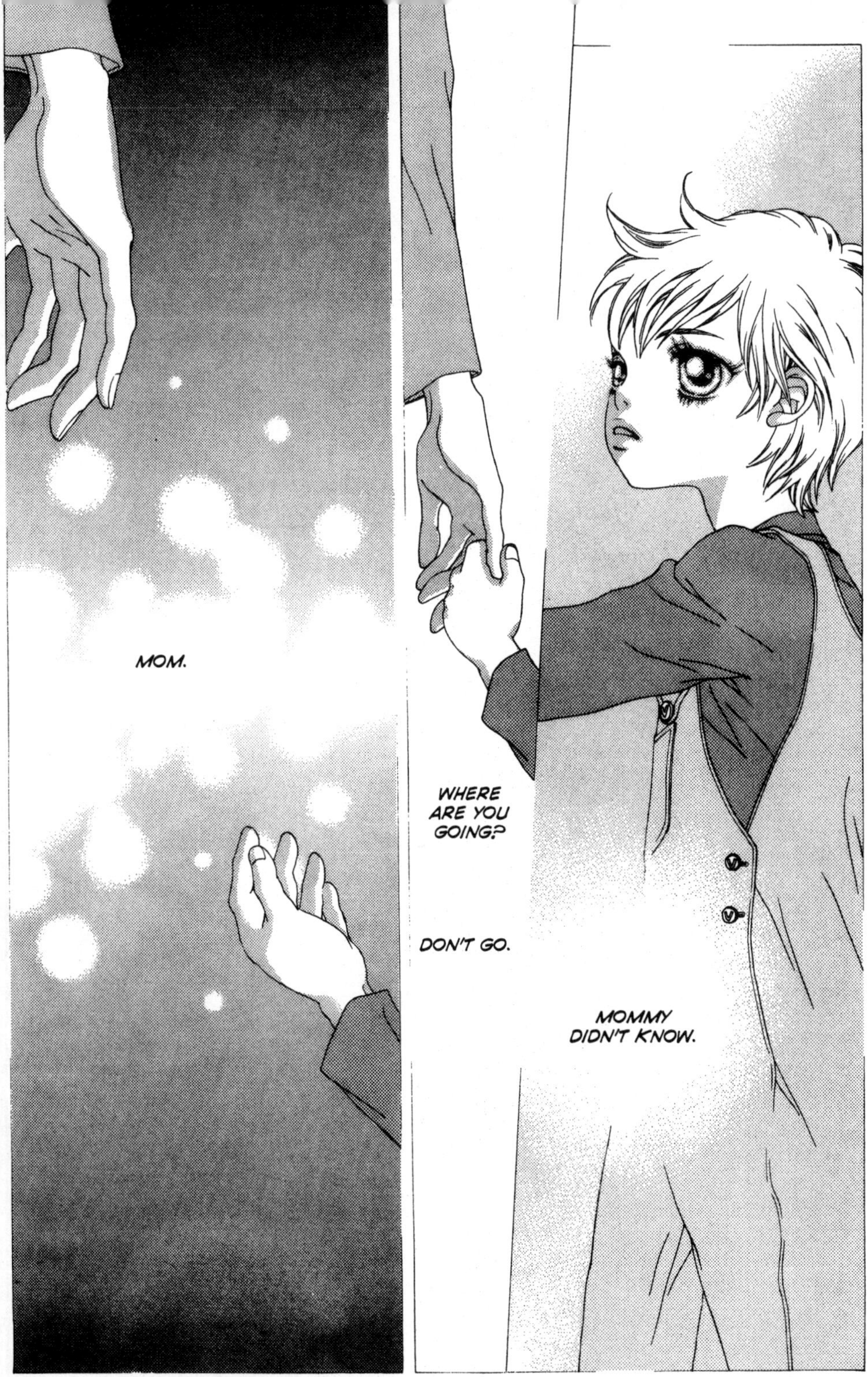
MOM.
WHERE ARE YOU GOING?
DON'T GO.
MOMMY DIDN'T KNOW.

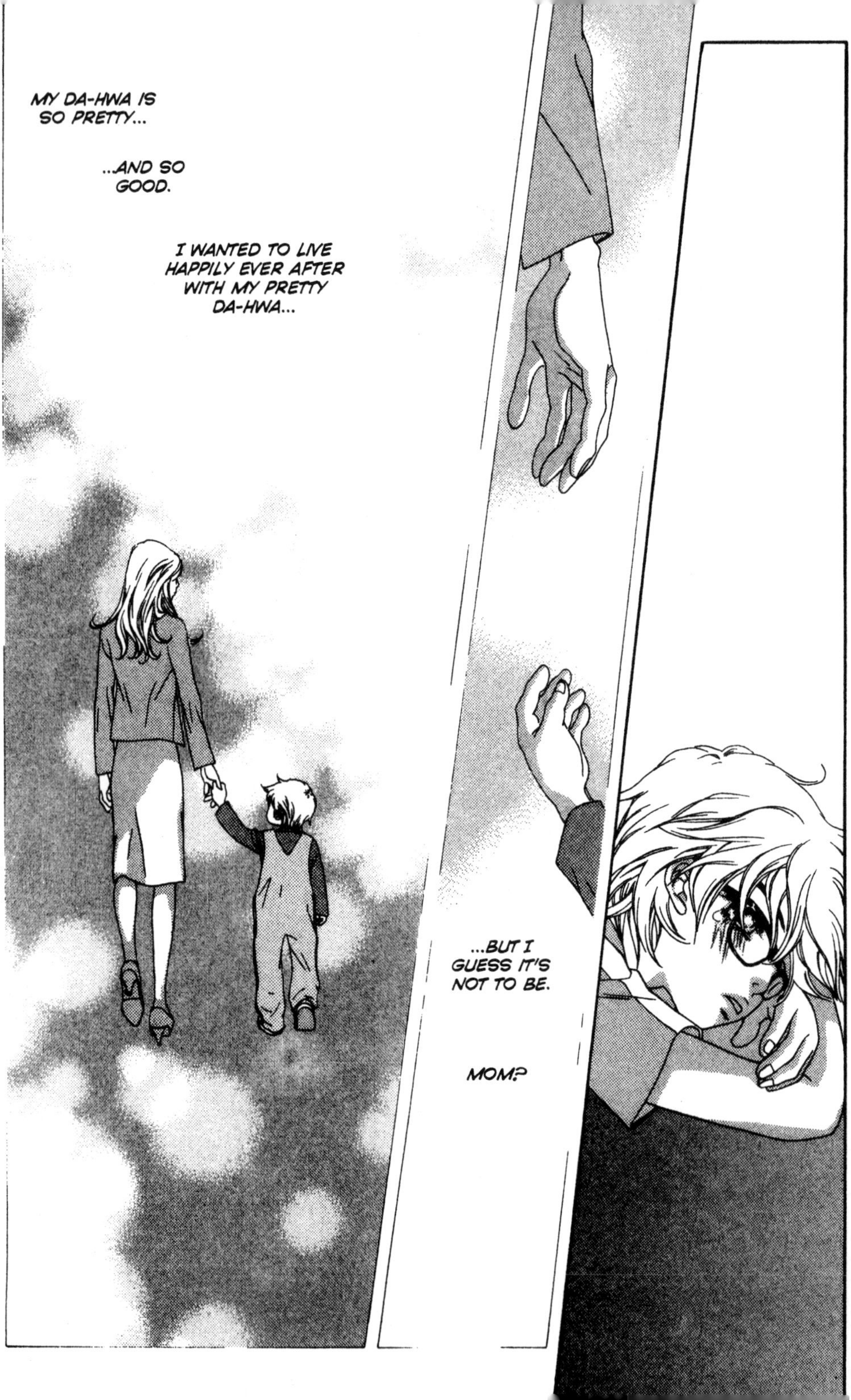
MY DA-HWA IS SO PRETTY...
...AND SO GOOD.
I WANTED TO LIVE HAPPILY EVER AFTER WITH MY PRETTY DA-HWA...
...BUT I GUESS IT'S NOT TO BE.
MOM?

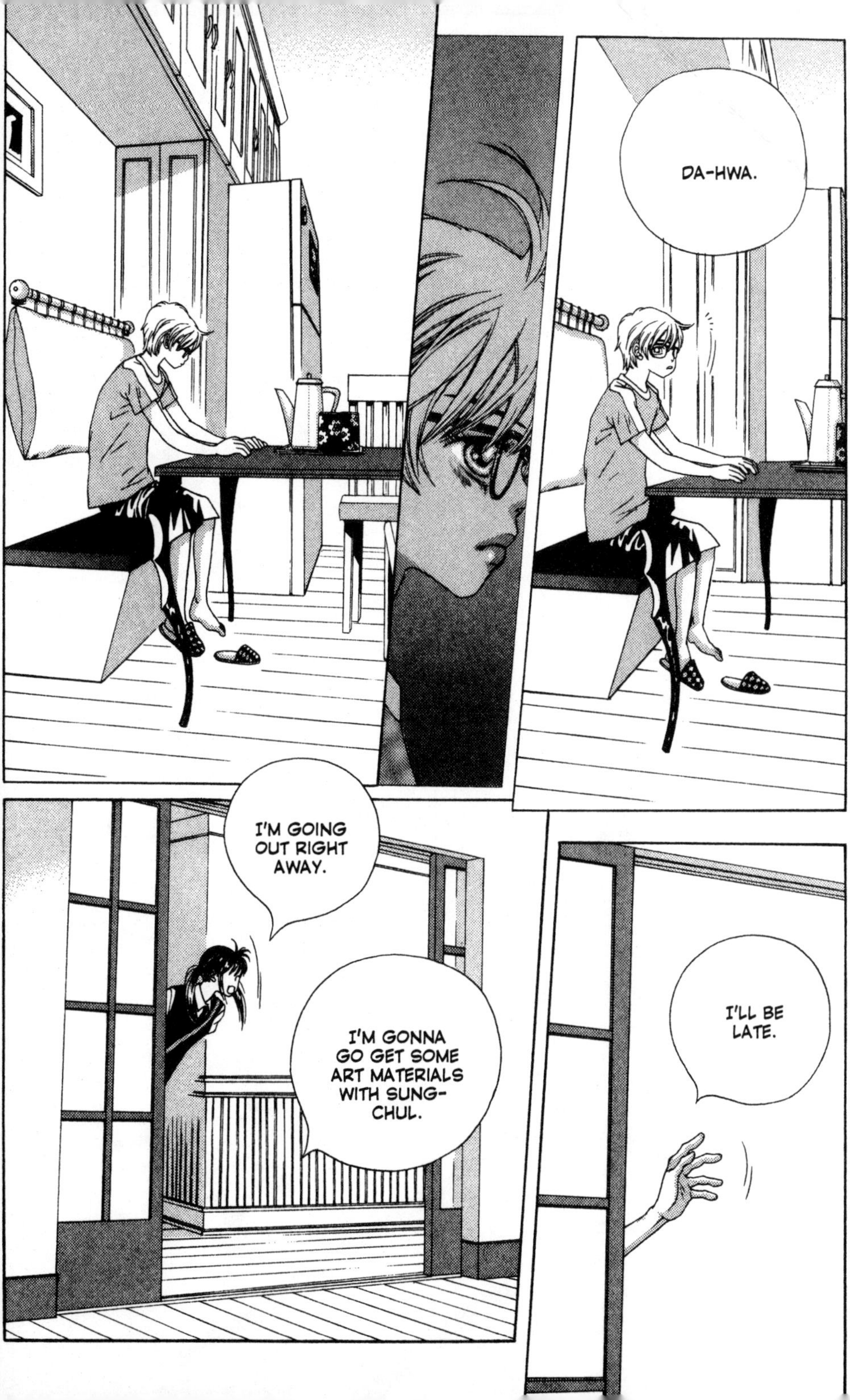
DA-HWA.
I'M GOING OUT RIGHT AWAY.
I'M GONNA GO GET SOME ART MATERIALS WITH SUNG-CHUL.
I'LL BE LATE.

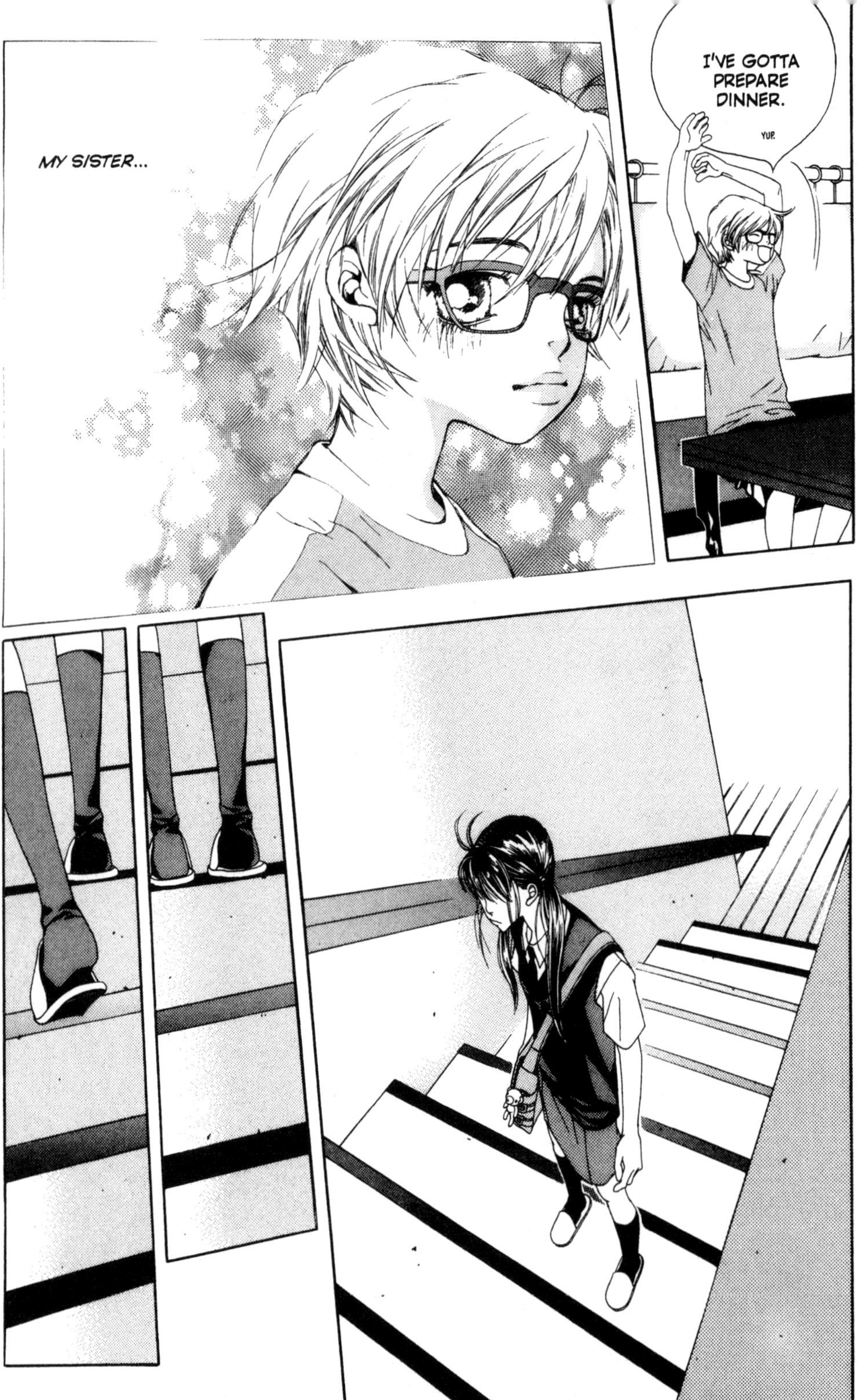
MY SISTER...
I'VE GOTTA PREPARE DINNER.
YUP.

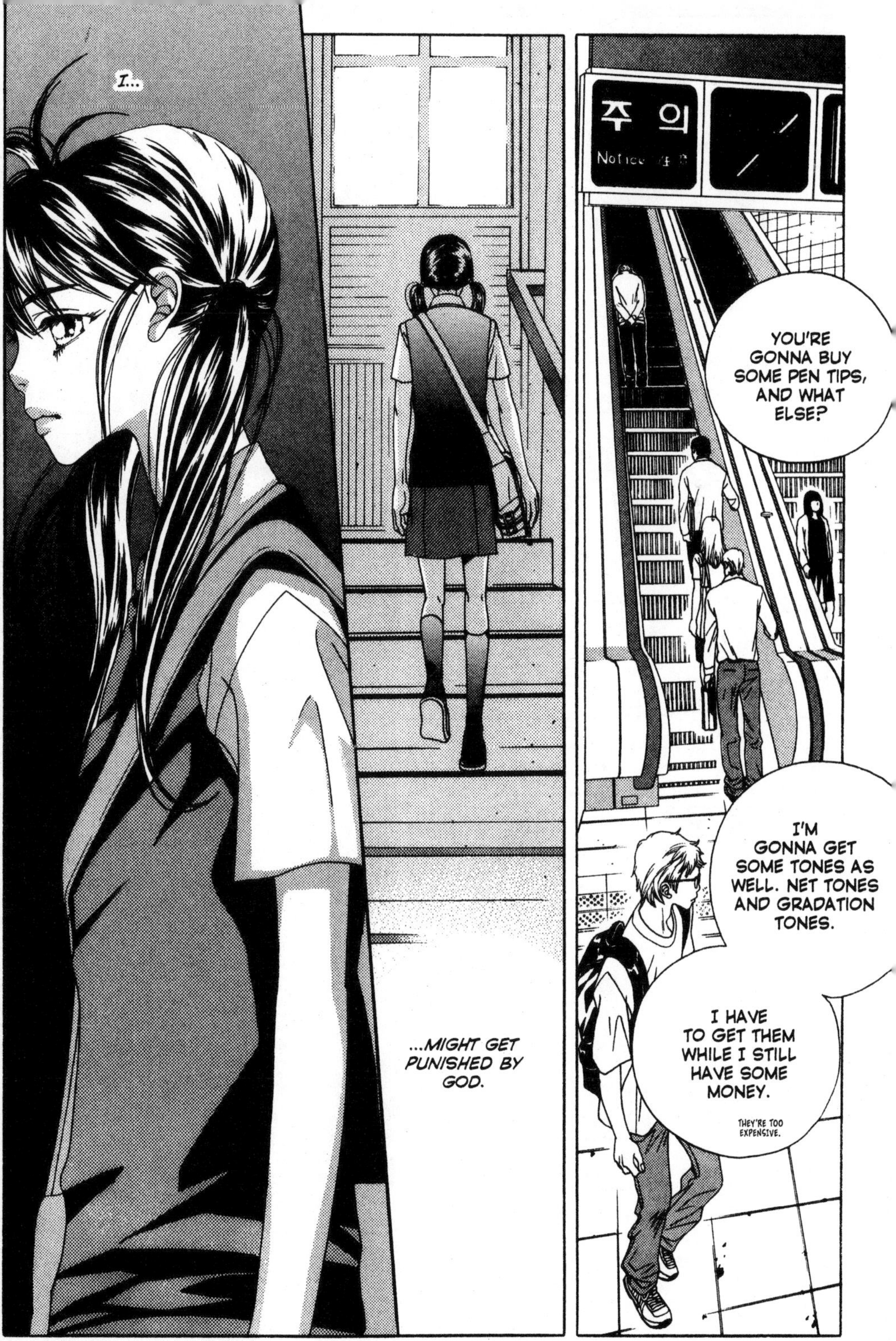
I...
...MIGHT GET PUNISHED BY GOD.
주의
Notice
YOU'RE GONNA BUY SOME PEN TIPS, AND WHAT ELSE?
I'M GONNA GET SOME TONES AS WELL. NET TONES AND GRADATION TONES.
I HAVE TO GET THEM WHILE I STILL HAVE SOME MONEY.
THEY'RE TOO EXPENSIVE.

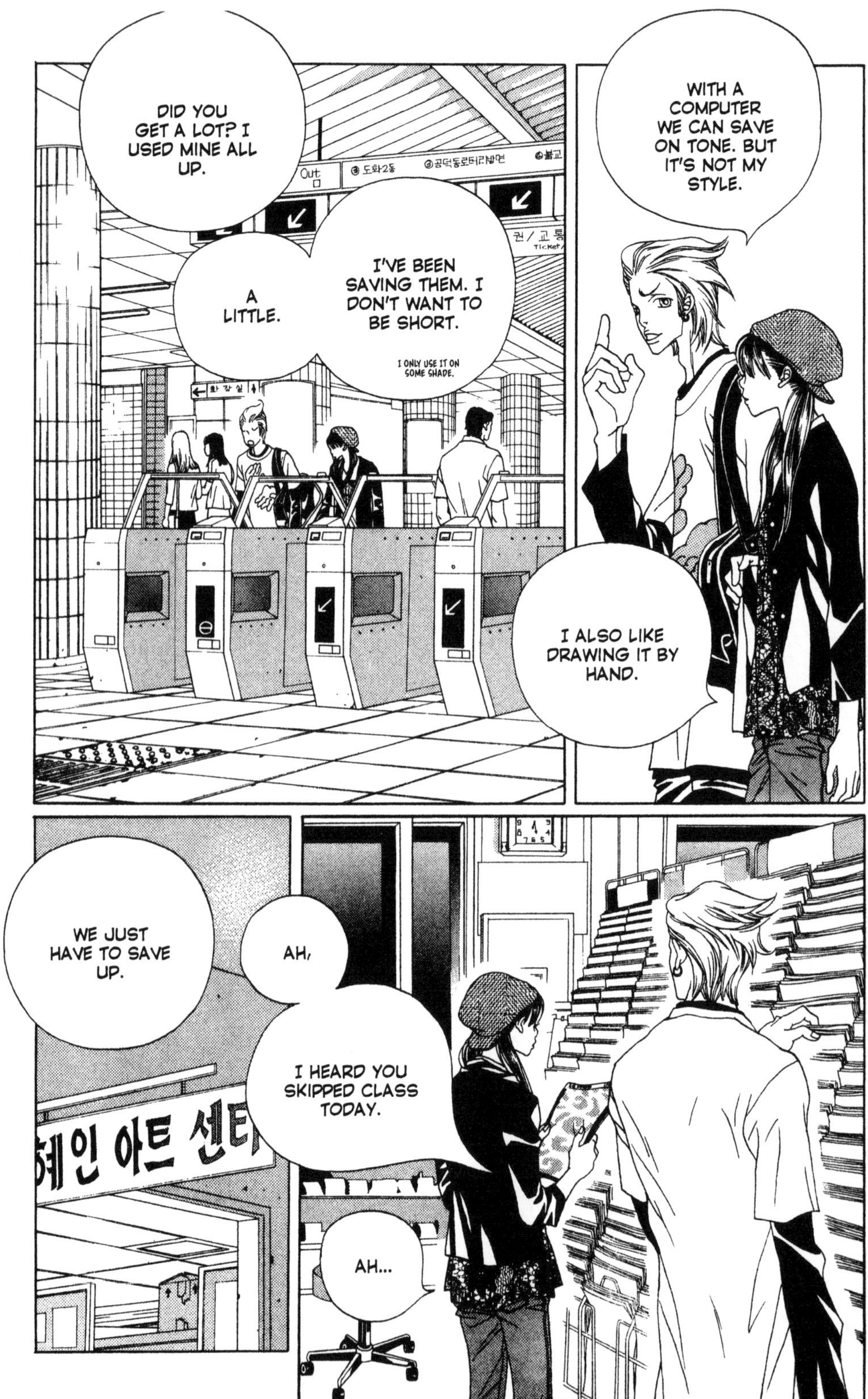
DID YOU GET A LOT? I USED MINE ALL UP.
Out
A LITTLE.
I'VE BEEN SAVING THEM. I DON'T WANT TO BE SHORT.
I ONLY USE IT ON SOME SHADE.
WITH A COMPUTER WE CAN SAVE ON TONE. BUT IT'S NOT MY STYLE.
I ALSO LIKE DRAWING IT BY HAND.
WE JUST HAVE TO SAVE UP.
혜인 아트 센터
AH,
I HEARD YOU SKIPPED CLASS TODAY.
AH...

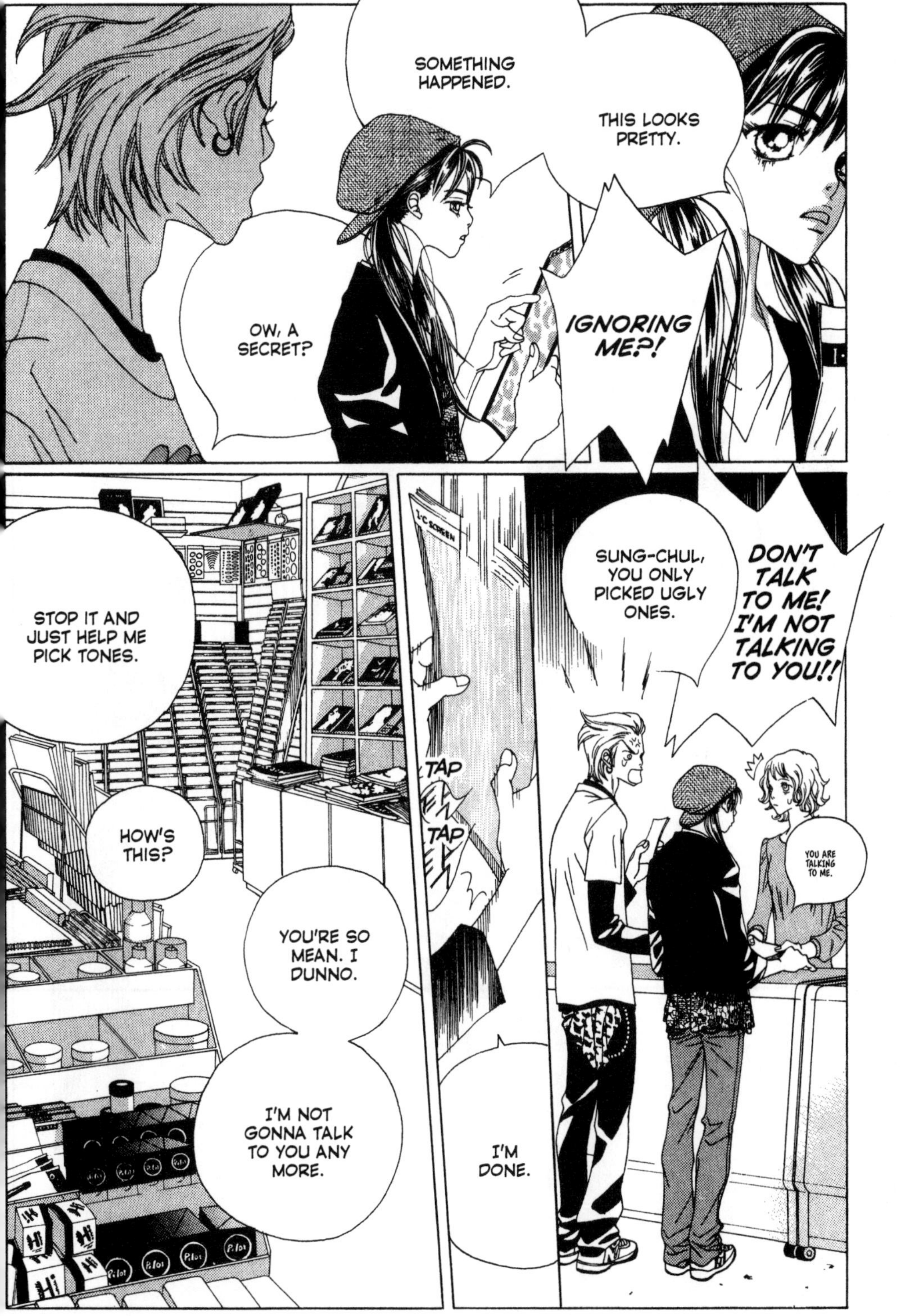
SOMETHING HAPPENED.
OW, A SECRET?
THIS LOOKS PRETTY.
IGNORING ME?!
STOP IT AND JUST HELP ME PICK TONES.
HOW'S THIS?
YOU'RE SO MEAN. I DUNNO.
I'M NOT GONNA TALK TO YOU ANY MORE.
TAP
TAP
I'M DONE.
SUNG-CHUL, YOU ONLY PICKED UGLY ONES.
DON'T TALK TO ME! I'M NOT TALKING TO YOU!!
YOU ARE TALKING TO ME.

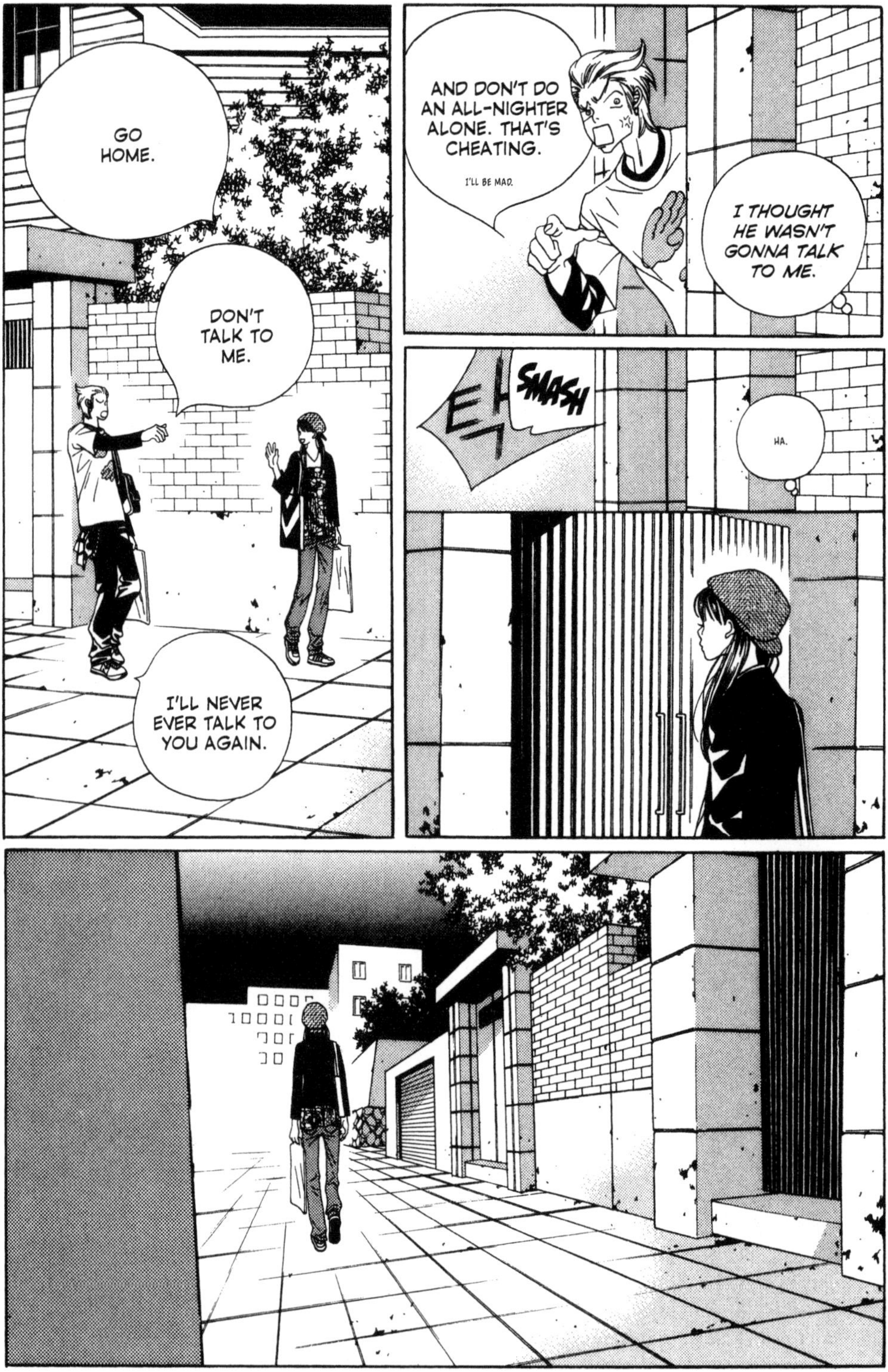
GO HOME.
DON'T TALK TO ME.
I'LL NEVER EVER TALK TO YOU AGAIN.
AND DON'T DO AN ALL-NIGHTER ALONE. THAT'S CHEATING.
I'LL BE MAD.
I THOUGHT HE WASN'T GONNA TALK TO ME.
SMASH
HA.

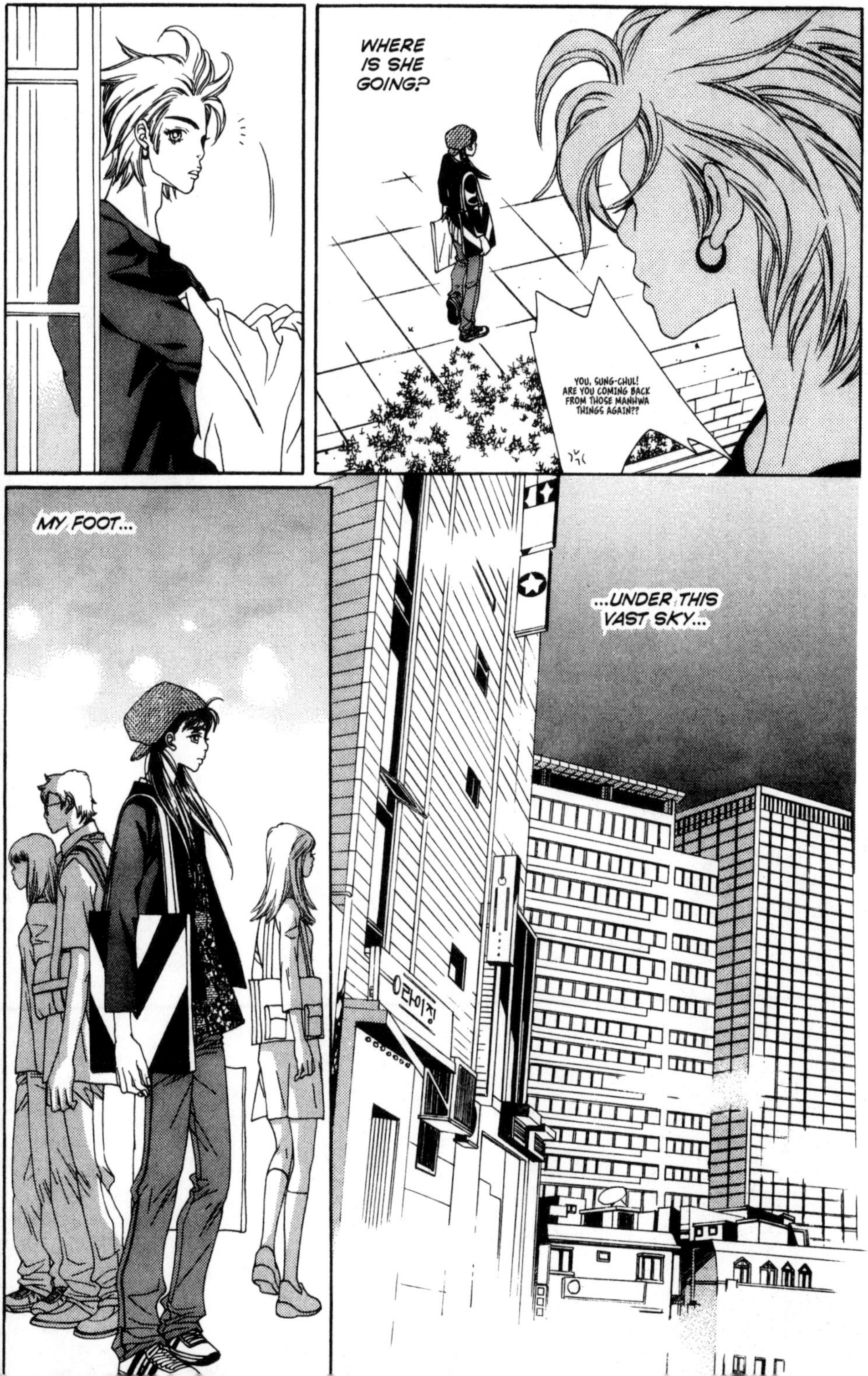
WHERE IS SHE GOING?
YOU, SUNG-CHUL! ARE YOU COMING BACK FROM THOSE MANHWA THINGS AGAIN??
MY FOOT...
...UNDER THIS VAST SKY...

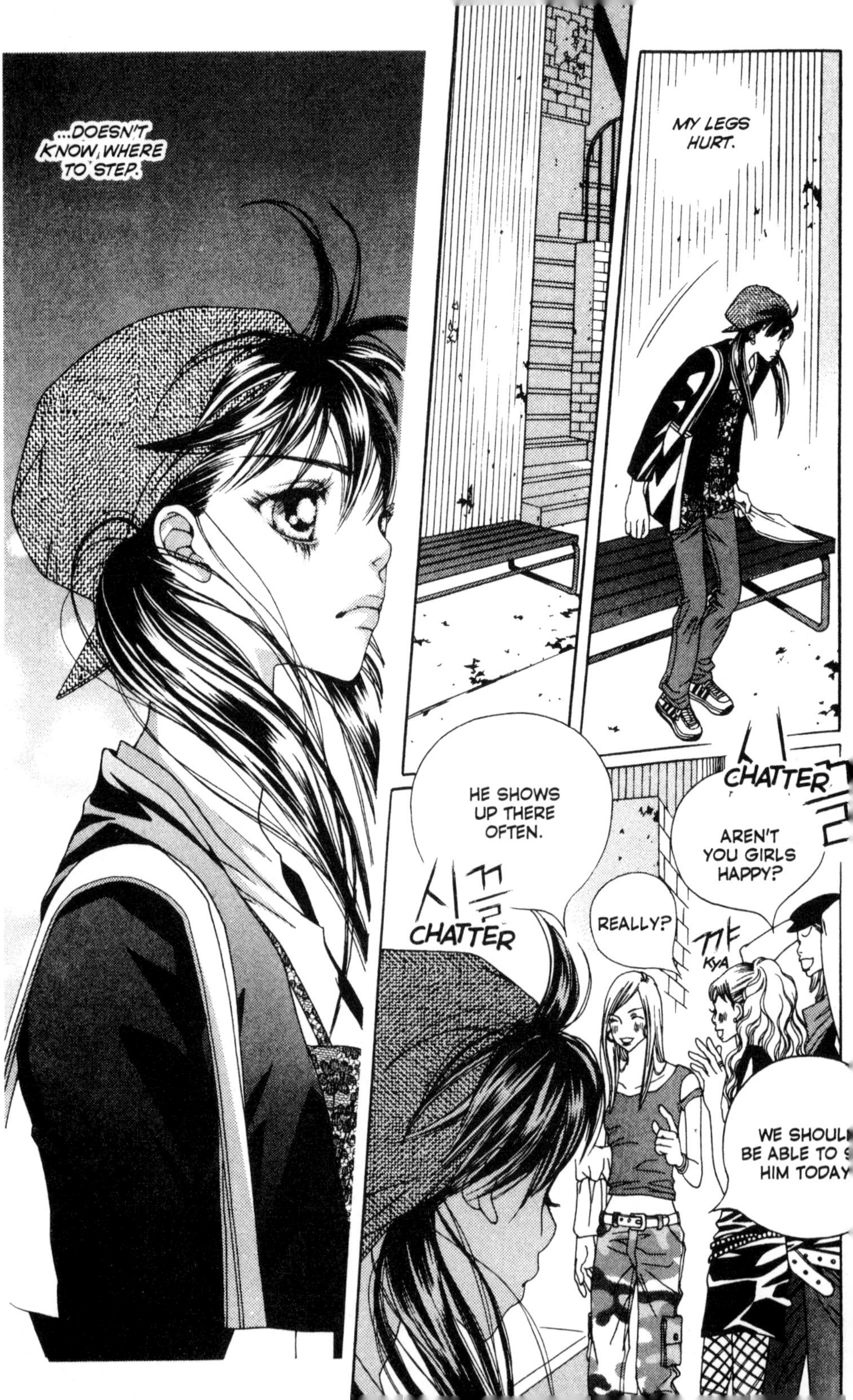
...DOESN'T KNOW WHERE TO STEP.
MY LEGS HURT.
HE SHOWS UP THERE OFTEN.
CHATTER
CHATTER
REALLY?
AREN'T YOU GIRLS HAPPY?
KYA
WE SHOUL
BE ABLE TO S
HIM TODAY

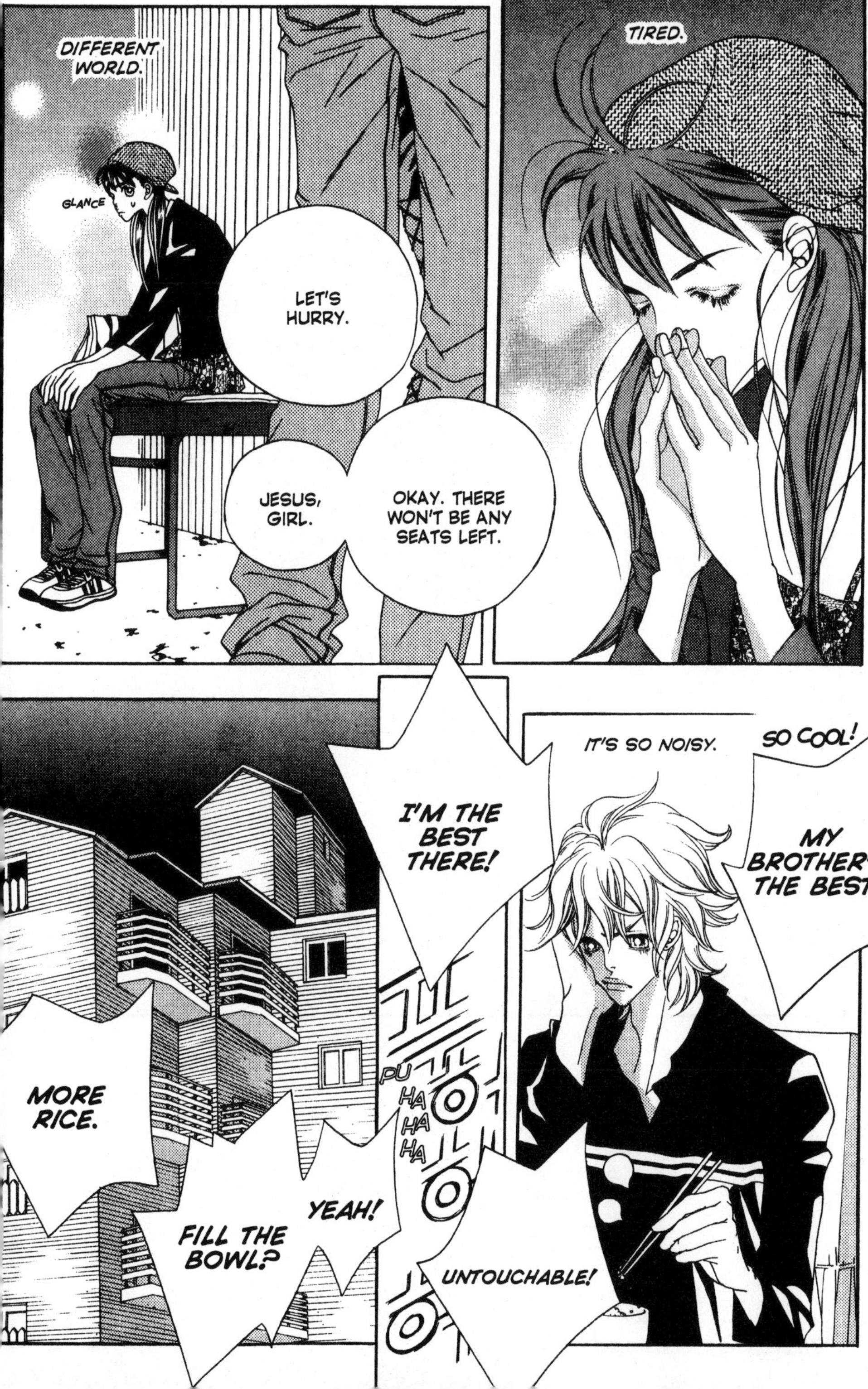
DIFFERENT WORLD.
GLANCE
LET'S HURRY.
JESUS, GIRL.
OKAY. THERE WON'T BE ANY SEATS LEFT.
TIRED.
MORE RICE.
FILL THE BOWL?
YEAH!
I'M THE BEST THERE!
IT'S SO NOISY.
SO COOL!
MY BROTHER'S THE BEST!
PU HA HA HA
UNTOUCHABLE!

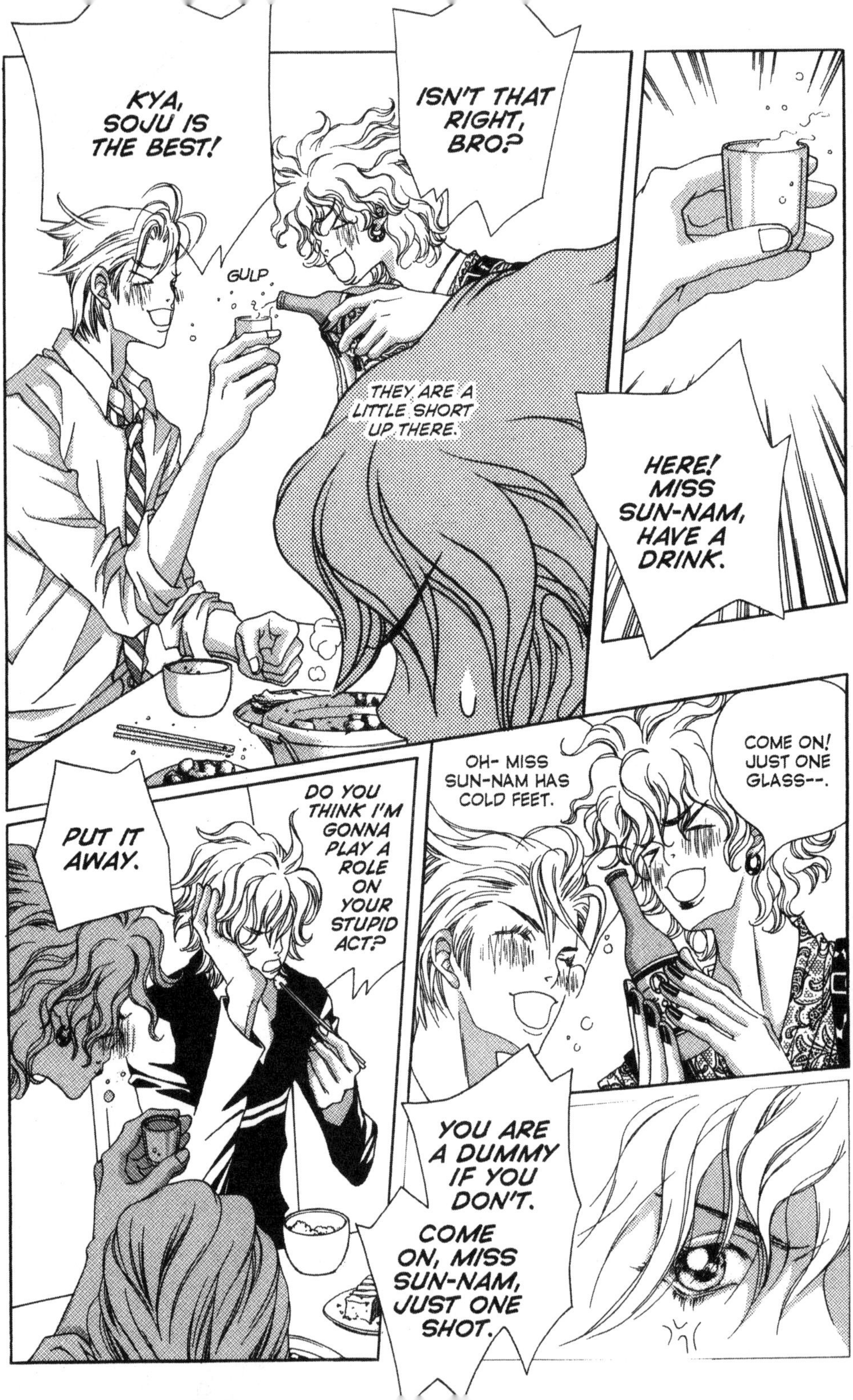
KYA, SOJU IS THE BEST!
ISN'T THAT RIGHT, BRO?
GULP
THEY ARE A LITTLE SHORT UP THERE.
HERE! MISS SUN-NAM, HAVE A DRINK.
PUT IT AWAY.
DO YOU THINK I'M GONNA PLAY A ROLE ON YOUR STUPID ACT?
OH- MISS SUN-NAM HAS COLD FEET.
COME ON! JUST ONE GLASS--.
YOU ARE A DUMMY IF YOU DON'T.
COME ON, MISS SUN-NAM, JUST ONE SHOT.

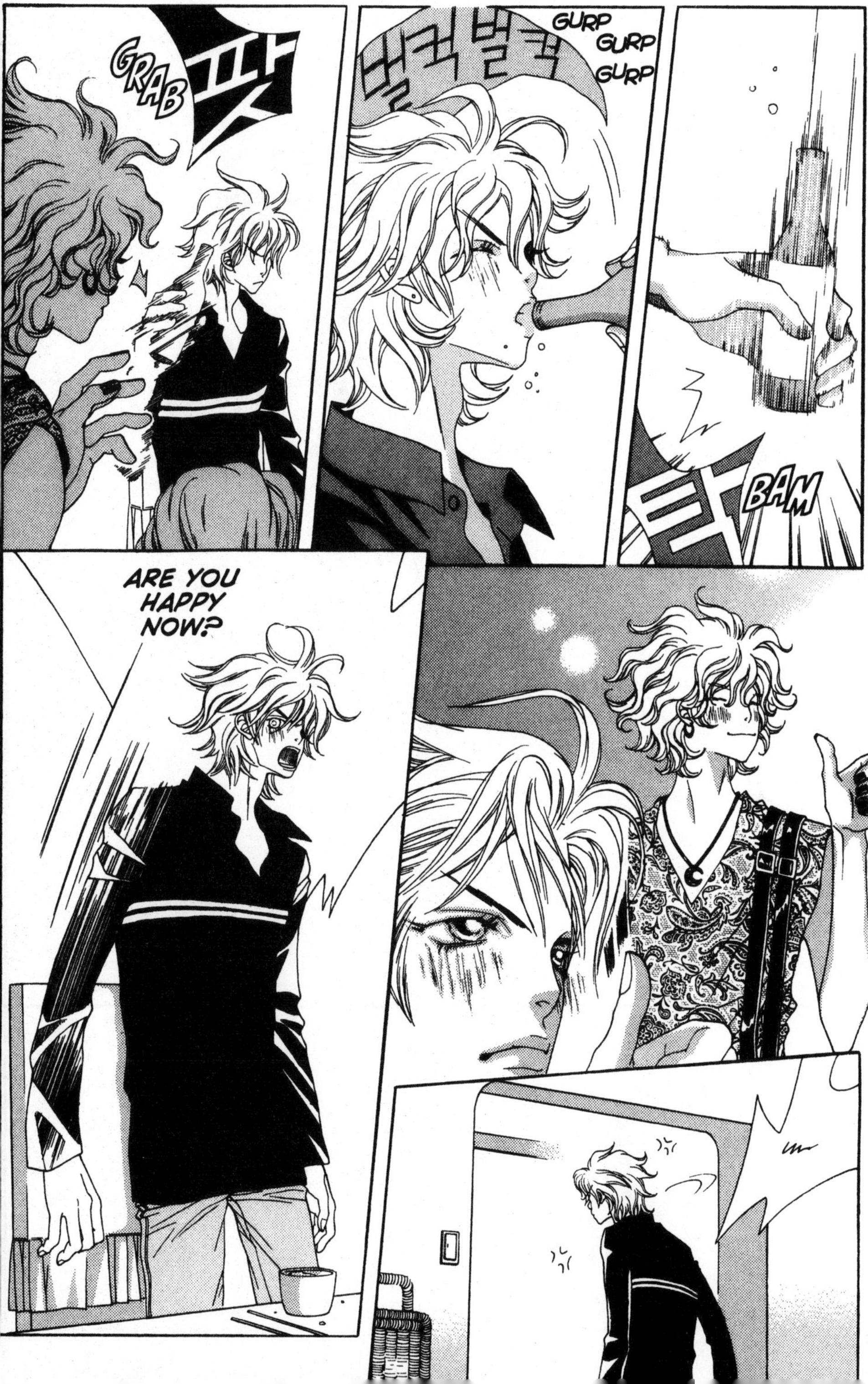
GRAB
벌컥벌컥
GURP GURP GURP
BAM
ARE YOU HAPPY NOW?

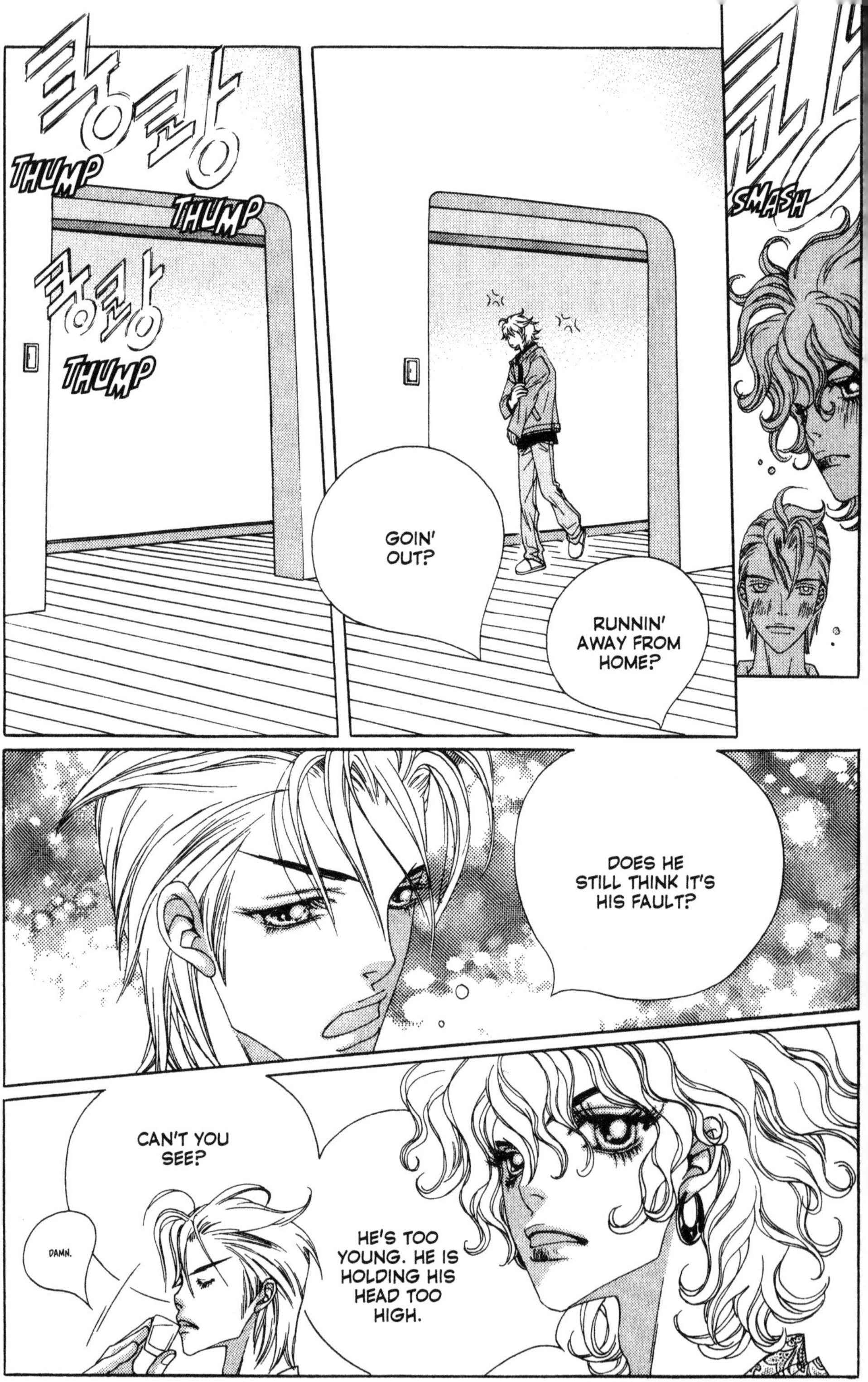
쿵쾅
THUMP
THUMP
쿵쾅
THUMP
GOIN' OUT?
RUNNIN' AWAY FROM HOME?
쾅
SMASH
DOES HE STILL THINK IT'S HIS FAULT?
CAN'T YOU SEE?
DAMN.
HE'S TOO YOUNG. HE IS HOLDING HIS HEAD TOO HIGH.

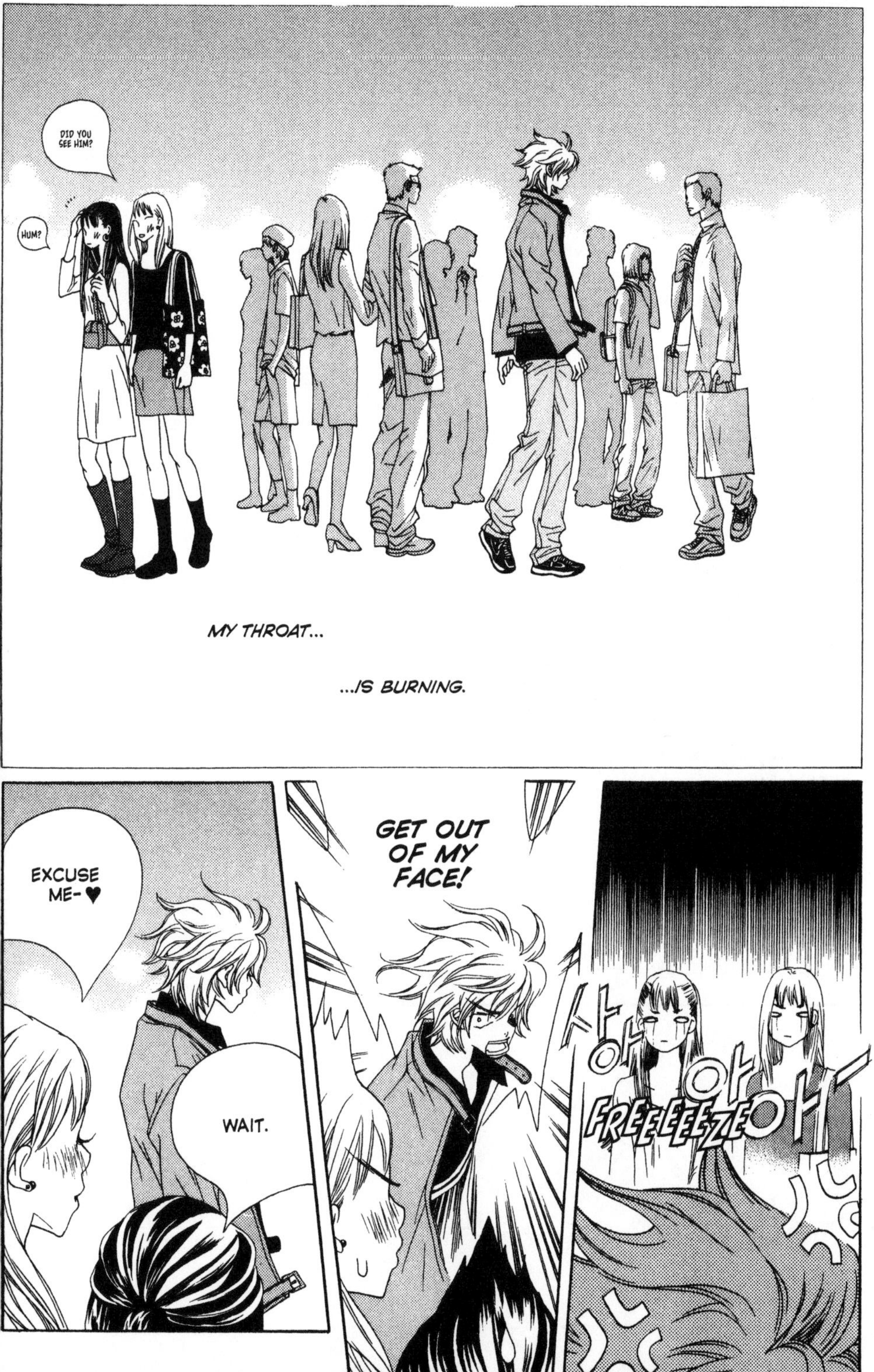
DID YOU SEE HIM?
HUM?
MY THROAT...
...IS BURNING.
EXCUSE ME-♥
WAIT.
GET OUT OF MY FACE!
FREEEEZE

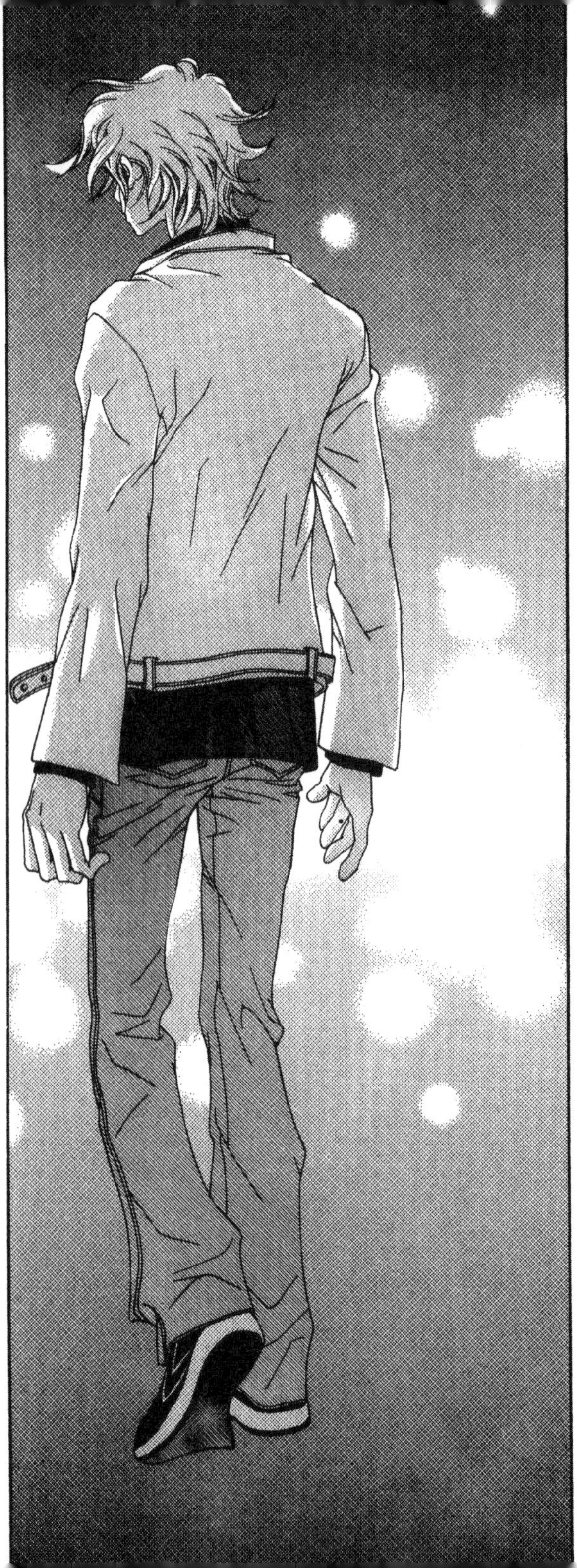

BITTER...

TOO BITTER.

IF THIS WAS POISON,

I WOULDN'T HAVE TO WORRY...

...ABOUT HOW MUCH OF A BAD GUY I HAVE TO BE OR HOW MUCH PAIN I'M IN...

IF THIS WAS POISON...

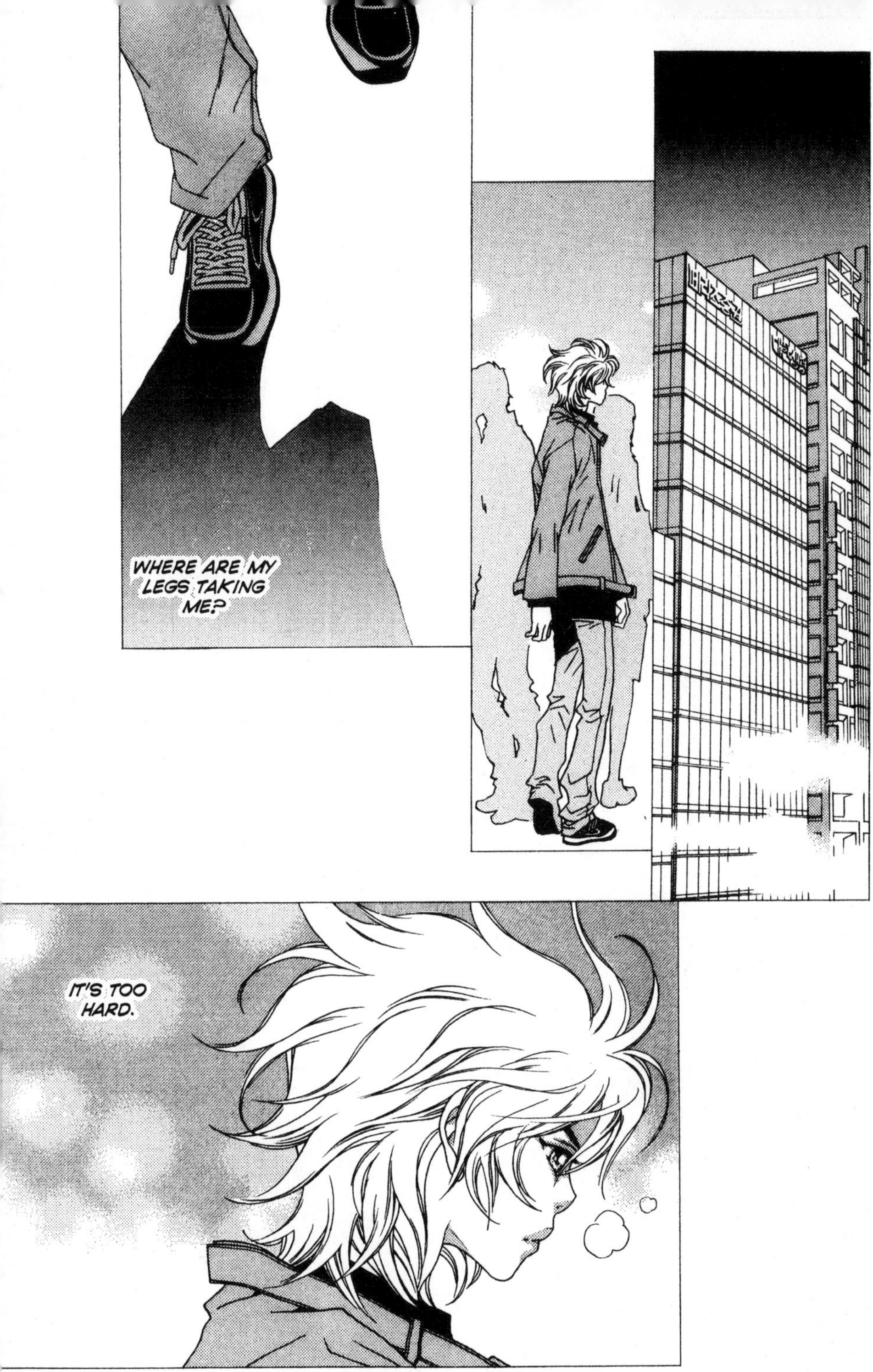
WHERE ARE MY LEGS TAKING ME?
IT'S TOO HARD.

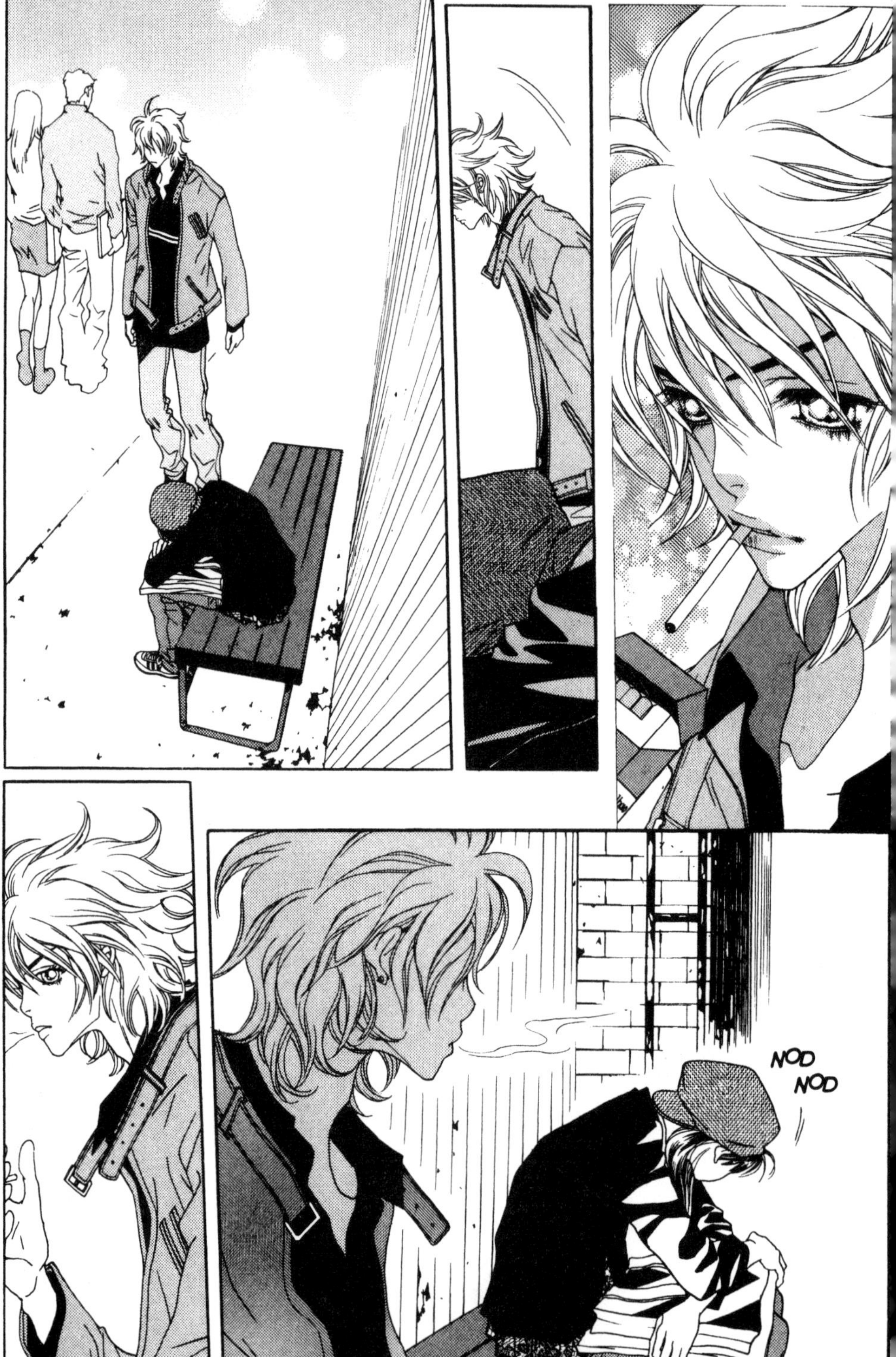
NOD
NOD

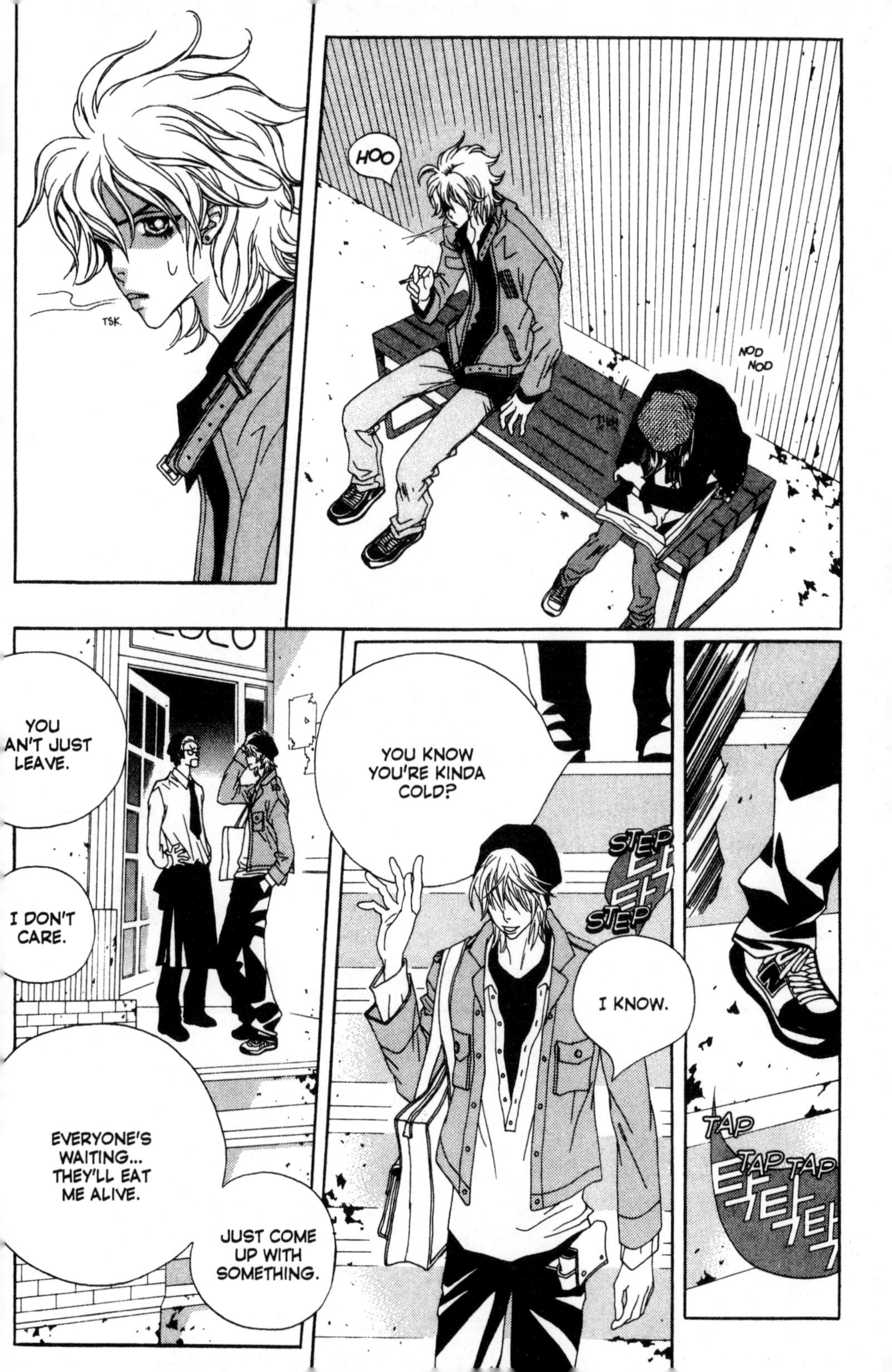
TSK.
HOO
NOD NOD
YOU AN'T JUST LEAVE.
I DON'T CARE.
EVERYONE'S WAITING... THEY'LL EAT ME ALIVE.
JUST COME UP WITH SOMETHING.
YOU KNOW YOU'RE KINDA COLD?
STEP
STEP
I KNOW.
TAP
TAP TAP

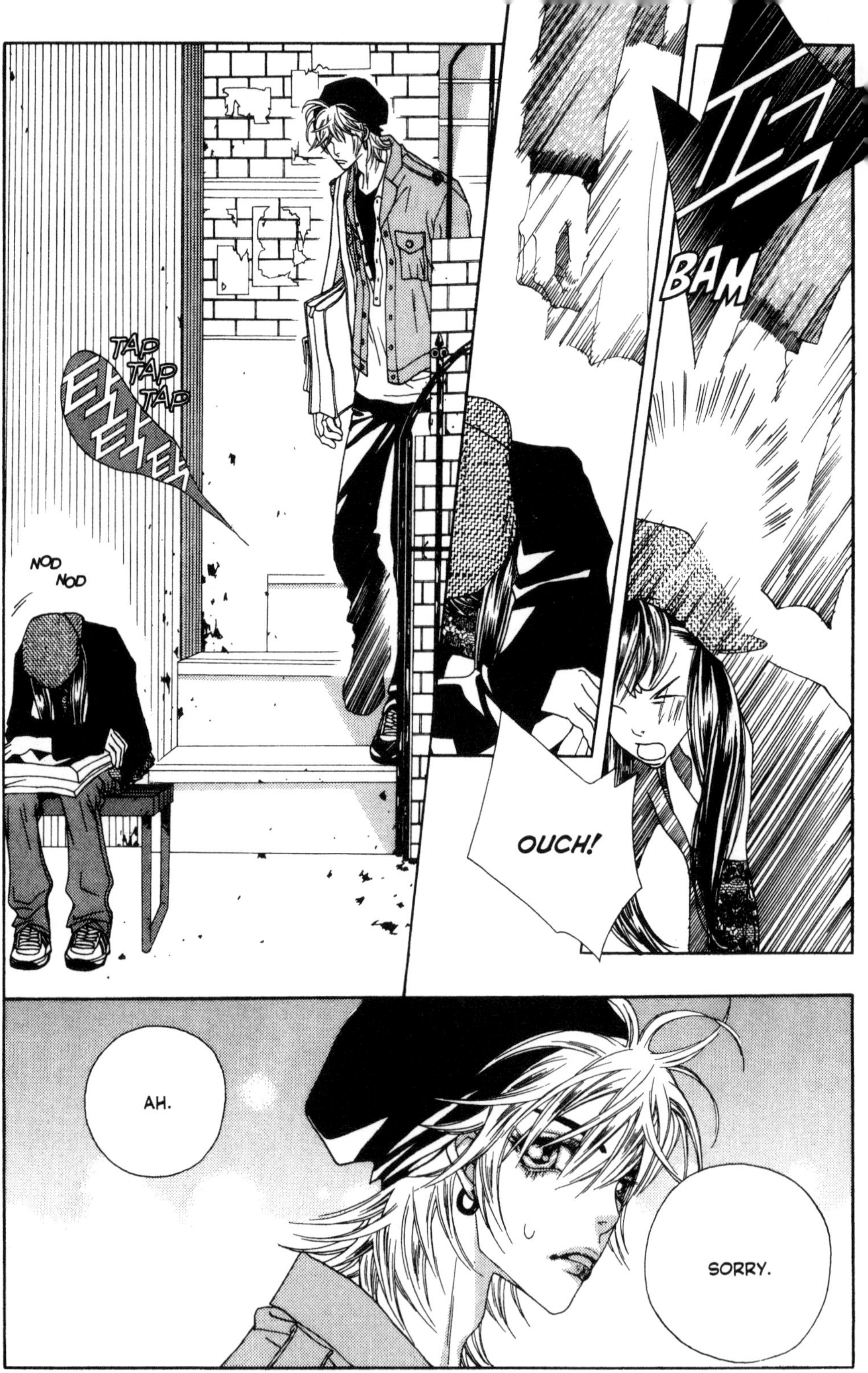

TAP TAP TAP
NOD NOD
BAM
OUCH!
AH.
SORRY.

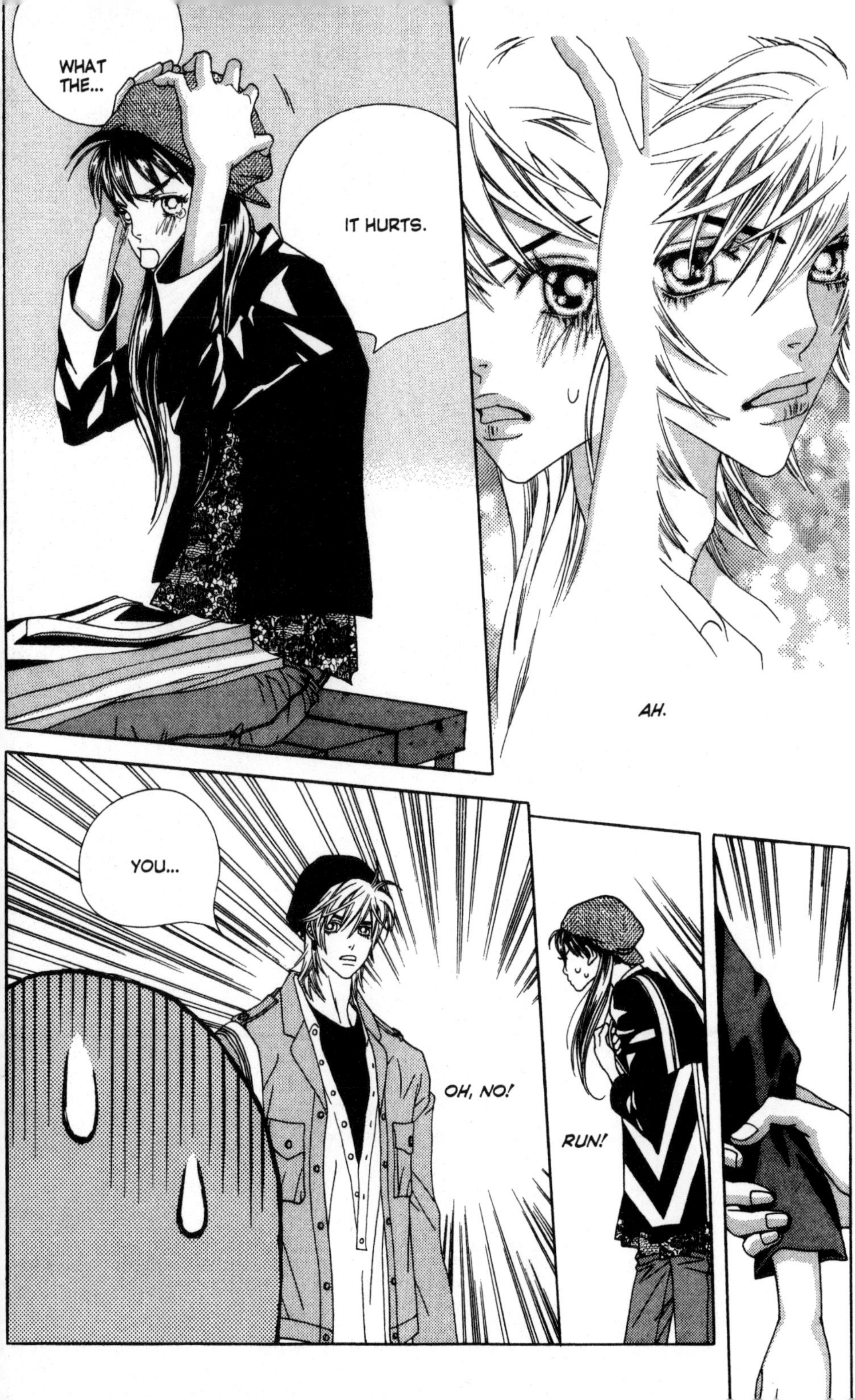
WHAT THE...
IT HURTS.
AH.
YOU...
OH, NO!
RUN!

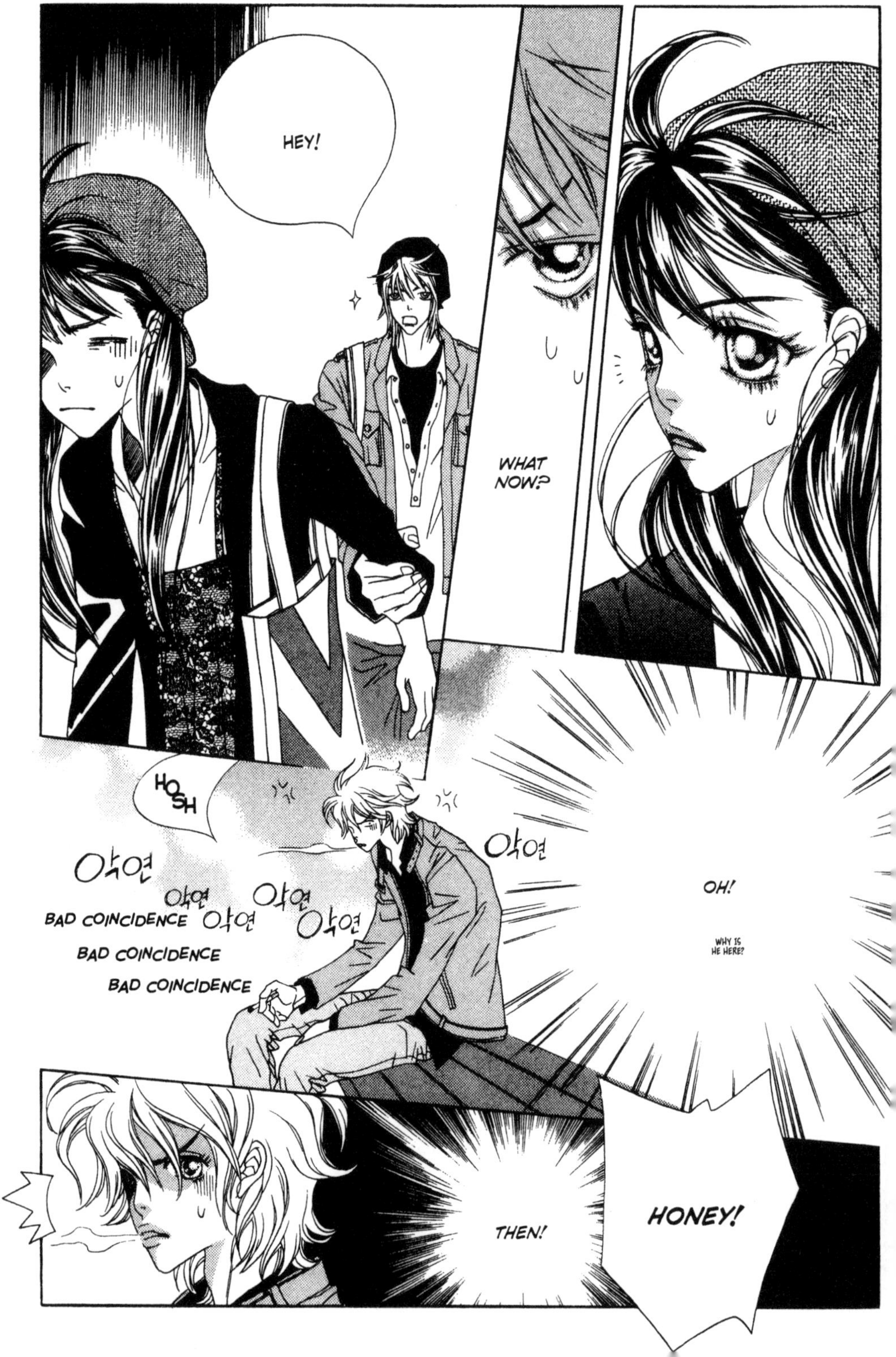
HEY!
WHAT NOW?
HOSH
악연
악연 악연 악연
BAD COINCIDENCE 악연
BAD COINCIDENCE
BAD COINCIDENCE
악연
OH!
WHY IS HE HERE?
THEN!
HONEY!

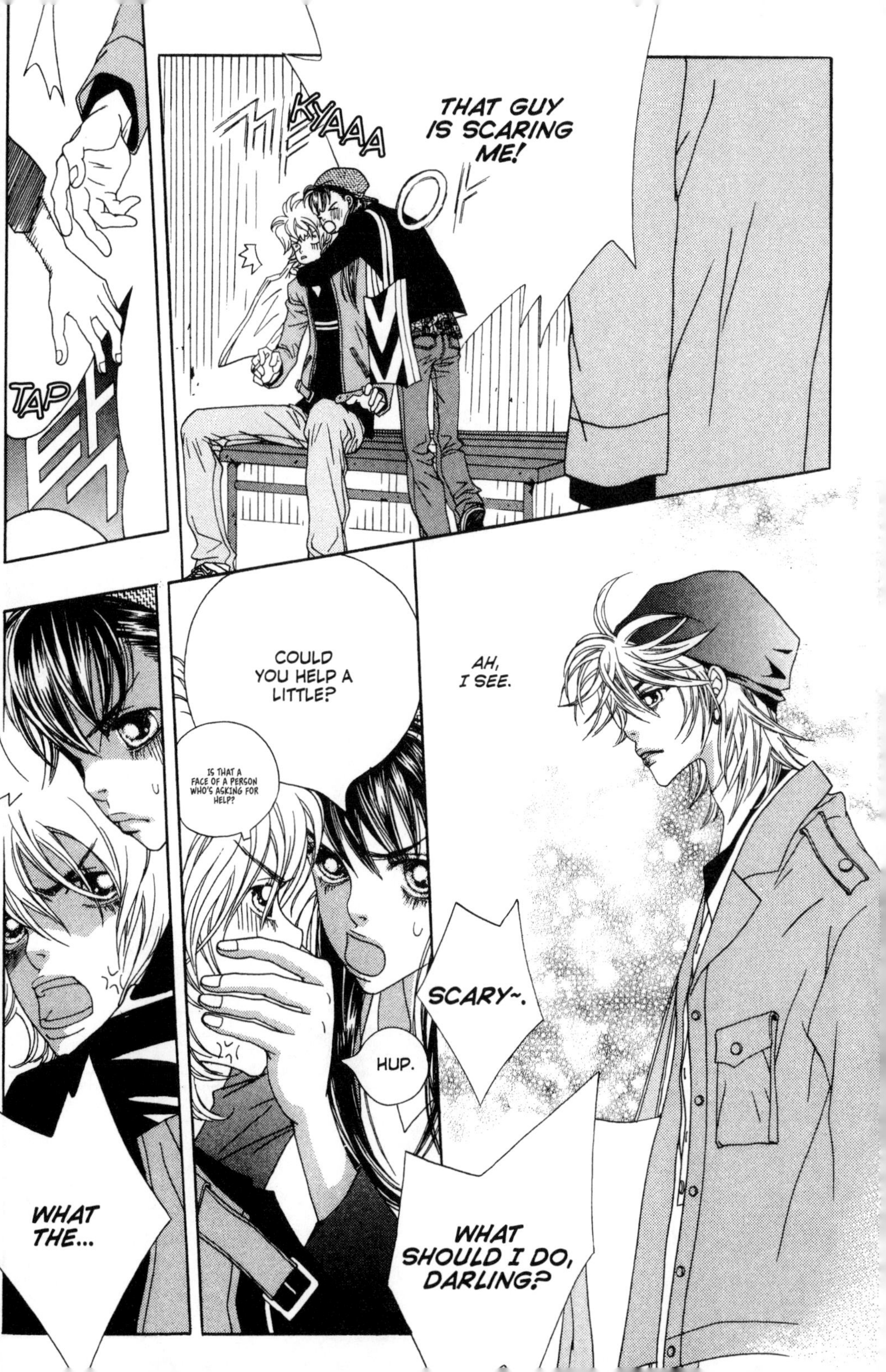
TAP
KYAAA
THAT GUY IS SCARING ME!
WHAT THE...
COULD YOU HELP A LITTLE?
IS THAT A FACE OF A PERSON WHO'S ASKING FOR HELP?
HUP.
AH, I SEE.
SCARY~.
WHAT SHOULD I DO, DARLING?

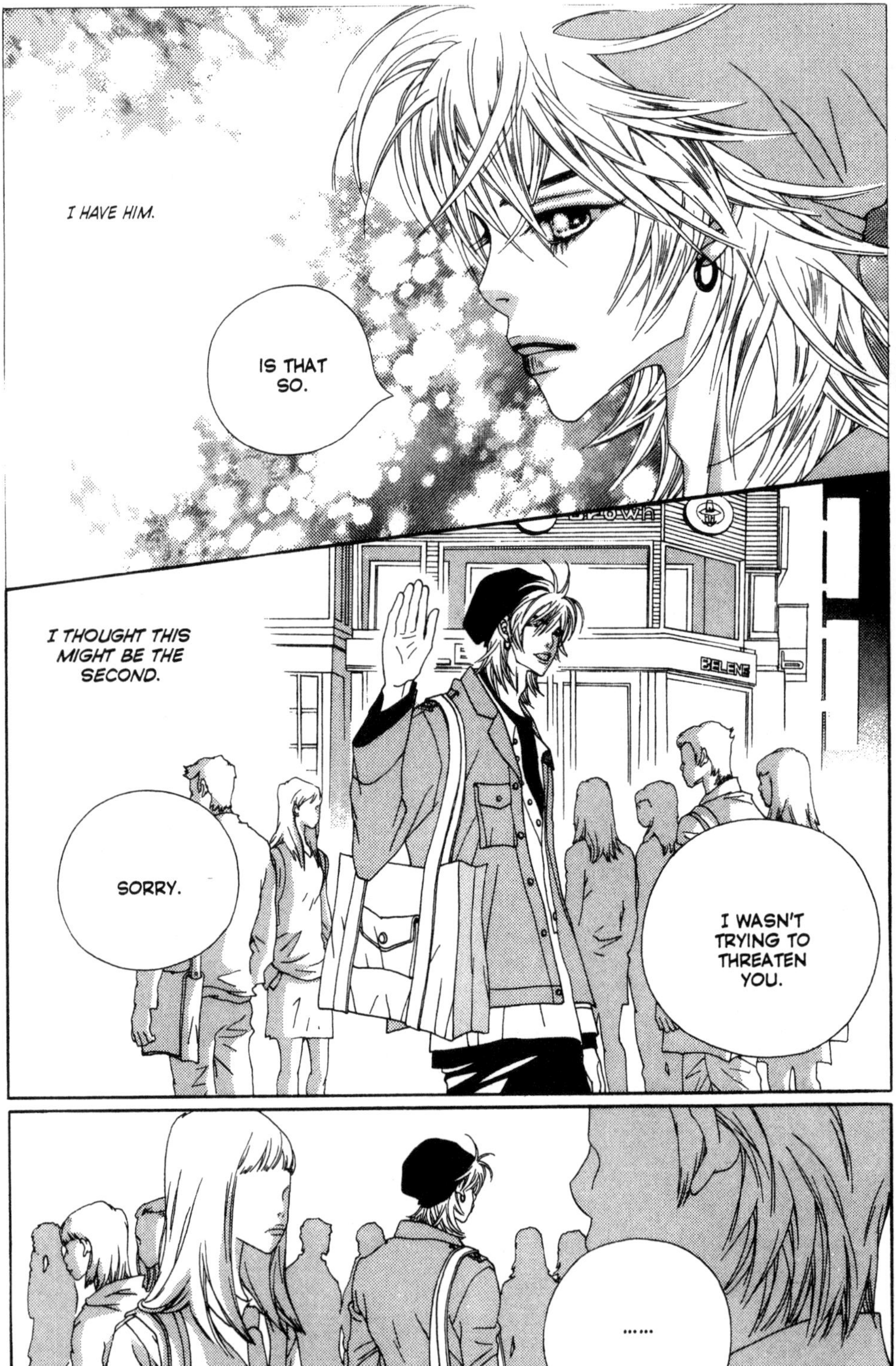
I HAVE HIM.
IS THAT SO.
I THOUGHT THIS MIGHT BE THE SECOND.
BELENE
SORRY.
I WASN'T TRYING TO THREATEN YOU.
……

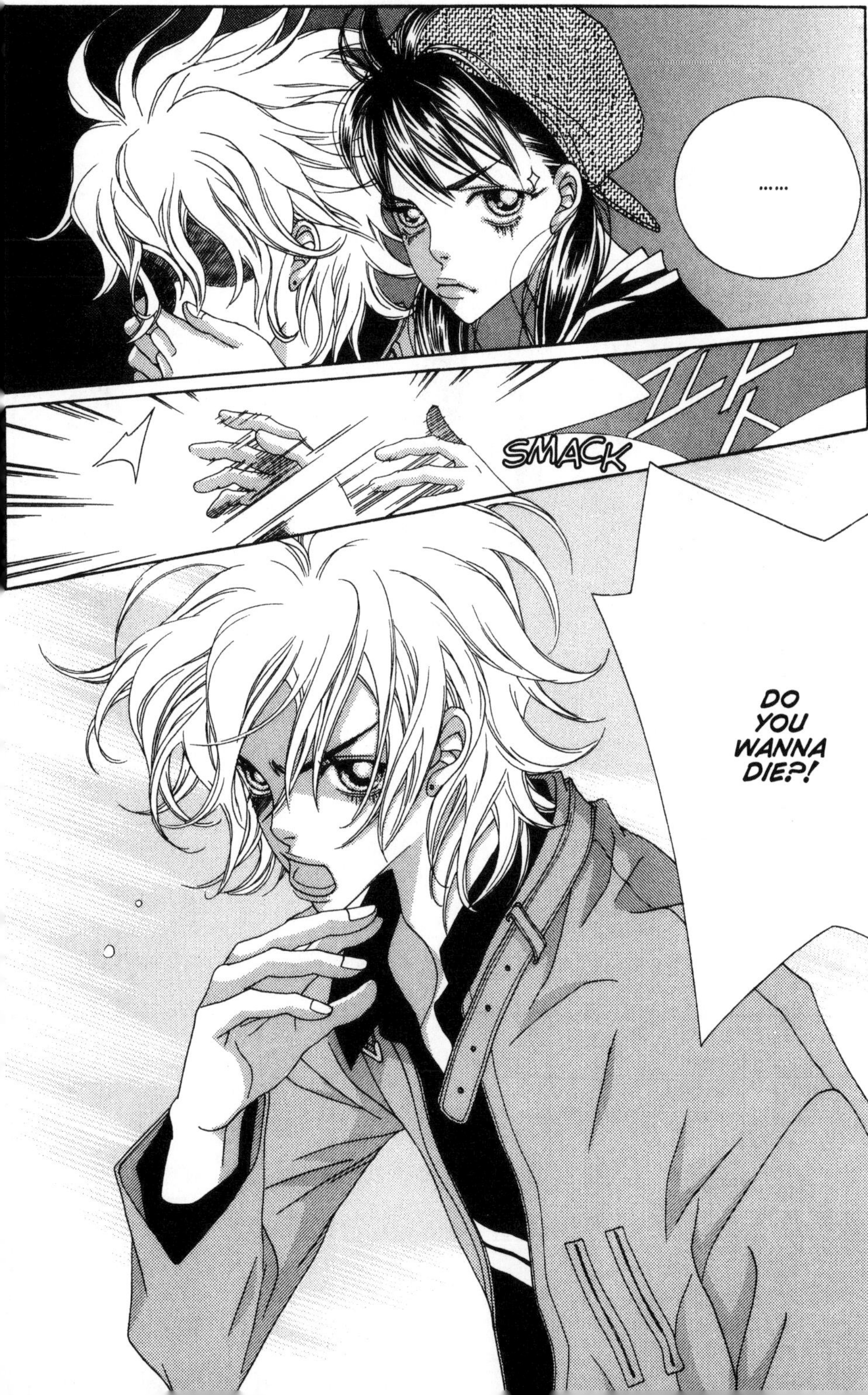
……
SMACK
DO YOU WANNA DIE?!

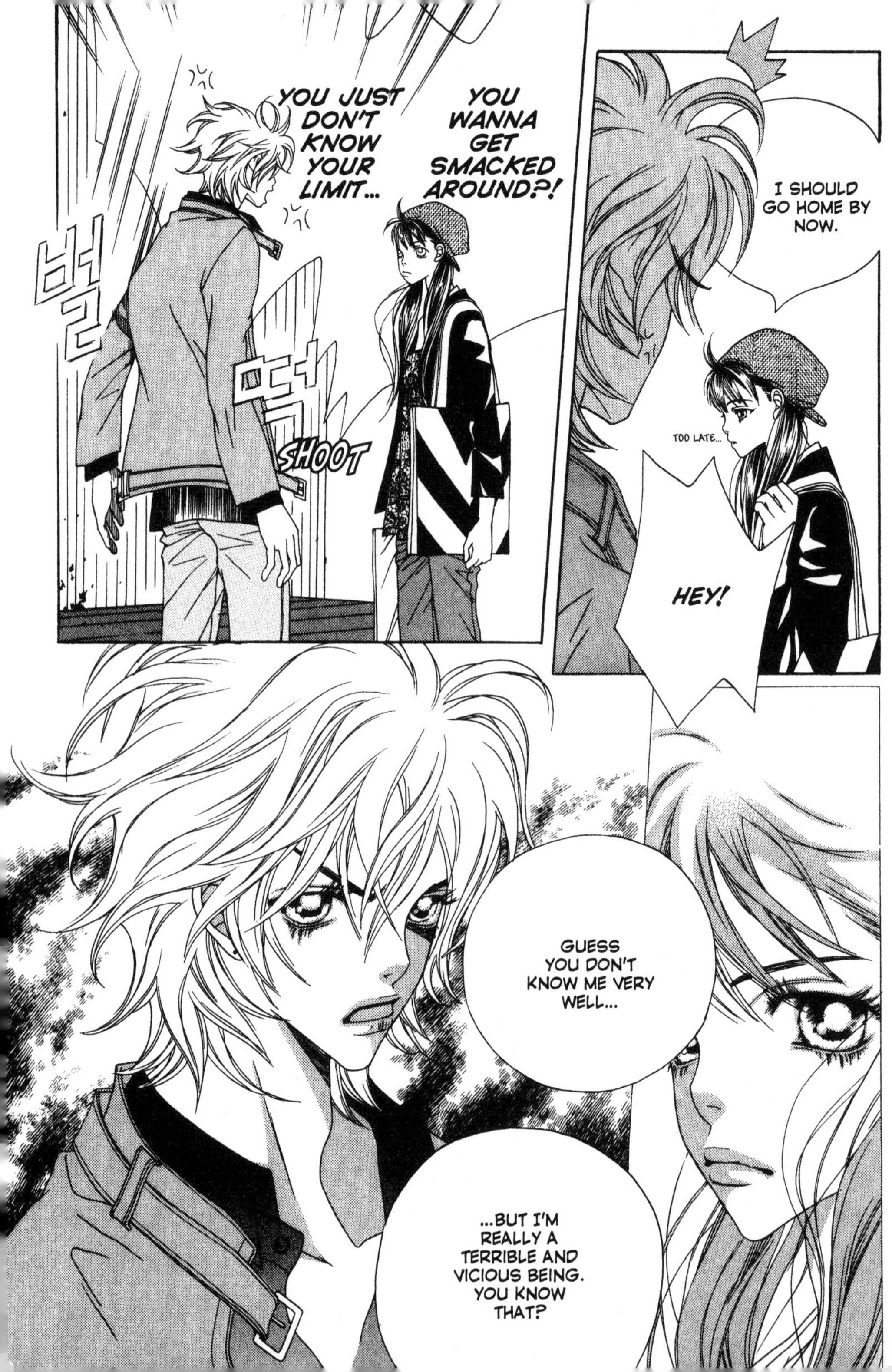

YOU JUST DON'T KNOW YOUR LIMIT...
YOU WANNA GET SMACKED AROUND?!
벌떡
SHOOT
I SHOULD GO HOME BY NOW.
TOO LATE...
HEY!
GUESS YOU DON'T KNOW ME VERY WELL...
...BUT I'M REALLY A TERRIBLE AND VICIOUS BEING. YOU KNOW THAT?

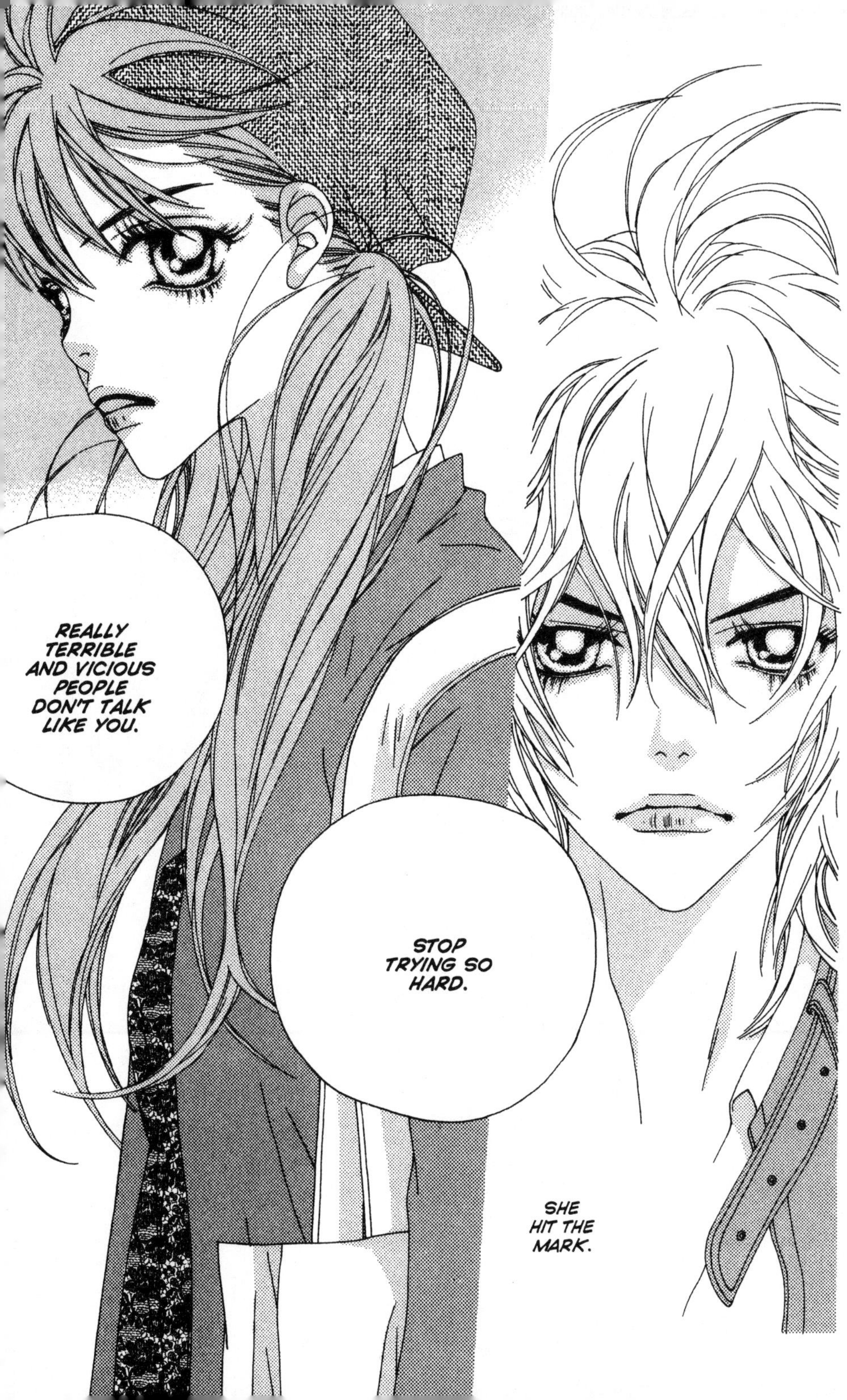
REALLY TERRIBLE AND VICIOUS PEOPLE DON'T TALK LIKE YOU.
STOP TRYING SO HARD.
SHE HIT THE MARK.

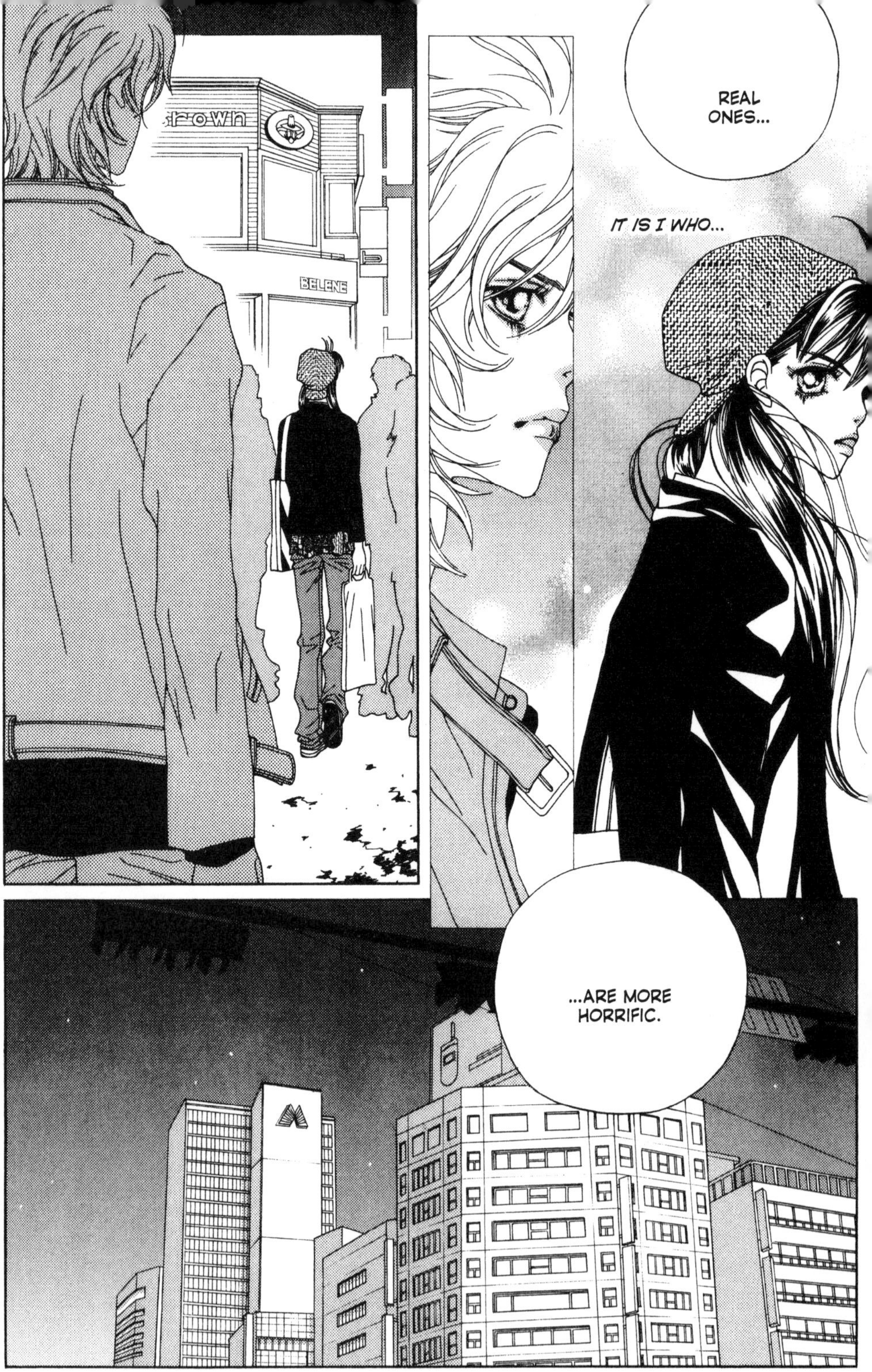
BELENE
REAL ONES...
IT IS I WHO...
...ARE MORE HORRIFIC.

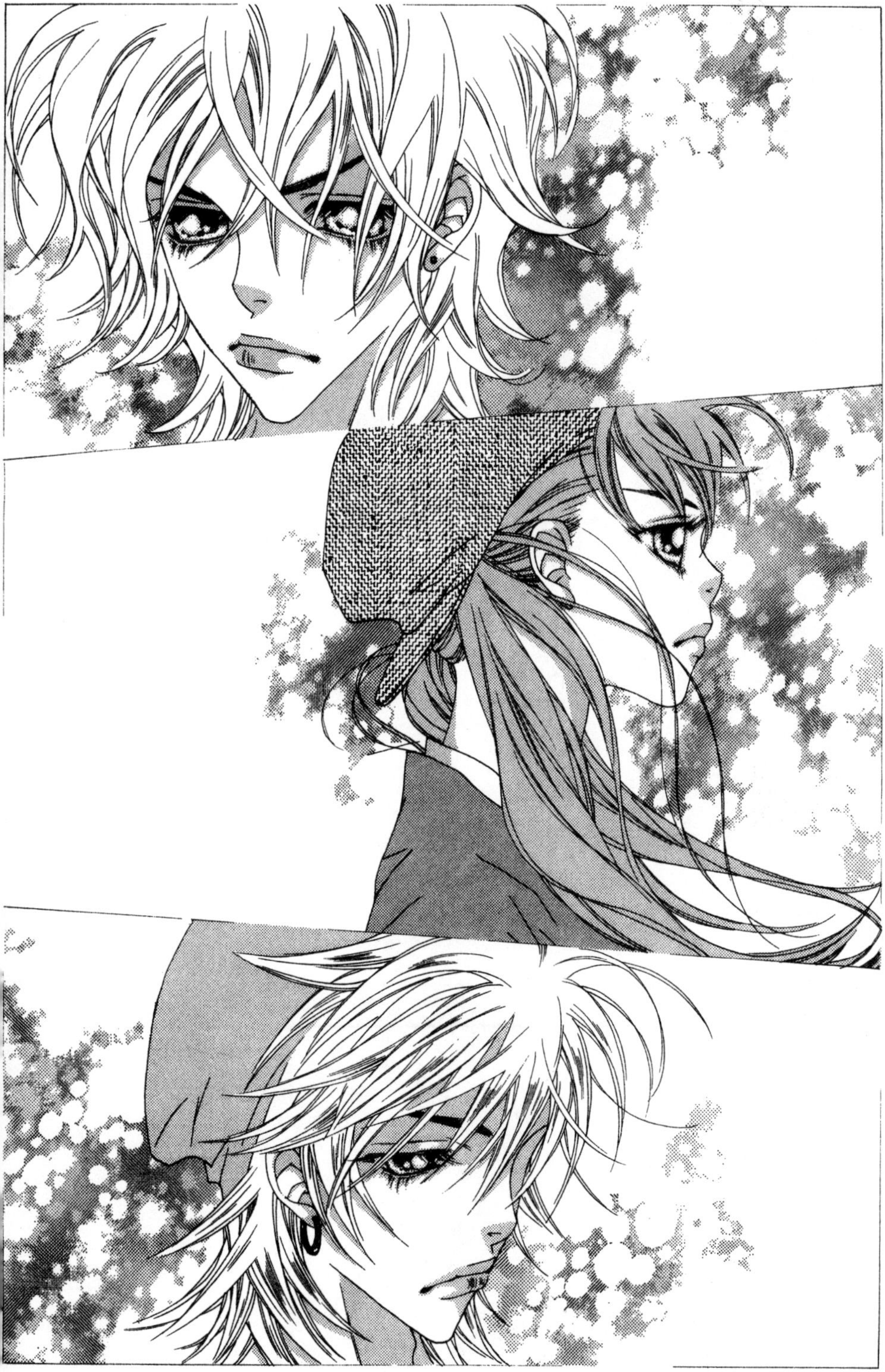

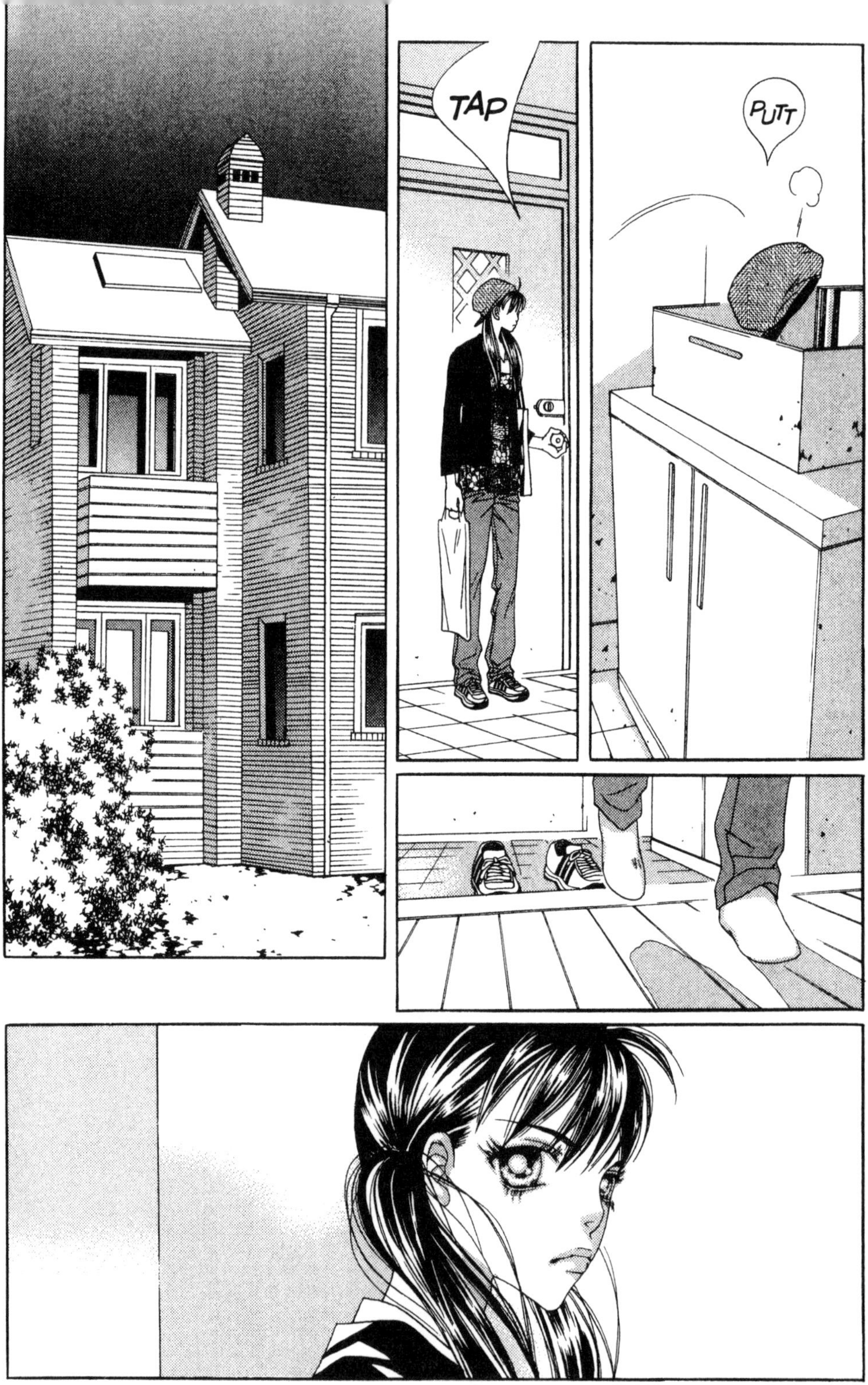
TAP
PUTT

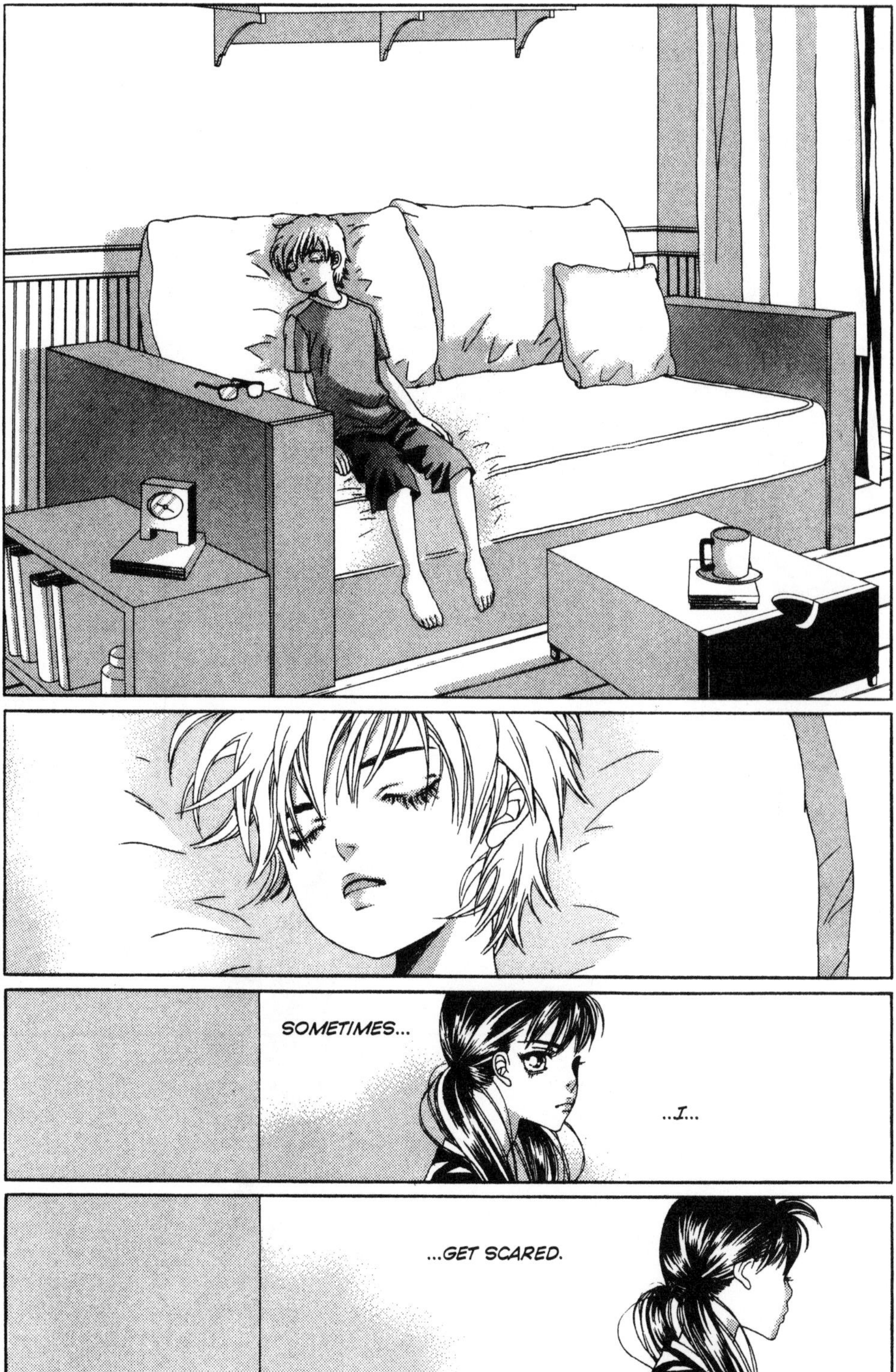
SOMETIMES...
...I...
...GET SCARED.

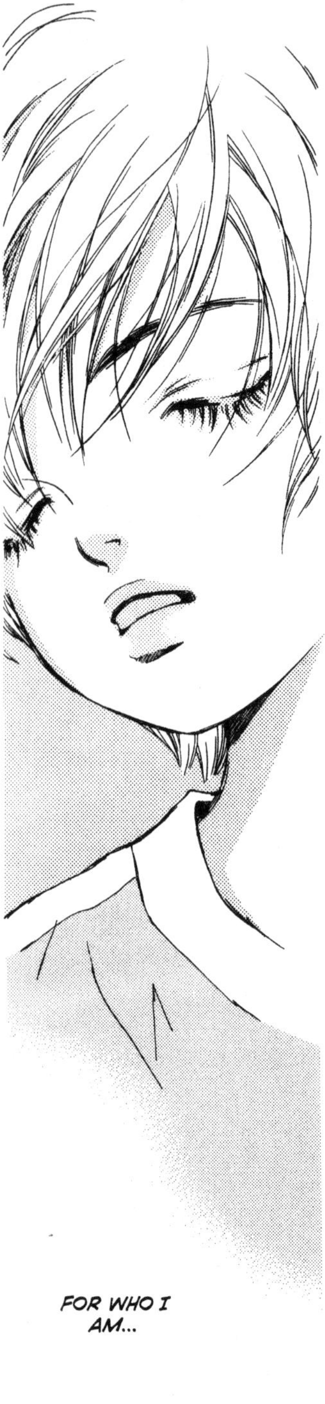
FOR WHO I AM...
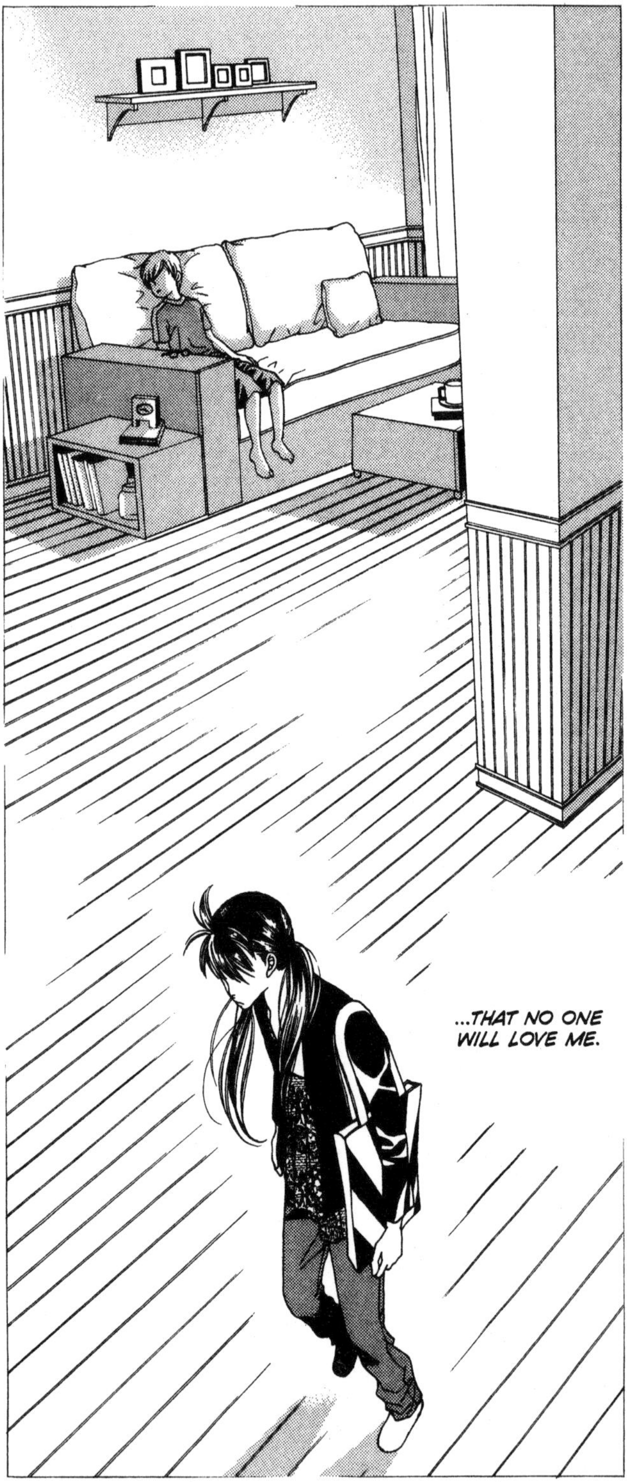
...THAT NO ONE WILL LOVE ME.

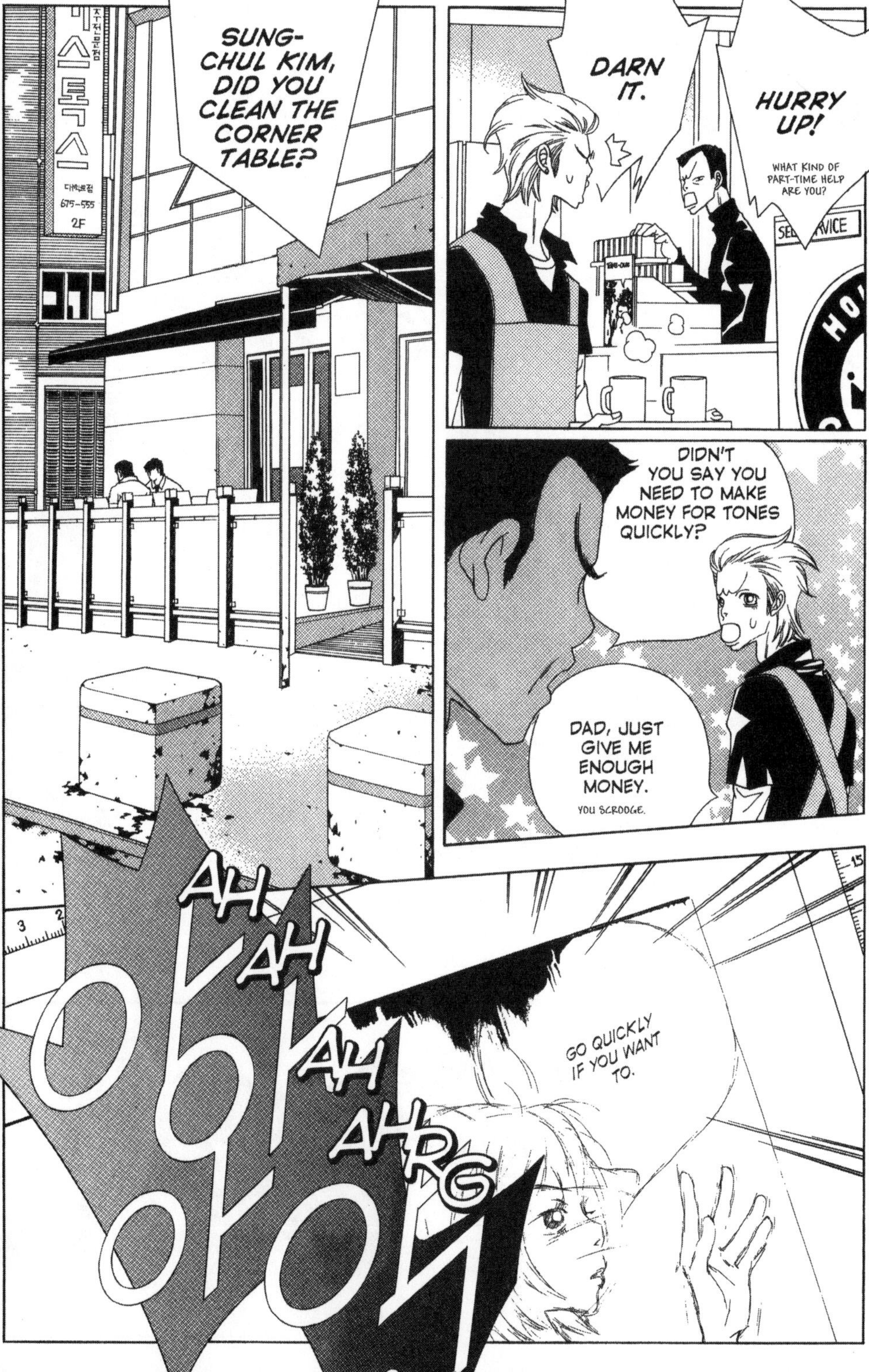
SUNG-CHUL KIM, DID YOU CLEAN THE CORNER TABLE?
675-555
2F
DARN IT.
HURRY UP!
WHAT KIND OF PART-TIME HELP ARE YOU?
DIDN'T YOU SAY YOU NEED TO MAKE MONEY FOR TONES QUICKLY?
DAD, JUST GIVE ME ENOUGH MONEY.
YOU SCROOGE.
AH AH AH AHRG
GO QUICKLY IF YOU WANT TO.

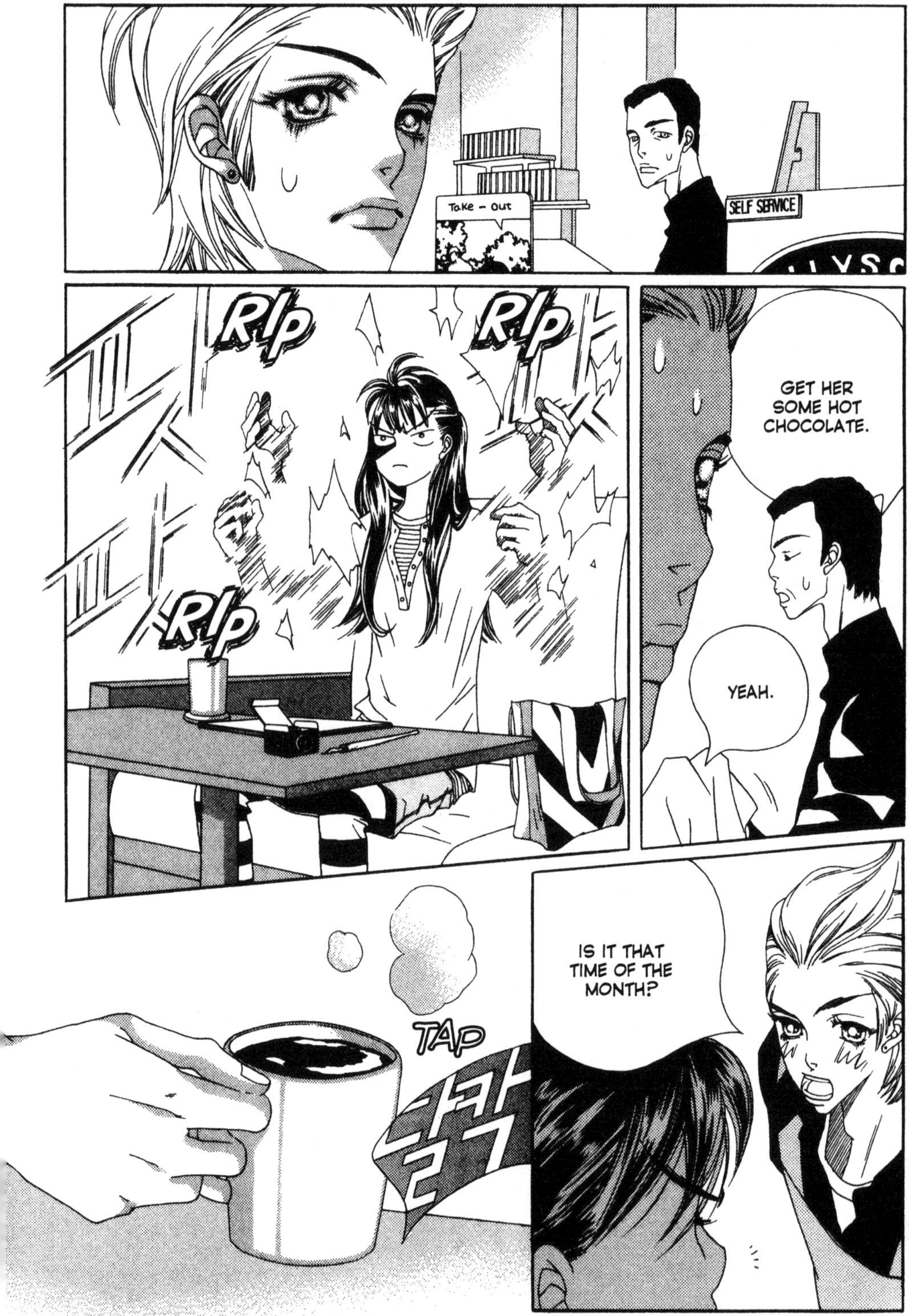
Take - out
SELF SERVICE
RIP
RIP
RIP
GET HER SOME HOT CHOCOLATE.
YEAH.
TAP
IS IT THAT TIME OF THE MONTH?

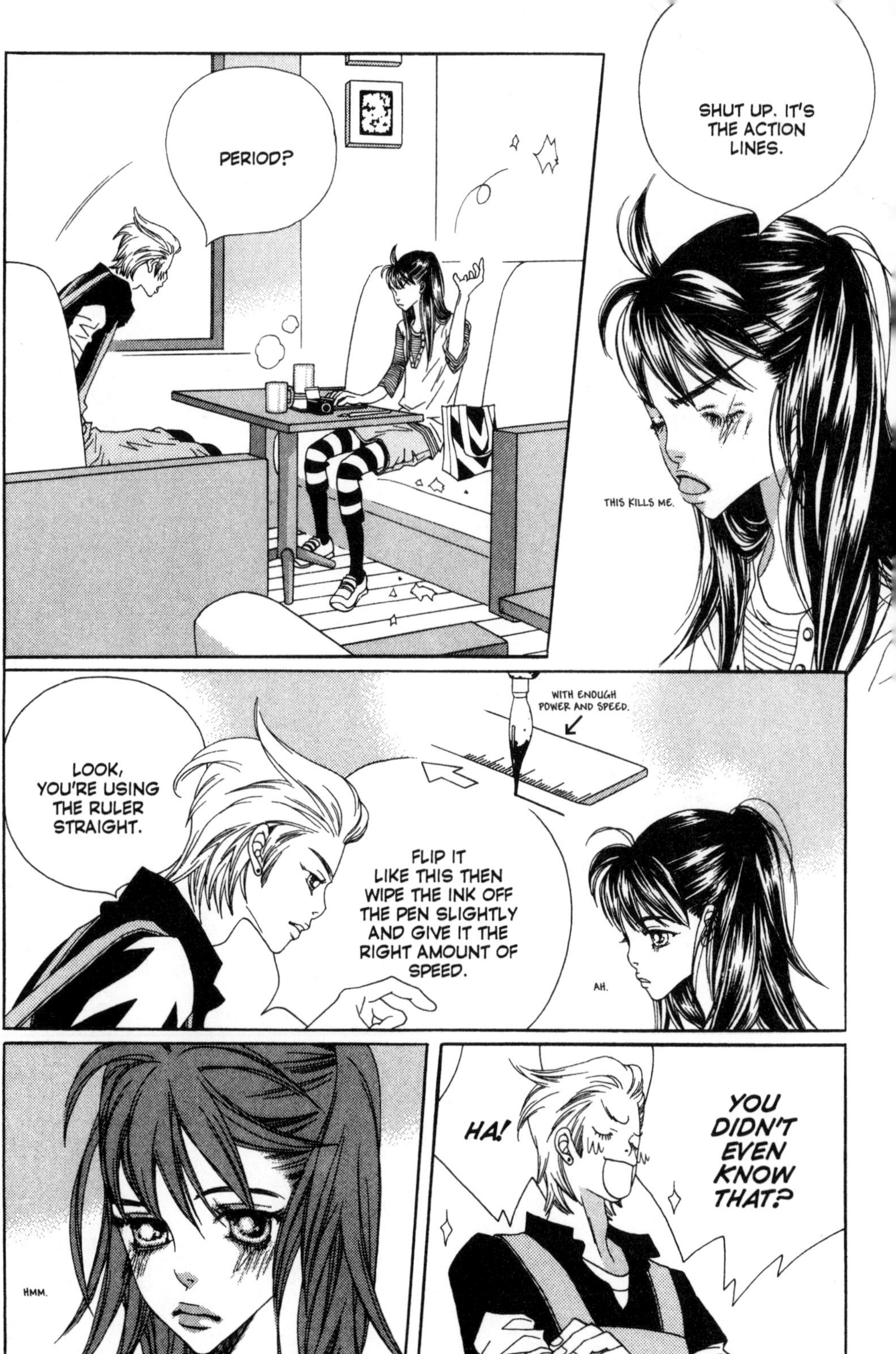
PERIOD?
SHUT UP. IT'S THE ACTION LINES.
THIS KILLS ME.
LOOK, YOU'RE USING THE RULER STRAIGHT.
WITH ENOUGH POWER AND SPEED.
FLIP IT LIKE THIS THEN WIPE THE INK OFF THE PEN SLIGHTLY AND GIVE IT THE RIGHT AMOUNT OF SPEED.
AH.
HMM.
HA!
YOU DIDN'T EVEN KNOW THAT?

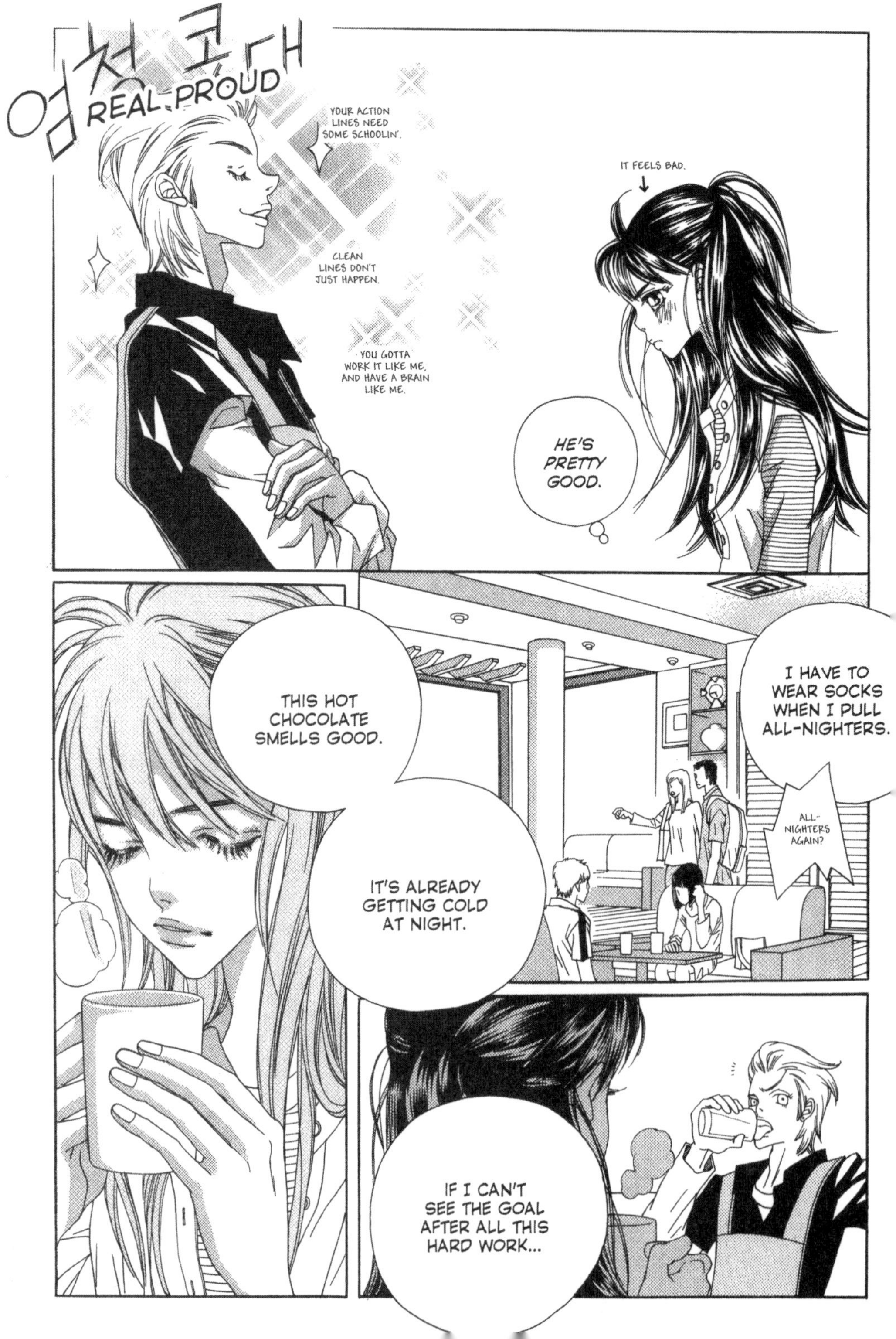
엄청 코대
REAL PROUD
YOUR ACTION LINES NEED SOME SCHOOLIN'.
CLEAN LINES DON'T JUST HAPPEN.
YOU GOTTA WORK IT LIKE ME, AND HAVE A BRAIN LIKE ME.
IT FEELS BAD.
HE'S PRETTY GOOD.
THIS HOT CHOCOLATE SMELLS GOOD.
IT'S ALREADY GETTING COLD AT NIGHT.
I HAVE TO WEAR SOCKS WHEN I PULL ALL-NIGHTERS.
ALL-NIGHTERS AGAIN?
IF I CAN'T SEE THE GOAL AFTER ALL THIS HARD WORK...

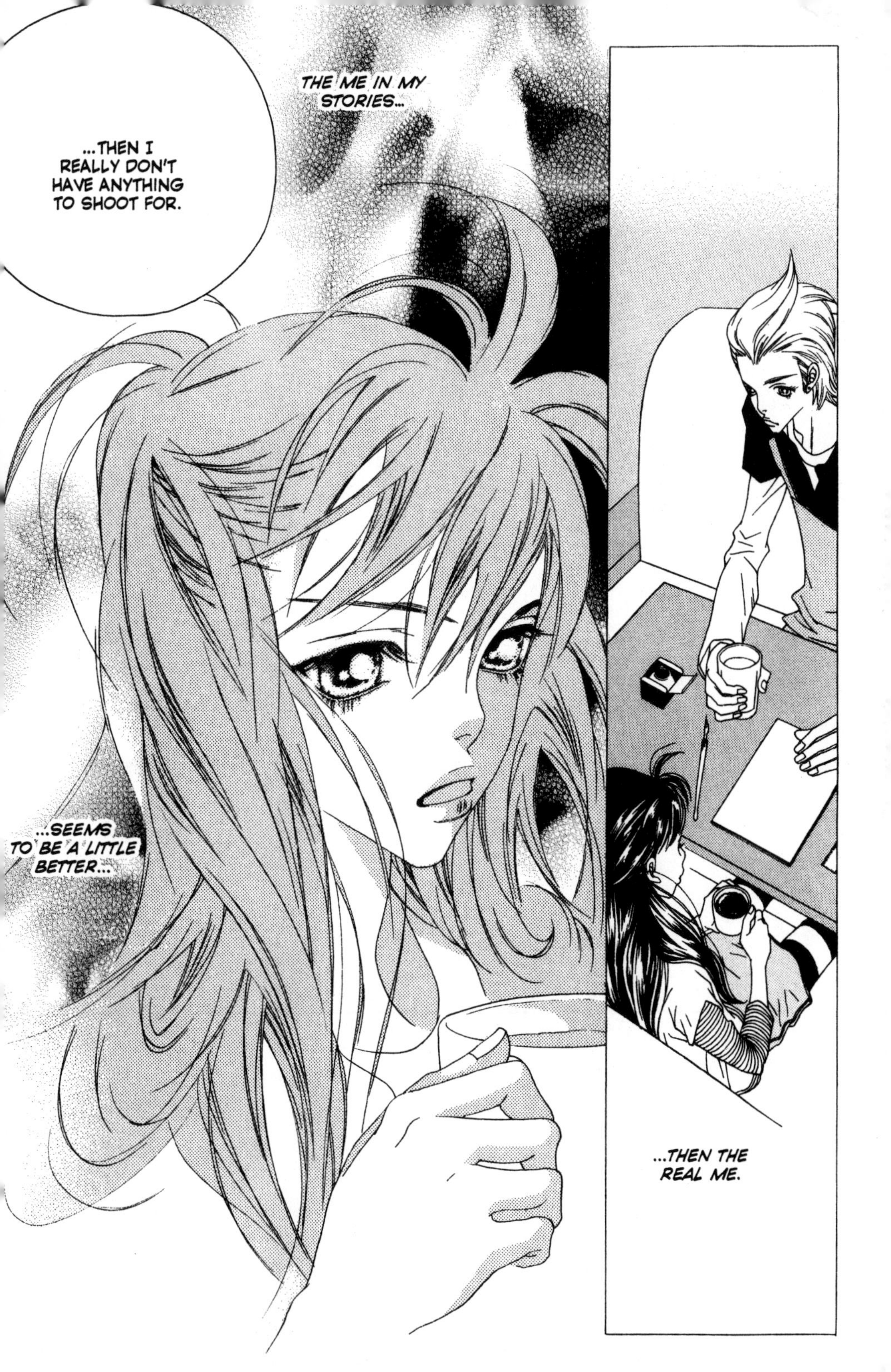
...THEN I REALLY DON'T HAVE ANYTHING TO SHOOT FOR.
THE ME IN MY STORIES...
...SEEMS TO BE A LITTLE BETTER...
...THEN THE REAL ME.

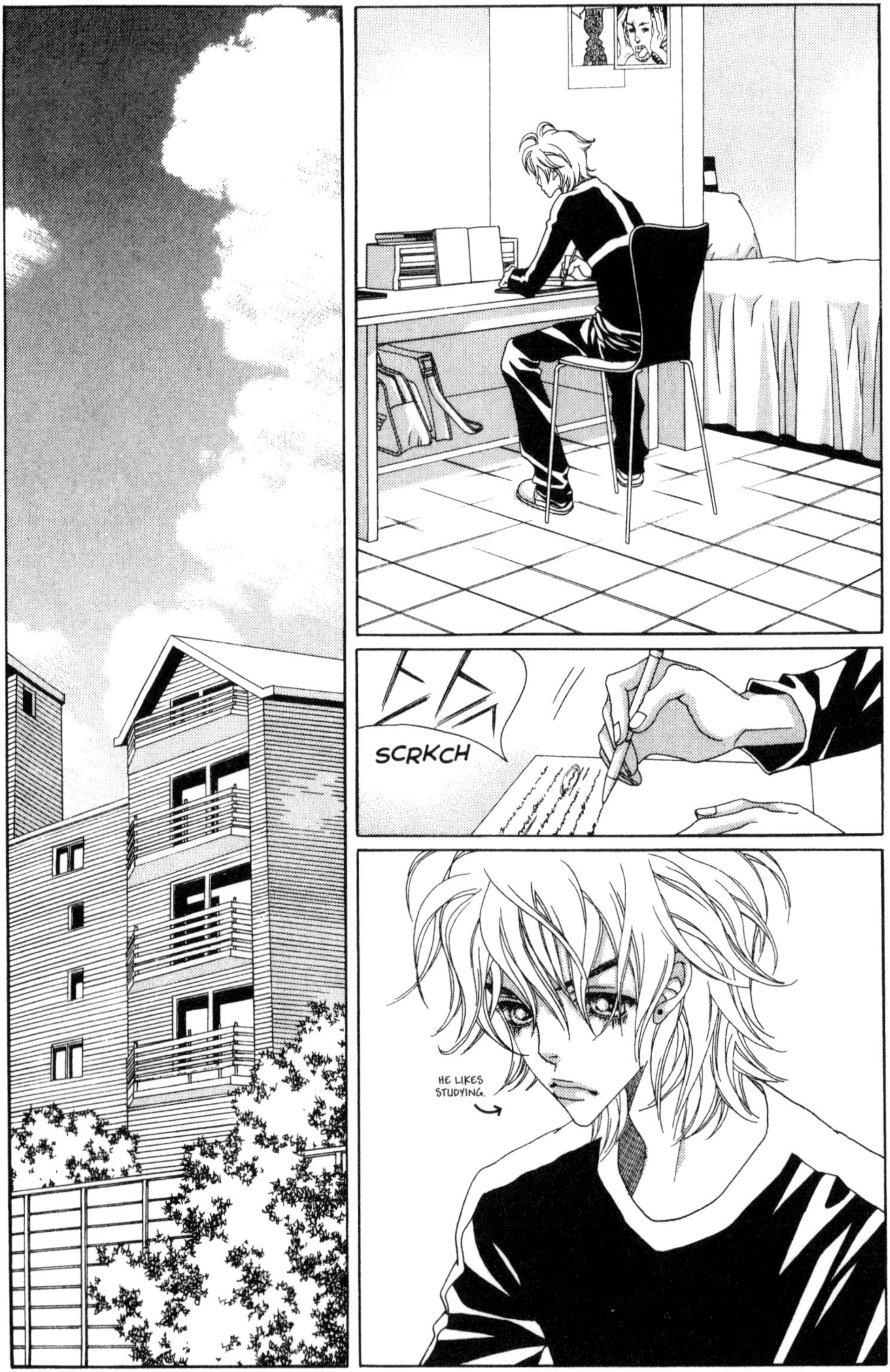
SCRKCH
HE LIKES STUDYING.

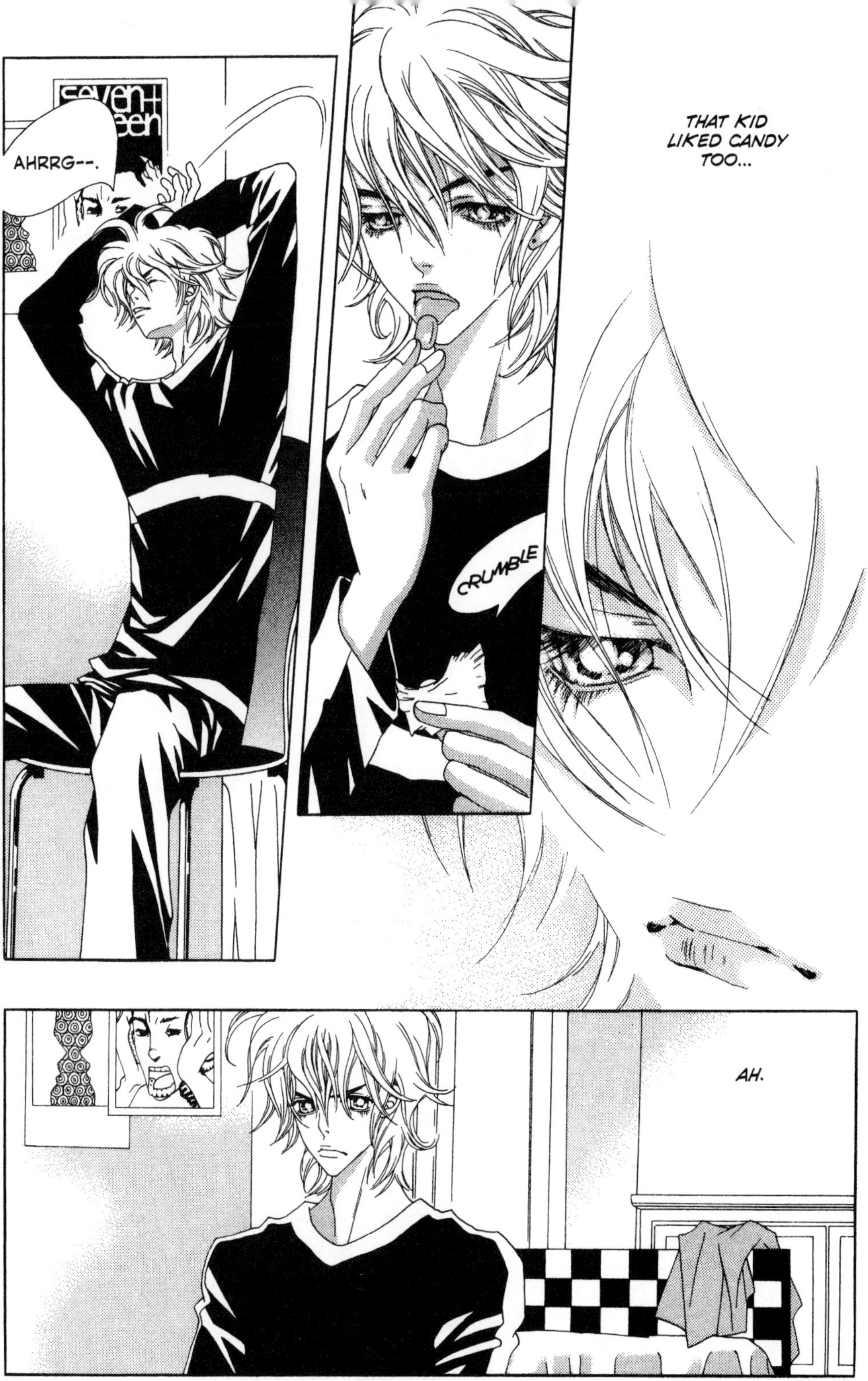
AHRRG--.
CRUMBLE
THAT KID LIKED CANDY TOO...
AH.

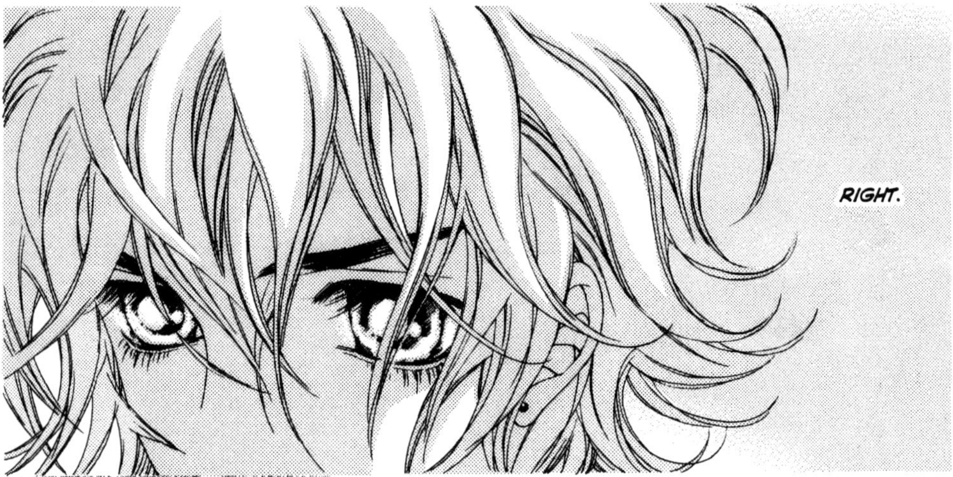
RIGHT.

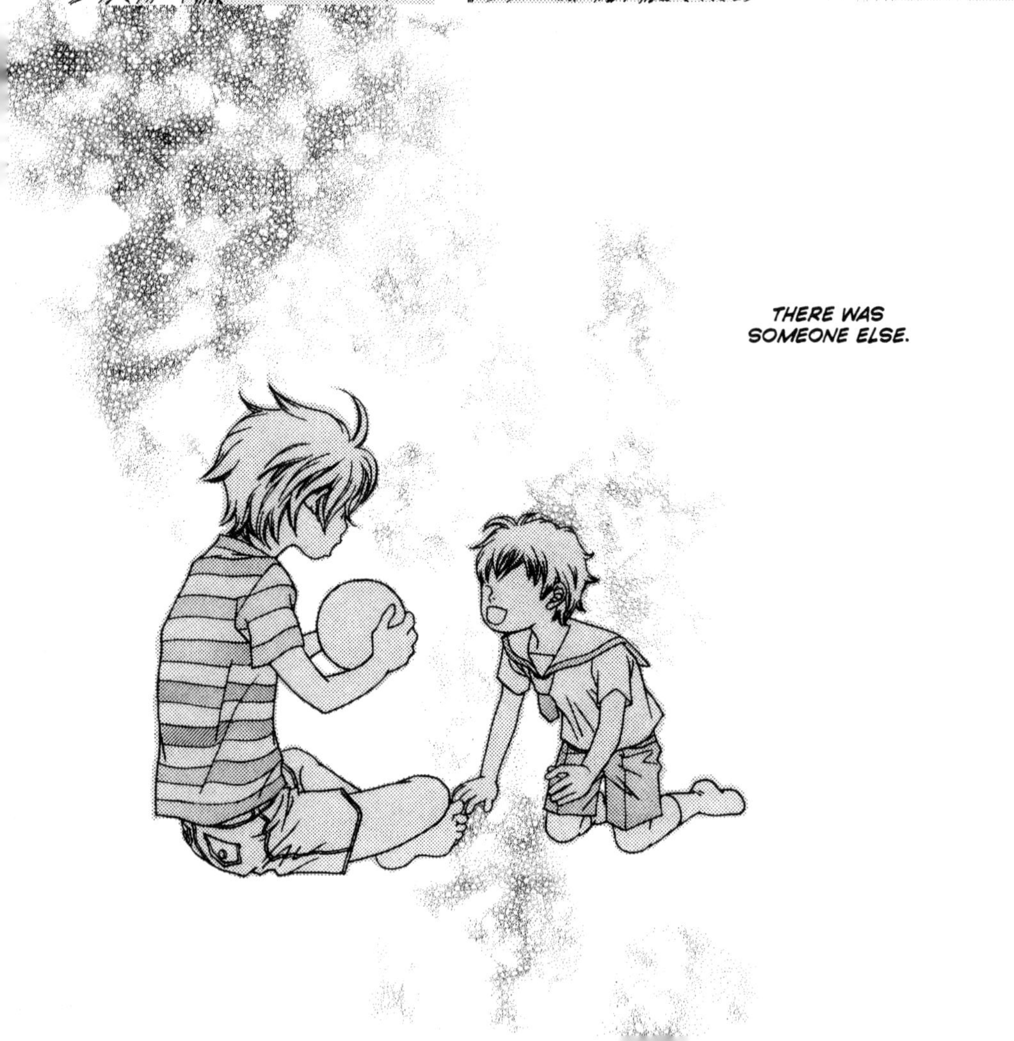
THERE WAS
SOMEONE ELSE.

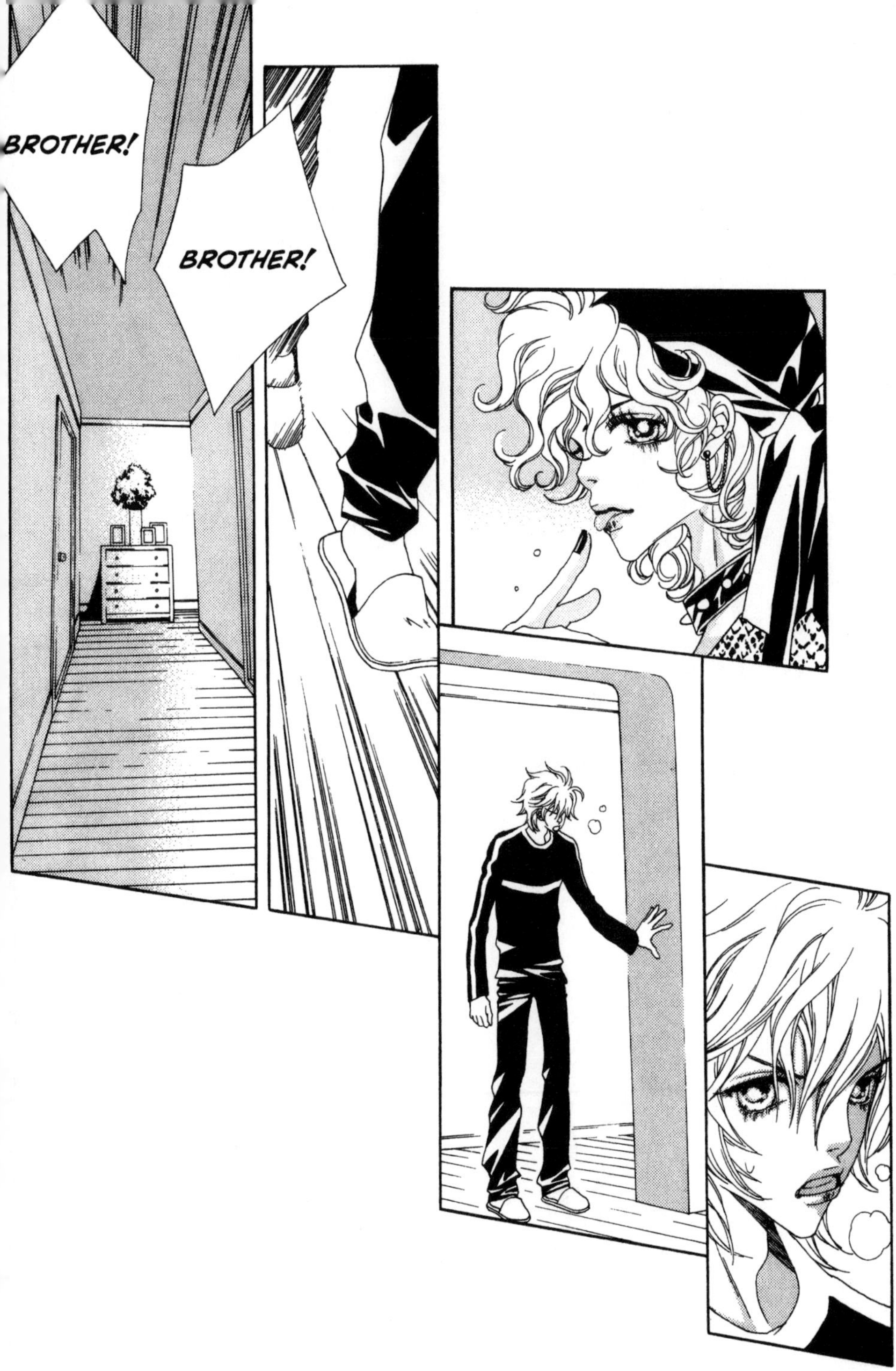
BROTHER!
BROTHER!

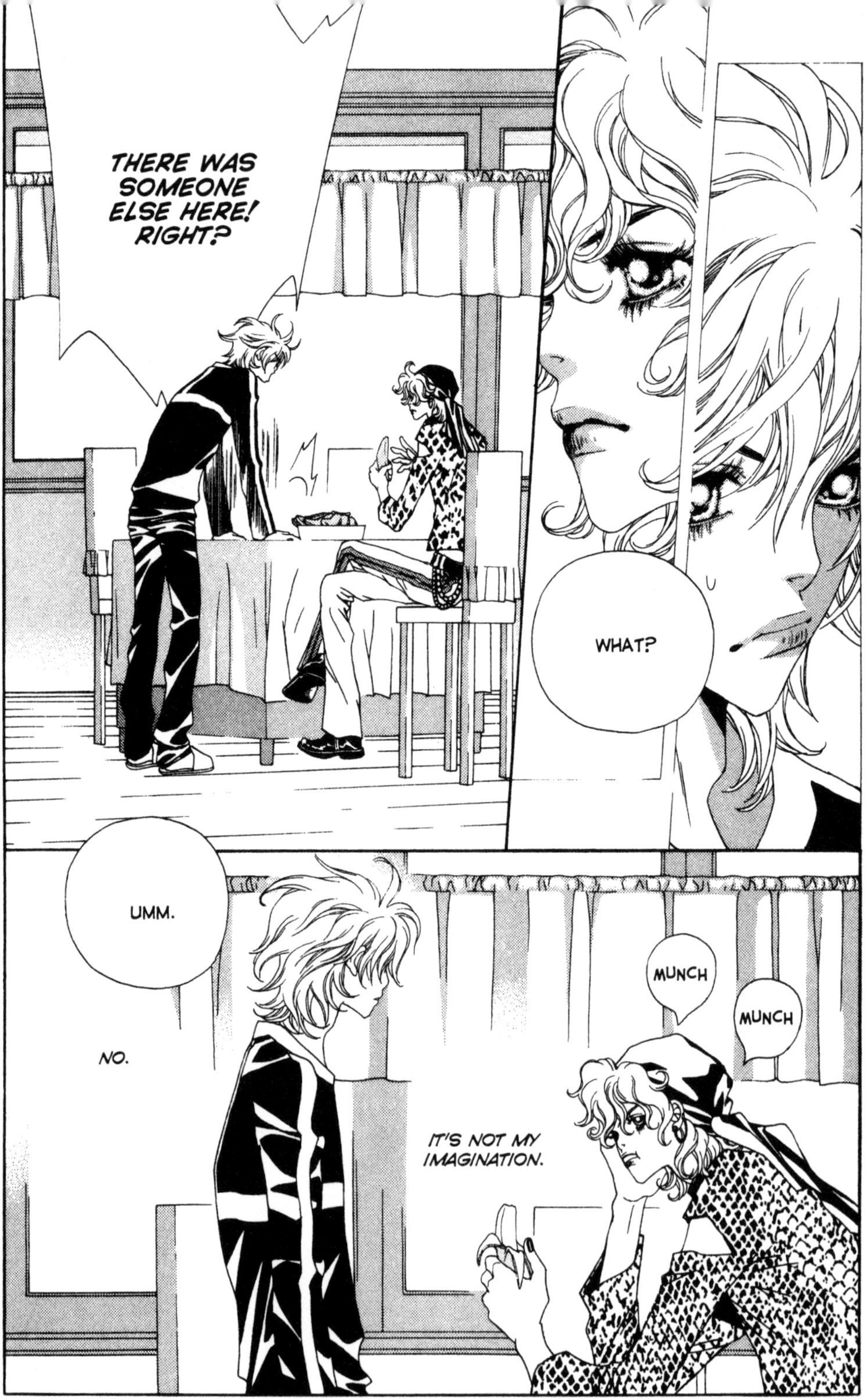

THERE WAS SOMEONE ELSE HERE! RIGHT?
WHAT?
UMM.
NO.
IT'S NOT MY IMAGINATION.
MUNCH
MUNCH

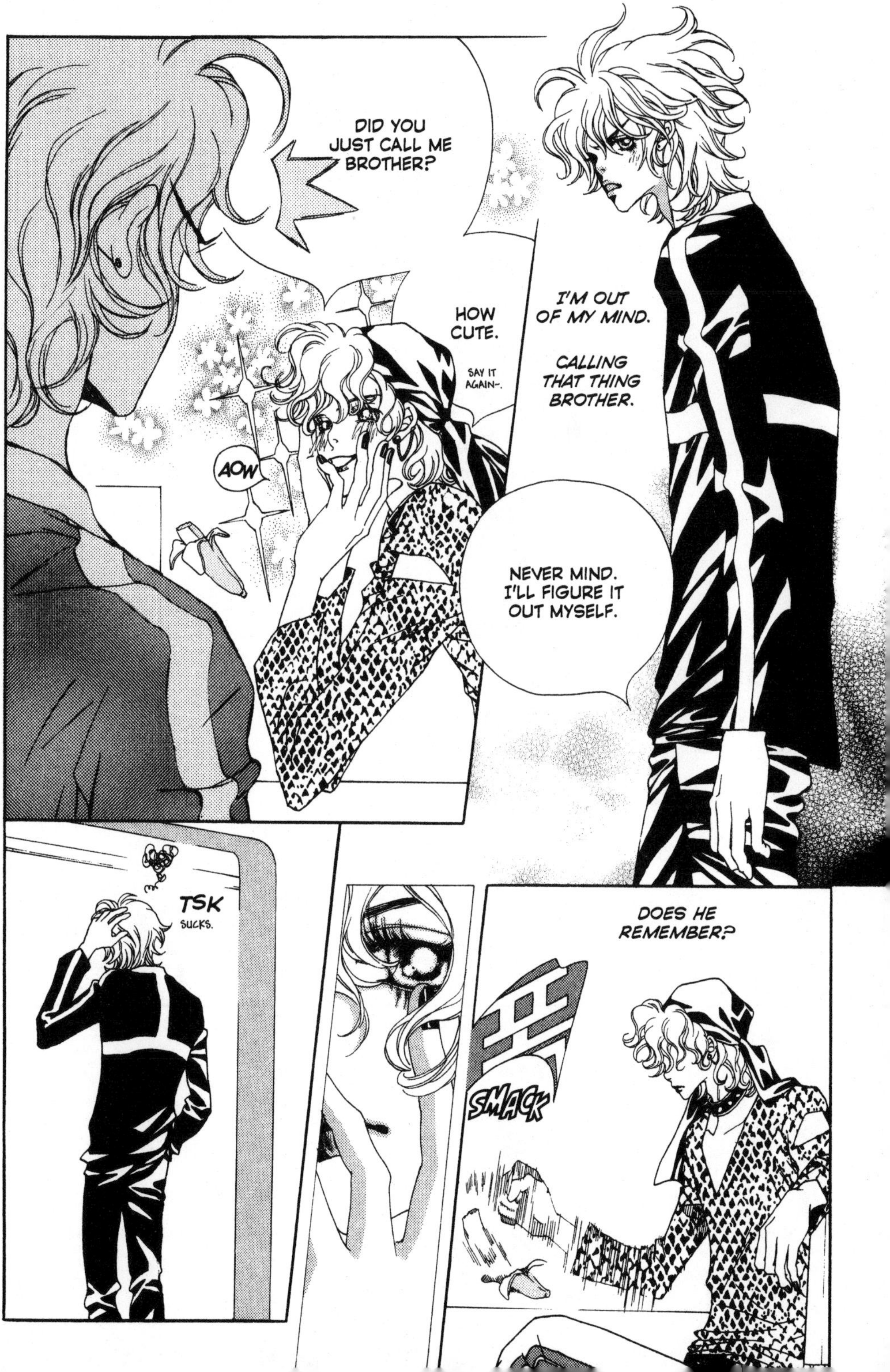
DID YOU JUST CALL ME BROTHER?
HOW CUTE.
SAY IT AGAIN~.
AOW
I'M OUT OF MY MIND.
CALLING THAT THING BROTHER.
NEVER MIND. I'LL FIGURE IT OUT MYSELF.
TSK
SUCKS.
DOES HE REMEMBER?
SMACK

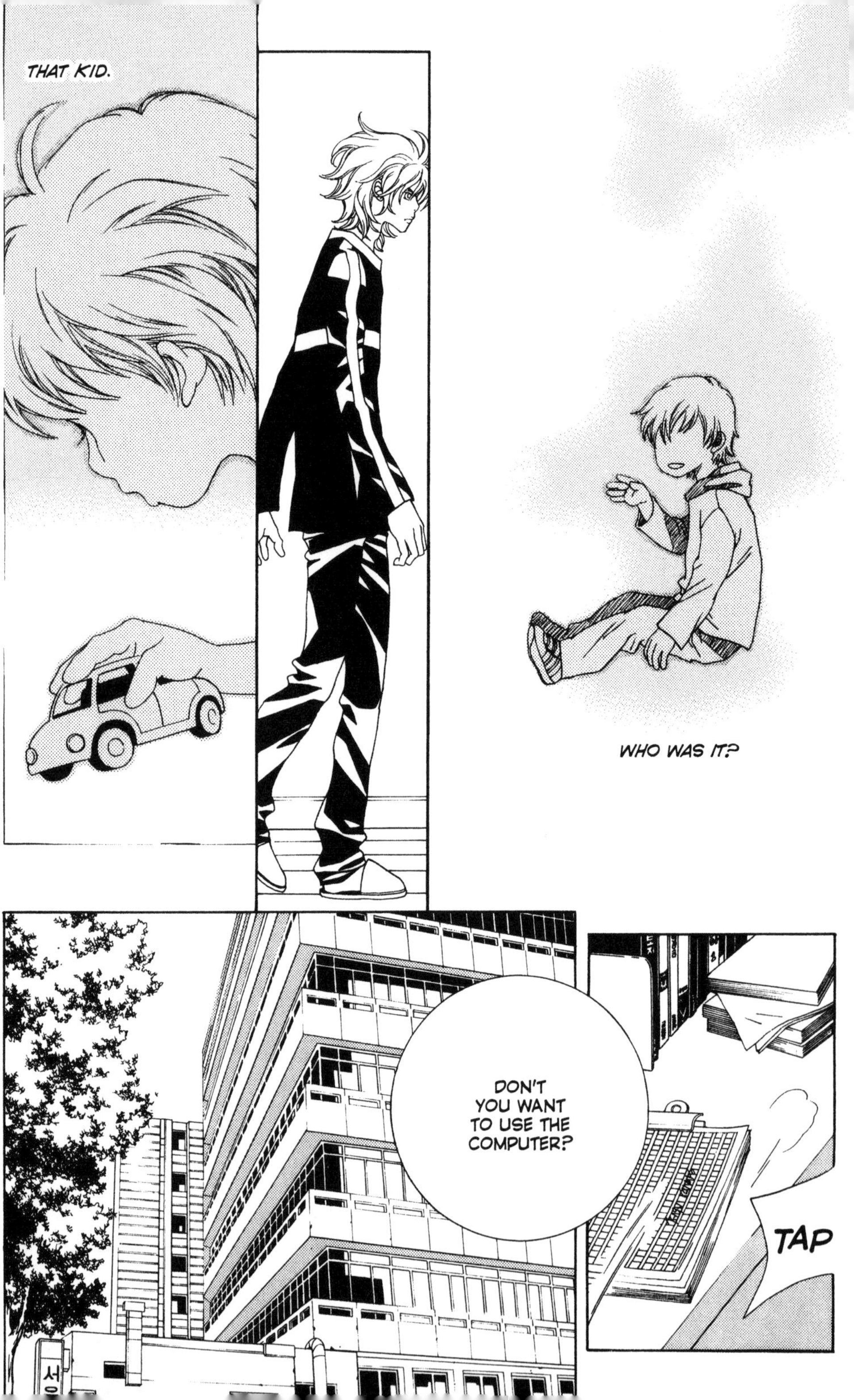
THAT KID.
WHO WAS IT?
DON'T YOU WANT TO USE THE COMPUTER?
TAP

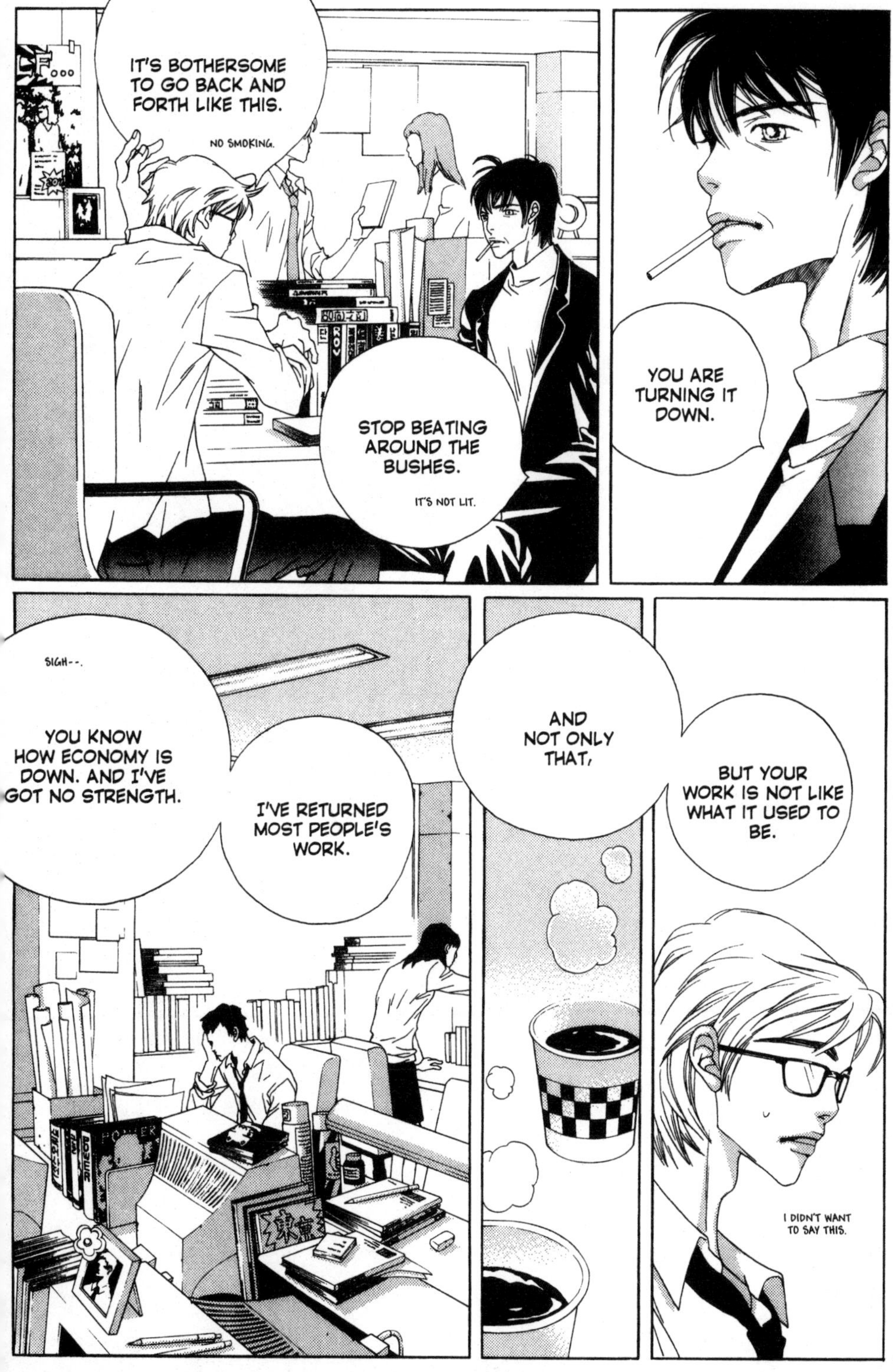
IT'S BOTHERSOME TO GO BACK AND FORTH LIKE THIS.
NO SMOKING.
STOP BEATING AROUND THE BUSHES.
IT'S NOT LIT.
YOU ARE TURNING IT DOWN.
SIGH--.
YOU KNOW HOW ECONOMY IS DOWN. AND I'VE GOT NO STRENGTH.
I'VE RETURNED MOST PEOPLE'S WORK.
AND NOT ONLY THAT,
BUT YOUR WORK IS NOT LIKE WHAT IT USED TO BE.
I DIDN'T WANT TO SAY THIS.

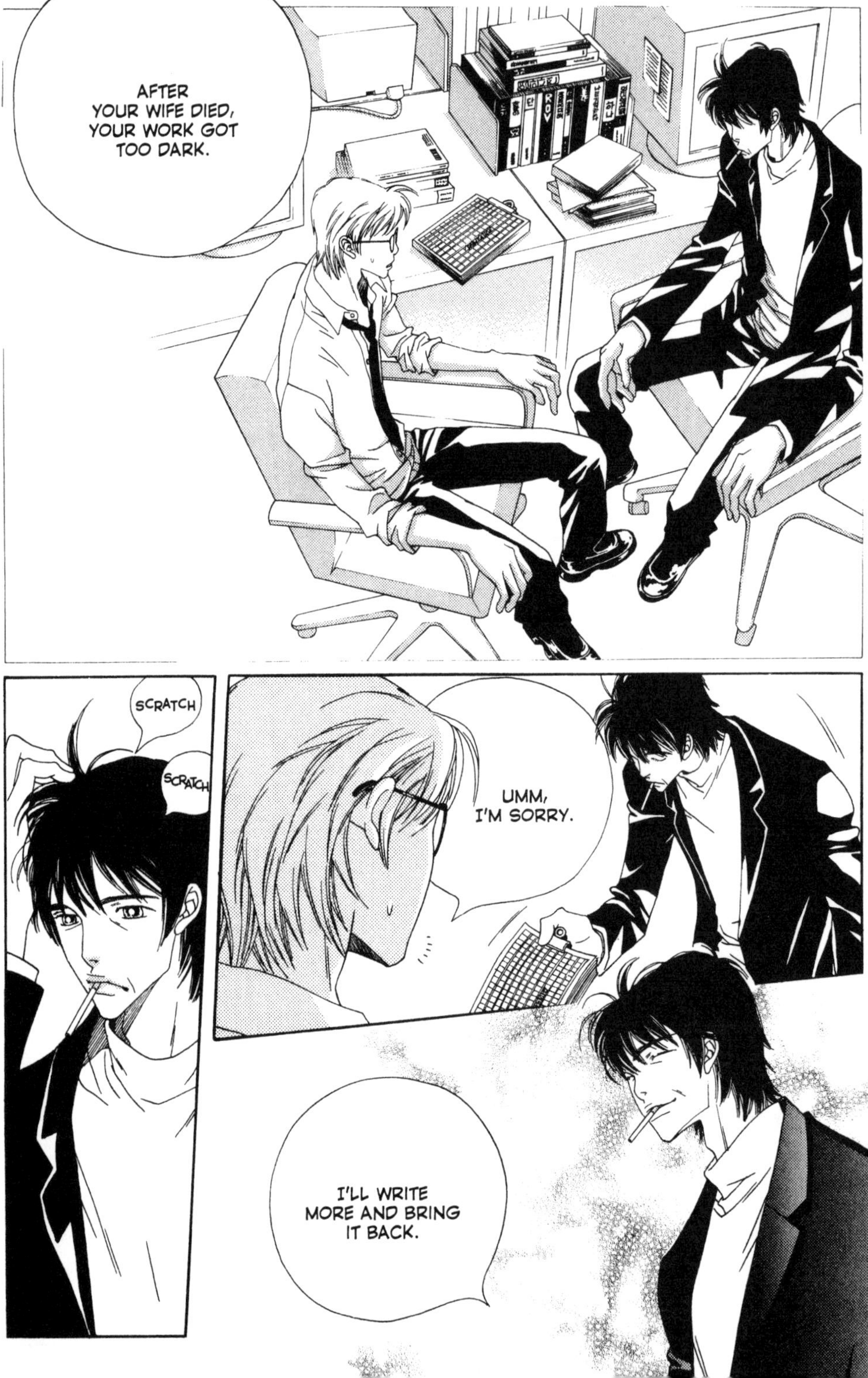
AFTER YOUR WIFE DIED, YOUR WORK GOT TOO DARK.
SCRATCH
SCRATCH
UMM, I'M SORRY.
I'LL WRITE MORE AND BRING IT BACK.

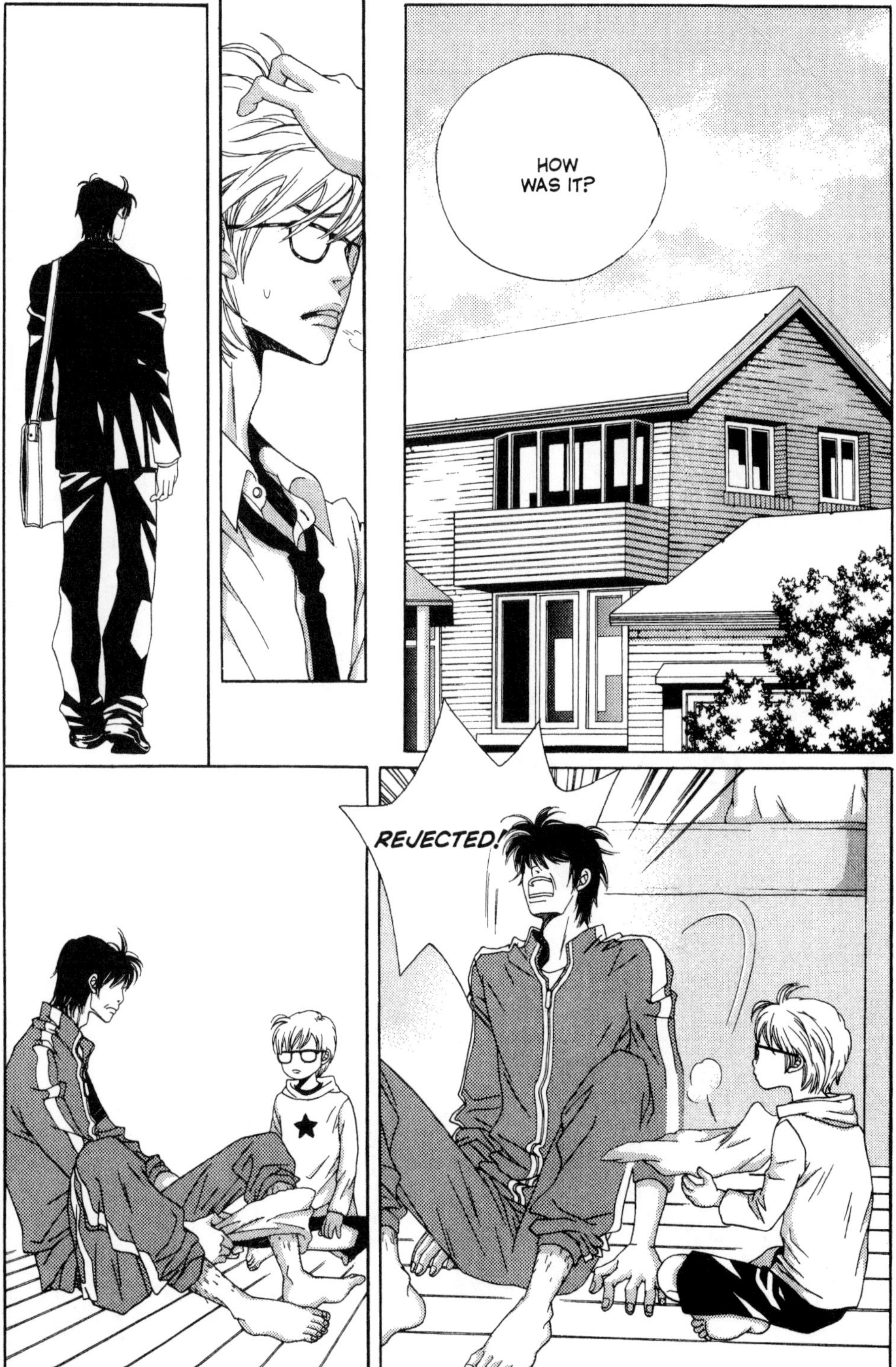
HOW WAS IT?
REJECTED!

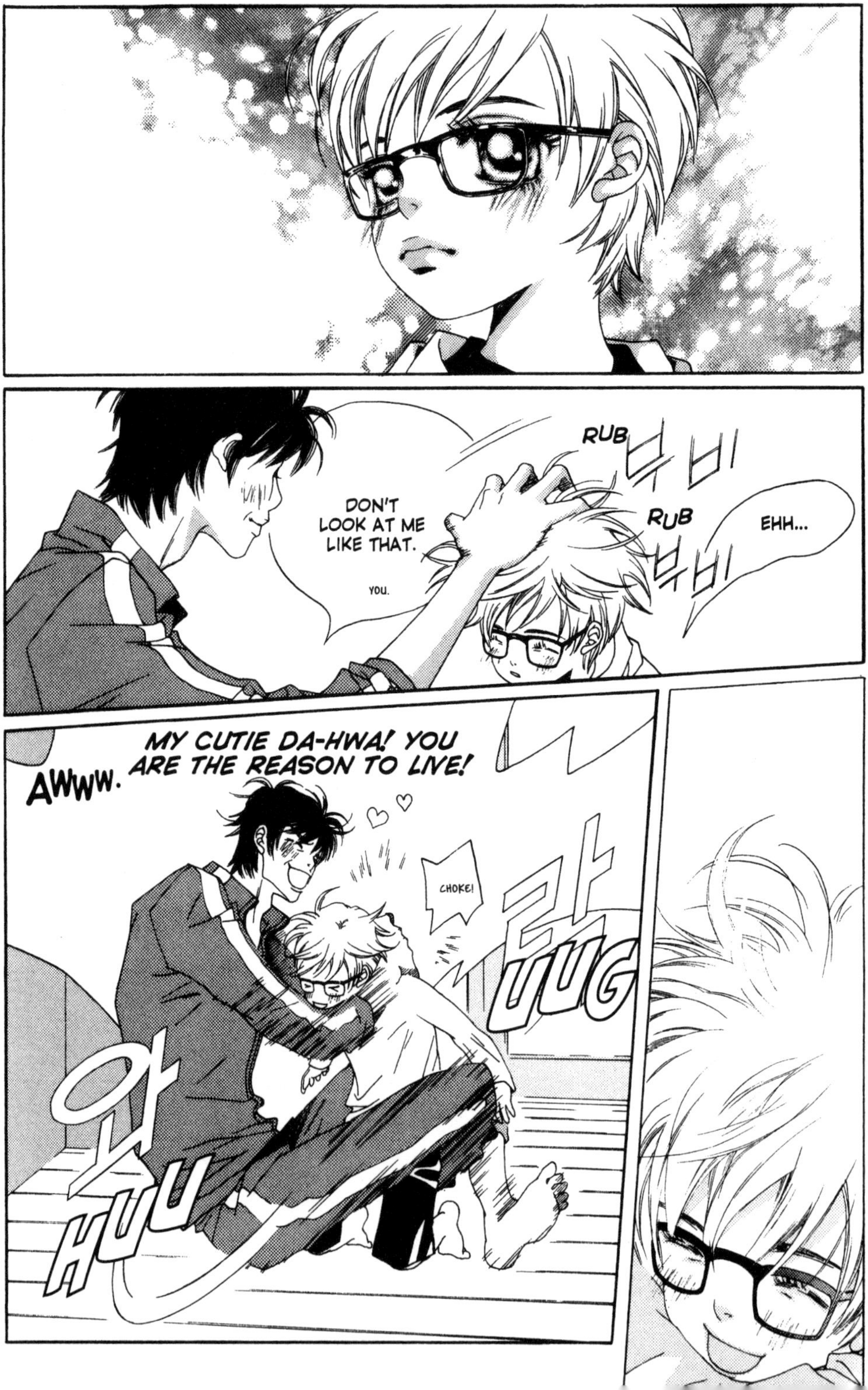
DON'T LOOK AT ME LIKE THAT.
YOU.
RUB
RUB
EHH...
AWWW.
MY CUTIE DA-HWA! YOU ARE THE REASON TO LIVE!
CHOKE!
UUG
HUU

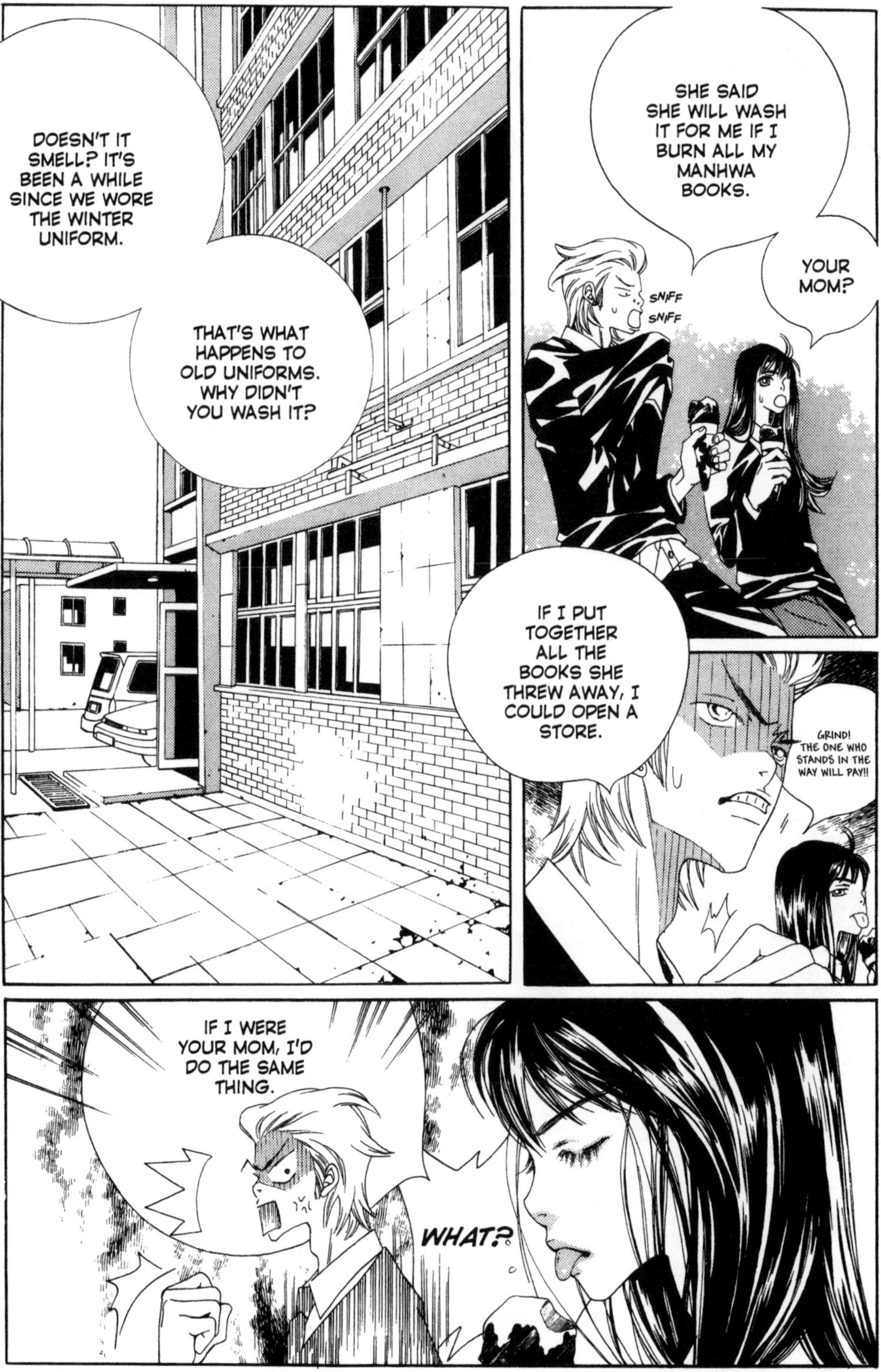
DOESN'T IT SMELL? IT'S BEEN A WHILE SINCE WE WORE THE WINTER UNIFORM.
THAT'S WHAT HAPPENS TO OLD UNIFORMS. WHY DIDN'T YOU WASH IT?
SHE SAID SHE WILL WASH IT FOR ME IF I BURN ALL MY MANHWA BOOKS.
SNIFF SNIFF
YOUR MOM?
IF I PUT TOGETHER ALL THE BOOKS SHE THREW AWAY, I COULD OPEN A STORE.
GRIND! THE ONE WHO STANDS IN THE WAY WILL PAY!!
IF I WERE YOUR MOM, I'D DO THE SAME THING.
WHAT?

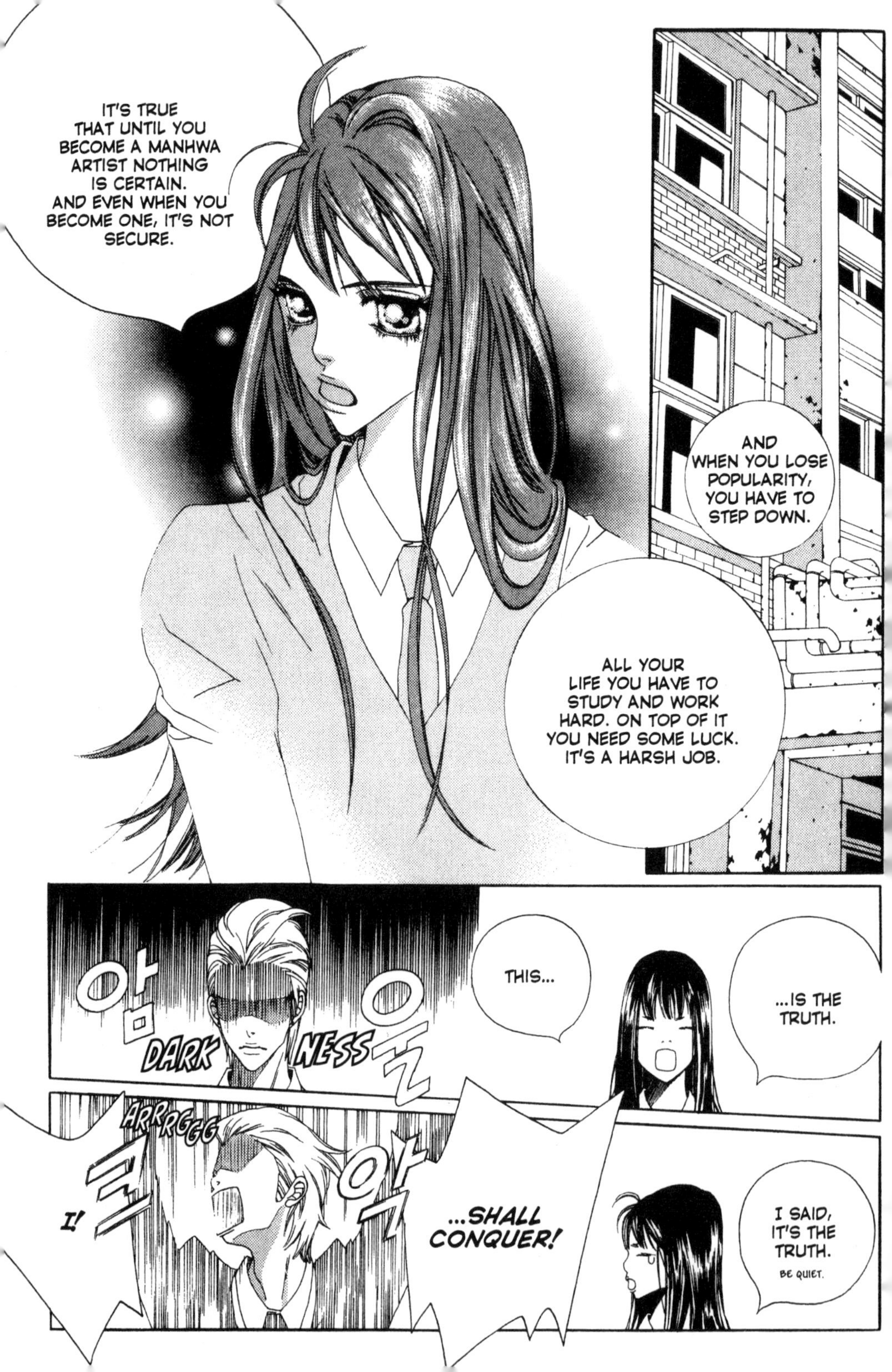
IT'S TRUE THAT UNTIL YOU BECOME A MANHWA ARTIST NOTHING IS CERTAIN. AND EVEN WHEN YOU BECOME ONE, IT'S NOT SECURE.
AND WHEN YOU LOSE POPULARITY, YOU HAVE TO STEP DOWN.
ALL YOUR LIFE YOU HAVE TO STUDY AND WORK HARD. ON TOP OF IT YOU NEED SOME LUCK. IT'S A HARSH JOB.
DARKNESS
THIS...
...IS THE TRUTH.
ARRRGGG
I!
...SHALL CONQUER!
I SAID, IT'S THE TRUTH.
BE QUIET.

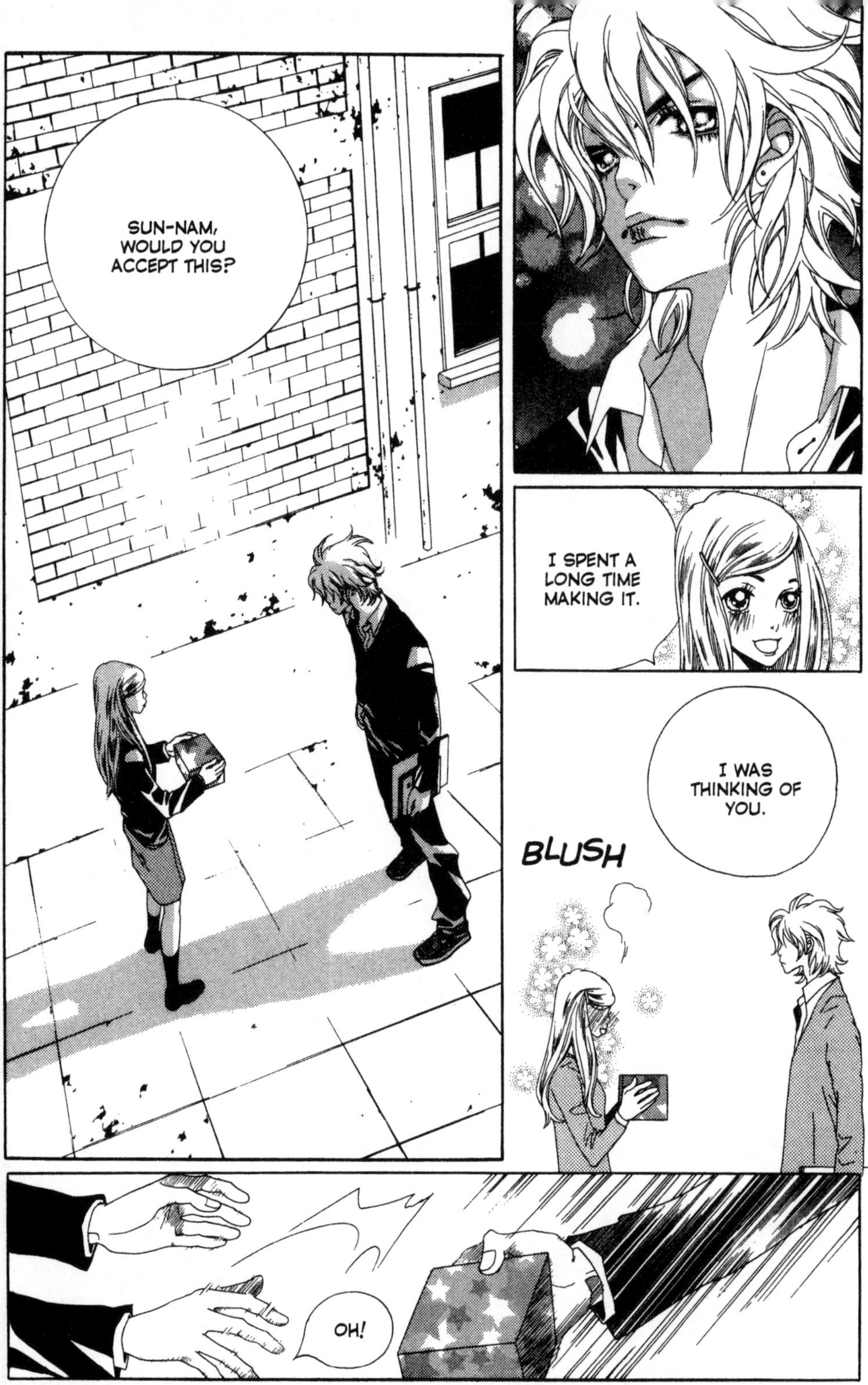
SUN-NAM, WOULD YOU ACCEPT THIS?
I SPENT A LONG TIME MAKING IT.
I WAS THINKING OF YOU.
BLUSH
OH!

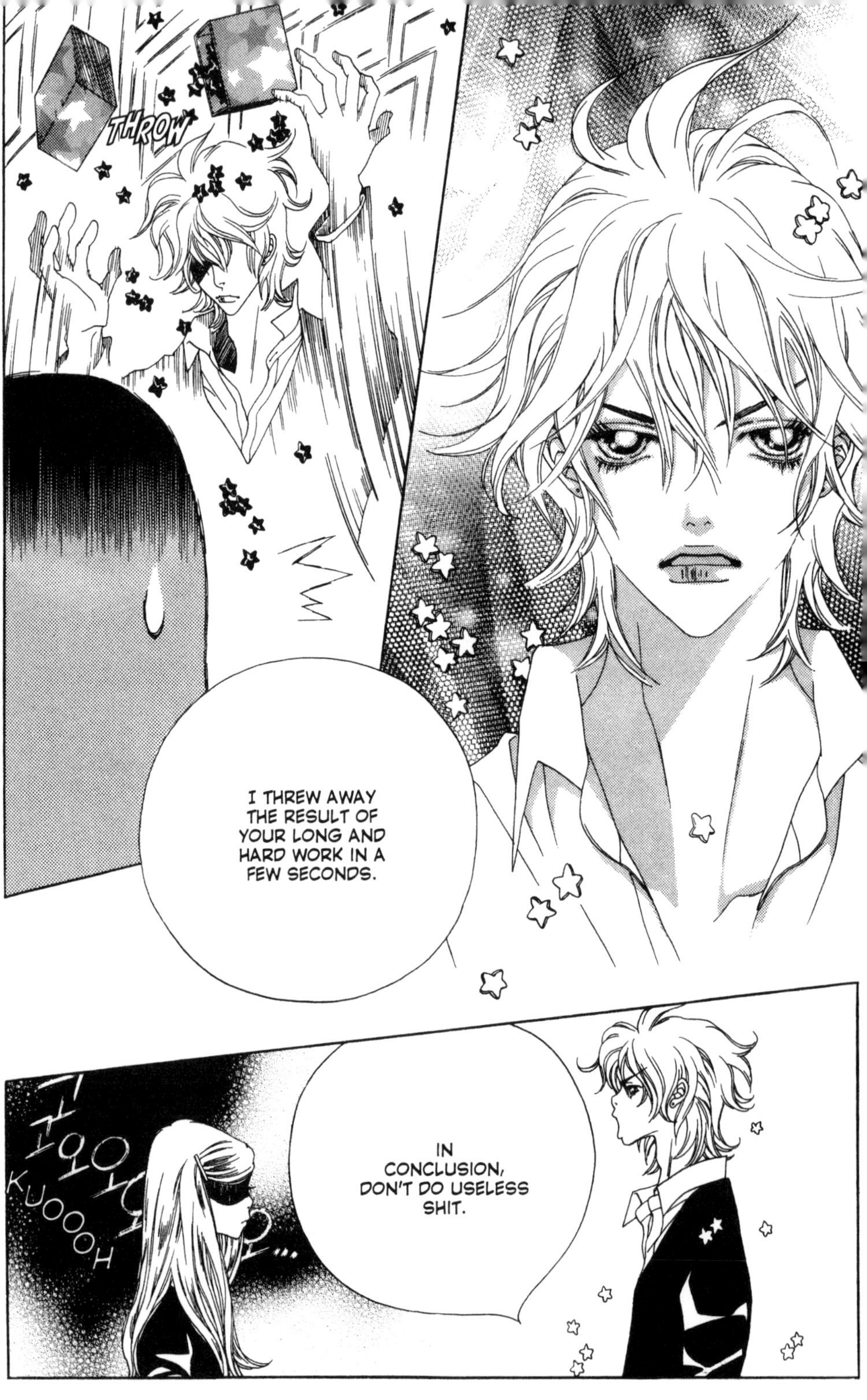
THROW
I THREW AWAY THE RESULT OF YOUR LONG AND HARD WORK IN A FEW SECONDS.
KUOOOH
IN CONCLUSION, DON'T DO USELESS SHIT.

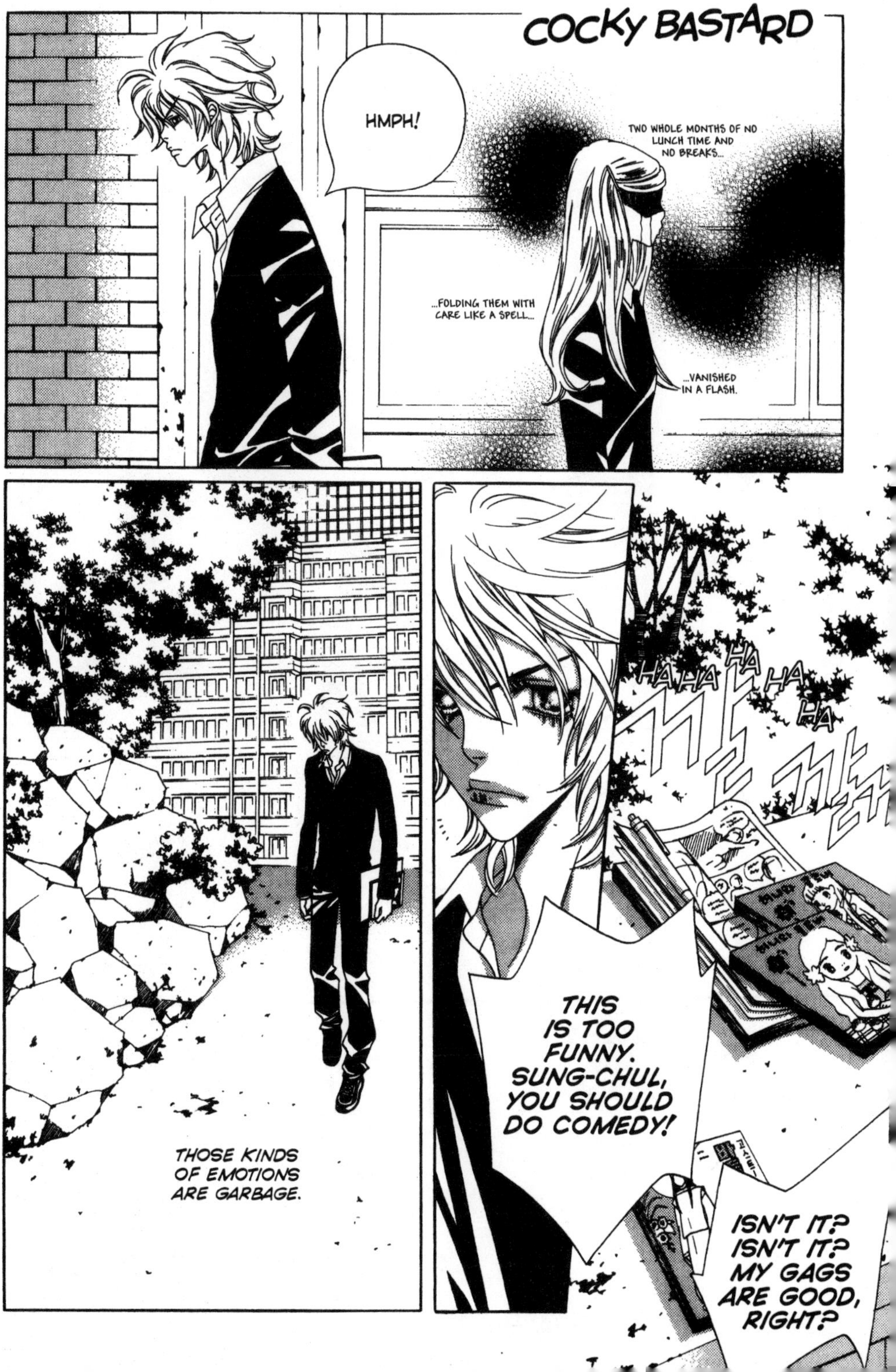
HMPH!
TWO WHOLE MONTHS OF NO LUNCH TIME AND NO BREAKS...
...FOLDING THEM WITH CARE LIKE A SPELL...
...VANISHED IN A FLASH.
THOSE KINDS OF EMOTIONS ARE GARBAGE.
HAHA HA HA HA
THIS IS TOO FUNNY. SUNG-CHUL, YOU SHOULD DO COMEDY!
ISN'T IT? ISN'T IT? MY GAGS ARE GOOD, RIGHT?

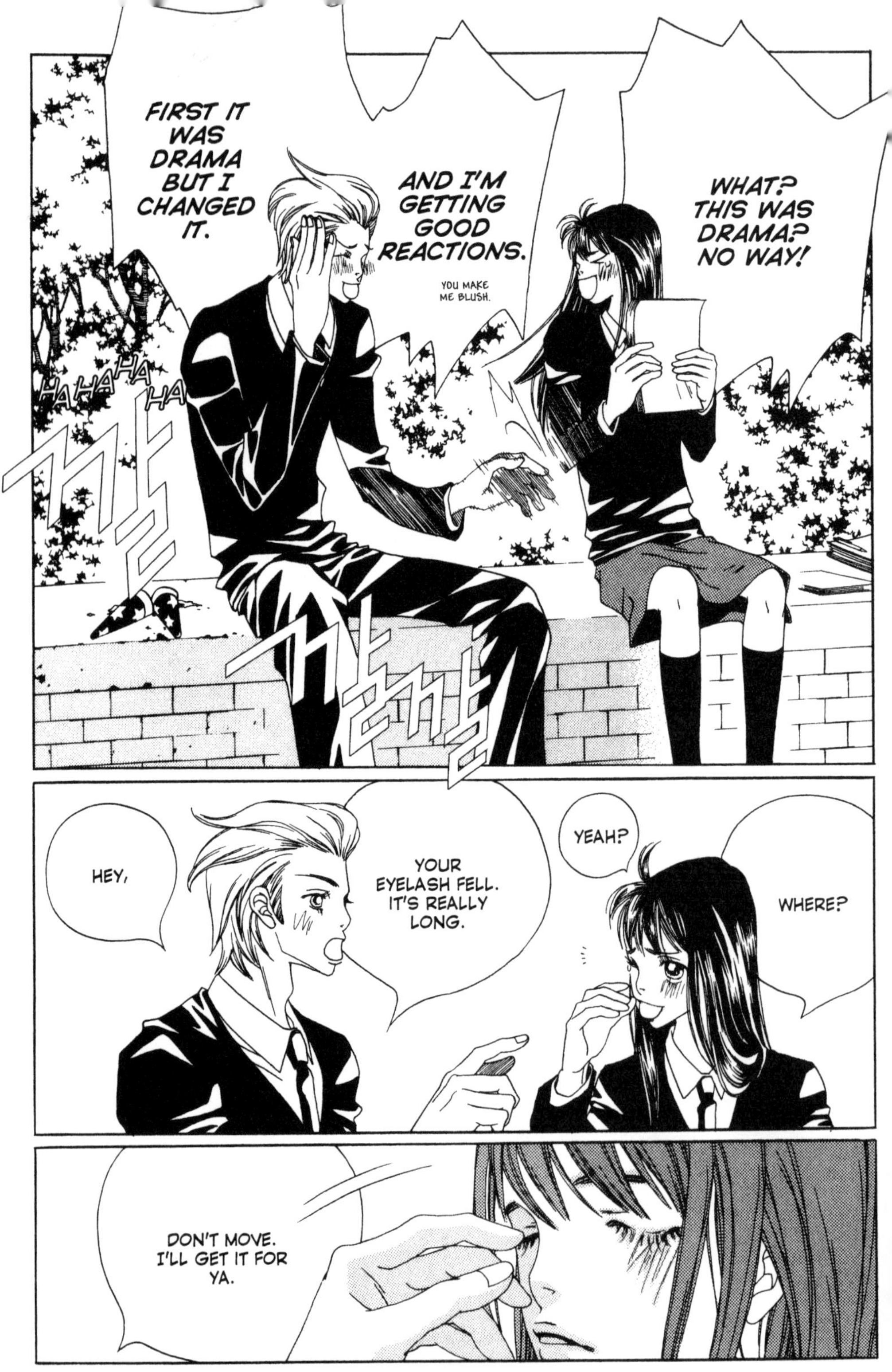
FIRST IT WAS DRAMA BUT I CHANGED IT.
AND I'M GETTING GOOD REACTIONS.
YOU MAKE ME BLUSH.
WHAT? THIS WAS DRAMA? NO WAY!
HAHAHAHA
HEY,
YOUR EYELASH FELL. IT'S REALLY LONG.
YEAH?
WHERE?
DON'T MOVE. I'LL GET IT FOR YA.

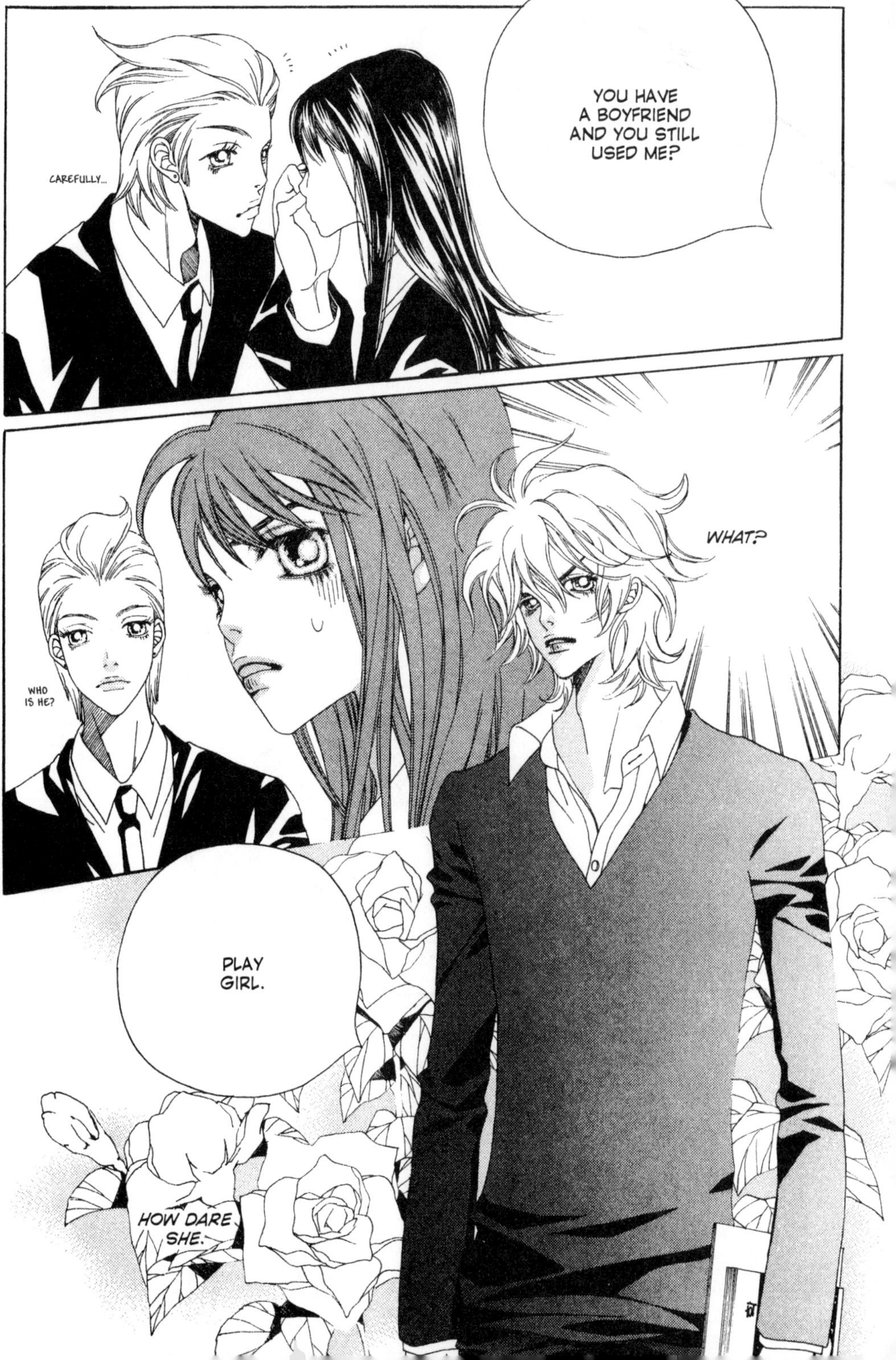
CAREFULLY...
YOU HAVE A BOYFRIEND AND YOU STILL USED ME?
WHO IS HE?
WHAT?
PLAY GIRL.
HOW DARE SHE.

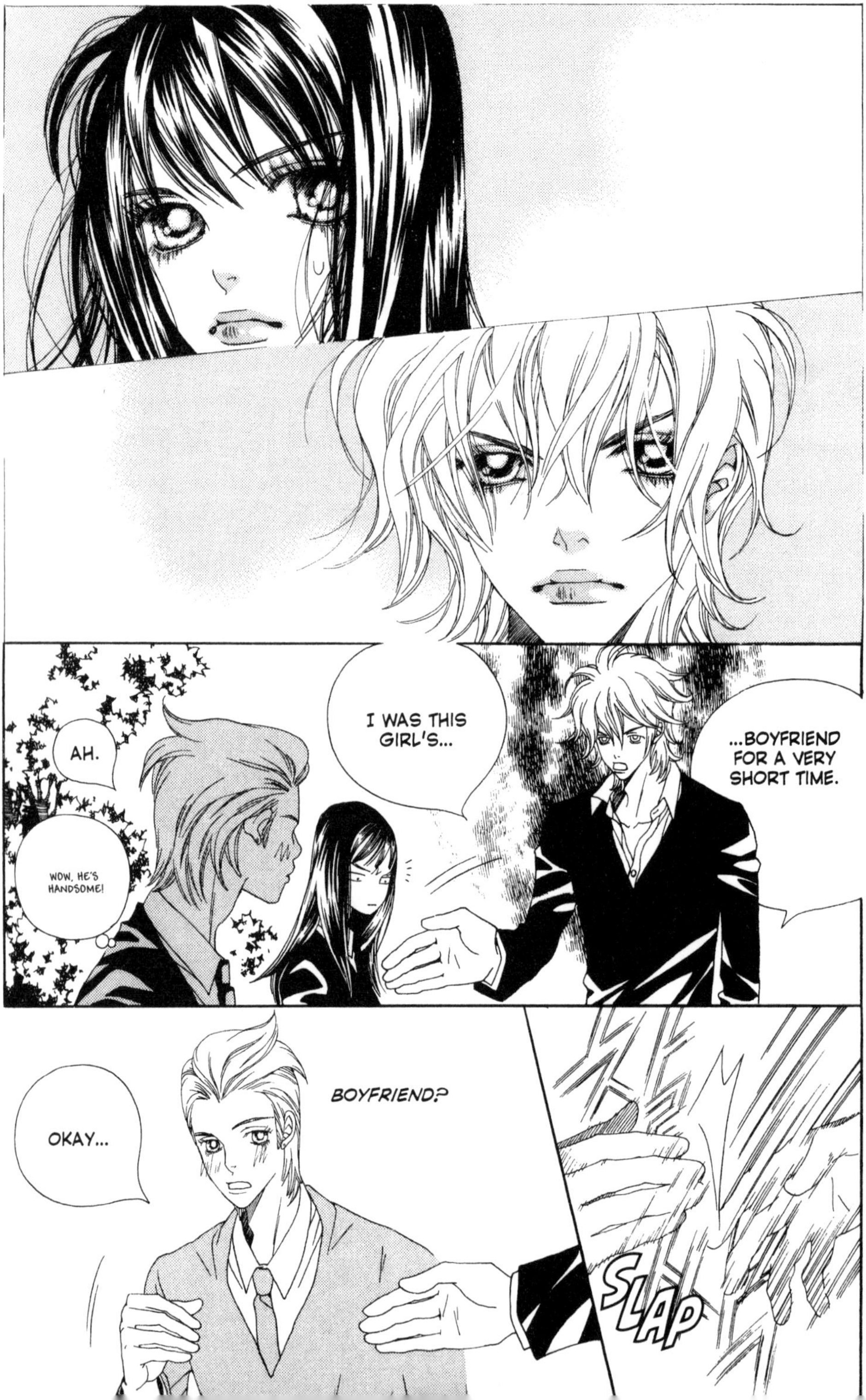
AH.
WOW, HE'S HANDSOME!
I WAS THIS GIRL'S...
...BOYFRIEND FOR A VERY SHORT TIME.
OKAY...
BOYFRIEND?
SLAP

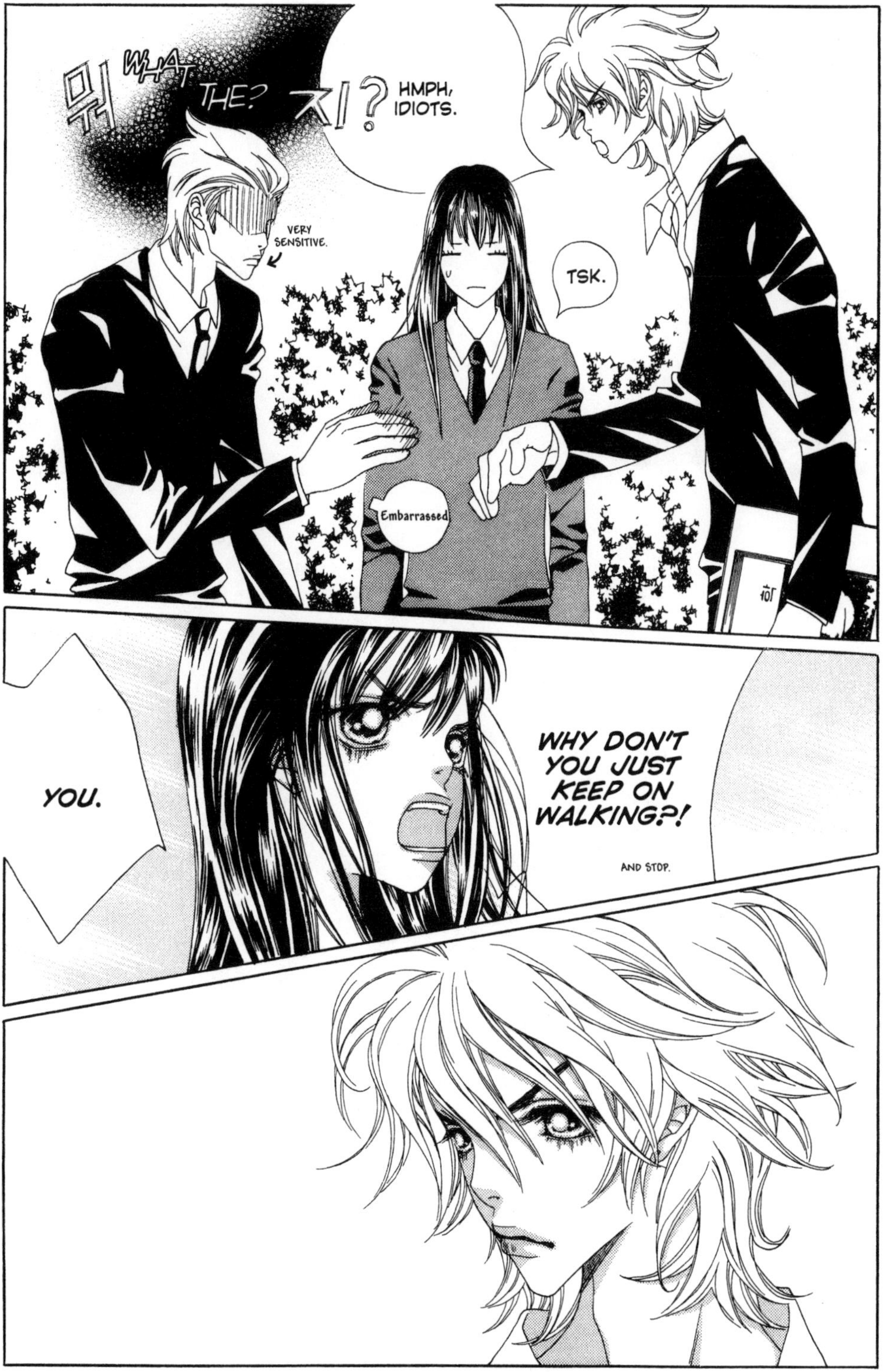
뭐
WHAT THE?
지?
HMPH, IDIOTS.
VERY SENSITIVE.
TSK.
Embarrassed
YOU.
WHY DON'T YOU JUST KEEP ON WALKING?!
AND STOP.

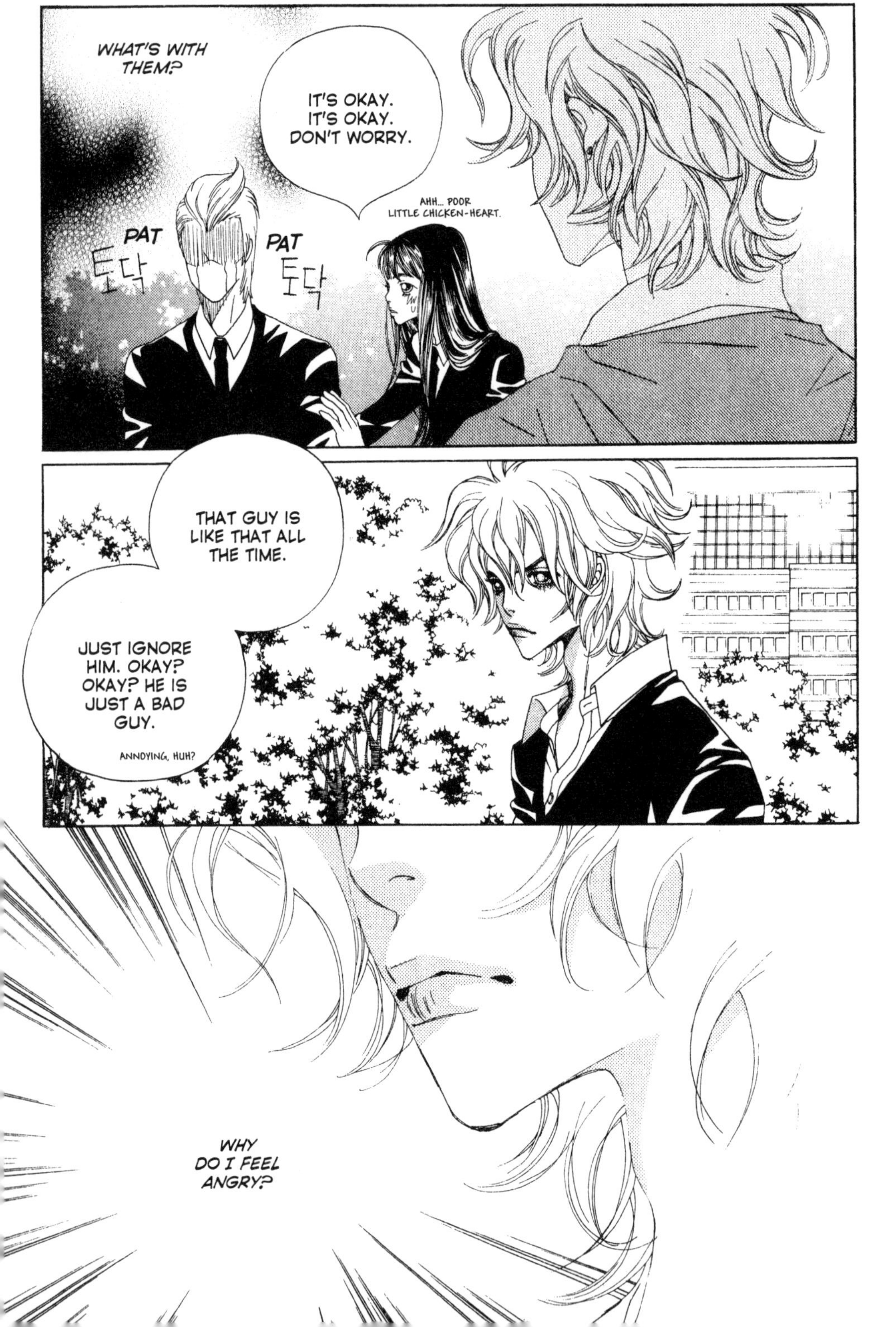
WHAT'S WITH THEM?
IT'S OKAY. IT'S OKAY. DON'T WORRY.
AHH... POOR LITTLE CHICKEN-HEART.
PAT 토닥
PAT 토닥
THAT GUY IS LIKE THAT ALL THE TIME.
JUST IGNORE HIM. OKAY? OKAY? HE IS JUST A BAD GUY.
ANNOYING, HUH?
WHY DO I FEEL ANGRY?

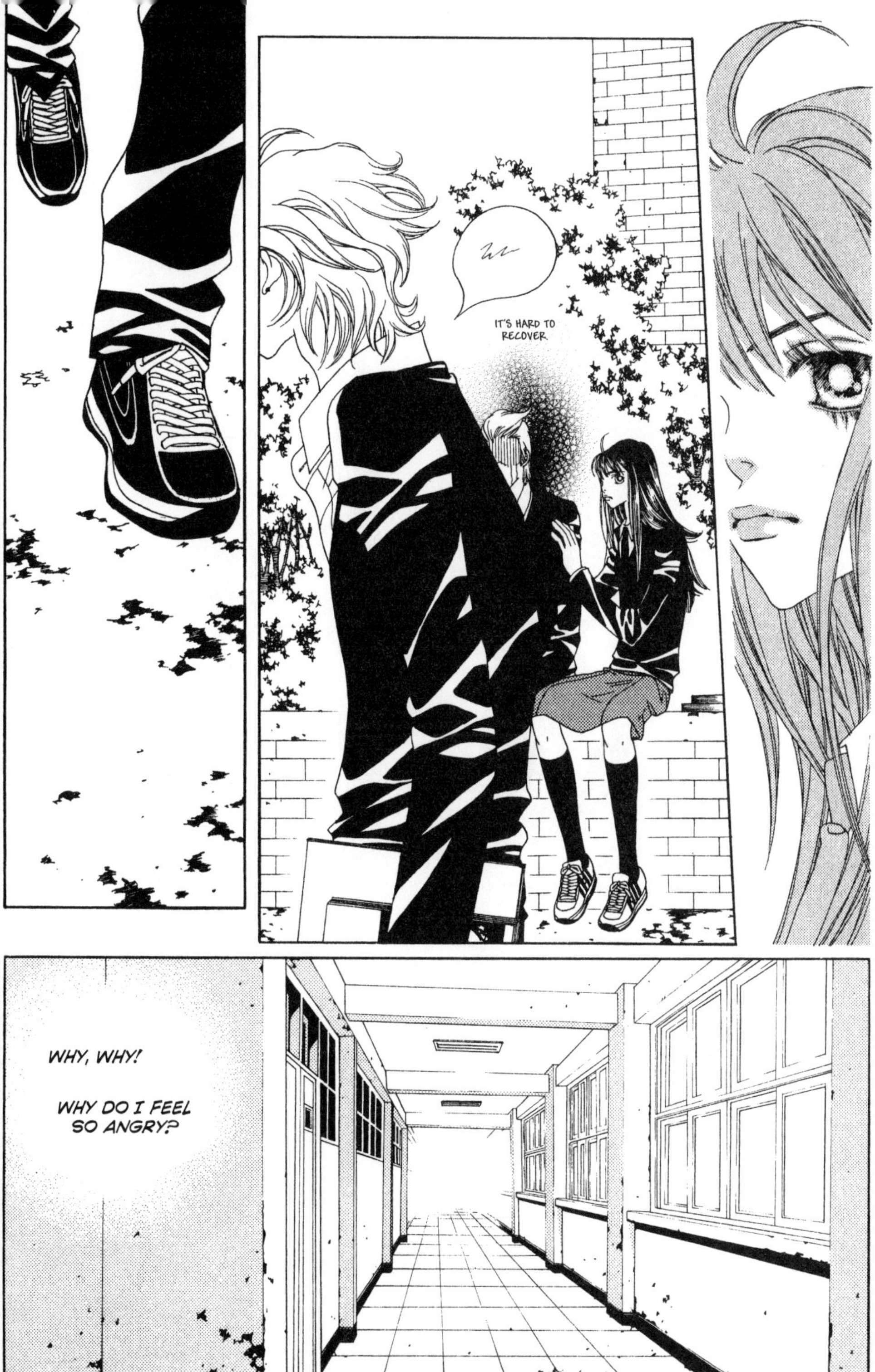
IT'S HARD TO RECOVER.
WHY, WHY!
WHY DO I FEEL SO ANGRY?

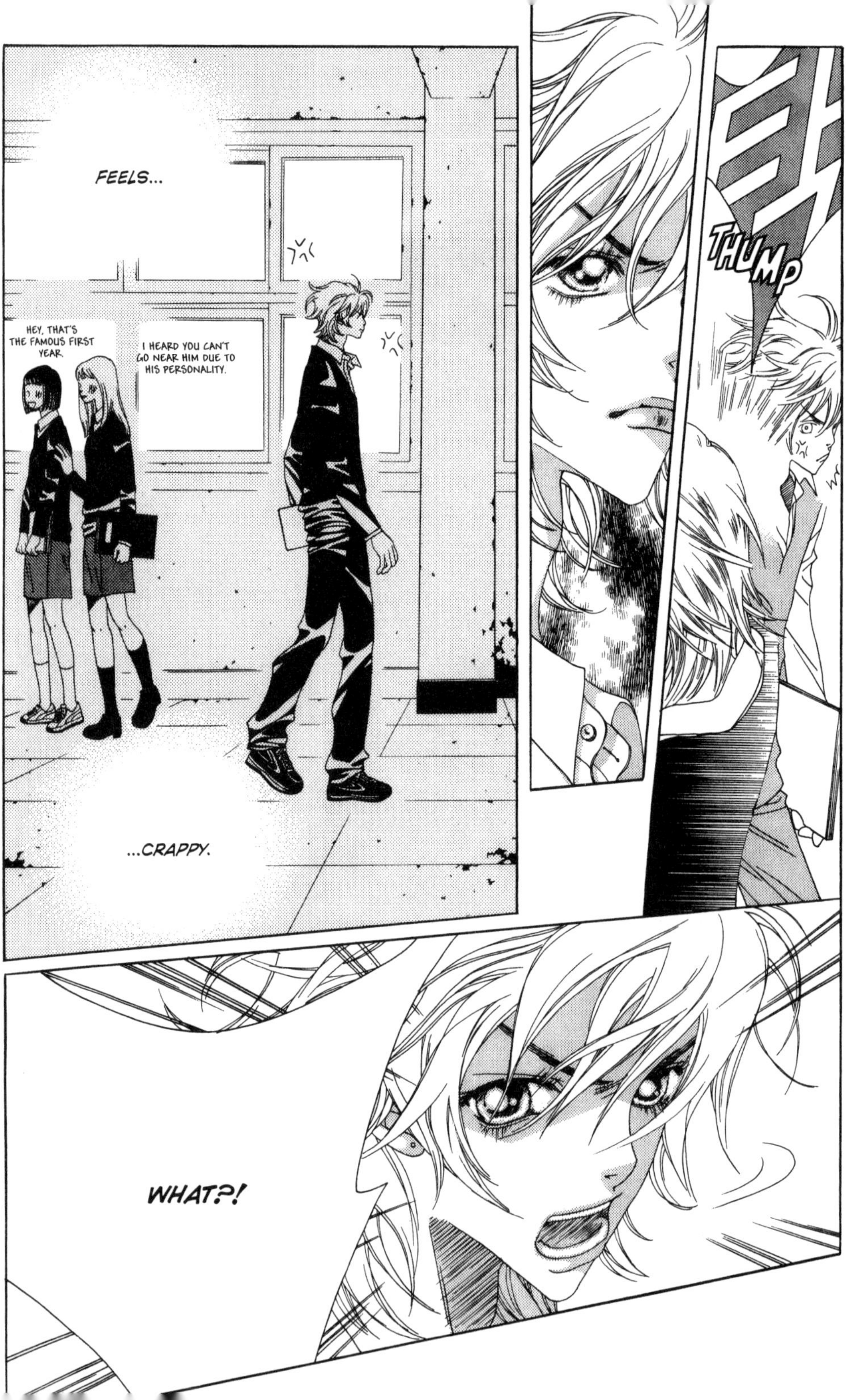
FEELS...
HEY, THAT'S THE FAMOUS FIRST YEAR.
I HEARD YOU CAN'T GO NEAR HIM DUE TO HIS PERSONALITY.
...CRAPPY.
THUMP
WHAT?!

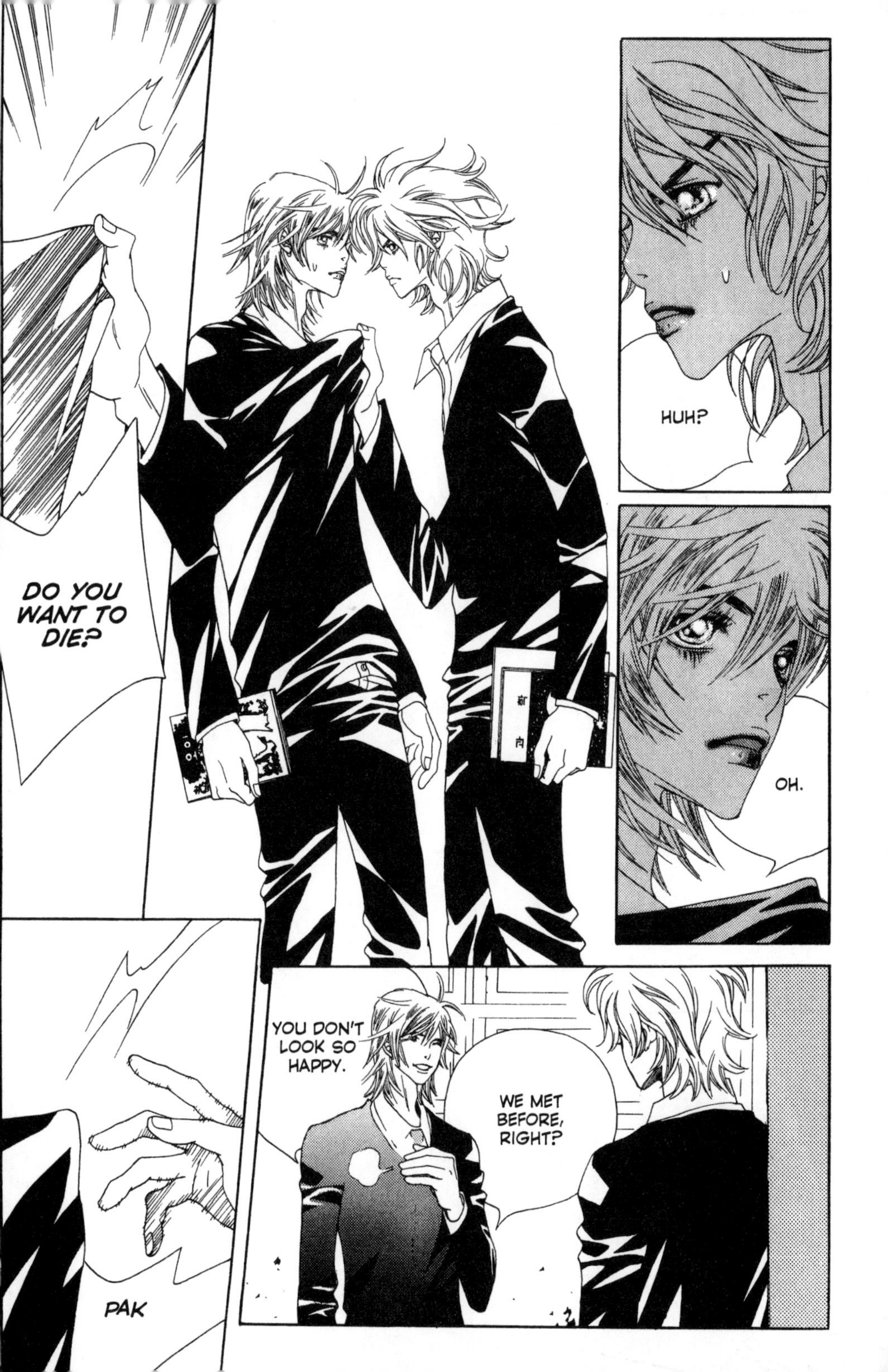
DO YOU WANT TO DIE?
HUH?
OH.
PAK
YOU DON'T LOOK SO HAPPY.
WE MET BEFORE, RIGHT?

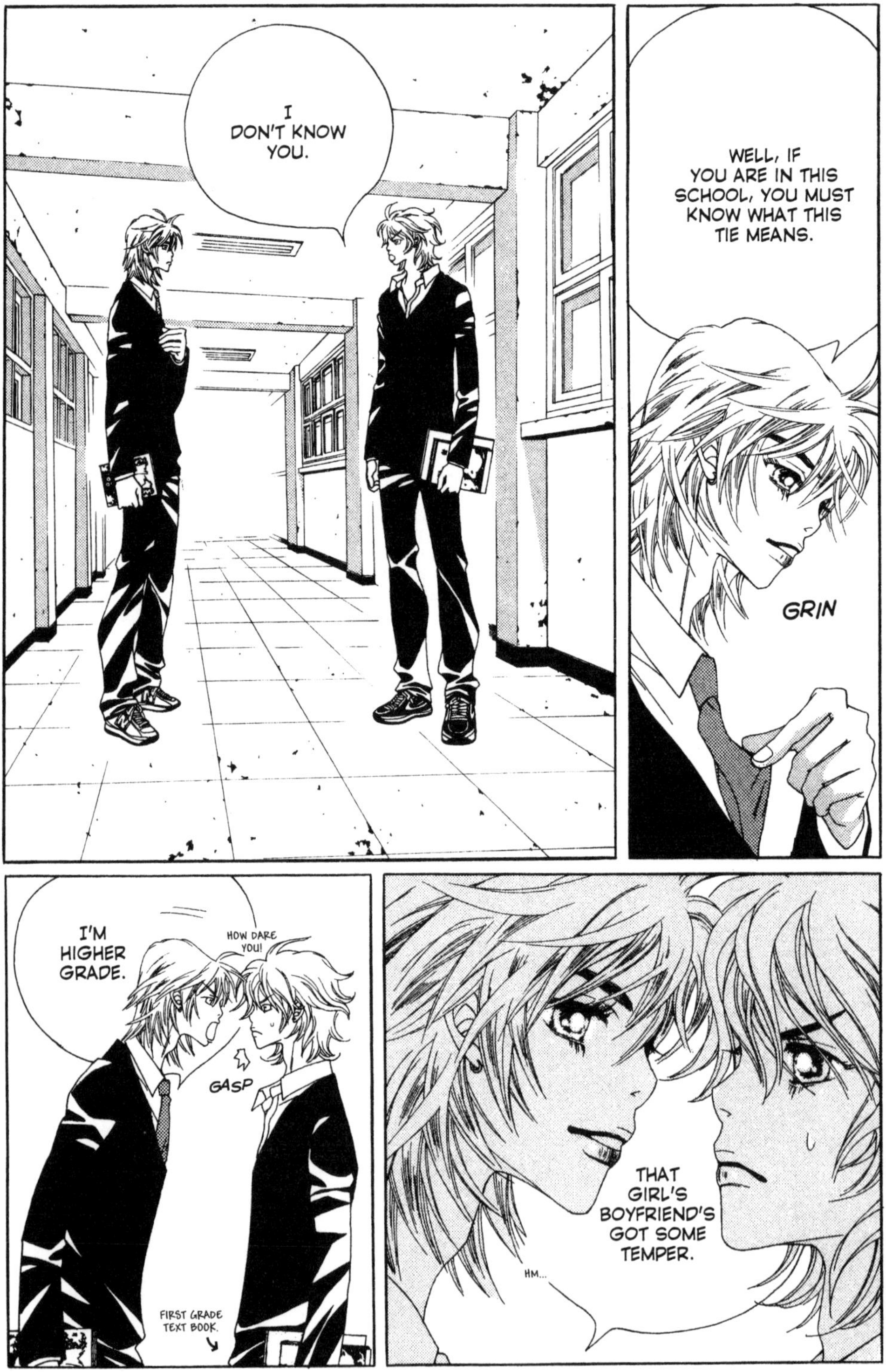
I DON'T KNOW YOU.
WELL, IF YOU ARE IN THIS SCHOOL, YOU MUST KNOW WHAT THIS TIE MEANS.
GRIN
I'M HIGHER GRADE.
HOW DARE YOU!
GASP
FIRST GRADE TEXT BOOK.
THAT GIRL'S BOYFRIEND'S GOT SOME TEMPER.
HM...

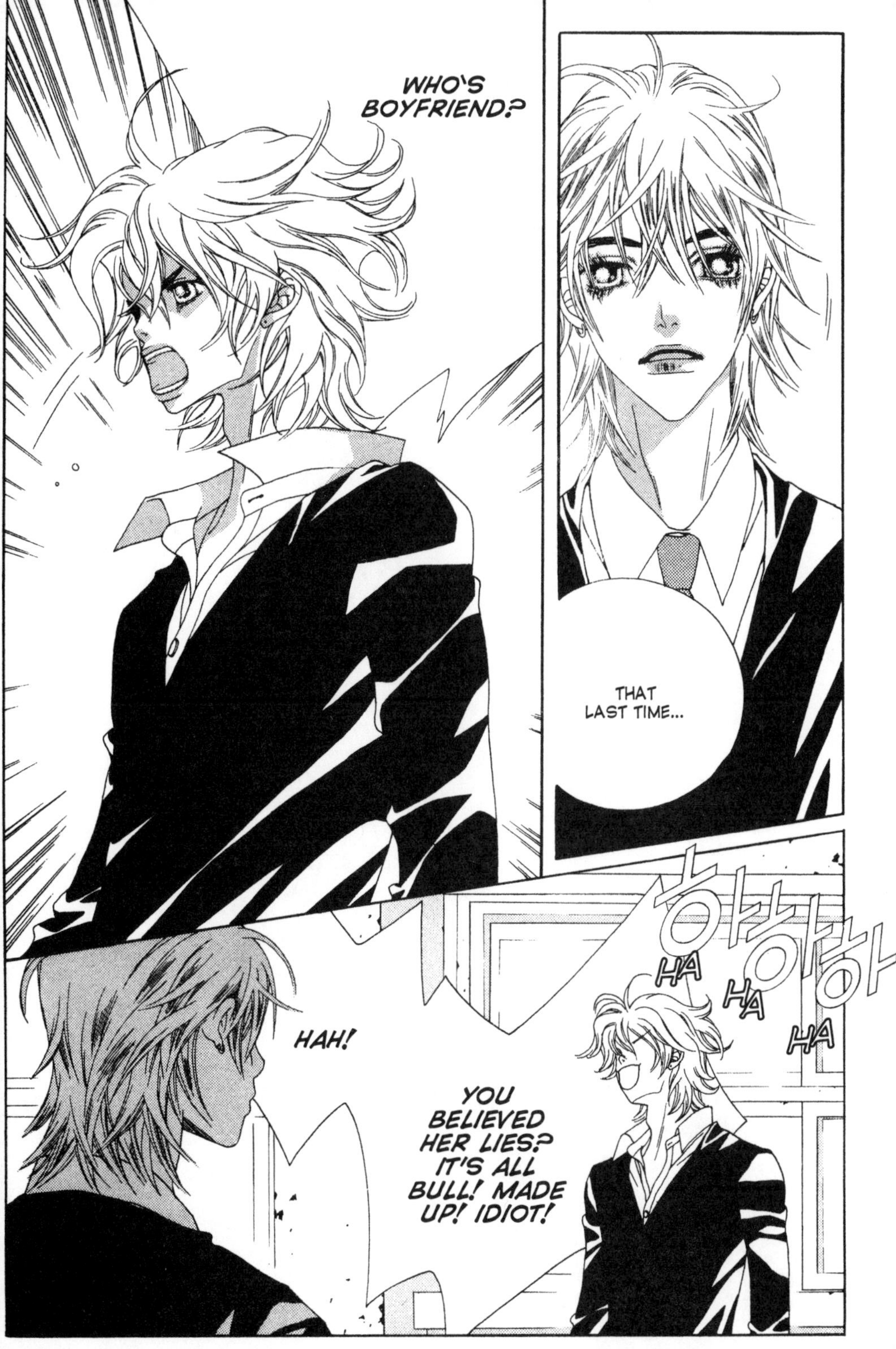

WHO'S BOYFRIEND?
THAT LAST TIME...
HAH!
YOU BELIEVED HER LIES? IT'S ALL BULL! MADE UP! IDIOT!
하하하
HA HA HA

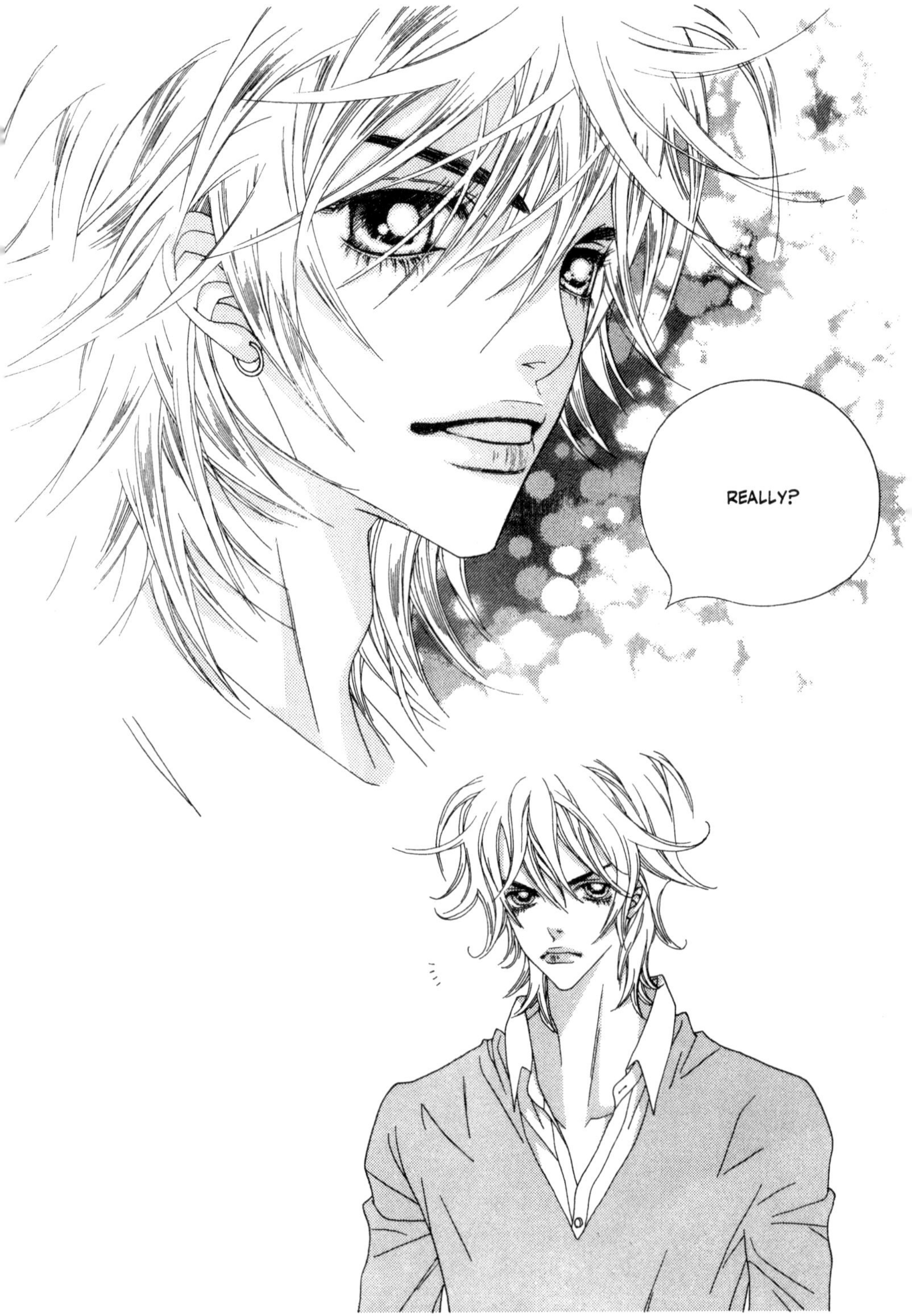
REALLY?

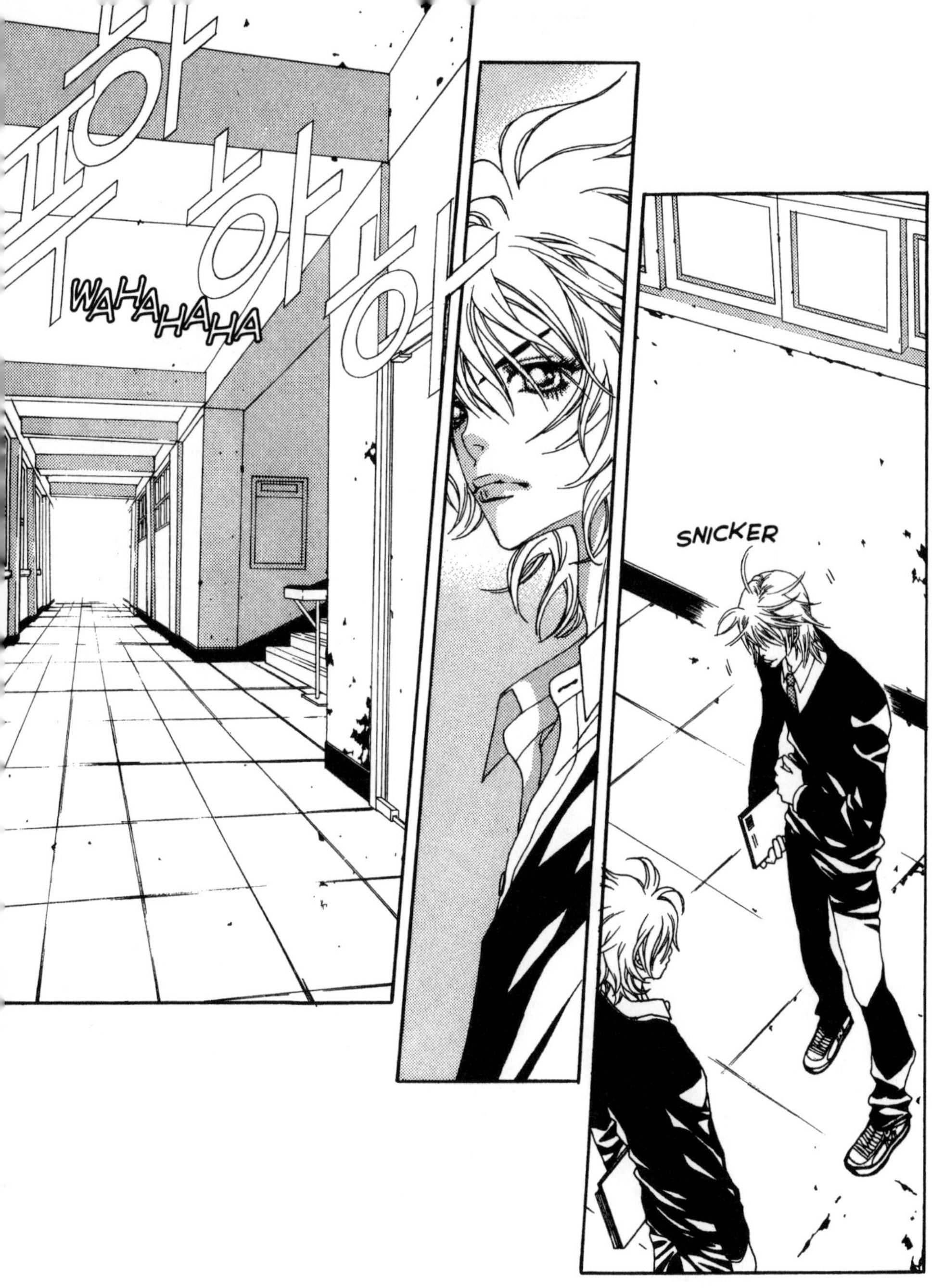
WAHAHAHA
SNICKER

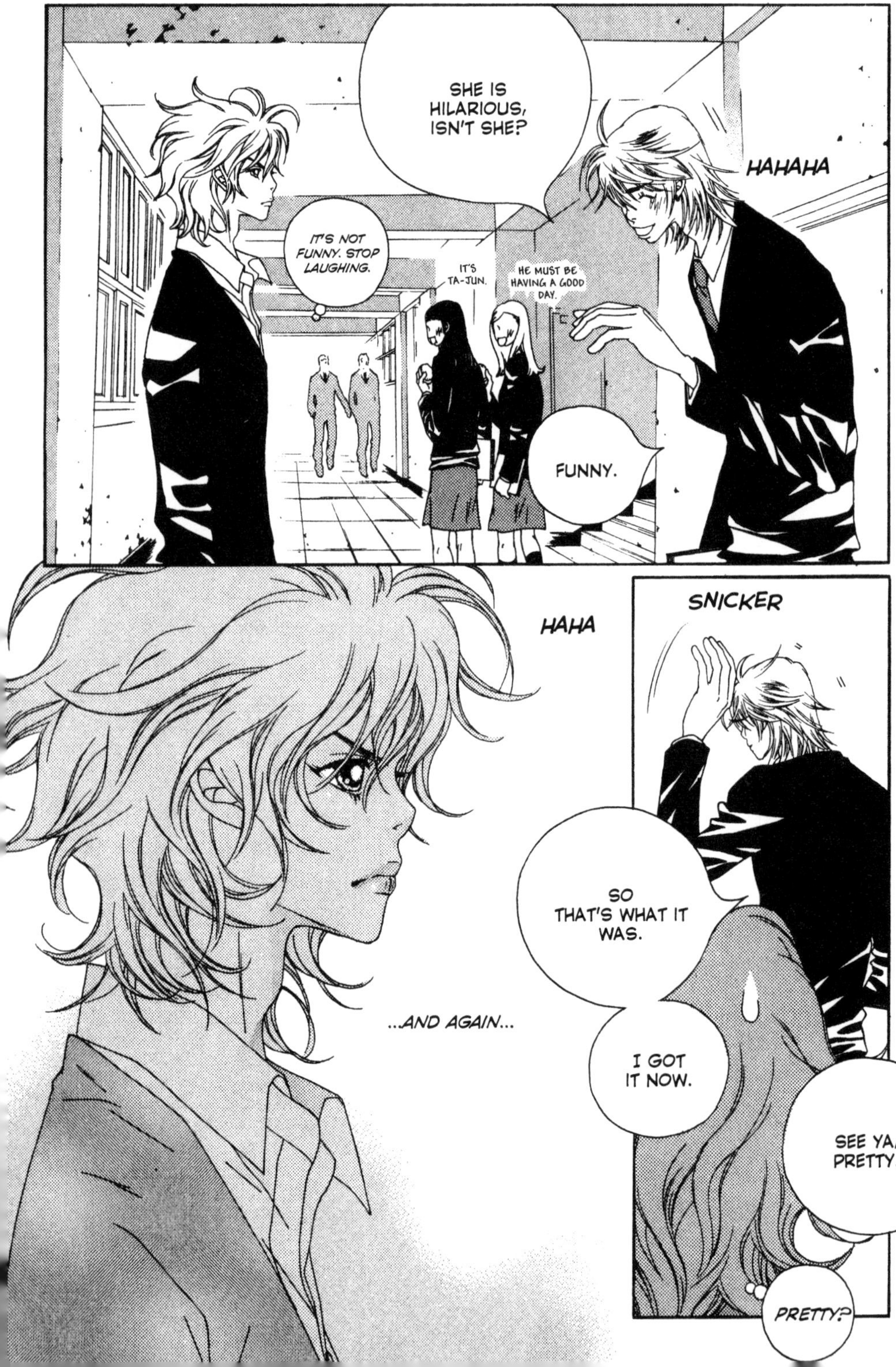
SHE IS HILARIOUS, ISN'T SHE?
HAHAHA
IT'S NOT FUNNY. STOP LAUGHING.
IT'S TA-JUN.
HE MUST BE HAVING A GOOD DAY.
FUNNY.
HAHA
...AND AGAIN...
SNICKER
SO THAT'S WHAT IT WAS.
I GOT IT NOW.
SEE YA, PRETTY.
PRETTY?

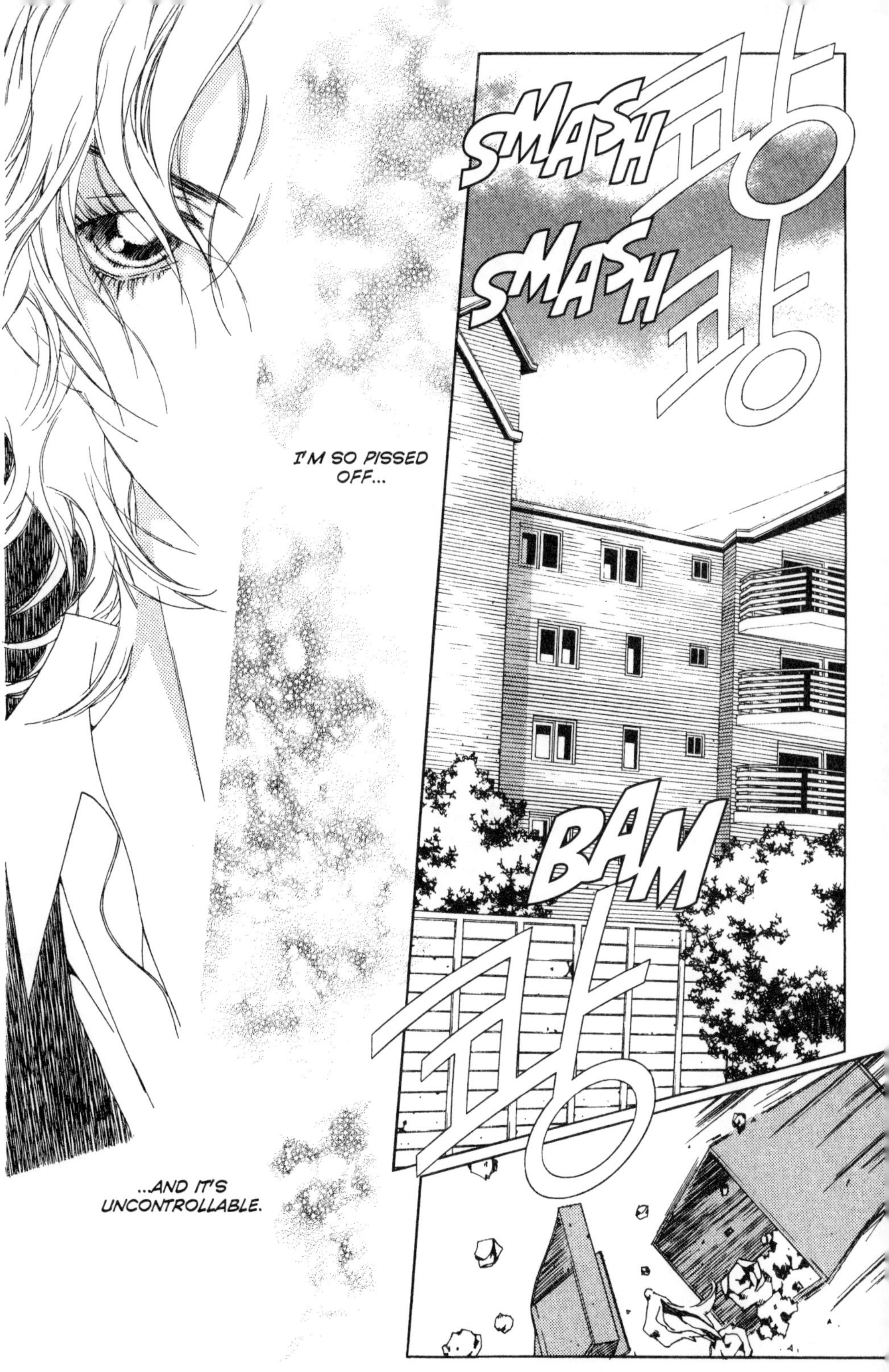
I'M SO PISSED OFF...
...AND IT'S UNCONTROLLABLE.
SMASH
SMASH
BAM

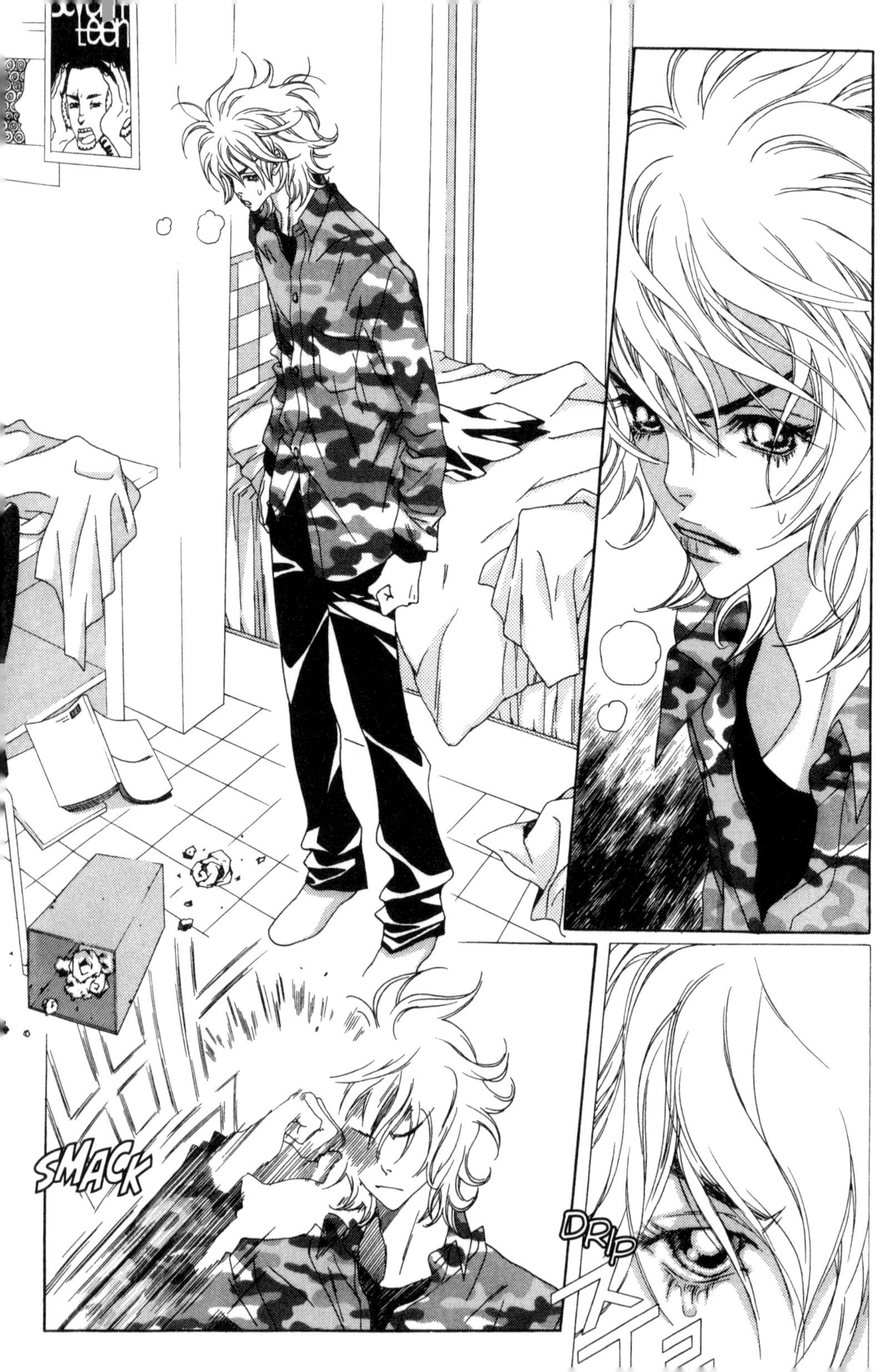
teen
SMACK
DRIP

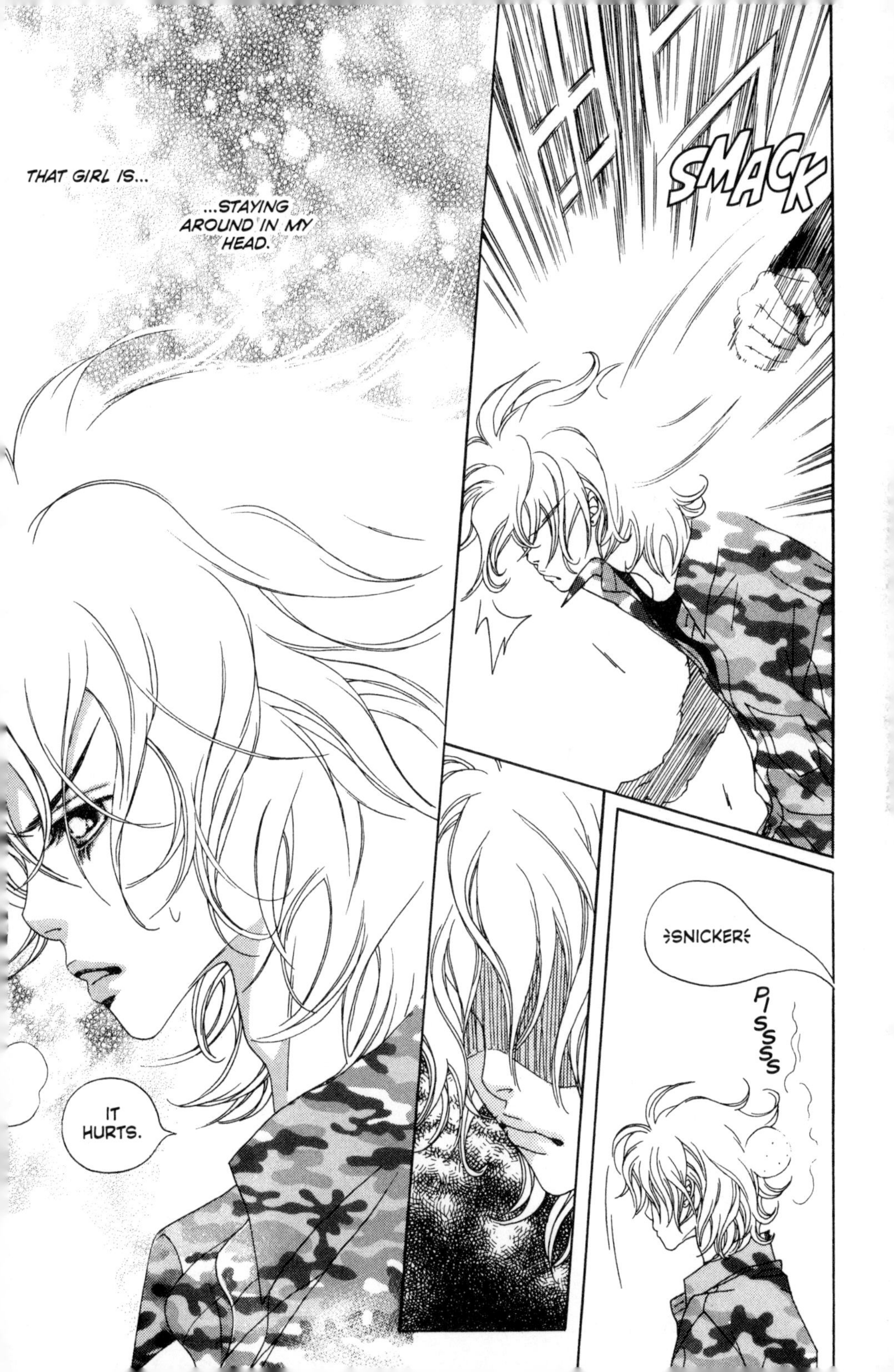
THAT GIRL IS...
...STAYING AROUND IN MY HEAD.
IT HURTS.
SMACK
SNICKER
PISSSS

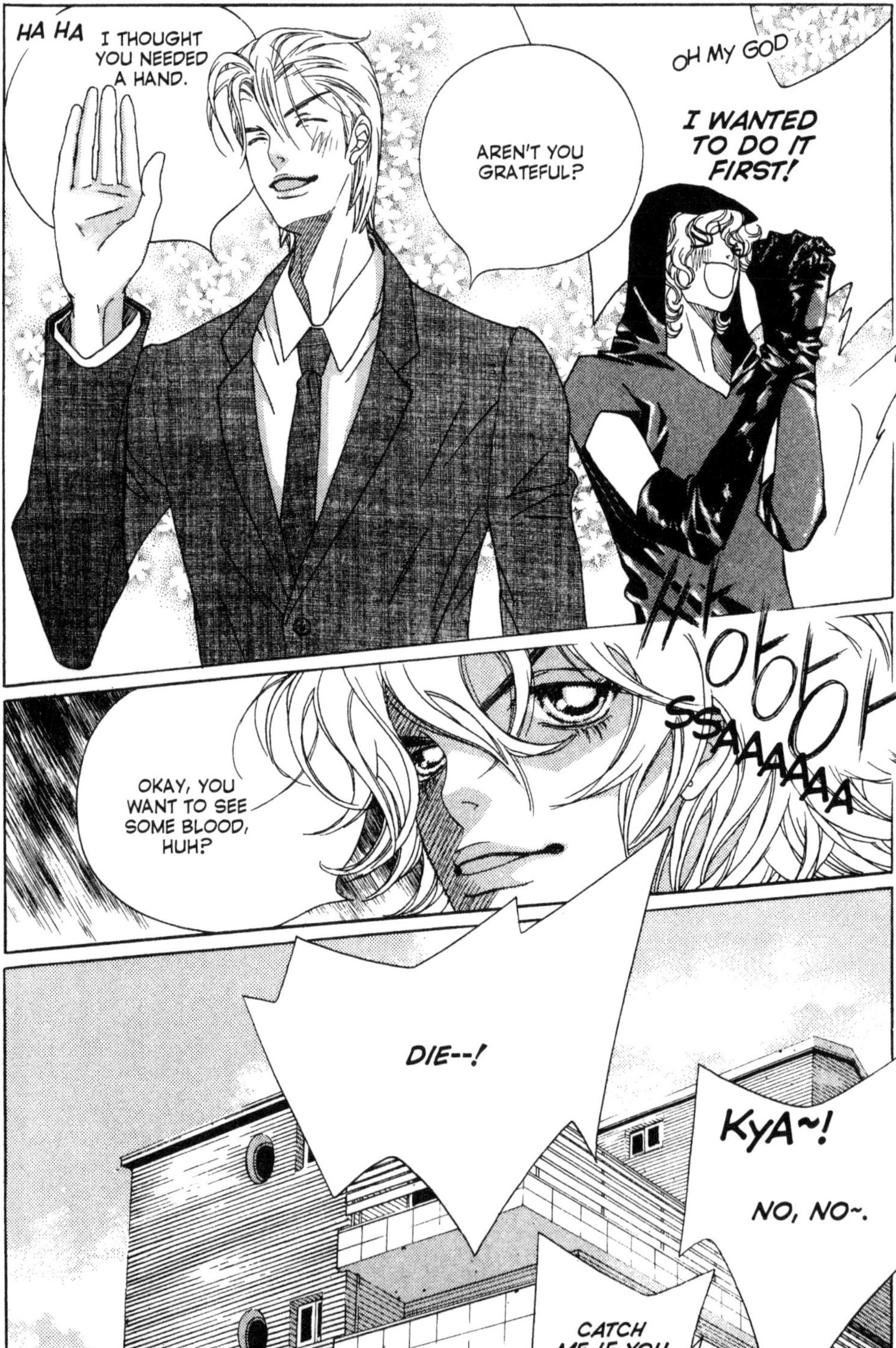
HA HA
I THOUGHT YOU NEEDED A HAND.
AREN'T YOU GRATEFUL?
OH MY GOD
I WANTED TO DO IT FIRST!
OKAY, YOU WANT TO SEE SOME BLOOD, HUH?
SSAAAAAAA
DIE--!
KYA~!
NO, NO~.
CATCH ME IF YOU CAN--.

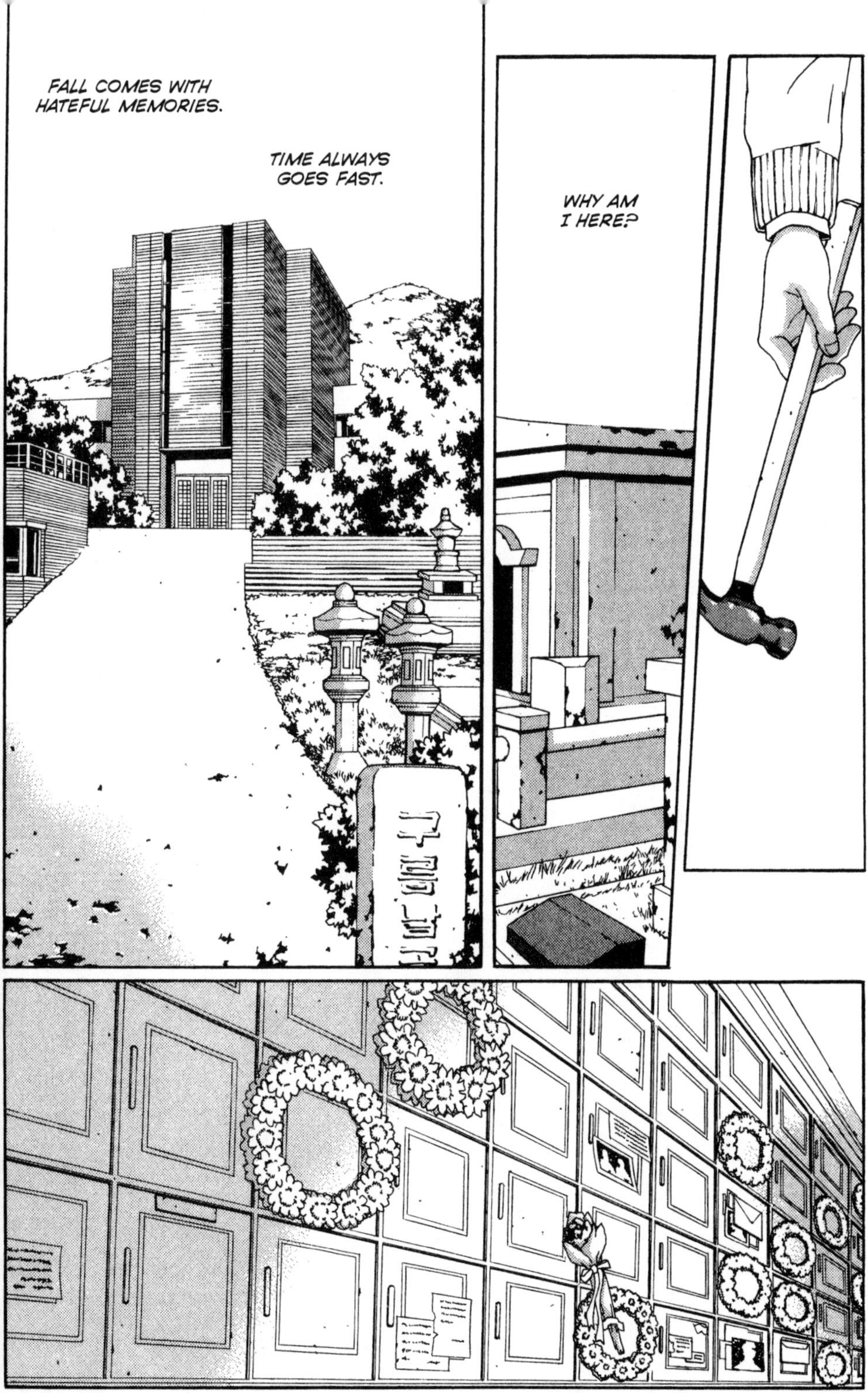
FALL COMES WITH HATEFUL MEMORIES.
TIME ALWAYS GOES FAST.
WHY AM I HERE?

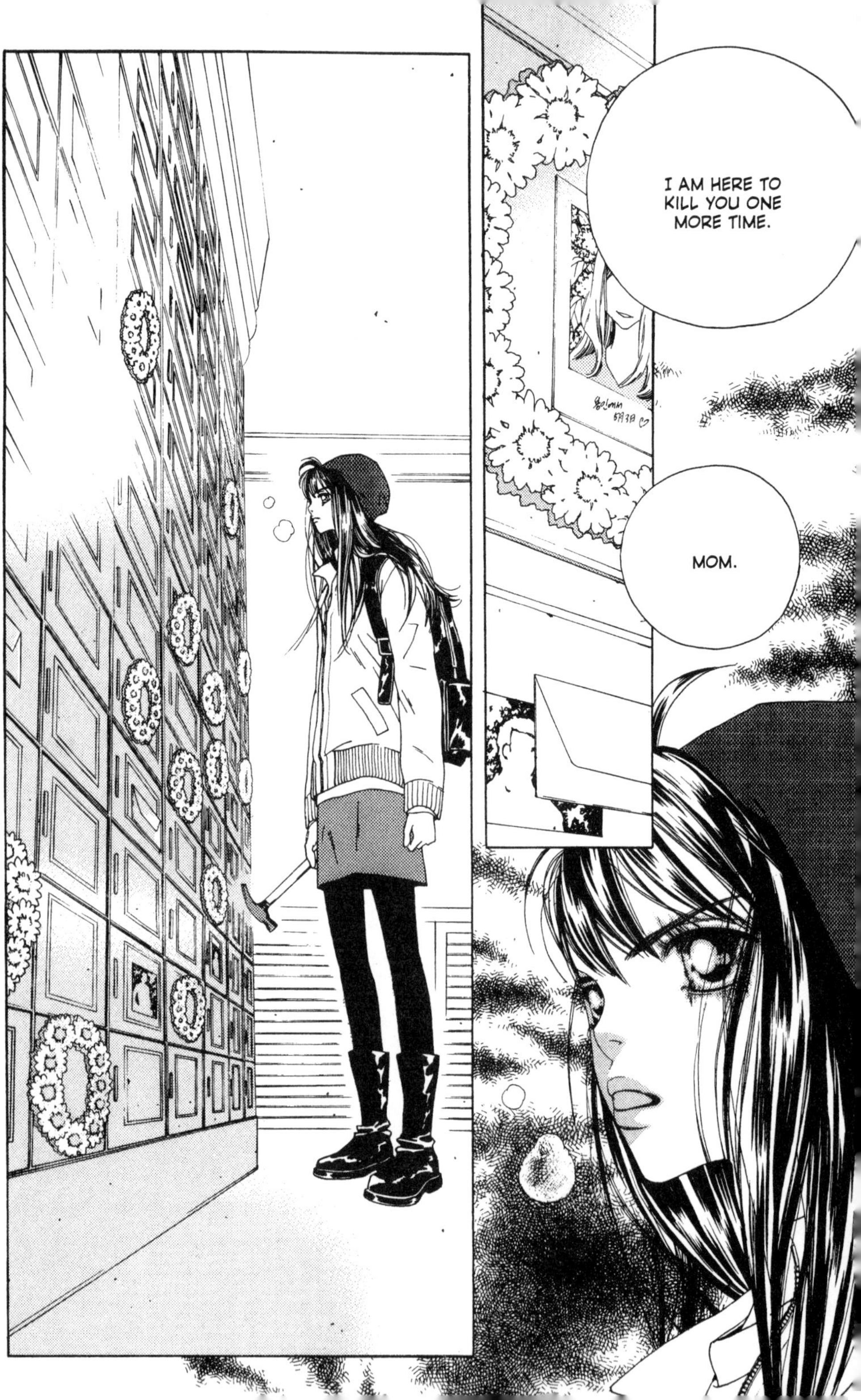
I AM HERE TO KILL YOU ONE MORE TIME.
MOM.

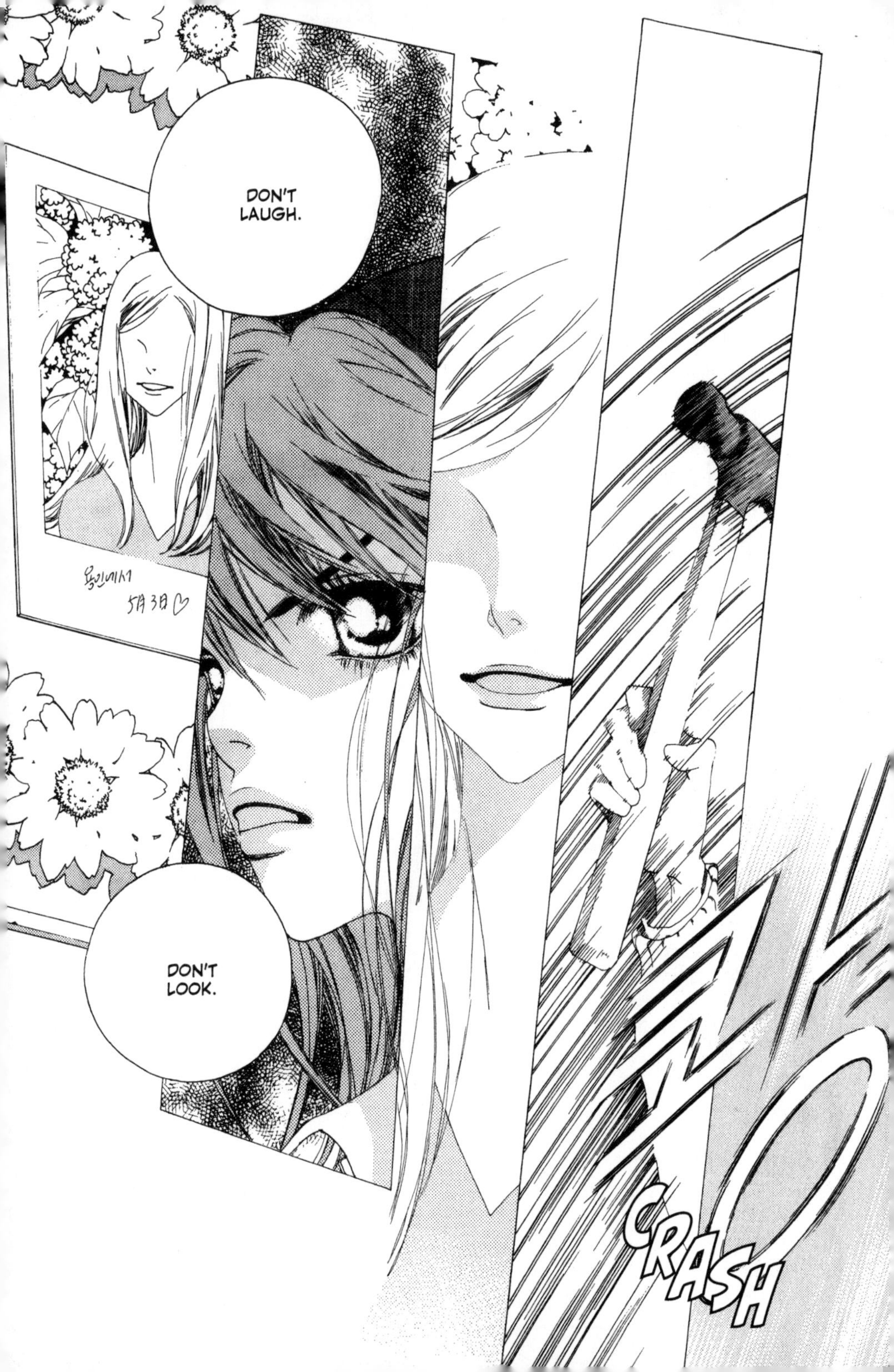
용인에서
5月 3日 ♡
DON'T LAUGH.
DON'T LOOK.
CRASH

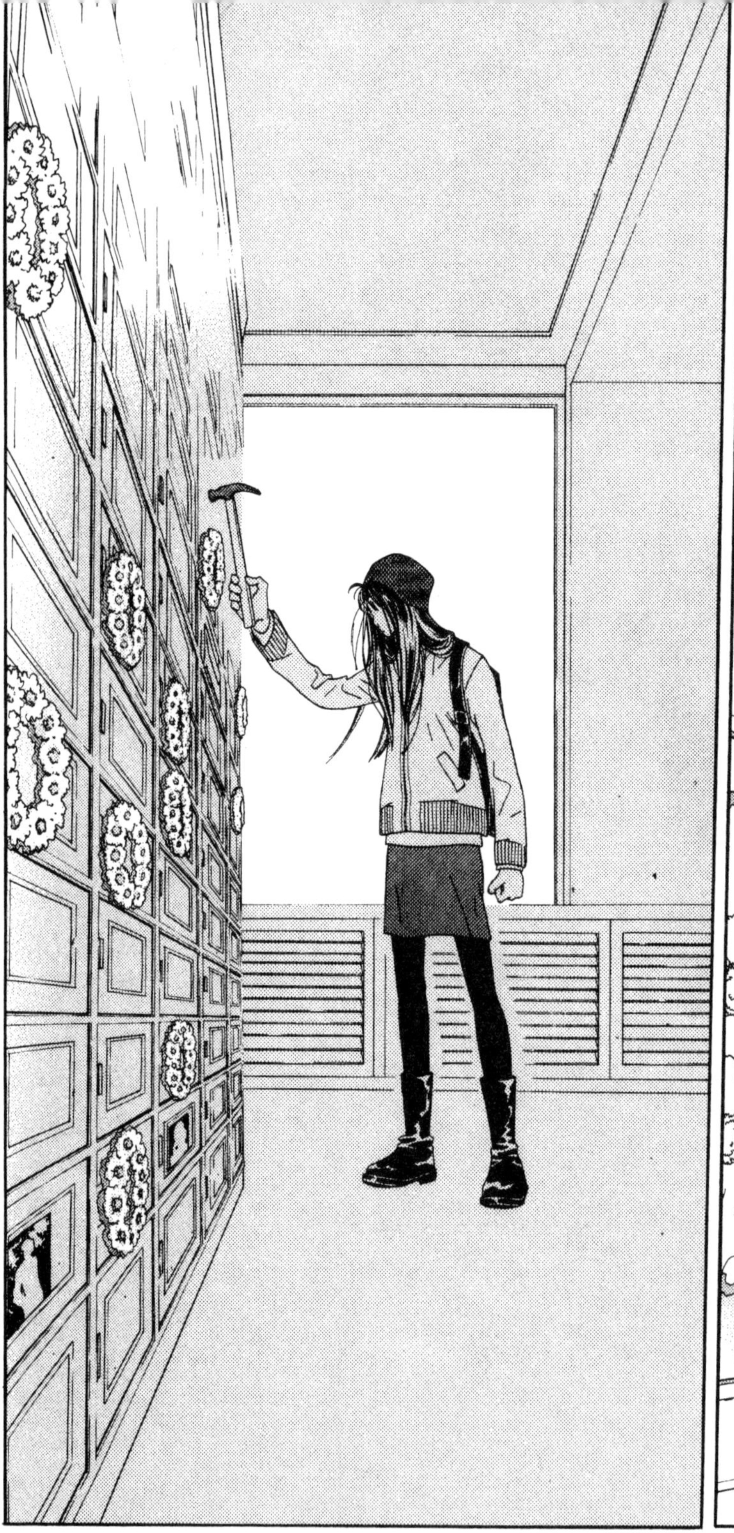
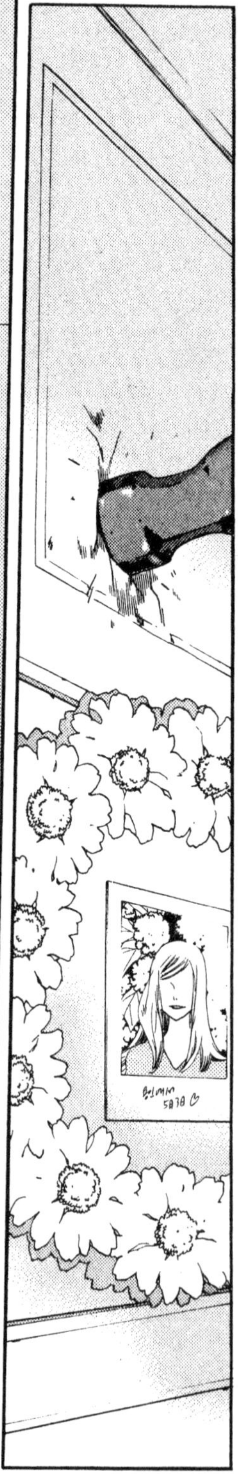

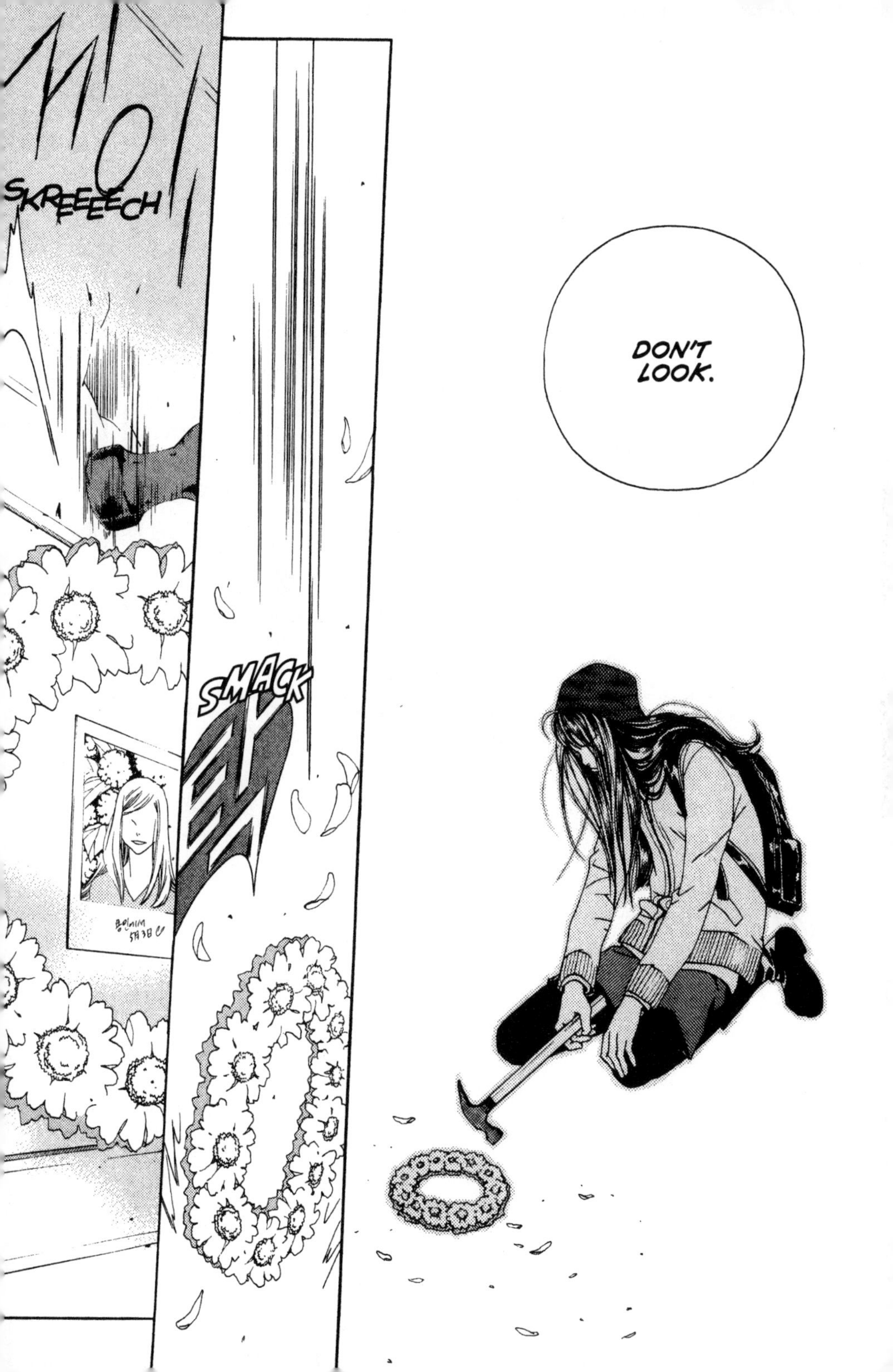
SKREEEECH
SMACK
DON'T LOOK.

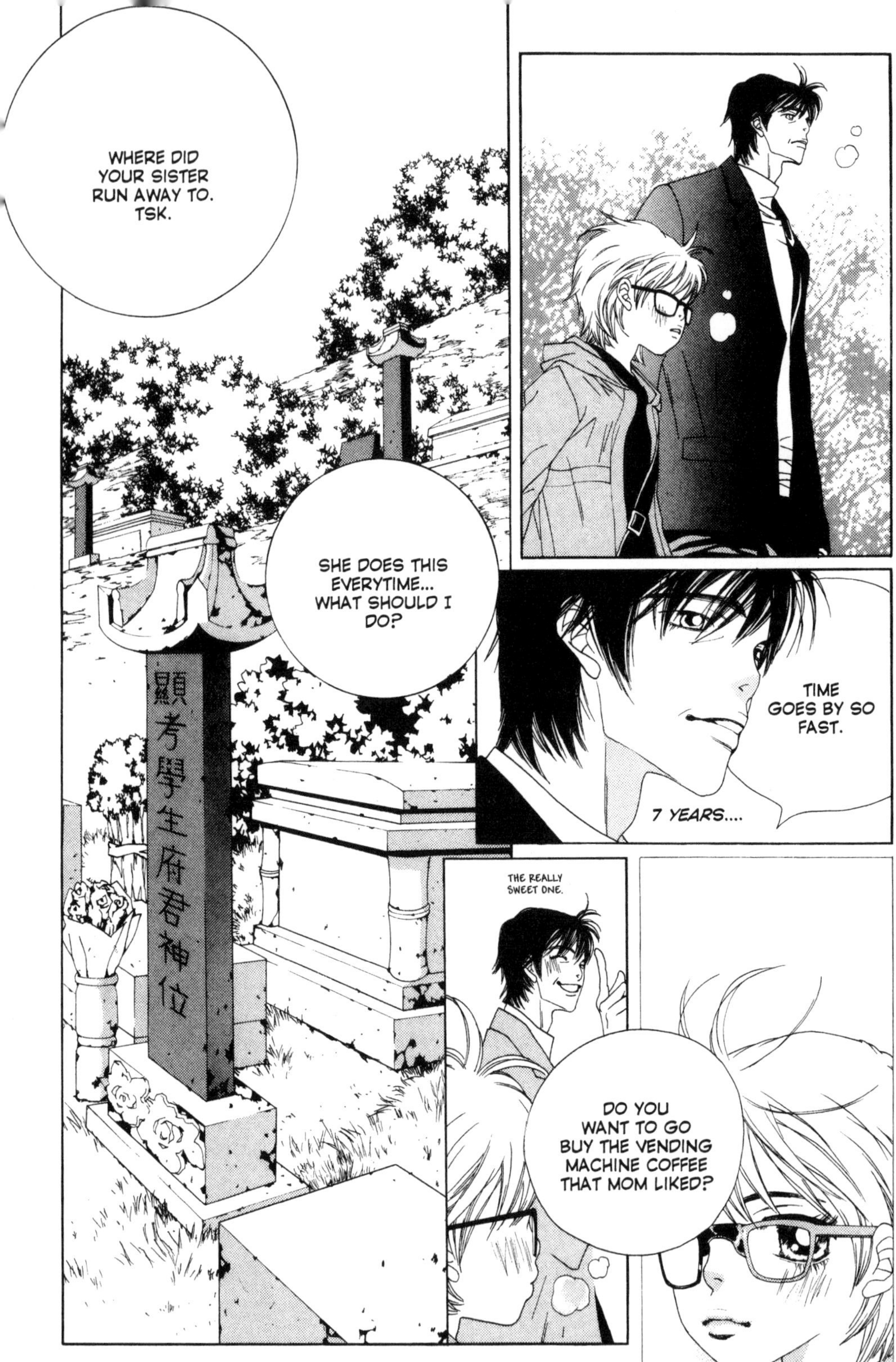
WHERE DID YOUR SISTER RUN AWAY TO. TSK.
顯考學生府君神位
SHE DOES THIS EVERYTIME... WHAT SHOULD I DO?
TIME GOES BY SO FAST.
7 YEARS....
THE REALLY SWEET ONE.
DO YOU WANT TO GO BUY THE VENDING MACHINE COFFEE THAT MOM LIKED?

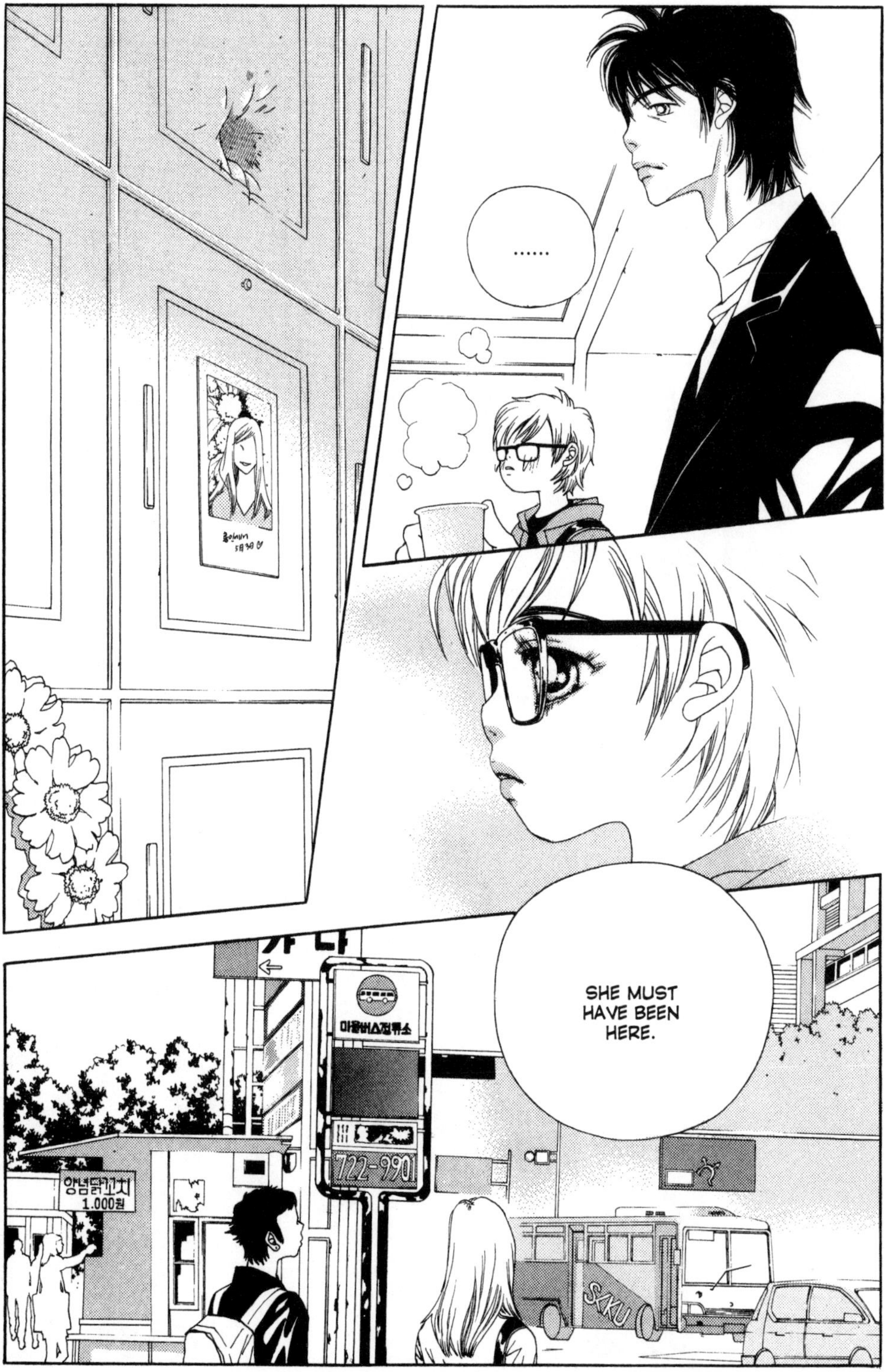
......
마을버스정류소
722-9901
양념닭꼬치
1.000원
SKKU
SHE MUST HAVE BEEN HERE.

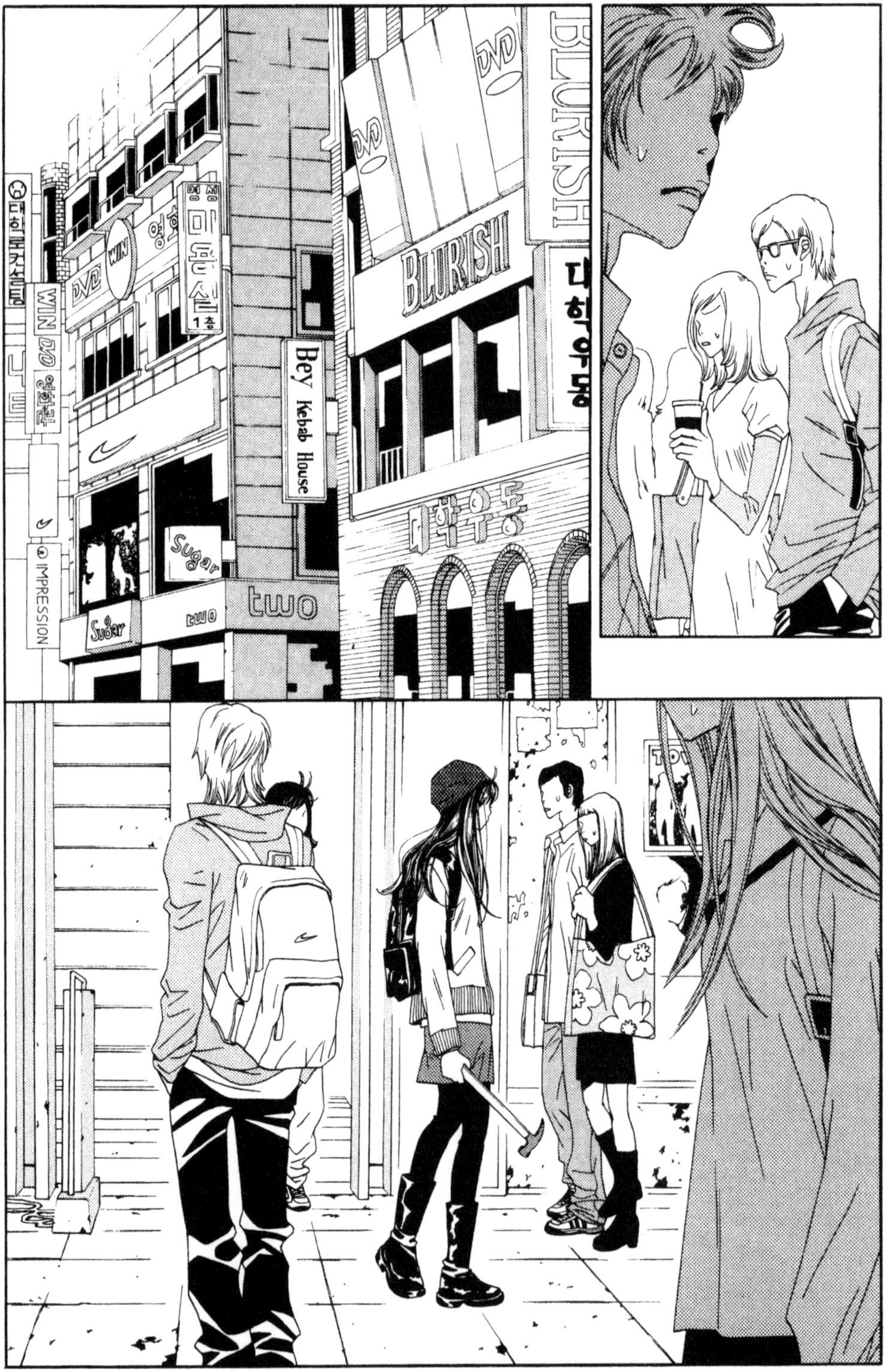
대학로컨설팅
WIN DVD 영화관
IMPRESSION
DVD WIN
미용실 1층
Sugar
two
Bey Kebab House
DVD
BLURISH
대학우동

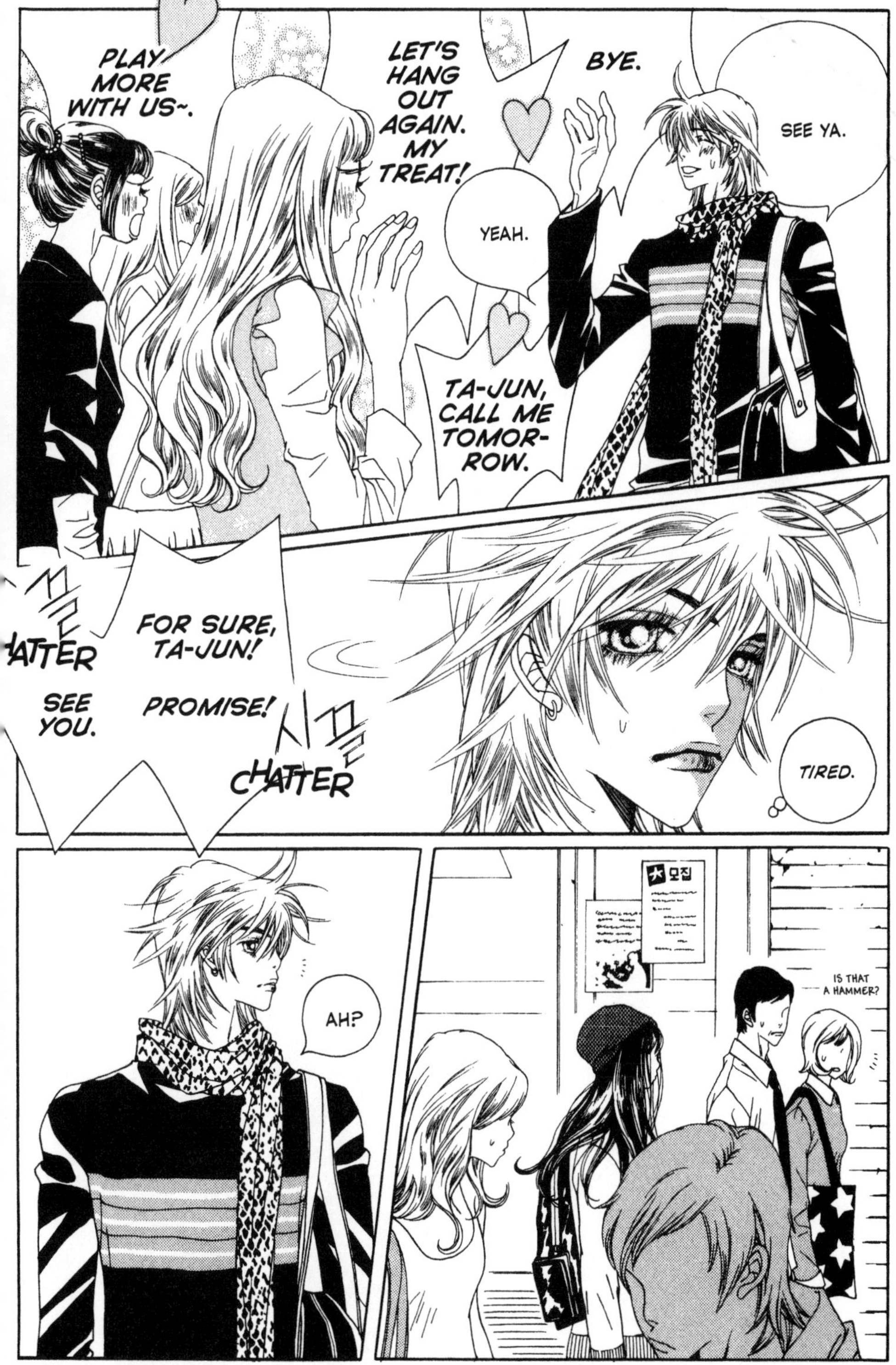
PLAY MORE WITH US~.
LET'S HANG OUT AGAIN. MY TREAT!
YEAH.
BYE.
SEE YA.
TA-JUN, CALL ME TOMORROW.
HATTER
FOR SURE, TA-JUN!
SEE YOU.
PROMISE!
시끌
CHATTER
TIRED.
AH?
모집
IS THAT A HAMMER?

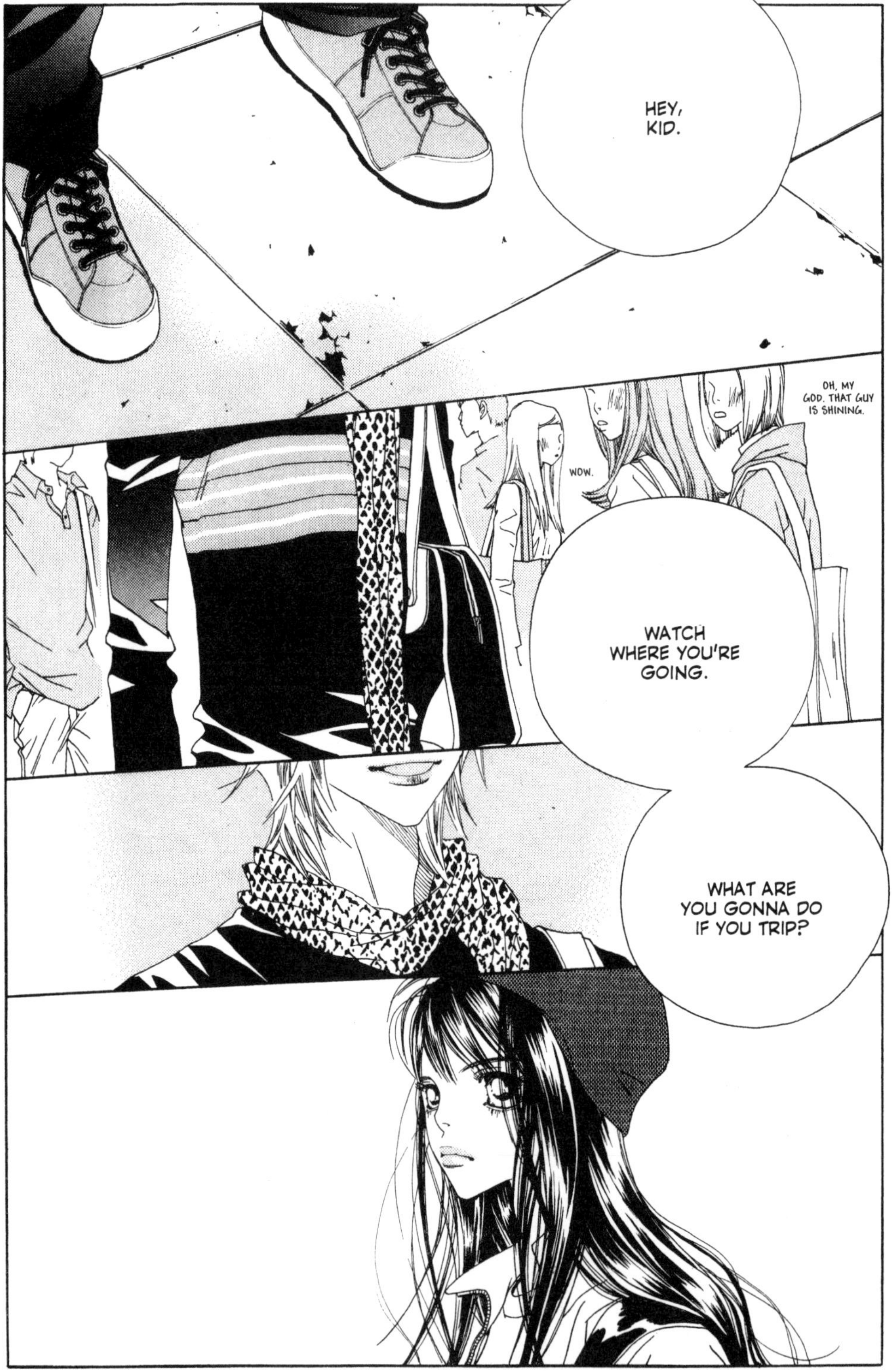
HEY, KID.
WOW.
OH, MY GOD. THAT GUY IS SHINING.
WATCH WHERE YOU'RE GOING.
WHAT ARE YOU GONNA DO IF YOU TRIP?

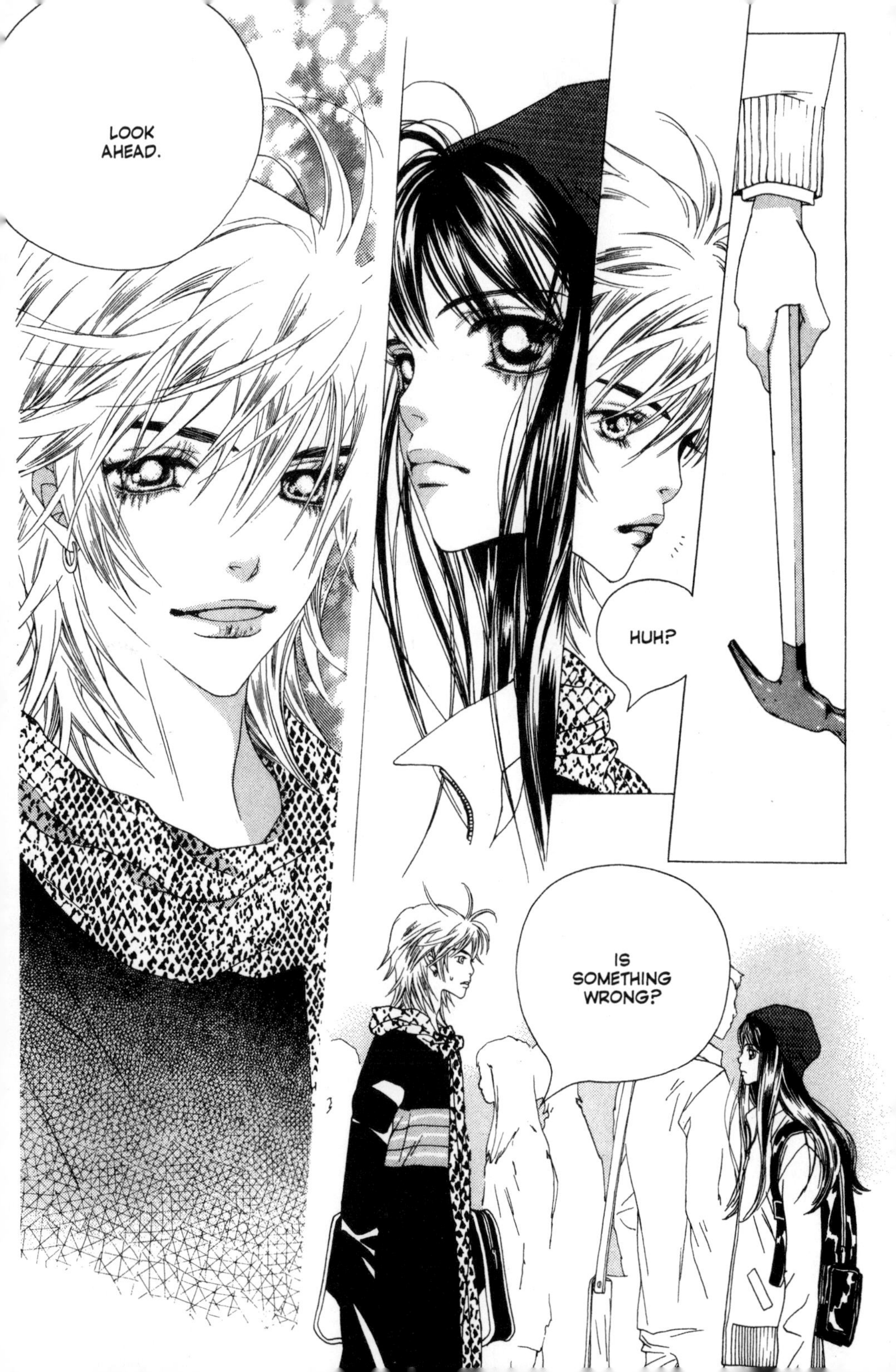

LOOK AHEAD.
HUH?
IS SOMETHING WRONG?

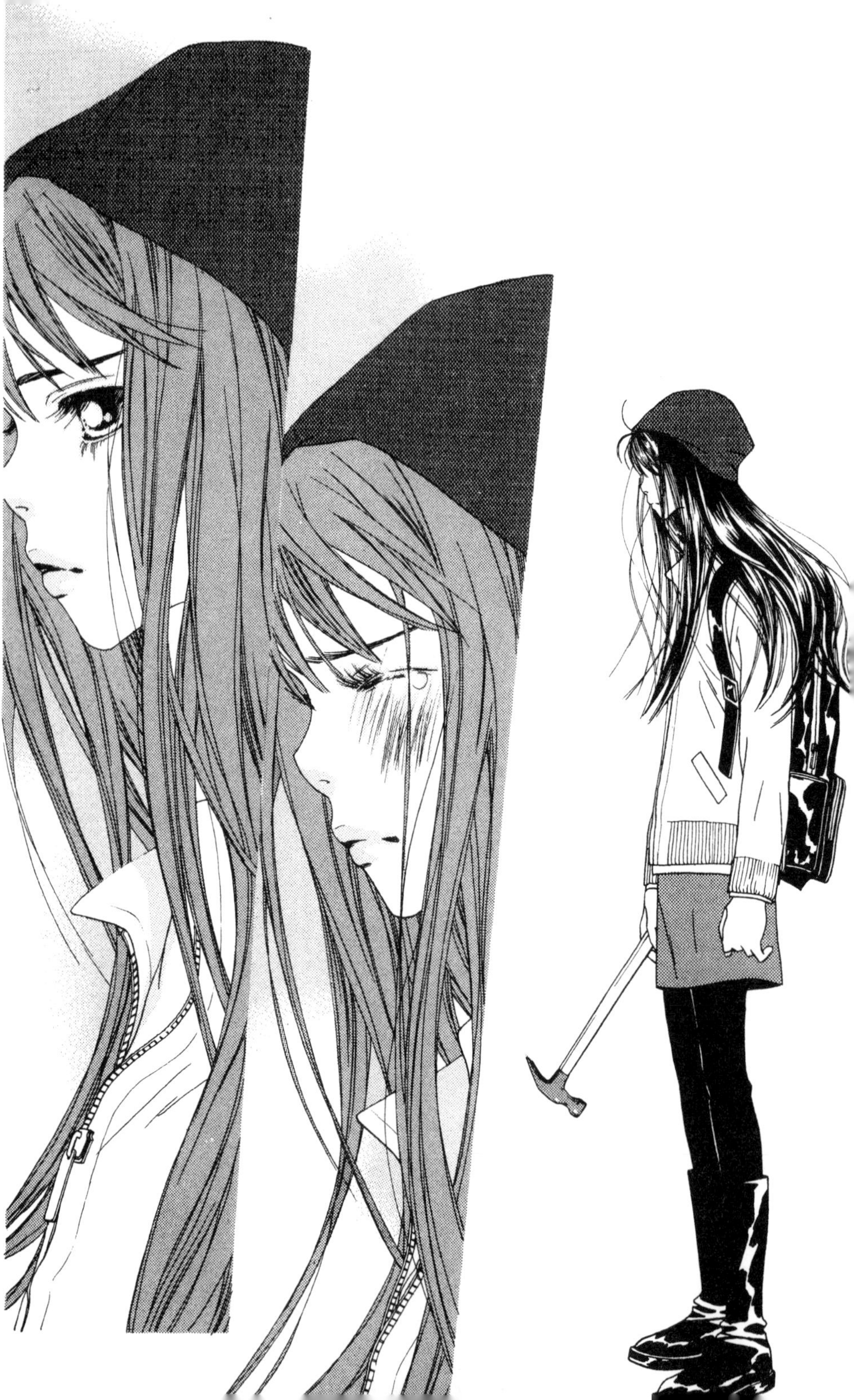

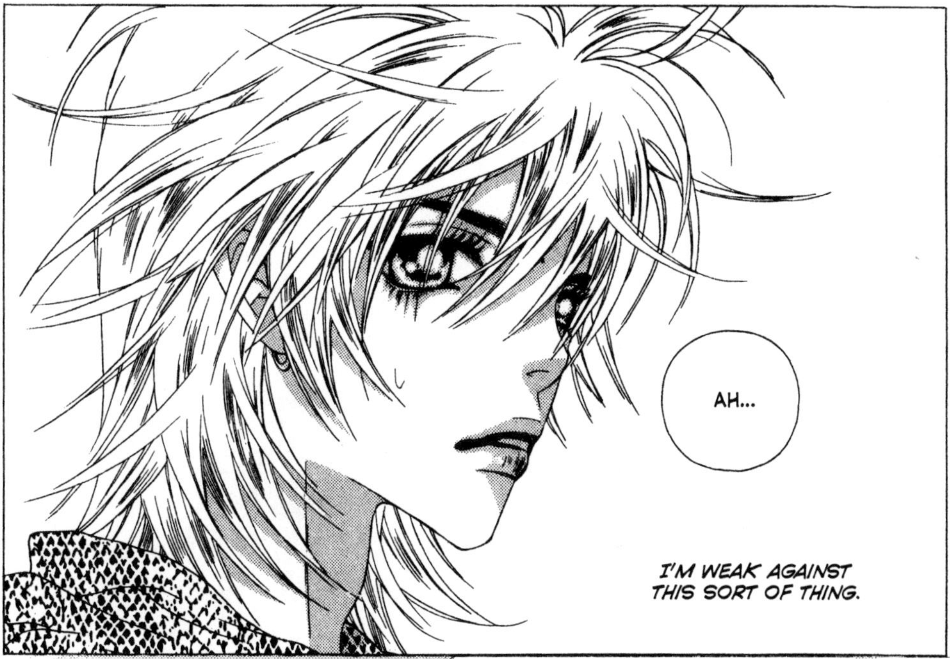
AH...
I'M WEAK AGAINST THIS SORT OF THING.
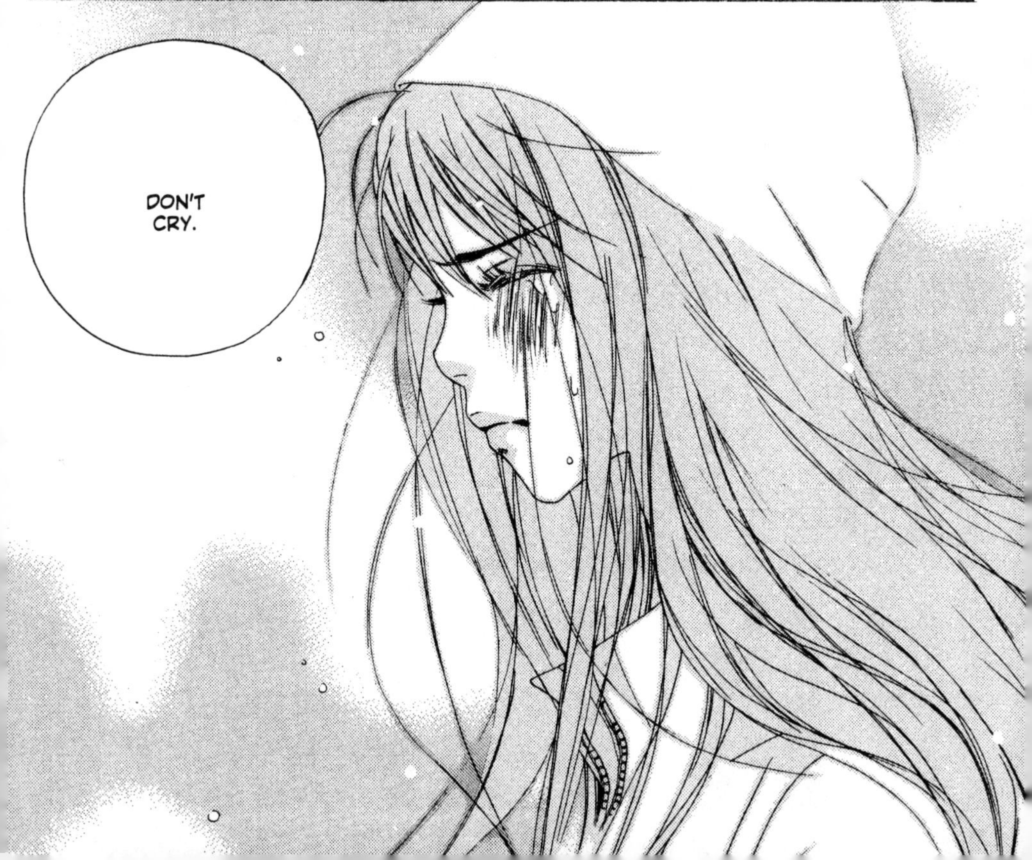
DON'T CRY.

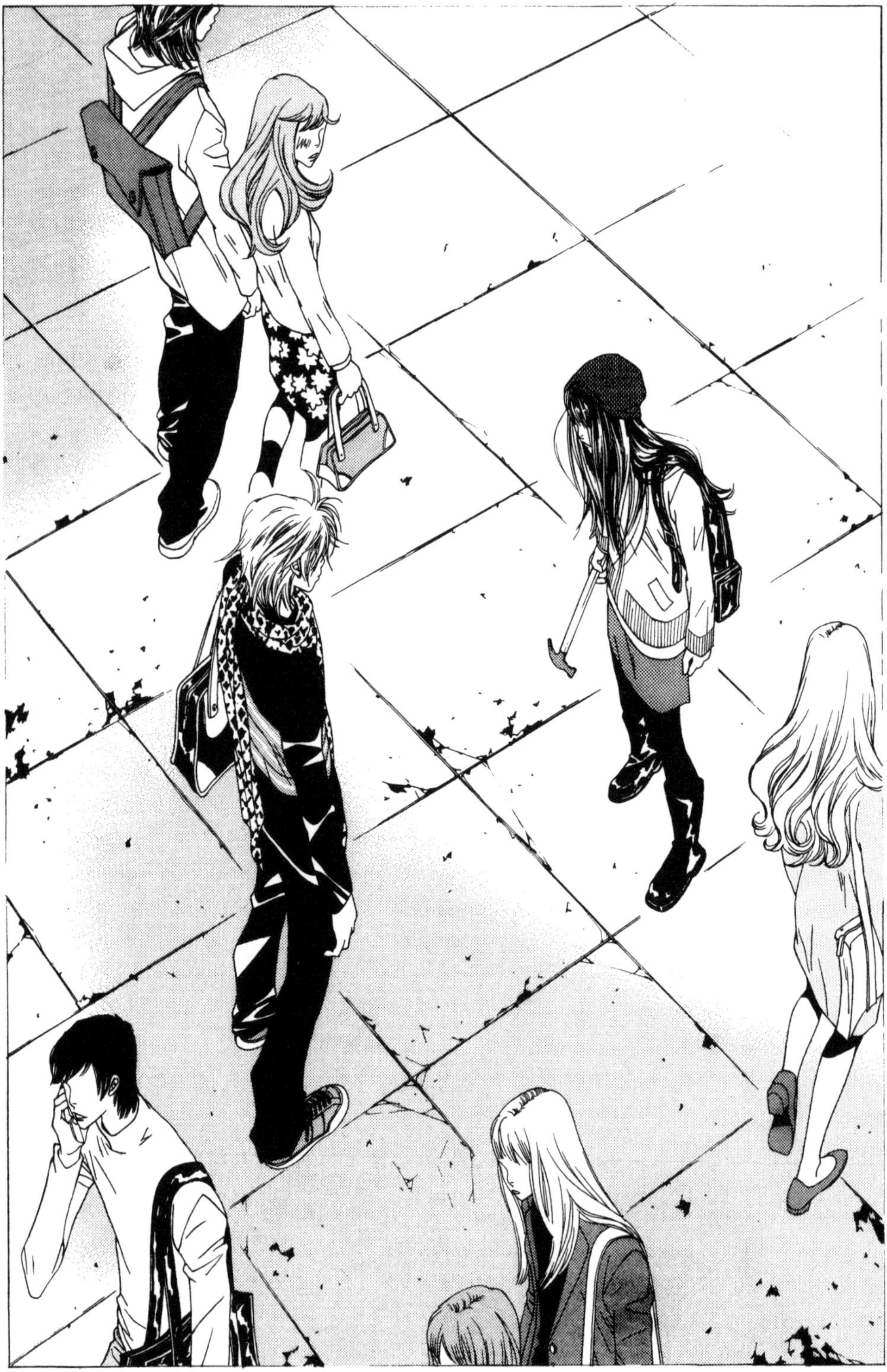

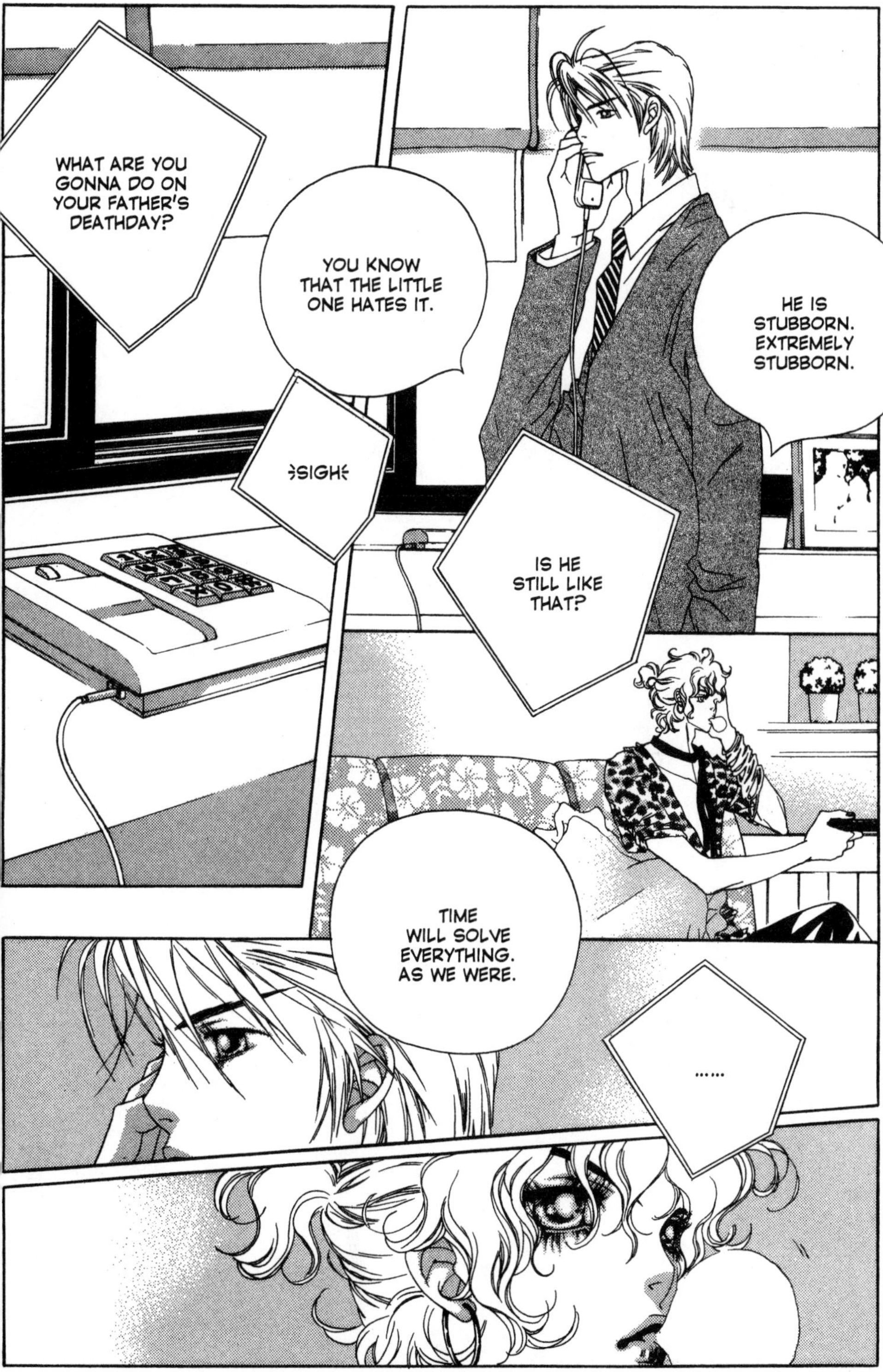
WHAT ARE YOU GONNA DO ON YOUR FATHER'S DEATHDAY?
YOU KNOW THAT THE LITTLE ONE HATES IT.
HE IS STUBBORN. EXTREMELY STUBBORN.
SIGH
IS HE STILL LIKE THAT?
TIME WILL SOLVE EVERYTHING. AS WE WERE.
......

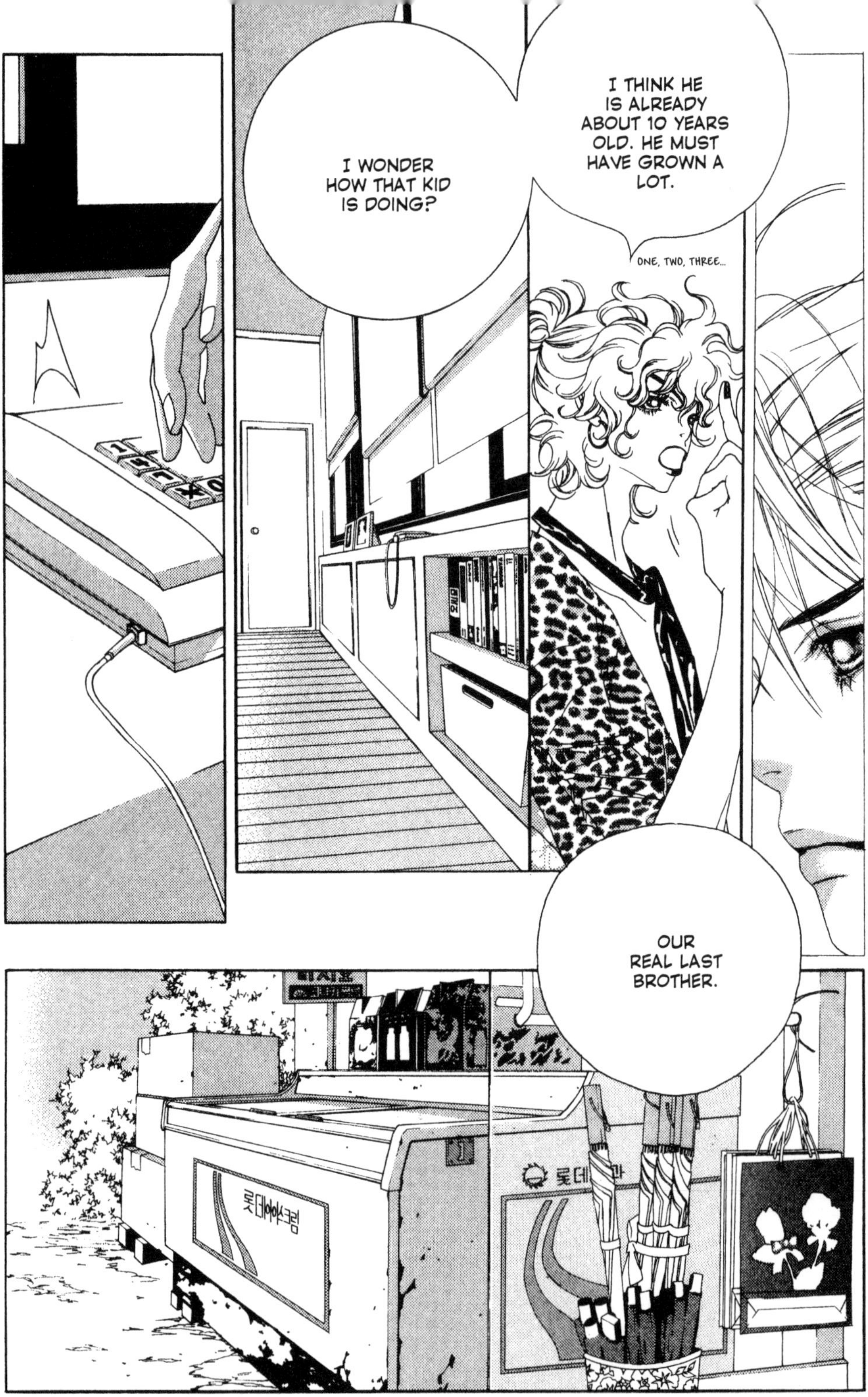
I WONDER HOW THAT KID IS DOING?
I THINK HE IS ALREADY ABOUT 10 YEARS OLD. HE MUST HAVE GROWN A LOT.
ONE, TWO, THREE...
OUR REAL LAST BROTHER.
롯데아이스크림

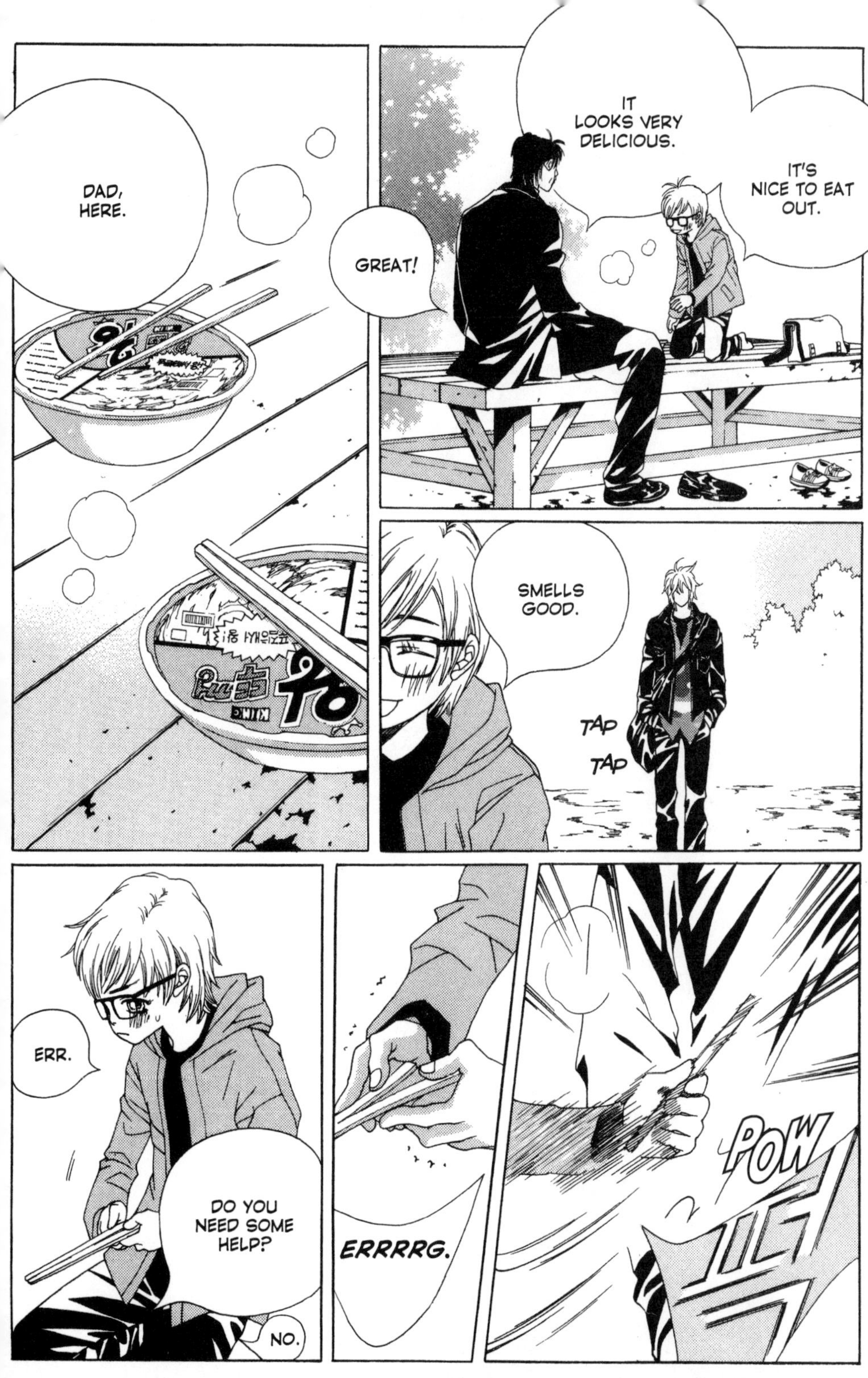
DAD, HERE.
GREAT!
IT LOOKS VERY DELICIOUS.
IT'S NICE TO EAT OUT.
SMELLS GOOD.
TAP
TAP
ERR.
DO YOU NEED SOME HELP?
NO.
ERRRRG.
POW

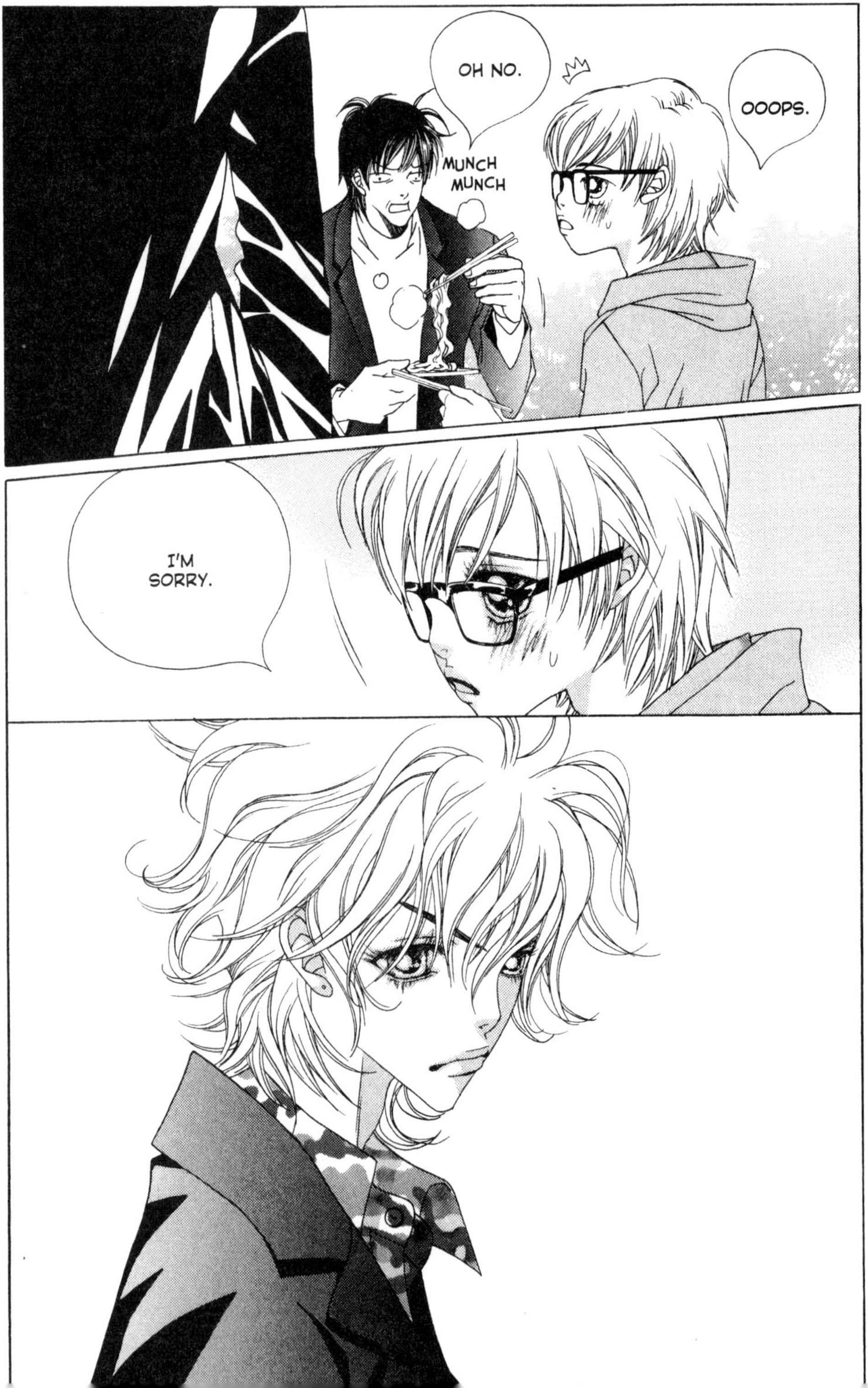
OH NO.
MUNCH MUNCH
OOOPS.
I'M SORRY.

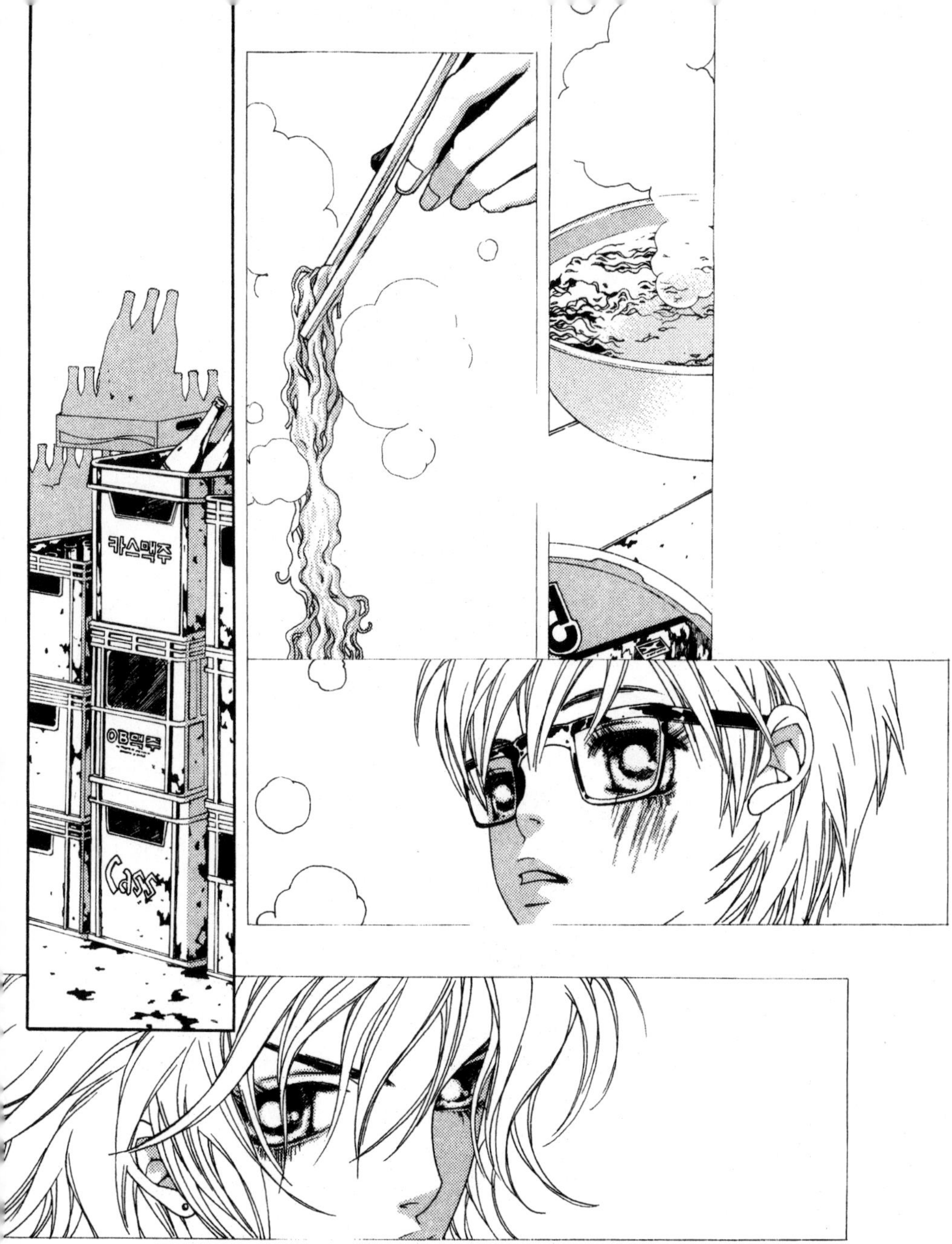
카스맥주
OB맥주
Cass

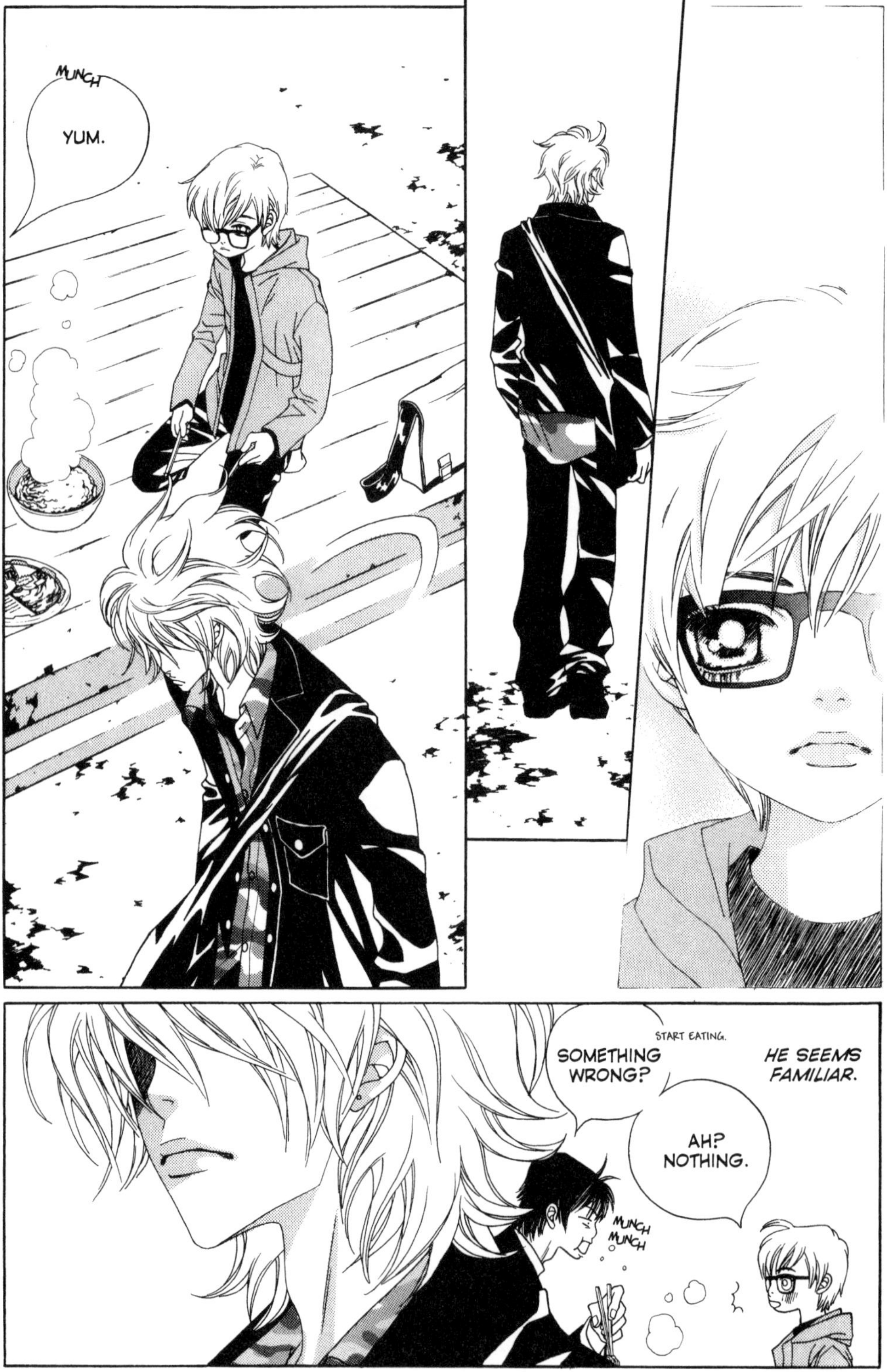
MUNCH
YUM.
SOMETHING WRONG?
START EATING.
HE SEEMS FAMILIAR.
AH? NOTHING.
MUNCH MUNCH

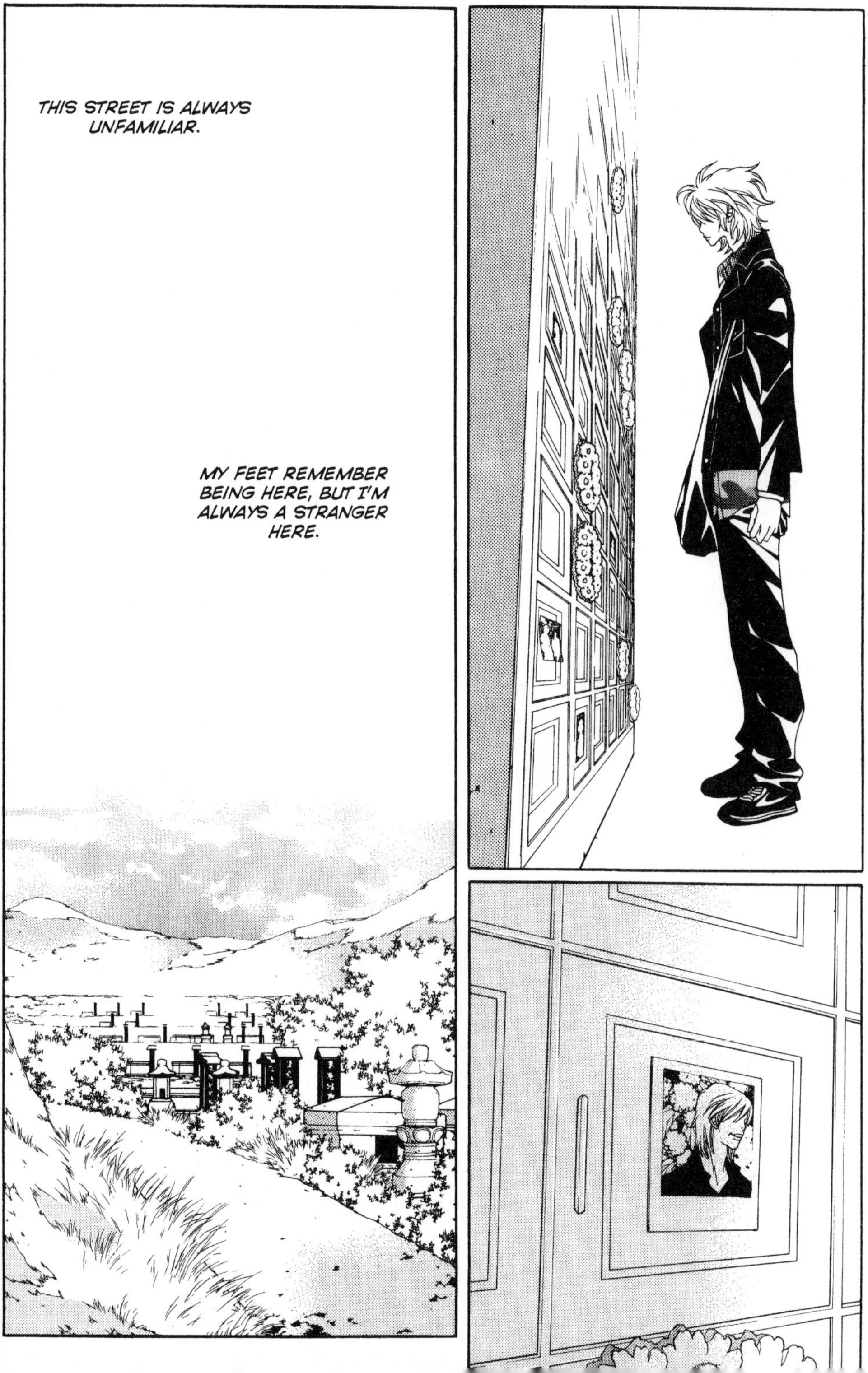
THIS STREET IS ALWAYS UNFAMILIAR.
MY FEET REMEMBER BEING HERE, BUT I'M ALWAYS A STRANGER HERE.

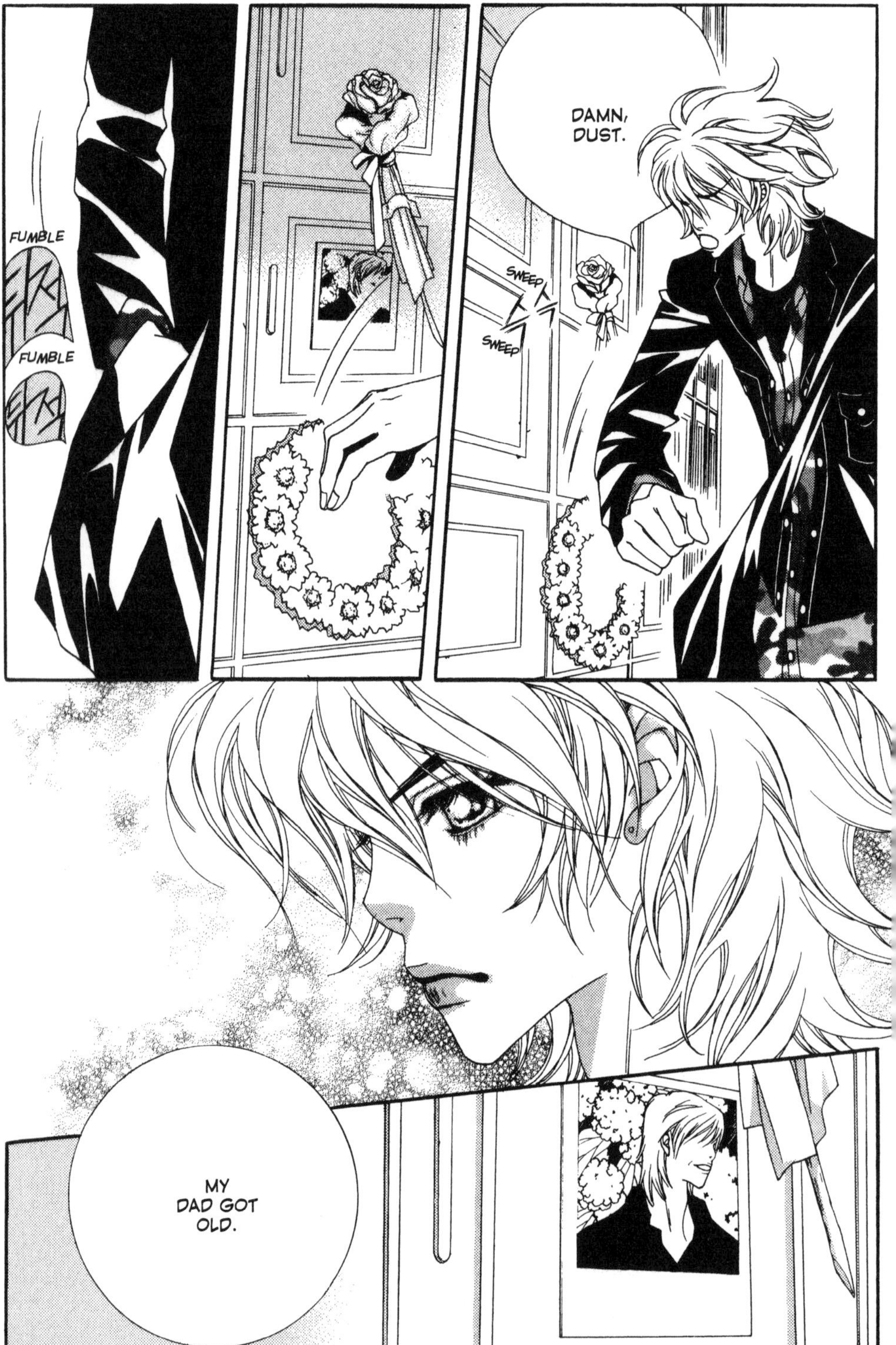
FUMBLE
FUMBLE
SWEEP
SWEEP
DAMN, DUST.
MY DAD GOT OLD.

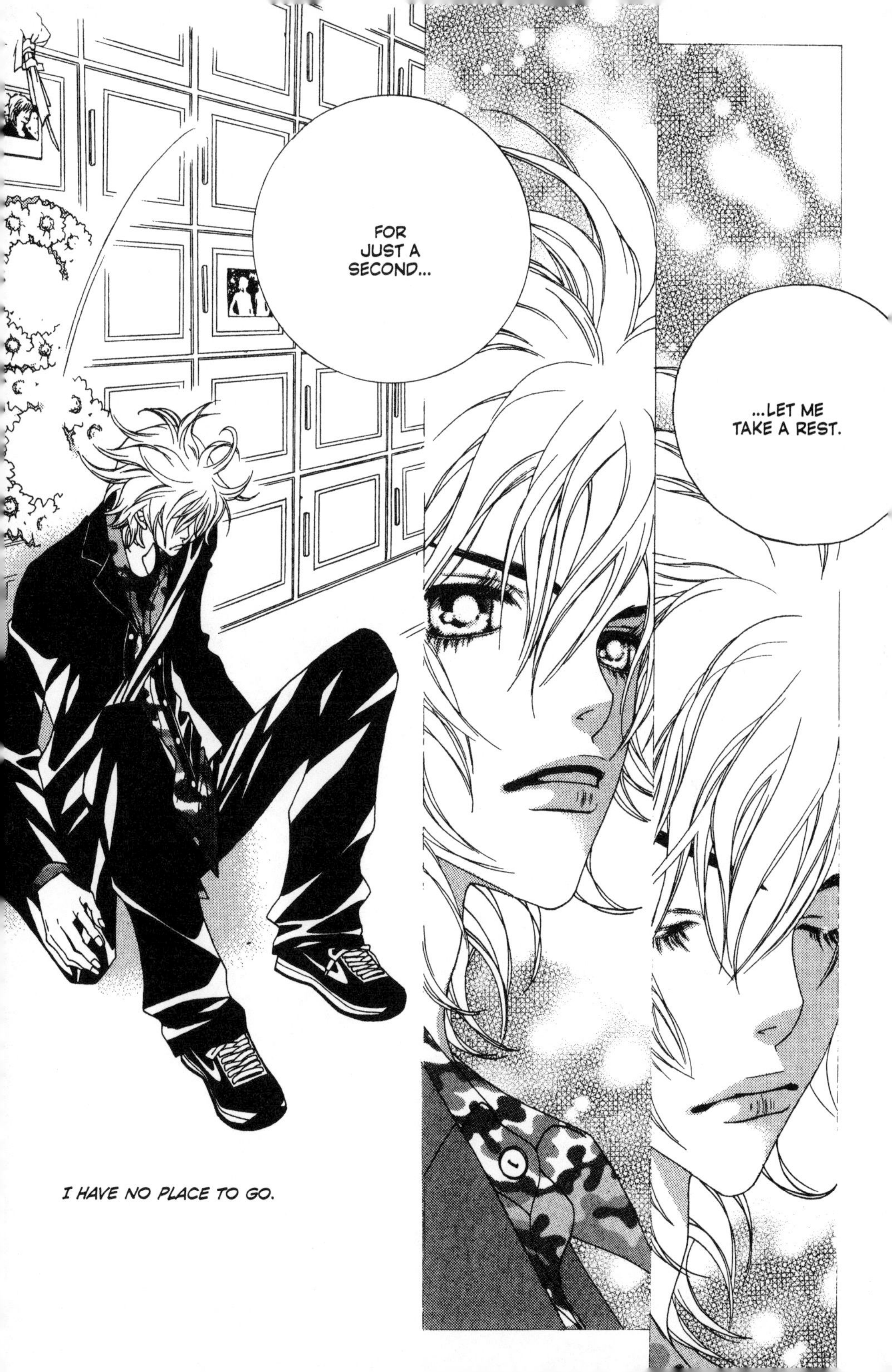
I HAVE NO PLACE TO GO.
FOR JUST A SECOND...
...LET ME TAKE A REST.

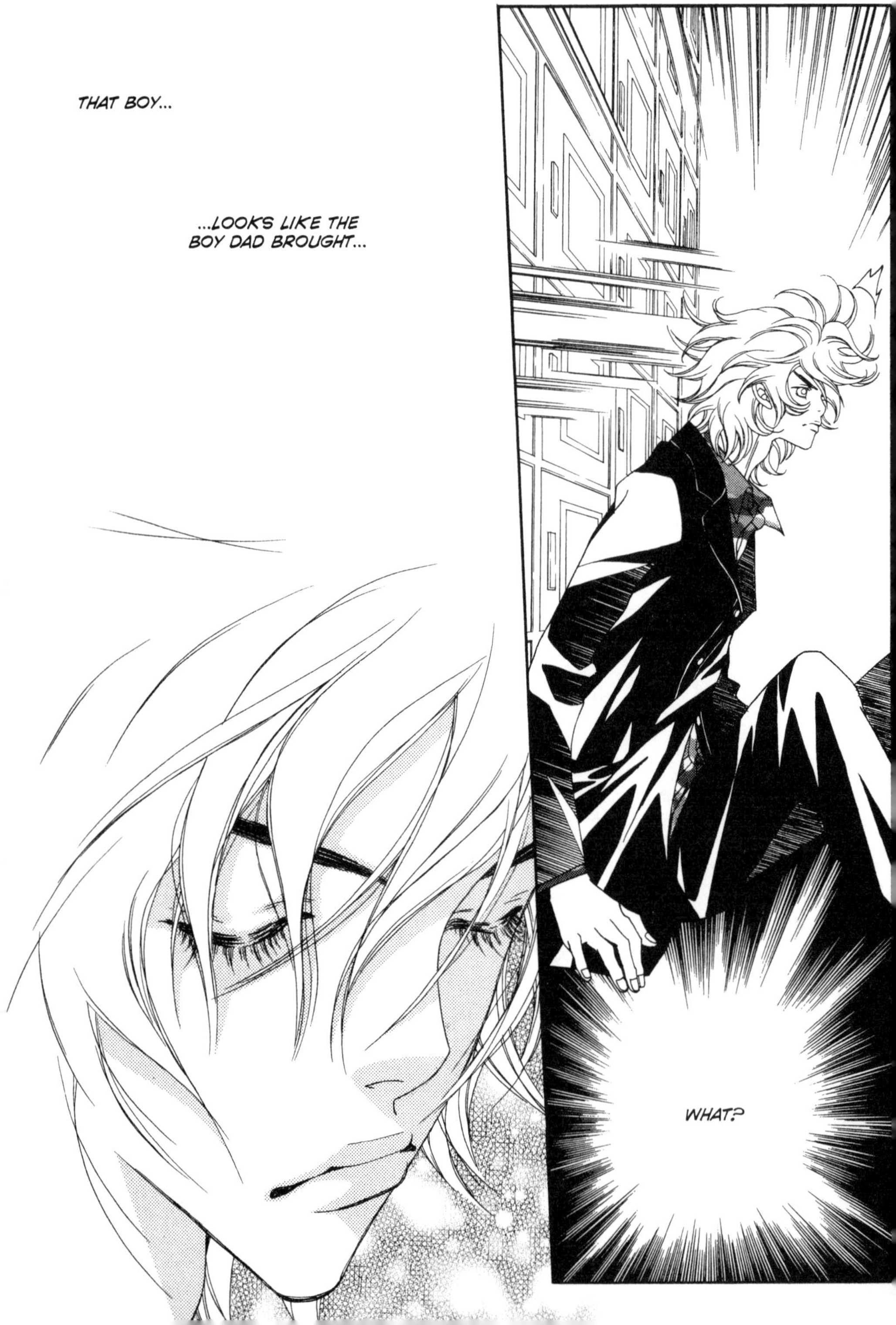
THAT BOY...
...LOOKS LIKE THE BOY DAD BROUGHT...
WHAT?

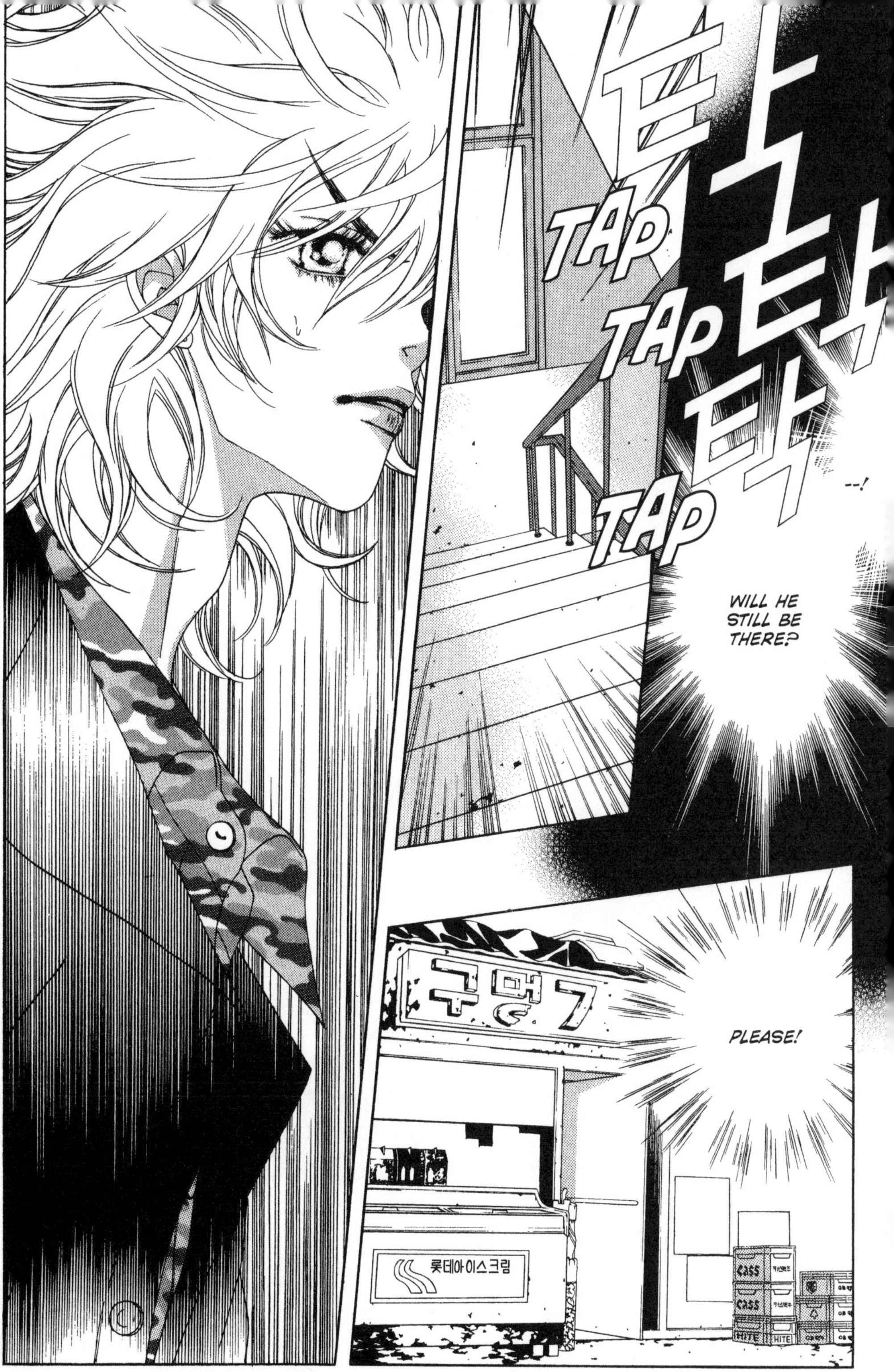
TAP
TAP
TAP
--!
WILL HE STILL BE THERE?
PLEASE!
롯데아이스크림

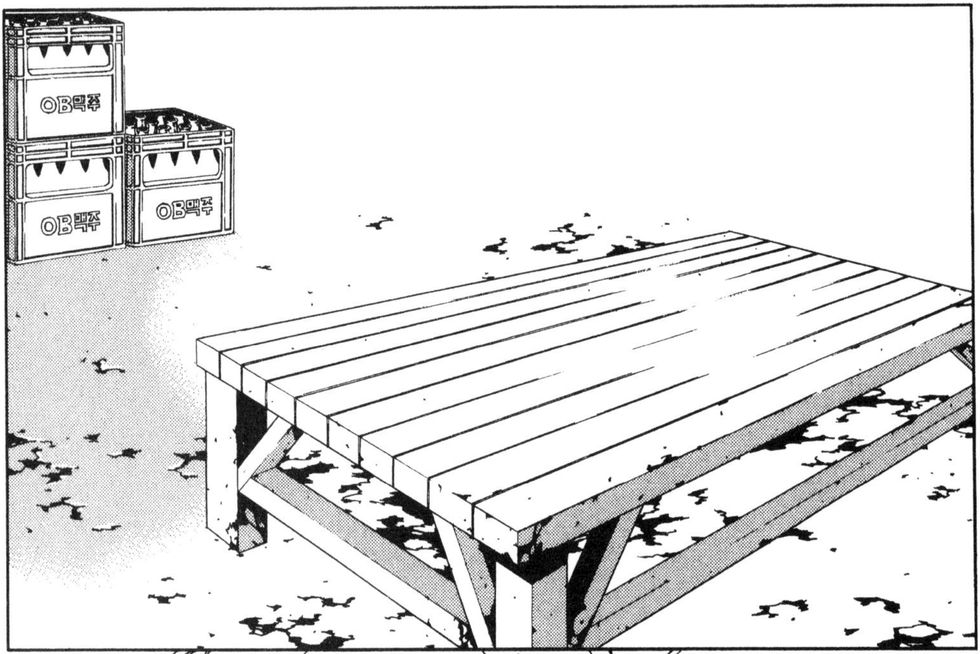
OB맥주
OB맥주
OB맥주

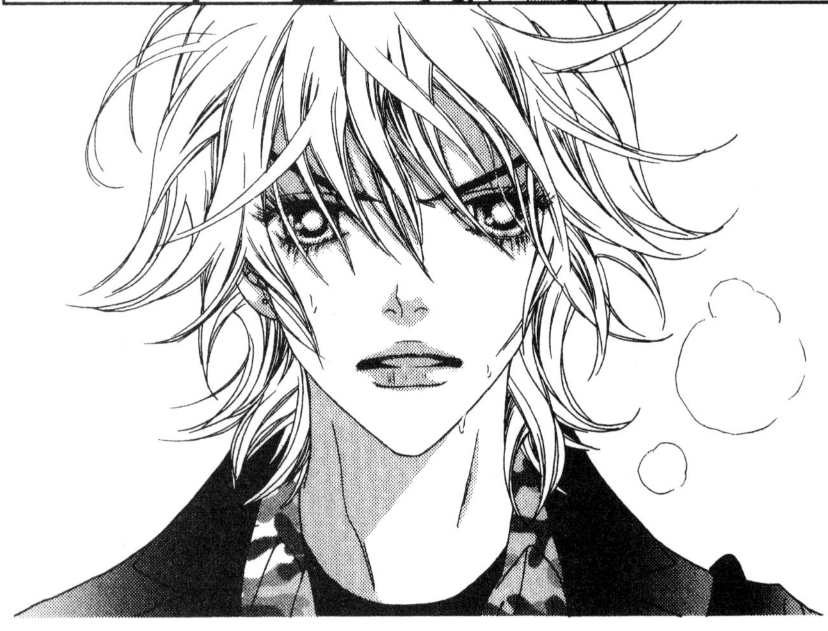
HE'S GONE...

TO BE CONTINUED IN **HISSING**, VOL. 2!

The Antique Gift Shop

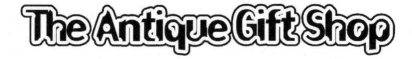

vol.2

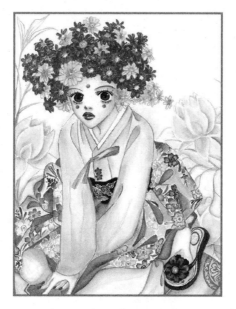

Lee Eun

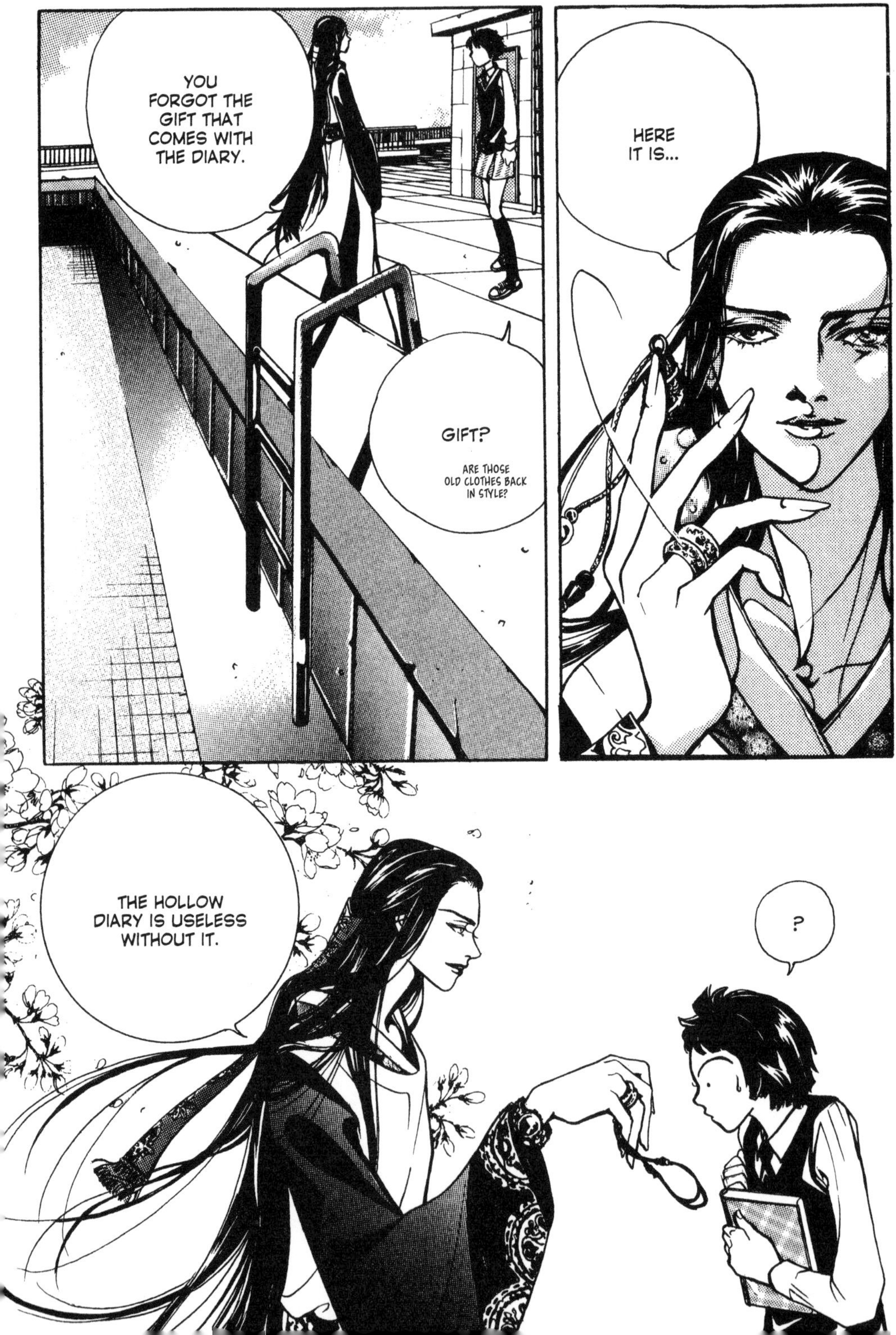
YOU FORGOT THE GIFT THAT COMES WITH THE DIARY.
GIFT?
ARE THOSE OLD CLOTHES BACK IN STYLE?
HERE IT IS...
THE HOLLOW DIARY IS USELESS WITHOUT IT.
?

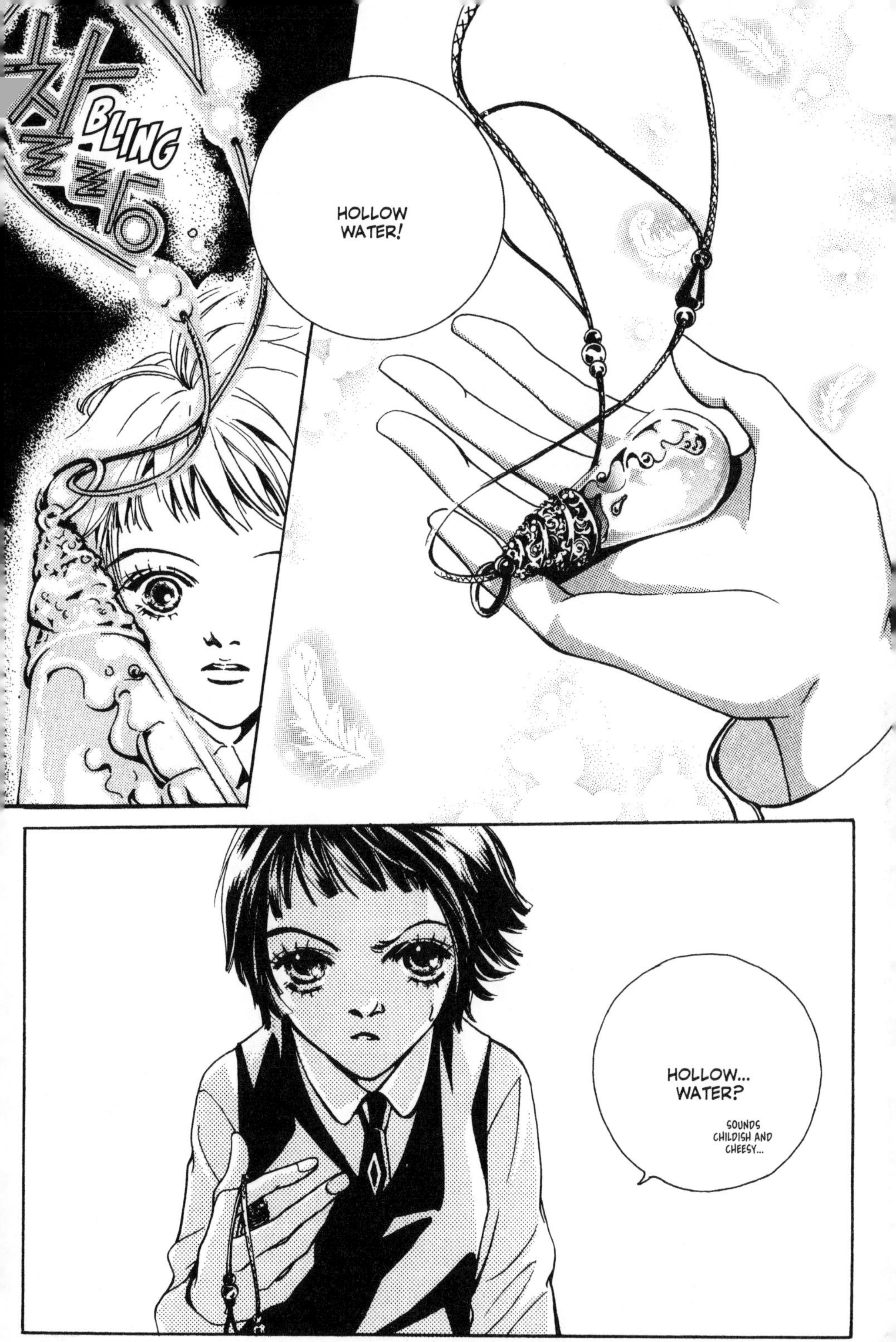
BLING
HOLLOW WATER!
HOLLOW... WATER?
SOUNDS CHILDISH AND CHEESY...

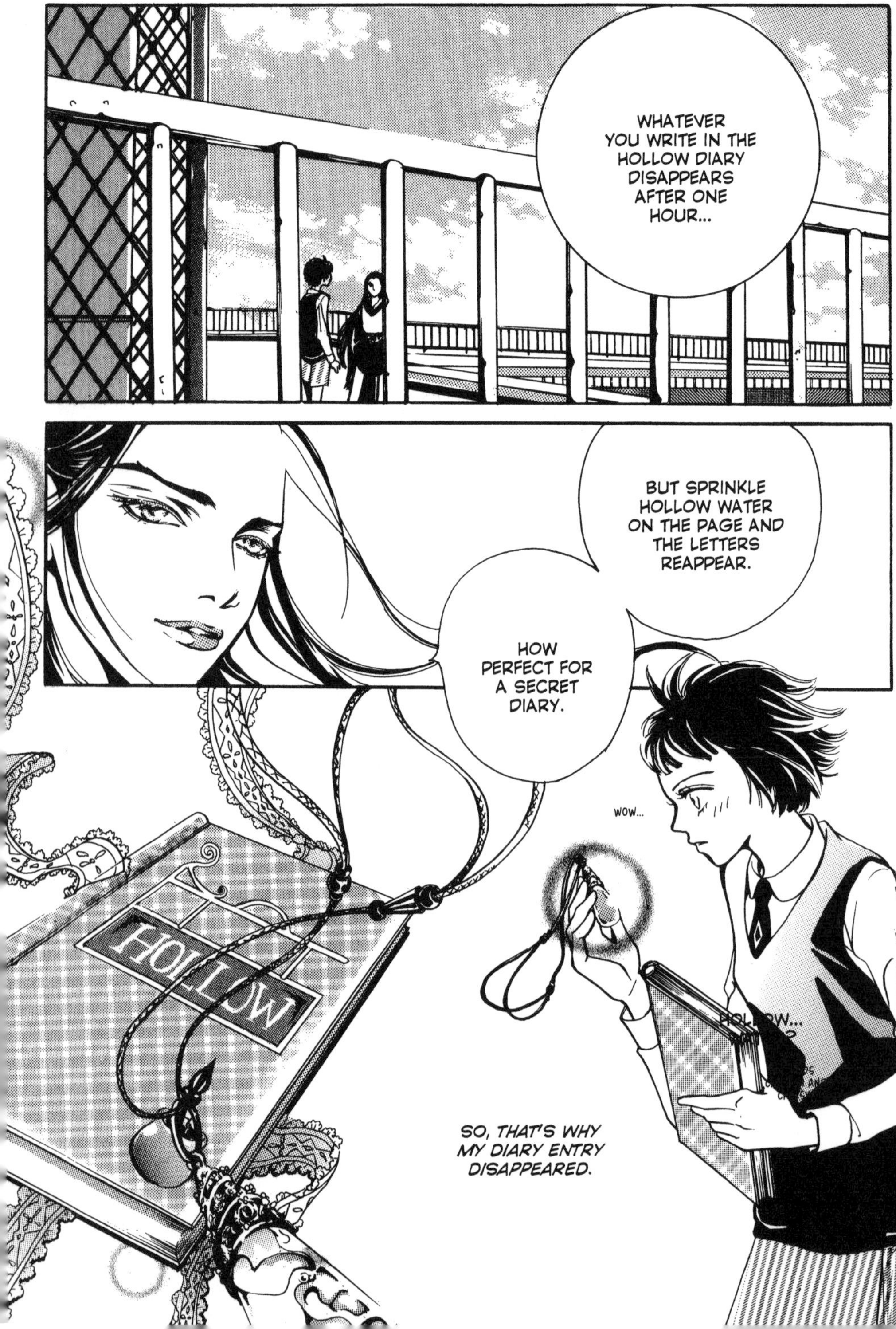
WHATEVER YOU WRITE IN THE HOLLOW DIARY DISAPPEARS AFTER ONE HOUR...
BUT SPRINKLE HOLLOW WATER ON THE PAGE AND THE LETTERS REAPPEAR.
HOW PERFECT FOR A SECRET DIARY.
HOLLOW
WOW...
SO, THAT'S WHY MY DIARY ENTRY DISAPPEARED.

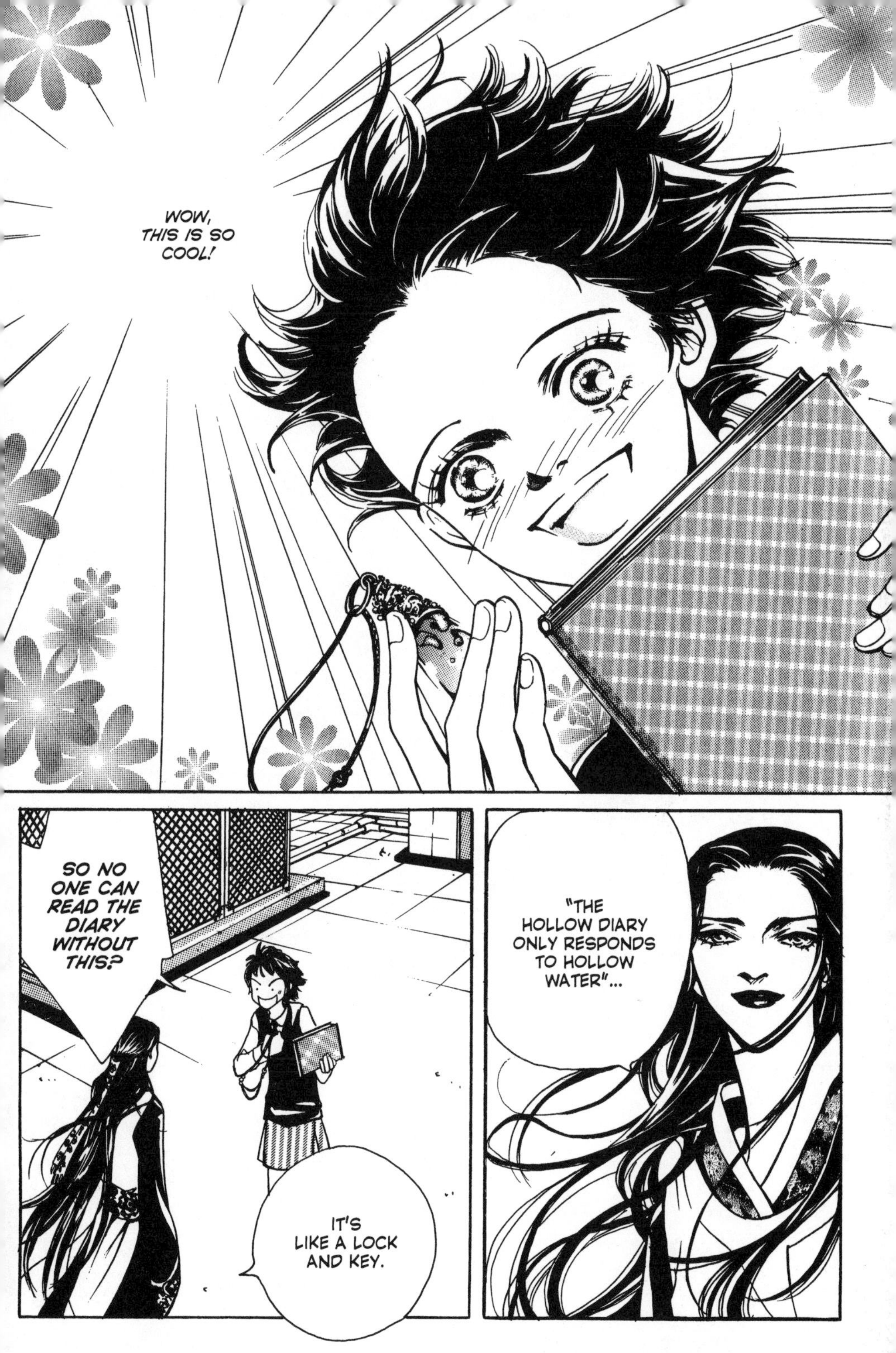
WOW, THIS IS SO COOL!
SO NO ONE CAN READ THE DIARY WITHOUT THIS?
IT'S LIKE A LOCK AND KEY.
"THE HOLLOW DIARY ONLY RESPONDS TO HOLLOW WATER"...

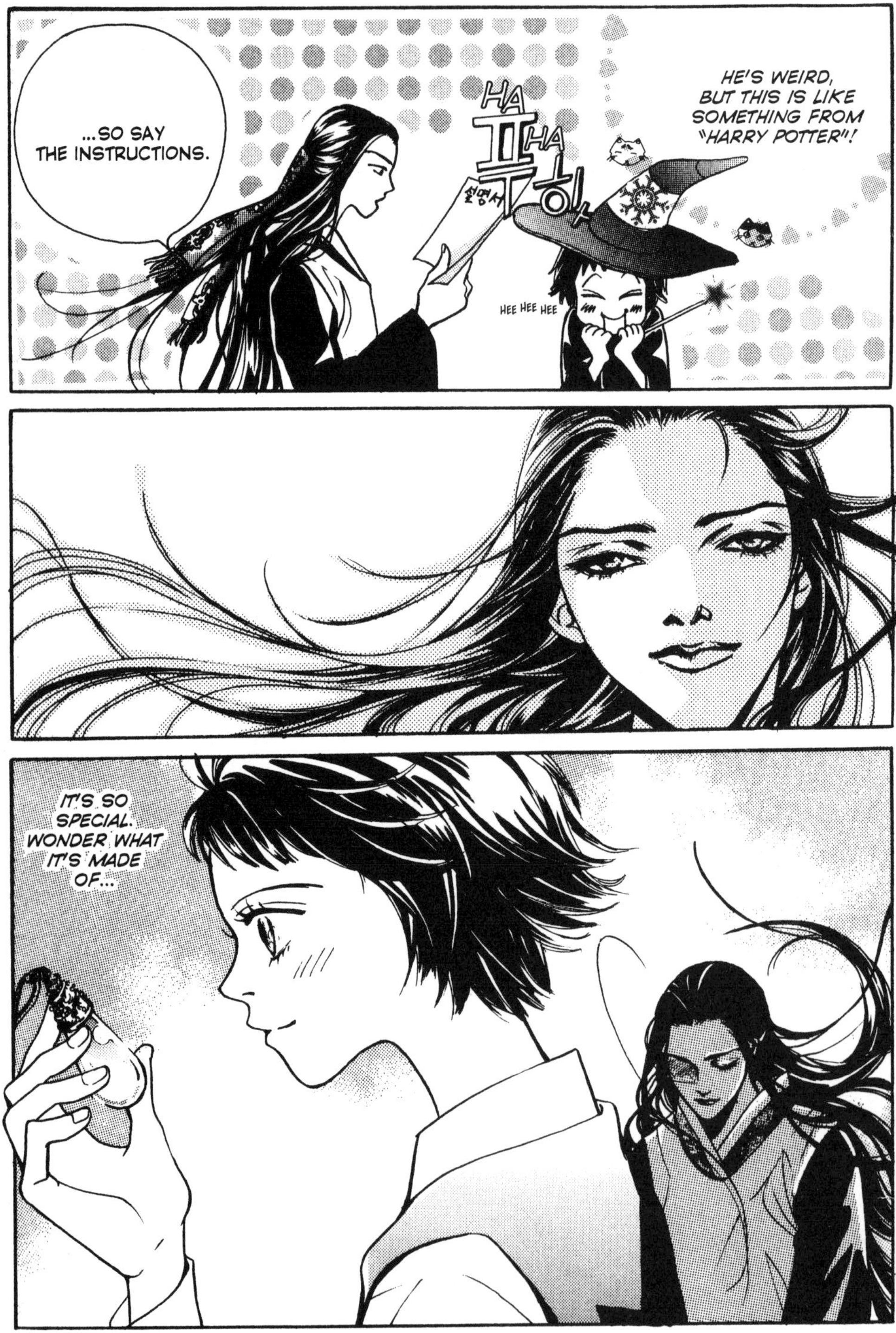
...SO SAY THE INSTRUCTIONS.
설명서
HA HA
HEE HEE HEE
HE'S WEIRD, BUT THIS IS LIKE SOMETHING FROM "HARRY POTTER"!
IT'S SO SPECIAL. WONDER WHAT IT'S MADE OF...

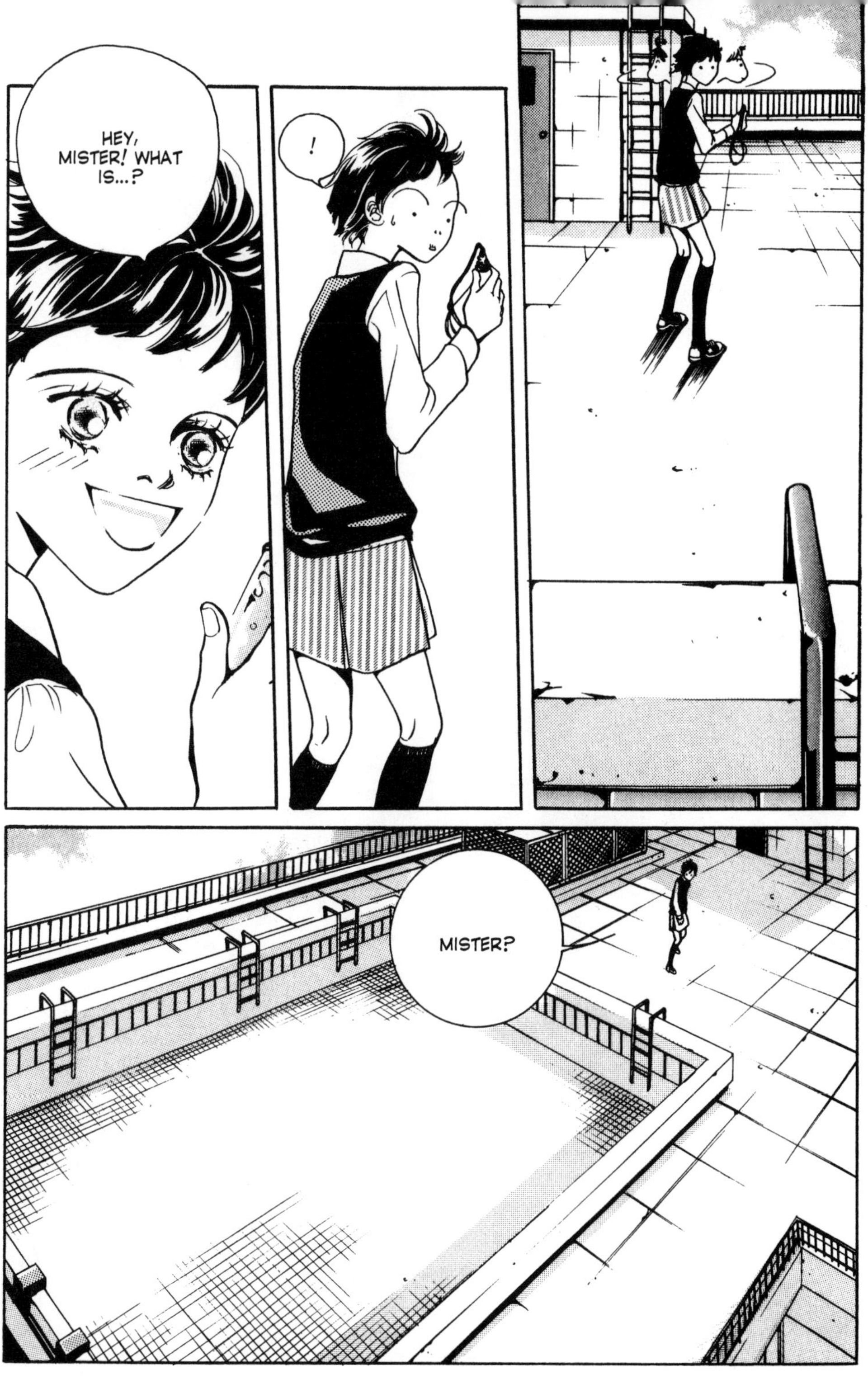
HEY, MISTER! WHAT IS...?
!
MISTER?

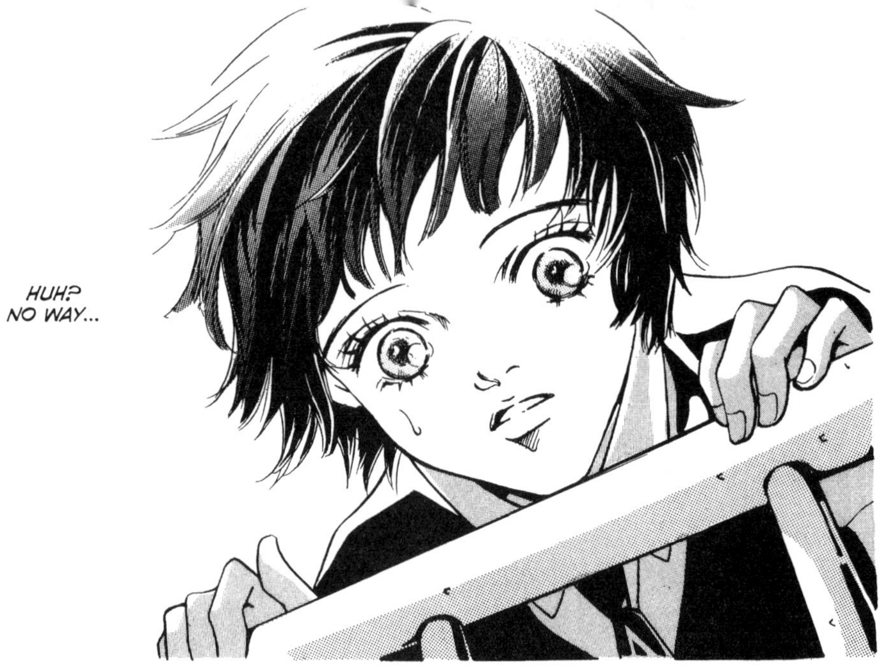
HUH?
NO WAY...

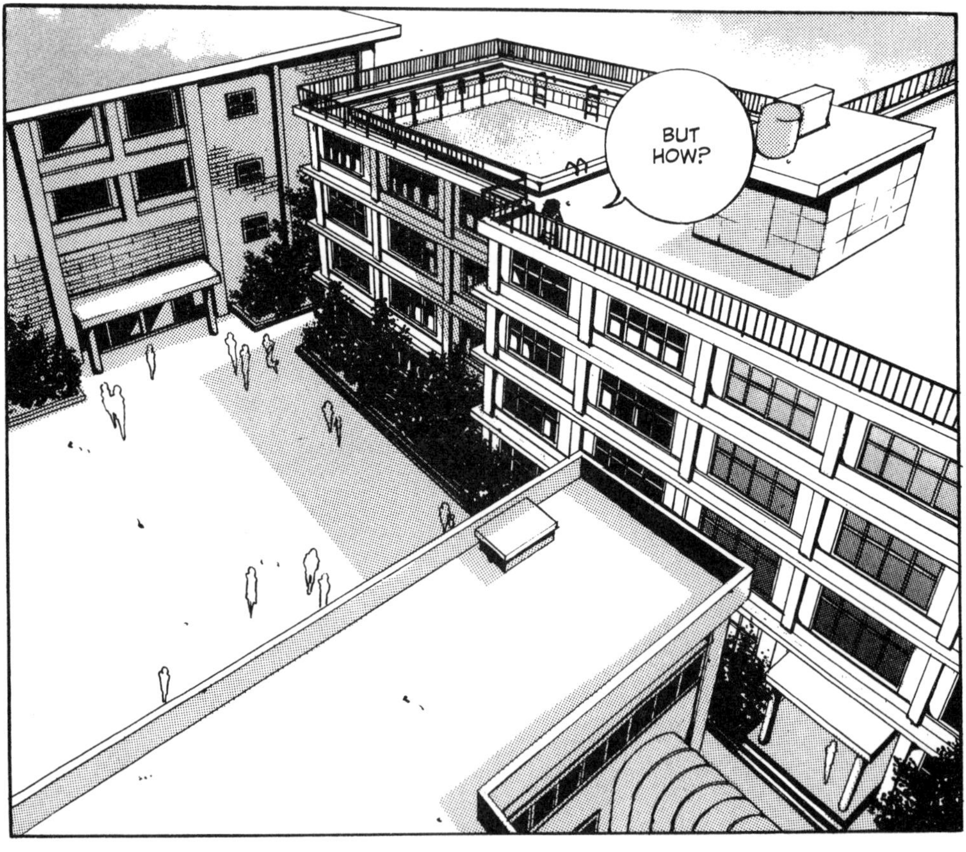
BUT
HOW?

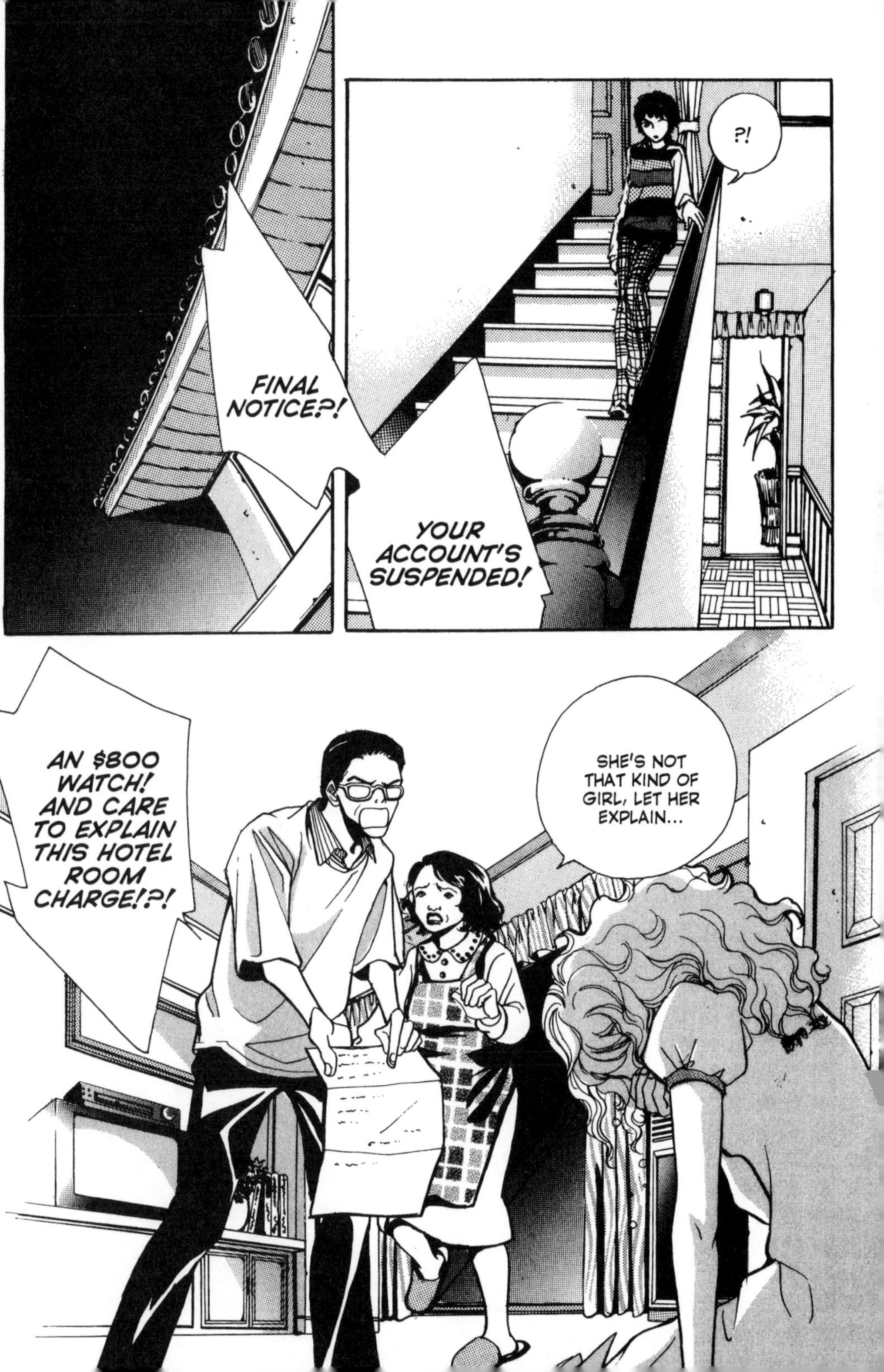
FINAL NOTICE?!
YOUR ACCOUNT'S SUSPENDED!
?!
AN $800 WATCH! AND CARE TO EXPLAIN THIS HOTEL ROOM CHARGE!?!
SHE'S NOT THAT KIND OF GIRL, LET HER EXPLAIN...

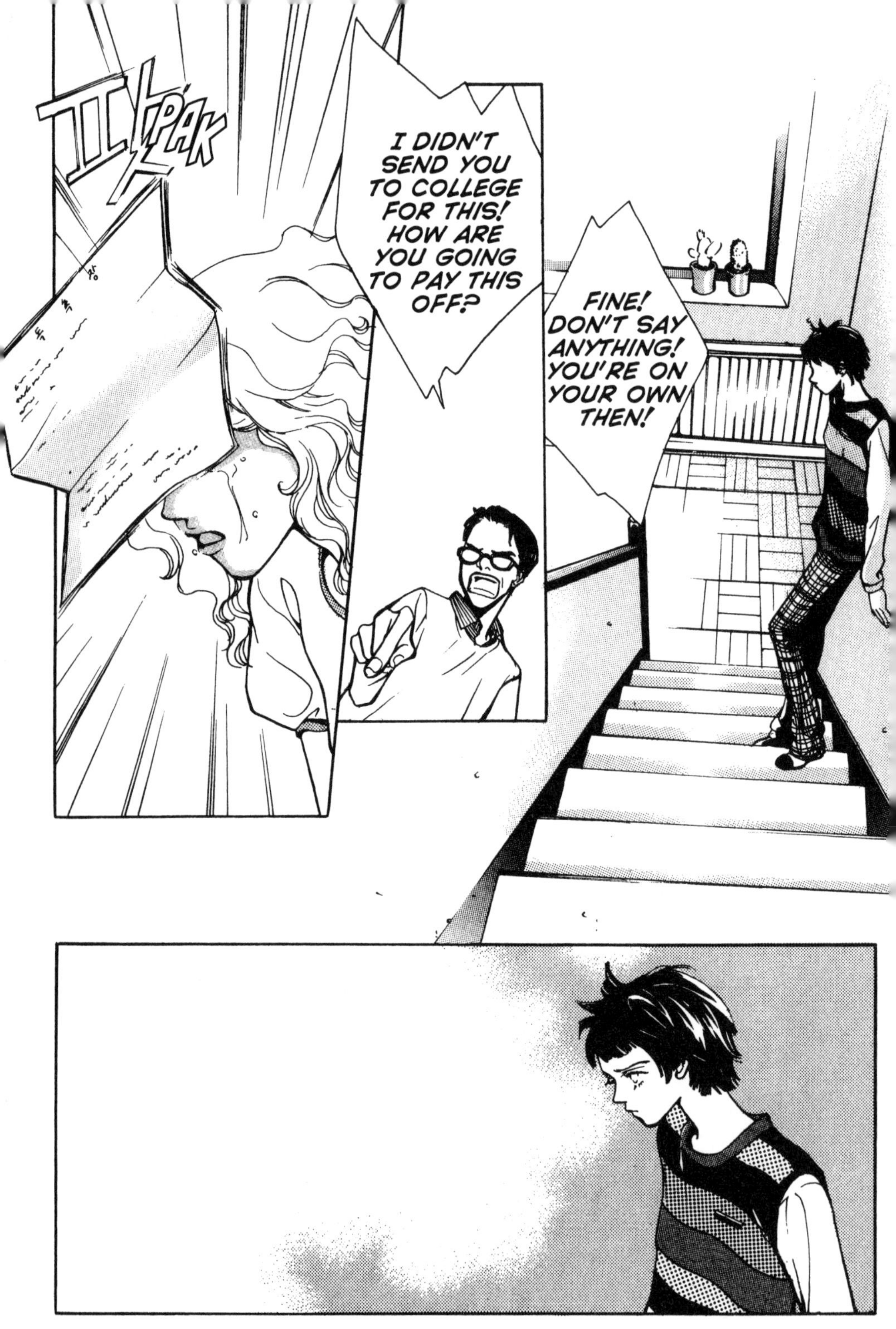
TIK PAK
I DIDN'T SEND YOU TO COLLEGE FOR THIS! HOW ARE YOU GOING TO PAY THIS OFF?
FINE! DON'T SAY ANYTHING! YOU'RE ON YOUR OWN THEN!

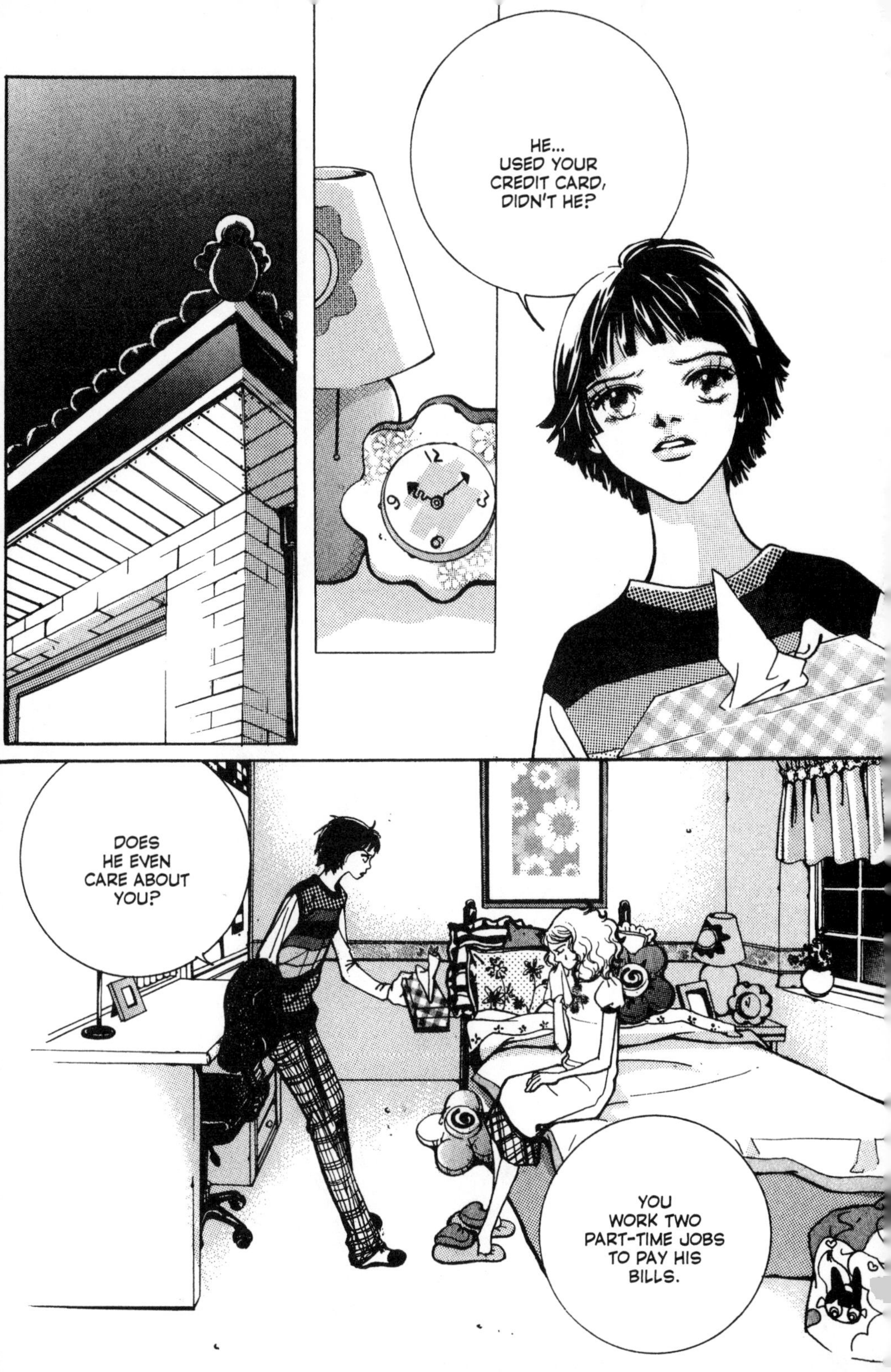
HE... USED YOUR CREDIT CARD, DIDN'T HE?
DOES HE EVEN CARE ABOUT YOU?
YOU WORK TWO PART-TIME JOBS TO PAY HIS BILLS.

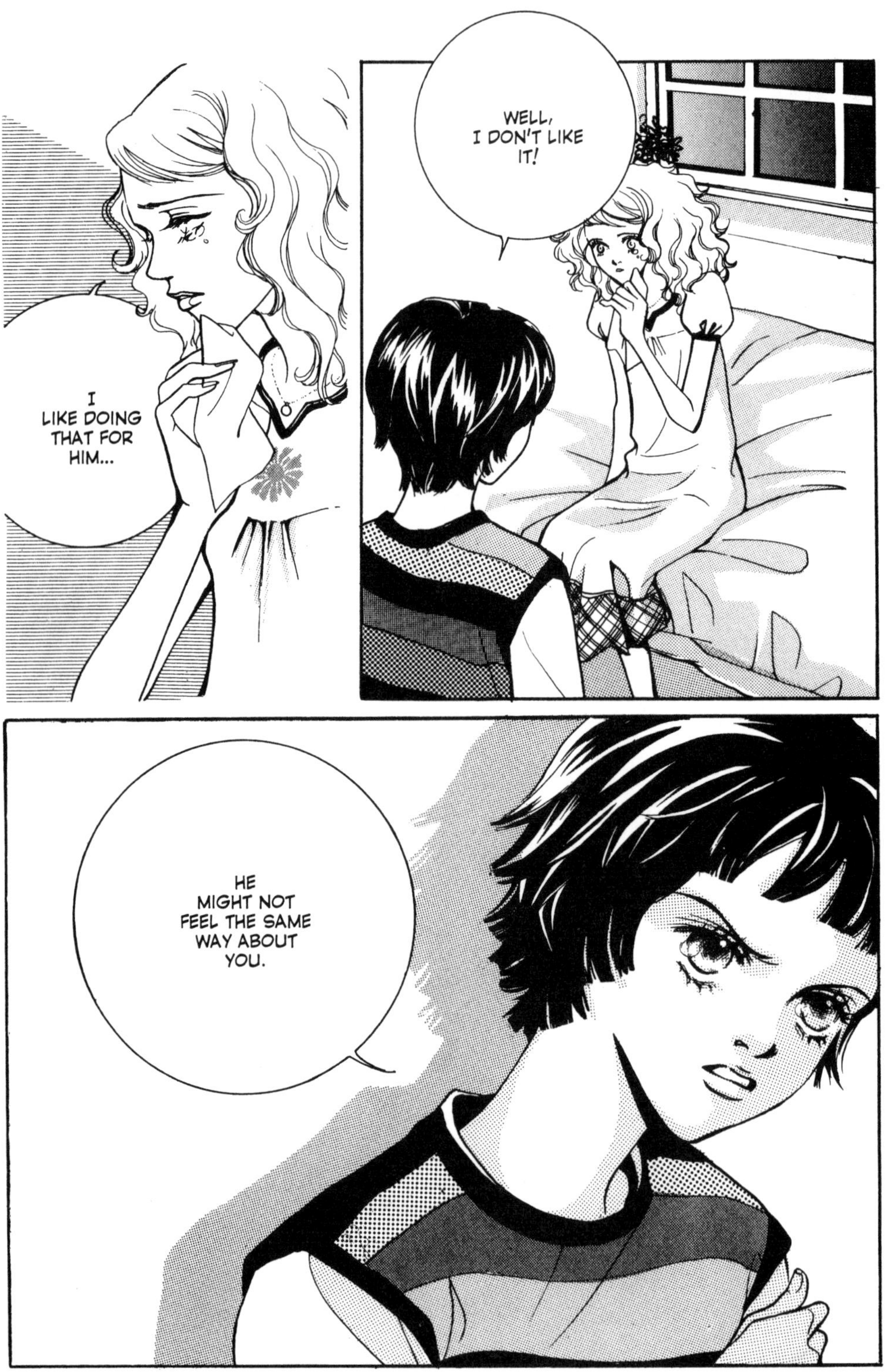
I LIKE DOING THAT FOR HIM...
WELL, I DON'T LIKE IT!
HE MIGHT NOT FEEL THE SAME WAY ABOUT YOU.

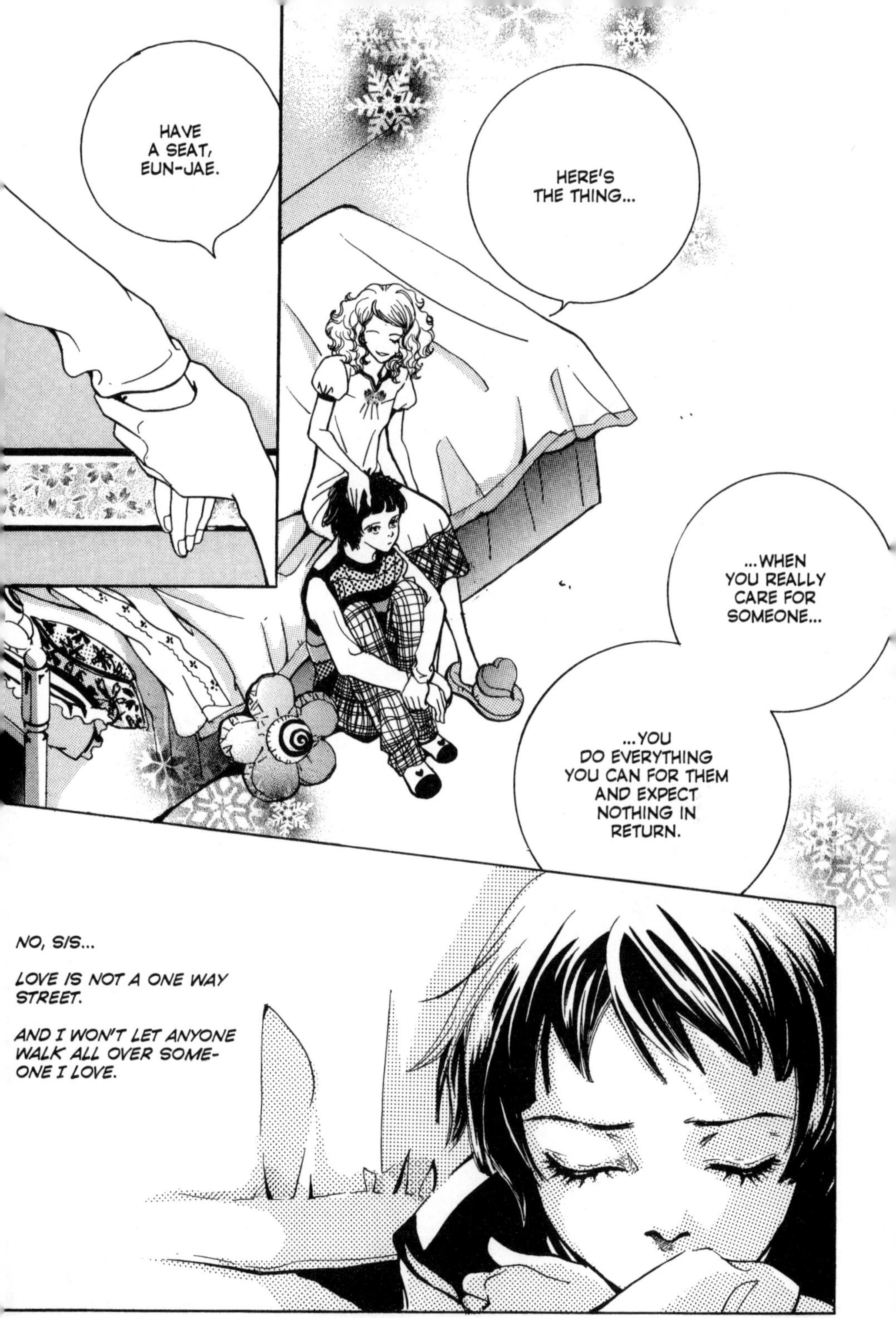
HAVE A SEAT, EUN-JAE.
HERE'S THE THING...
...WHEN YOU REALLY CARE FOR SOMEONE...
...YOU DO EVERYTHING YOU CAN FOR THEM AND EXPECT NOTHING IN RETURN.
NO, SIS...
LOVE IS NOT A ONE WAY STREET.
AND I WON'T LET ANYONE WALK ALL OVER SOME-ONE I LOVE.

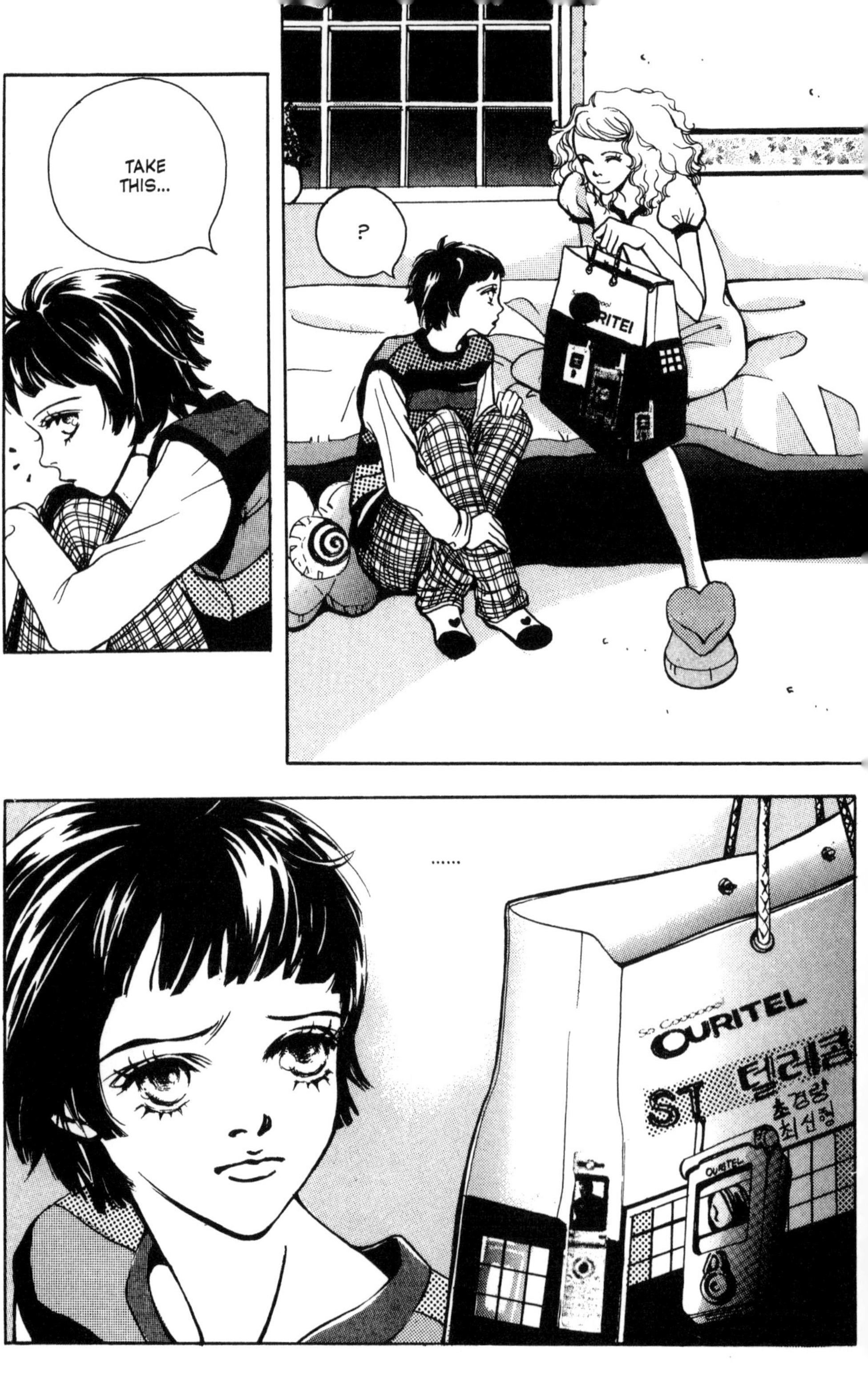
TAKE THIS...
?
......
OURITEL
ST 텔레콤
초경량
최신형

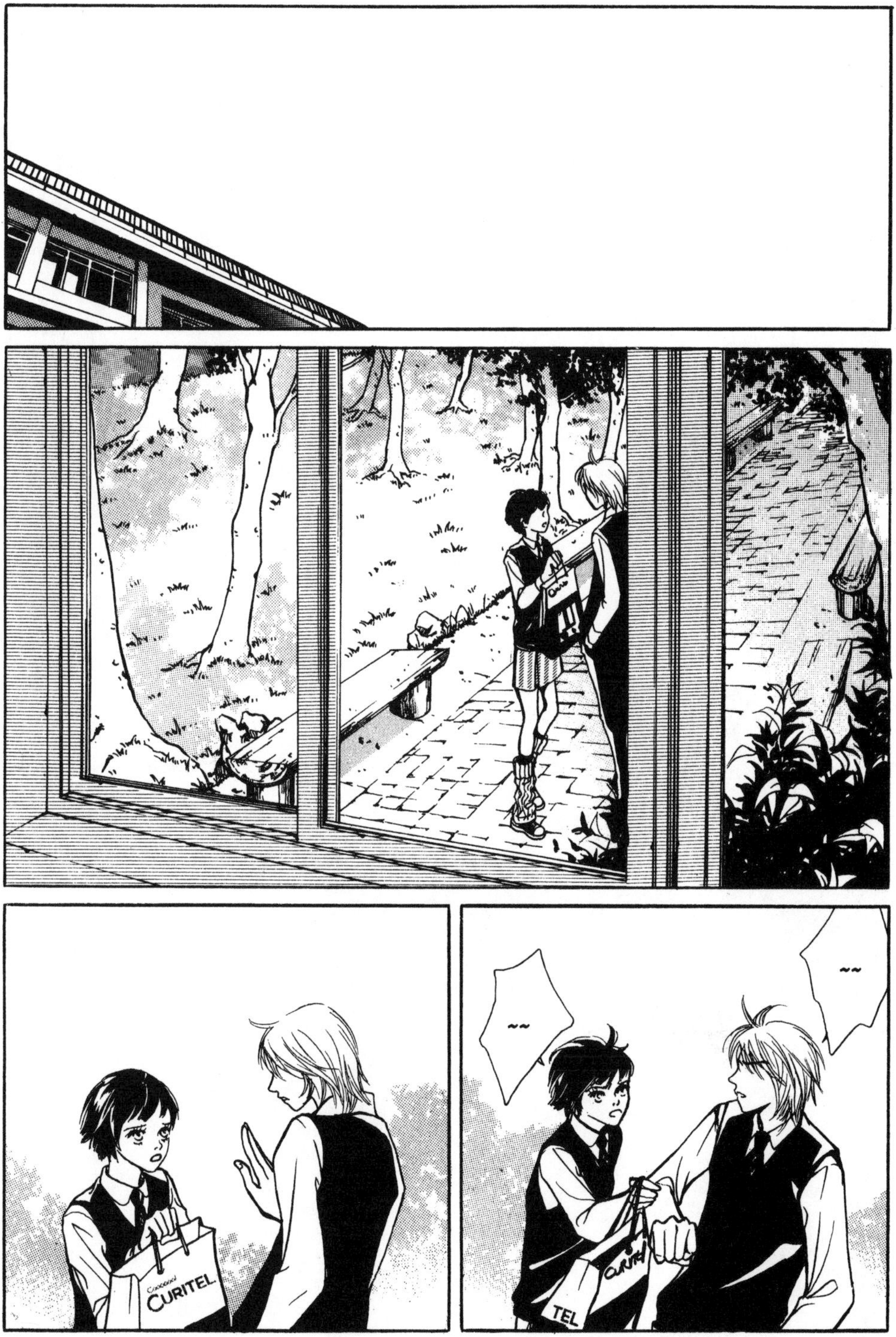
CURITEL
~~
~~
CURITEL
TEL

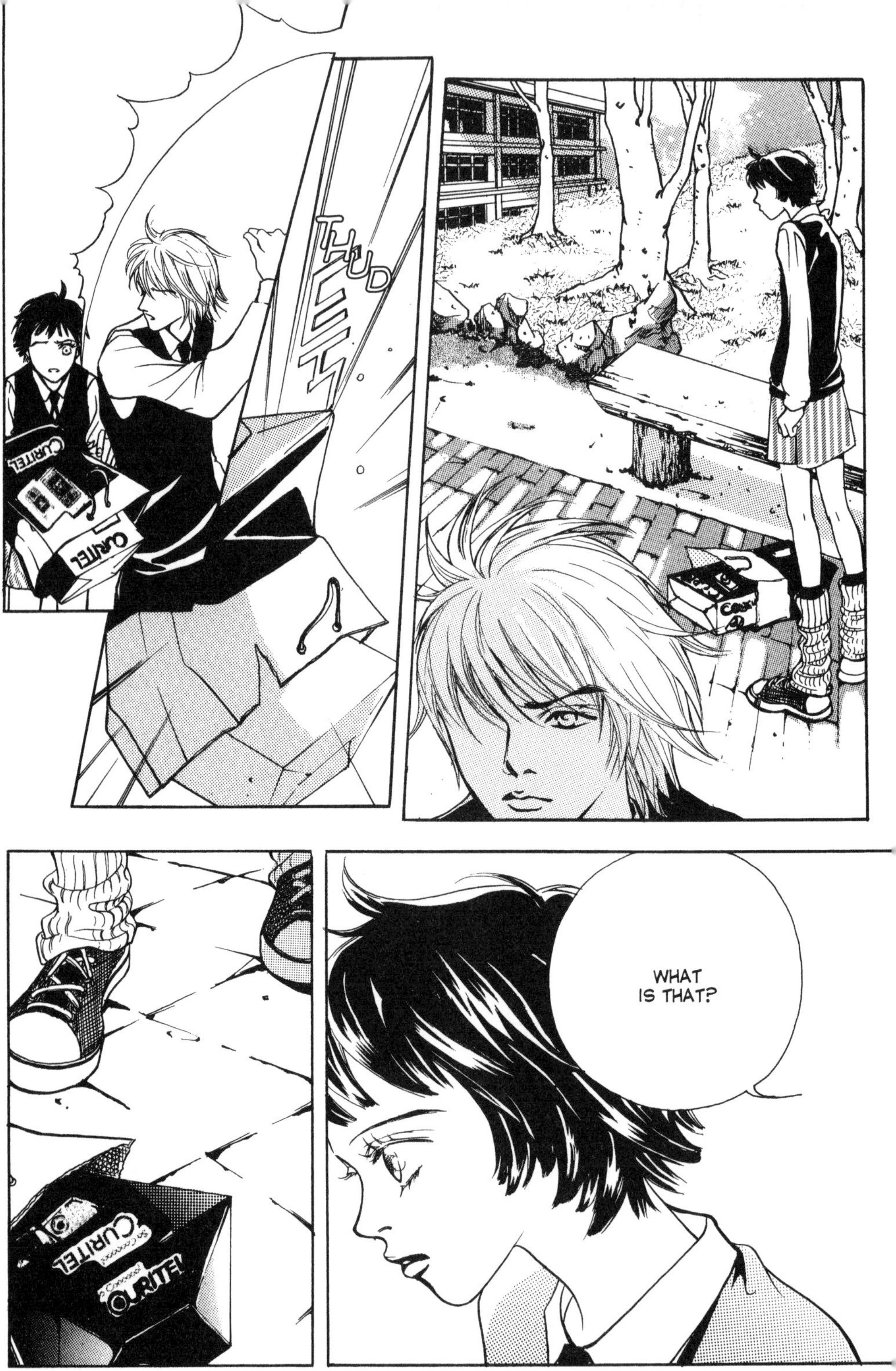
CURITEL
CURITEL
THUD
CURITEL
CURITEL
WHAT IS THAT?

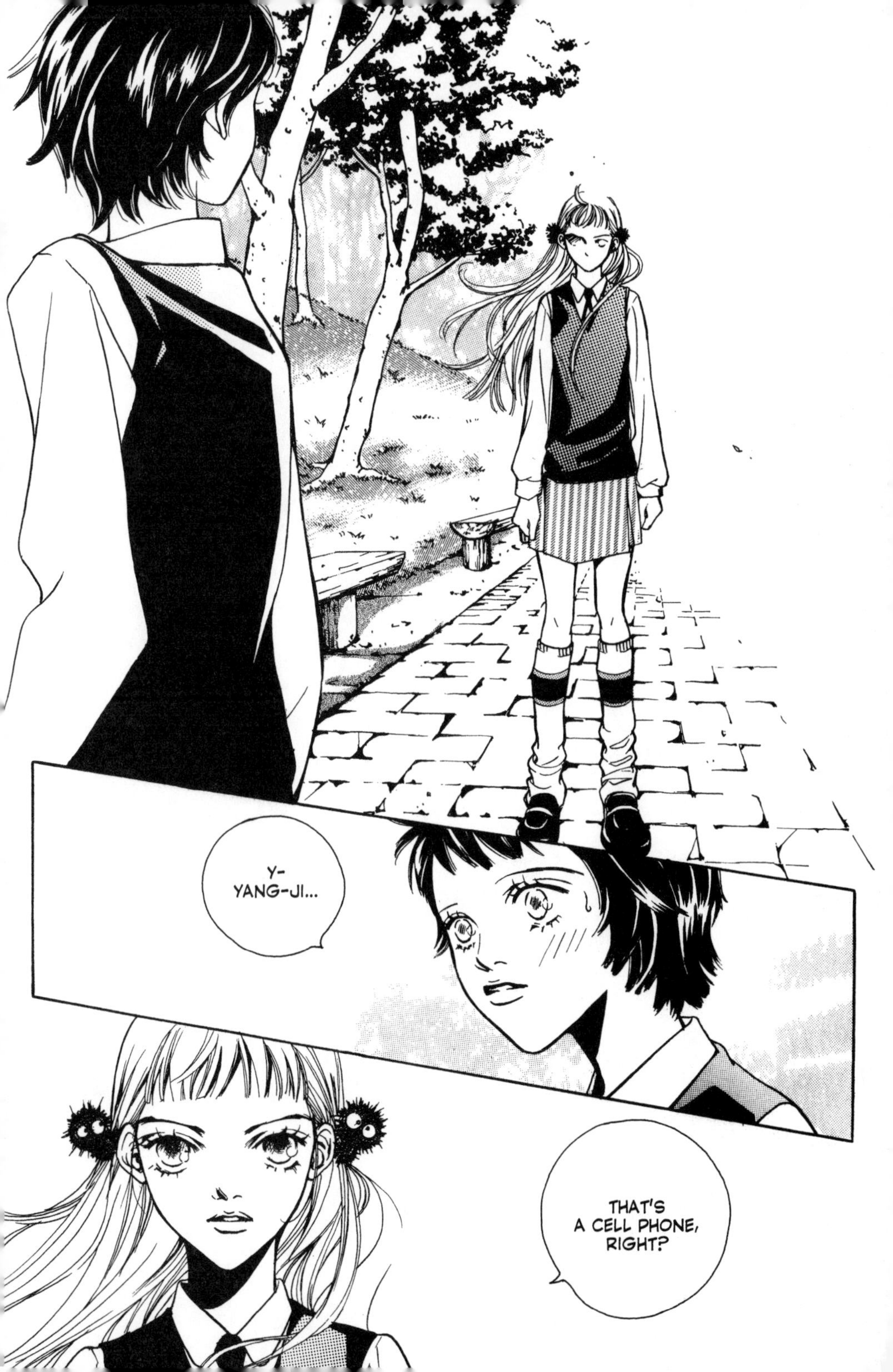
Y-
YANG-JI...
THAT'S
A CELL PHONE,
RIGHT?

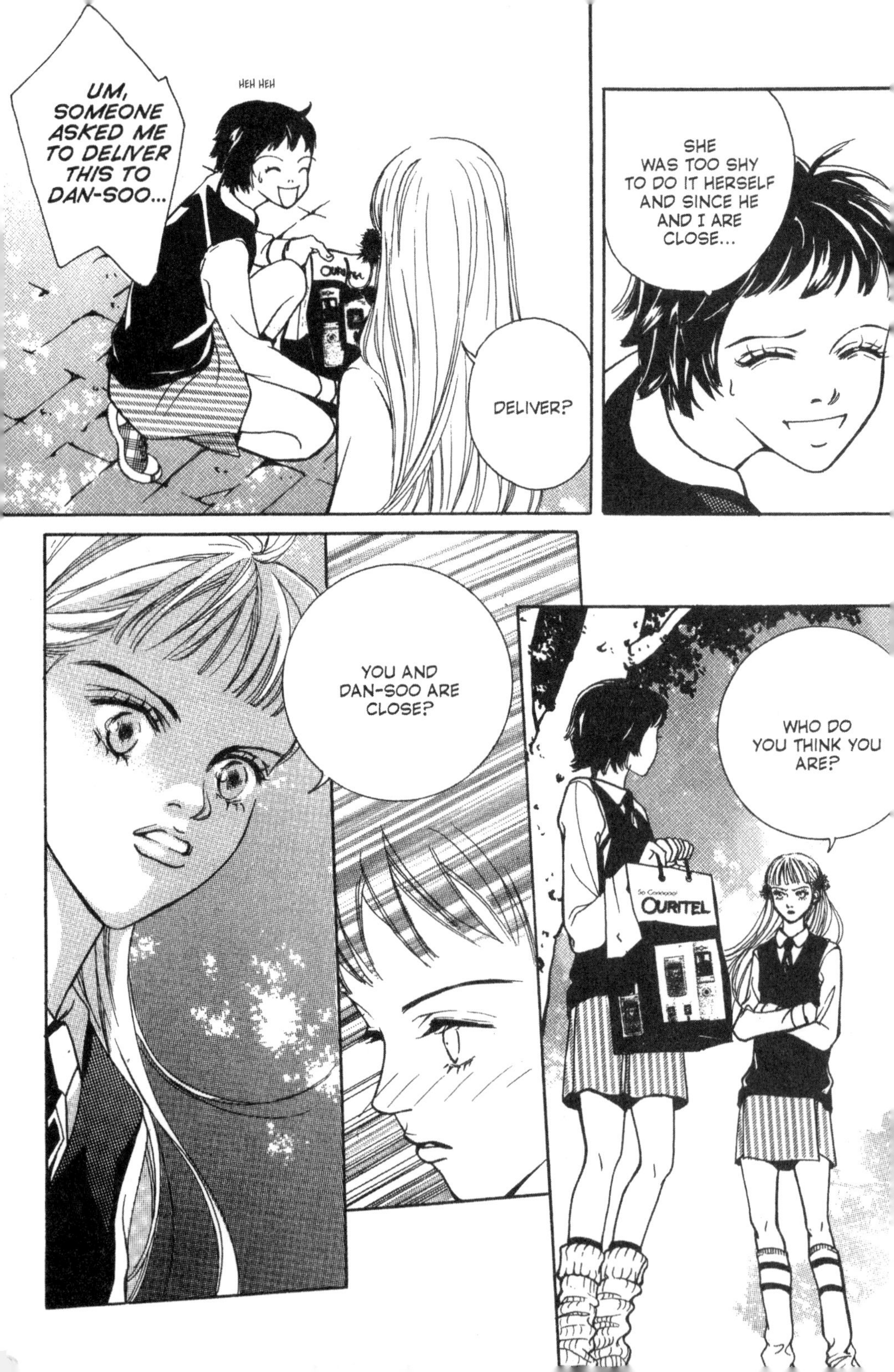

UM, SOMEONE ASKED ME TO DELIVER THIS TO DAN-SOO...
HEH HEH
DELIVER?
SHE WAS TOO SHY TO DO IT HERSELF AND SINCE HE AND I ARE CLOSE...
YOU AND DAN-SOO ARE CLOSE?
WHO DO YOU THINK YOU ARE?
OURITEL

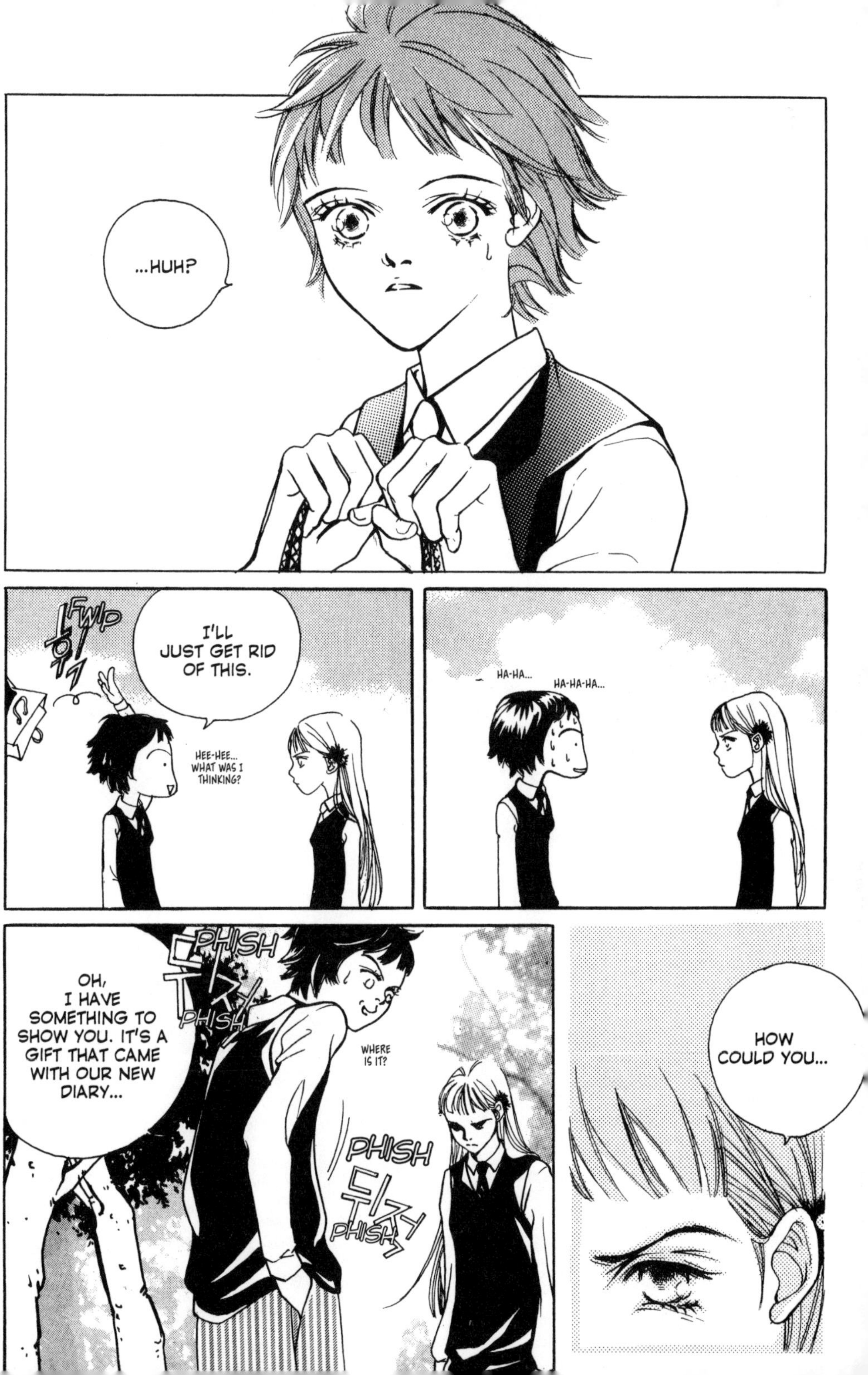
...HUH?
FWIP
I'LL JUST GET RID OF THIS.
HEE-HEE... WHAT WAS I THINKING?
HA-HA...
HA-HA-HA...
PHISH
PHISH
OH, I HAVE SOMETHING TO SHOW YOU. IT'S A GIFT THAT CAME WITH OUR NEW DIARY...
WHERE IS IT?
PHISH
PHISH
HOW COULD YOU...

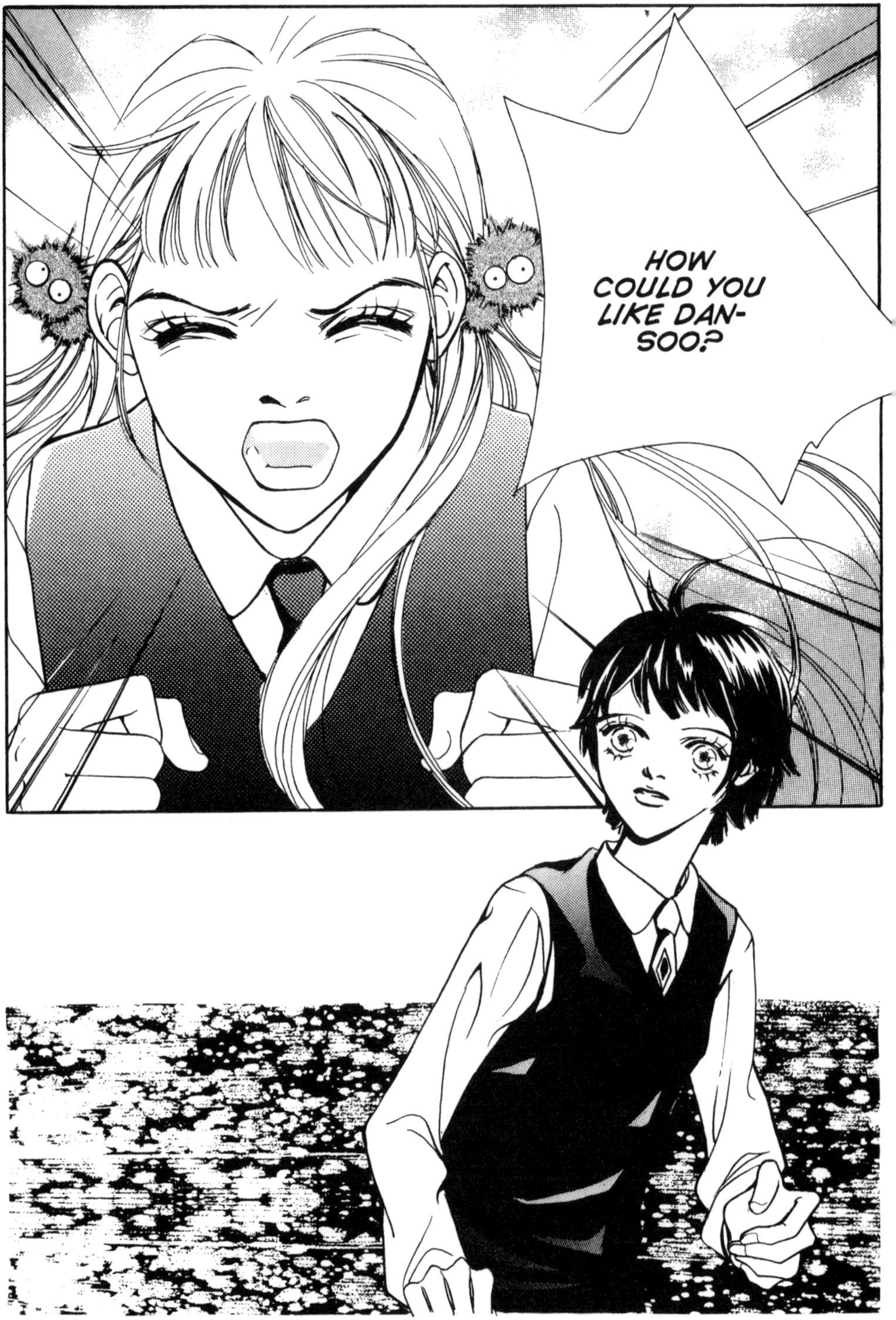
HOW COULD YOU LIKE DAN-SOO?

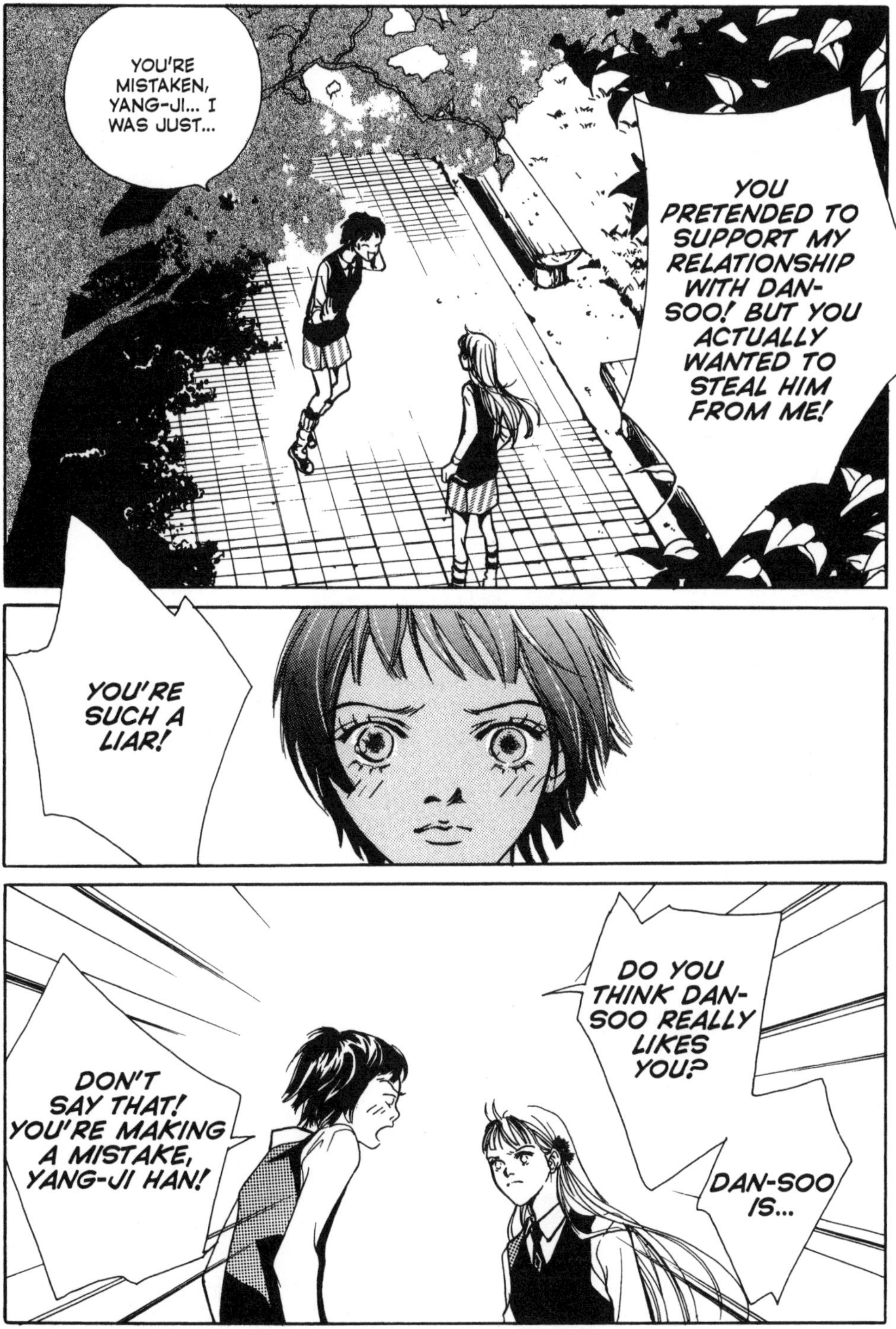
YOU'RE MISTAKEN, YANG-JI... I WAS JUST...
YOU PRETENDED TO SUPPORT MY RELATIONSHIP WITH DAN-SOO! BUT YOU ACTUALLY WANTED TO STEAL HIM FROM ME!
YOU'RE SUCH A LIAR!
DON'T SAY THAT! YOU'RE MAKING A MISTAKE, YANG-JI HAN!
DO YOU THINK DAN-SOO REALLY LIKES YOU?
DAN-SOO IS...

Hissing vol. 1

Story and art by EunYoung Kang

Translation: June Um
English Adaptation: Marie P. Croall
Lettering: Terri Delgado · Marshall Dillon

Yen Press
Hachette Book Group USA
237 Park Avenue, New York, NY 10017

Visit our Web sites at www.HachetteBookGroupUSA.com and www.YenPress.com.

Yen Press is an imprint of Hachette Book Group USA, Inc. The Yen Press name and logo are trademarks of Hachette Book Group USA, Inc.

First English Printing: June 2006
First Yen Press Edition: July 2008

ISBN-10: 89-527-4463-2
ISBN-13: 978-89-527-4463-0

10 9 8 7 6 5 4 3 2

BVG

Printed in the United States of America